INTERNATIONAL MARKETING RELATIONSHIPS

INTERNATIONAL MARKETING RELATIONSHIPS

Sue Bridgewater and Colin Egan

palgrave

First published 2002 by
PALGRAVE
Houndmills, Basingstoke, Hampshire RG21 6XS and
175 Fifth Avenue, New York, N. Y. 10010
Companies and representatives throughout the world

PALGRAVE is the new global academic imprint of
St. Martin's Press LLC Scholarly and Reference Division and
Palgrave Publishers Ltd (formerly Macmillan Press Ltd).

ISBN 0–333–73377–0 hardback
ISBN 0–333–73378–9 paperback

This book is printed on paper suitable for recycling and
made from fully managed and sustained forest sources.

Cataloguing-in-publication data

A catalogue record for this book is available
from the British Library.

A catalogue record for this book is available
from the Library of Congress.

10   9   8   7   6   5   4   3   2   1
11   10   09   08   07   06   05   04   03   02

Printed and bound in Great Britain by
Antony Rowe Ltd, Chippenham, Wiltshire

For Andrew, James and Samuel – Sue
For Sonia – Colin

CONTENTS

List of Figures	xiv
List of Maps	xv
List of Tables	xvi
List of Boxes	xvii
List of Case Studies	xviii
Foreword	xix
Preface and Acknowledgements	xxi

PART I **RELATIONSHIP AND NETWORK PERSPECTIVES ON INTERNATIONAL MARKETING**

1	**Theoretical Background: A Review of Relationship and Network Perspectives of Marketing**	**3**
	Introduction	3
	Relationship Perspectives on Marketing	3
	Interaction studies	3
	Interaction processes	5
	Types of distance between suppliers and buyers	5
	Developing relationships	5
	Are long-term relationships beneficial?	6
	Relationship marketing	7
	Network Studies of Marketing	9
	Markets as networks	9
	Key themes in the markets as networks literature	11
	Comparing the Interaction, Relationship and Network Literature	12
	Unit of analysis	13
	Description or prescription?	13
	Static or dynamic?	14
	Relationship and Network Perspectives on International Marketing	14
	Bibliography	16

PART II **MACRO-LEVEL CONTEXT**

2	**The Cultural Environment**	**23**
	Introduction	23
	The Traditional Perspective	24
	Influences on national culture	24
	Cultural stereotypes	26
	Classifying national culture	26
	Long-term versus short-term orientation (LTO)	27
	Country-of-origin effects	27

The Relationship Perspective   28
  The impact of culture in international relationships   29
  Criticisms of cultural and psychic distance   32
  Assessing cultural perceptions at the individual level   33
The Network Perspective   33
  Are there culturally different network structures?   33
  Psychic distance in networks   35
Summary   36
Bibliography   36

3   **The Technological Context**   38
Introduction   38
The Traditional Perspective   38
  The innovation imperative   38
  Technology and changing markets   39
  The real impact of the Internet   39
The Relationship Perspective   42
  Distinctive characteristics of technological assets   42
  Technology relationships   42
  Issues for consideration in technology relationships   44
  International technology co-operation   46
  Virtual relationships   46
The Network Perspective   50
  Rapidly changing network structures   50
  Types of exchange   50
  Networks in technology industries   53
  International technology networks   54
Summary   54
Bibliography   55

4   **The Economic and Political Context**   57
Introduction   57
The Traditional Perspective   58
  Classical economic theories   58
  Competitive advantage of nations   59
  Critique of Porter's 'diamond framework'   61
The Relationship Perspective   63
  Global interlinkage of economies   63
  Operation in a globally interlinked economy   63
  Impacts of the Euro on international marketing   65
  Supranational economic and political challenges   66
The Network Perspective   67
  The interface between an organization and its macro-context   67
  A network view of the economic context   68
Case Study 4.1: Bofors in India   73
Summary   78
Bibliography   78

PART III   INTERNATIONAL MARKETING STRATEGIES

5   **International Marketing Strategy**   83
     Introduction   83
     The Traditional Perspective   84
         International marketing strategies for a gobal economy   84
         Arguments for global standardization   85
         Arguments against global standardization   86
         Globalization   87
     The Relationship Perspective   87
         Decoupling the value chain   87
         Value constellations   87
         Branding   88
         Managing international relationships   89
     The Network Perspective   91
         Macro-level network relationships   91
         Inter-organizational network relationships   92
         Building positions in international markets   94
     Case Study 5.1: Budweiser A   96
     Summary   102
     Bibliography   103

6   **Assessing Market Attractiveness**   105
     Introduction   105
     The Traditional Perspective   105
         Uncertainty and risk   105
         Risk assessment techniques   106
         International marketing planning in
         the new millennium   110
     The Relationship Perspective   113
         Knowledge, learning and international markets   113
     The Network Perspective   116
         The knowledge economy   116
         Knowledge flows and networks   116
     Case Study 6.1: Scenarios for the Future of China   119
     Summary   120
     Bibliography   120

7   **The Mode of International Operation**   123
     Introduction   123
     The Traditional Perspective   124
         Economics-based theories   124
     The Relationship Perspective   128
         Classifying co-operative ventures   129
         How can joint venture effectiveness be improved?   130
         Creating successful joint ventures   131
     The Network Perspective   131
         The network as an organizational type   131

Case Study 7.1: Bohomin Steel Works   134
Summary   136
Bibliography   136

8   **The Process of Internationalization**   **139**
     Introduction   139
     The Traditional Perspective   139
        The process of internationalization   139
        Sequential models of internationalization   140
        Theoretical analysis of the Uppsala model   141
        Simultaneous models of internationalization   144
        Manufacturing firms   145
        Service firms   145
        Retailers   146
        Multinational and global firms   148
        Small firms   148
     The Relationship Perspective   150
        Retailer–supplier relationships   150
        Relationships between small and large firms   150
     The Network Perspective   151
        A network view of internationalization   151
     The Internationalization Process   152
     Case Study 8.1: The Internationalization Process
     of CigaretteCo in Central Europe   154
     Summary   155
     Bibliography   156

PART IV	THE INTERNATIONAL MARKETING MIX

9   **International Pricing**   **161**
     Introduction   161
     The Traditional Perspective   161
        Market oriented pricing   161
        International pricing strategies   162
     The Relationship Perspective   168
        Countertrade   168
        The development of countertrade relationships   168
     The Network Perspective   168
        Interrelationships and international pricing   168
        Transfer pricing   169
        Co-operative international buying groups   169
        Parallel pricing or grey markets   170
        Countertrade networks   171
     Summary   171
     Bibliography   172

10	**Promotion**	**173**
	Introduction	173
	The Traditional Perspective	173
	Challenges in international promotional strategies	174
	The Relationship Perspective	180
	Advertising agency–client relationships	180
	Successful creative relationships	181
	Implementing creative strategies	182
	Defining relationship scope	182
	Global creative relationships	182
	Global key account management	183
	The Network Perspective	187
	Integrated marketing communications	187
	Summary	189
	Bibliography	189

PART V REGIONAL ISSUES

11	**The Americas**	**193**
	Introduction	193
	The Traditional Perspective	193
	The challenges	195
	The Relationship Perspective	195
	Bilateral and multilateral free trade agreements	195
	The 'double diamond' of competitive advantage	200
	The Network Perspective	201
	Networks in the Americas	201
	Network structures in the USA	202
	Network structures in Canada	203
	Case Study 11.1 Banana Wars: Complex Webs of Old and New	
	Trading Relationships	204
	Summary	205
	Bibliography	205

12	**Europe**	**207**
	Introduction	207
	The Traditional Perspective	207
	Challenges	207
	The reality of pan-European marketing	209
	The Relationship Perspective	212
	Europe as a trading bloc	212
	European interaction studies	213
	Strategic alliances in Europe	215
	The Network Perspective	215
	Network evolution	215
	Network organizations	216
	Summary	217
	Bibliography	217

13   **Asia-Pacific**   220
     Introduction   220
     The Traditional Perspective   221
         The Japanese miracle   221
         The East Asian crisis   222
         'Post-bubble' East Asia   223
     The Relationship Perspective   223
         Relationships within Asia-Pacific   223
         Relationships in Asia-Pacific   224
         The role of relationships in Asian societies   225
         Cross-cultural adjustment   226
     The Network Perspective   226
         Guanxi networks   226
         Keiretsu   227
     Summary   228
     Bibliography   228

14   **Emerging Mega-Markets**   231
     Introduction   231
     The Traditional Perspective   231
         Definitions   231
         Market data   232
         Opportunity and risk in emerging markets   232
         Challenges   234
     The Relationship Perspective   236
         Joint ventures and emerging markets   237
     The Network Perspective   238
         From Soviet hierarchy to Russian network   241
     Case Study 14.1: Budweiser B   243
     Summary   250
     Bibliography   250

15   **Less Developed Markets**   253
     Introduction   253
     The Traditional Perspective   253
         Defining LDCs   253
         Challenges   254
     The Relationship Perspective   256
         The role of multinational corporations   256
         Multinationals and politics in LDCs   257
         Ethical policy and duty of care   257
         Power in relationships between multinationals and LDCs   258
         Technology transfer in relationships: partners in progress   259
         Relationships with local distributors   260
     The Network Perspective   260
     Case Study 15.1: Shell in Ogoni Land   262
     Summary   263
     Bibliography   264

PART VI INTERNATIONAL MARKETING ORGANIZATIONS

16 **International Marketing Organization**   267
    Introduction   267
    The Traditional Perspective   268
        Creating marketing oriented organizations   268
        International organization   269
        Global organizations: reality or myth?   270
    The Relationship Perspective   271
    The Network Perspective   272
        Communication   272
        Location of research and development activities   272
        Control over subsidiary activities   273
    Summary   273
    Bibliography   273

    Index   277

LIST OF FIGURES

1.1	Understanding business-to-business relationships	4
1.2	Checklist of IMP relationships	4
1.3	Database marketing contrasted with relationship marketing	8
1.4	The six markets model: a broader view of marketing relationships	9
1.5	Network levels	10
1.6	Traditional relationship and network perspectives on marketing: similarities and differences	14
1.7	The perspectives on marketing distinguished in this book	15
II.1	Understanding Relationships	21
2.1	Perceptions of psychic distance	30
4.1	Simplified network at the time of the Pergau Dam incident	71
5.1	Young and Rubicam's Brand Asset Valuator	90
5.2	The Brand Power Grid	90
5.3	Building positions in international markets	92
5.4	Firm interdependency	95
5.5	Anheuser-Busch, international sales, 1981–94 (million barrels)	99
6.1	Scenario planning	109
6.2	X and Y grid of scenarios for the future of retailing	113
6.3	SWOT analysis: Ukraine	114
7.1	Trading off modes of market entry	128
7.2	SWOT analysis: Bohomin	135
9.1	Pressures for price harmonization	170
10.1	Industry globalization drivers	184
10.2	The IMC network	188
11.1	Network relationships in NAFTA	202
11.2	Network relationships in the Caribbean Basin	202
12.1	The network context of a subsidiary	217
14.1	Relationships (a) under central planning, (b) in transition	239
14.2	Budvar's major export markets, 1994	246
14.3	Budvar's production and exports, 1975–94	248
14.4	Budvar's revenues and profits, 1989–94 (million (2K))	248
15.1	Appropriate marketing strategies for LDCs	256
15.2	Attitudes towards corporate social responsibility	258
15.3	Philosophical approaches to international business ethics	258

LIST OF MAPS

11.1 The Americas 194
11.2 Positive and negative impacts of banana wars dispute on a network of relationships 204
12.1 Europe 208
13.1 Asia-Pacific 221
14.1 Emerging and mega-markets 232
15.1 Africa 254

LIST OF TABLES

2.1	What countries are believed to be good at	28
2.2	Ranking of countries by psychic distance from Sweden	30
2.3	Cultural distance measured from Australia outwards	32
2.4	Cultural distance measured from the UK	32
3.1	Potential benefits of international marketing via the Internet	41
3.2	Barriers to international marketing via the Internet	41
5.1	Anheuser-Busch, sales in Europe, 1993	100
6.1	Classifications of 'uncertainty'	107
8.1	Ranking of explanations of incremental entry mode behaviour	142
8.2	Wal Mart and Carrefour: geographic scope, 2000	147
9.1	Who determines the price and on what basis?	162
9.2	International pricing	162
9.3	Exporter strategies under varying currency conditions	164
12.1	EU members, 2001	208
12.2	European enlargement	209
12.3	Current level of standardization across Europe	210
12.4	Will a greater level of standardization be possible in future?	211
12.5	What advantages has the SEM offered your firm?	211
12.6	What disadvantages has the SEM created for your firm?	211
12.7	Has the SEM resulted in a change in your business performance?	212
14.1	Primary research into investment in East and Central Europe	236
14.2	Entry modes used in East and Central Europe	236

LIST OF BOXES

2.1 Country-of-Origin Effects: The Case of the New Russia   28
2.2 Diaspora and Distance   31
3.1 The Real Impacts of the Internet on International Marketing   41
3.2 Apple and IBM   43
3.3 Supplying Marks and Spencer: Boundary Spanning Roles   45
4.1 Strategy, Structure and Rivalry?   60
4.2 The Pergau Dam Incident   70
5.1 Young and Rubicam's Brand Asset Valuator Framework   90
5.2 The 'Bix Six' Accounting Firms in Eastern Europe   93
6.1 Scenario Planning Narratives   112
8.1 ComputerCo   141
8.2 AuditCo   144
8.3 Global Retail: Battle of the Titans?   147
8.4 Simultaneous or Sequential Internationalization: Small Firm Experiences 149
8.5 TelecomCo   152
9.1 Johnson Wax in Ukraine   163
9.2 Sterling on Steroids: The Impact on UK Exporters   164
9.3 The Impact of Channels to Market for Home Fashion Products
     in the UK and France   166
9.4 Price Differentiation in the Automobile Industry   167
10.1 Dust Up Over Hoover Promotion   175
11.1 Winners and Losers After NAFTA   197
11.2 Chicken Arbitrage and Tomato Tariffs   198
12.1 The 'Euro Consumer'   210
14.1 Seagram's Strategy in the CEE Countries   233
14.2 Ins and Pre-Ins in Eastern Europe   233
14.3 China's Difficult Choices   234
14.4 Network Issues in Ukraine: Dislocation   239
14.5 Network Issues in Ukraine: Opacity   240
14.6 Network Issues in Ukraine: An Emerging Network   241

LIST OF CASE STUDIES

4.1	Bofors in India	73
5.1	Budweiser A	96
6.1	Scenarios for the future of China	119
7.1	Bohomin Steel Works	134
8.1	The internationalization process of CigaretteCo in Central Europe	154
11.1	Banana wars: complex webs of old and new trading relationships	204
14.1	Budweiser B	243
15.1	Shell in Ogoni Land	262

FOREWORD

The emerging recognition of the importance of interaction processes and the development of inter-organizational relationships is an important and perhaps historic development in marketing theory. Although considerable theoretical evolution and empirical research have occurred during the past twenty years or so, few texts have been written that recognize and incorporate these developments.

This book is therefore an important welcome contribution to the literature. It not only focuses on international marketing, covering in depth and breadth the more traditional thinking in this field, but also, in a proactive and exciting way, encompasses current thinking on relationships, interaction and networks.

Few scholars could have brought the depth of scholarship and the ability to integrate the two fields as do Sue Bridgwater and Colin Egan. Equally important is the precision and coherence of the presentation. The material is comprehensive, cohesive and intellectually stimulating.

There are many international marketing texts, many of which are very good, and a few are seminal, but this is unique in that it integrates the important, and still emerging, paradigm of marketing as a process of developing and managing relationships with traditional international marketing theory. A formidable task yet executed with insight and intelligence by the authors.

The evolution of a new paradigm in management is always both exciting and challenging; this book is both; intellectually challenging, exciting, comprehensive and very readable. I commend it wholeheartedly; it will, I believe, prove to be one of the 'classics' of international marketing.

Peter Turnbull

FOREWORD

PREFACE AND ACKNOWLEDGEMENTS

In his introduction to *Culture's Consequences*, Hofstede (1980, p. 15) says of studying social sciences:

> Social scientists approach...social reality as the blind men from the Indian fable approached the elephant; the one who gets hold of a leg thinks it is a tree, the one who gets the tail thinks it is a rope, but none of them understands what the whole animal is like. We will never be more than blind men in front of the social elephant; but by joining forces with other blind men and women and approaching the animal from as many different angles as possible, we may find out more about it than we could ever do alone.

In the 1990s, global marketing is an inescapable reality for practitioners and academics alike. The challenges of building ongoing relationships with customers and consumers in domestic markets are compounded by operation across different market environments, fraught with the complexity of differences in levels of economic development, political regimes, cultural norms and technical standards. It may be difficult to fully comprehend the whole. Studying the issues from a number of different perspectives, as Hofstede suggests, may give a fuller picture of the whole 'elephant'.

Although marketers increasingly recognize the importance of ongoing relationships to successful marketing, the majority of marketing literature still analyzes static marketing situations. There is a tendency to focus on a static cross-section of data rather than studying marketing phenomena over time. Relationship perspectives reflect the real-world challenges for marketers. Building relationships with customers is a dynamic process. When this occurs across international borders, as is increasingly the case, these relationships must be developed against a backcloth of diverse cultures and political systems and differing levels of economic and technological development.

This book owes its genesis to the work of a number of influential schools of marketing literature. First, it is informed to a considerable extent by the work of the Industrial Marketing and Purchasing Group (IMP). The group's work sparked the original idea that, to reflect the richness of its contribution to marketing knowledge, international marketing should be studied from a number of different 'angles'. Secondly, it draws to no little extent on the parallel literature in relationship marketing which has developed over recent decades.

Our understanding of international marketing – from all of the perspectives covered in this book – stems from our reading and research in these areas but also from our experience as executive teachers and consultants to a number of blue chip international organizations including IBM, Nestlé, Philips, KPMG, HSBC and Arthur Andersen. As academics we are fortunate in being exposed to contemporary international marketing issues and having the resources and knowledge of our institutions, Warwick Business School and De Montfort University, to give us scope to reflect and write about them. We hope the end result is valuable both to practitioners and managers.

As with any project as complex and lengthy as the development, writing and publication of this book, we have been assisted and encouraged by a number of people. Without their help we might never have reached the point of publication! Particular thanks are offered to Peter Turnbull for suggesting we write this book. Tim Ambler and Ian Wilkinson responded rapidly to panic requests for articles in their respective areas of expertise, and David Wilson and Robin Wensley from Warwick Business School offered support and guidance along the way.

In attempting to incorporate the range of perspectives on each topic we have had to take some liberties with the various strands of literature and hope the final work does not cause any offence to any of those whose work we reference. As ever, any errors of omission or commission in the final work are ours, not theirs. Two anonymous reviewers also provided valuable suggestions on how we might improve the book.

Since we started writing this book, the project has been supported by a number of Macmillan (or Palgrave, as it is now) editors, including Jane Powell, Sam Whittaker, Sarah Brown, Ursula Gavin and Ruth Lake. We would like to thank them all for their patience and hope the wait was worth it . . .

Finally all our thanks to our families for their support and for putting up with the burden that our involvement in this book has put on them without complaint.

SUE BRIDGEWATER
COLIN EGAN

Note from Colin Egan

A number of personal circumstances meant that Sue carried much the greater burden of work than is normally the case in co-authored texts. This embraced both intellectual input and administrative chores. Many thanks, Sue.

PART I

RELATIONSHIP AND NETWORK PERSPECTIVES ON INTERNATIONAL MARKETING

This book begins with a review of the interaction, relationship and network perspectives on marketing. From this review a number of similarities and differences are drawn, on the basis of which a framework for this book is proposed. This framework takes into account both pragmatism and academic rigour. It is desirable to study international marketing from different perspectives to gain as full as possible an understanding of the issues. Too many different strands may, however, result in duplication of material.

The framework developed in this first part, therefore, proposes three perspectives: traditional (or transactional), relationship and network perspectives. The principal distinction between these approaches is that the traditional perspective assumes a competitive environment with uncontrollable environmental forces posing opportunities and threats for international marketers. The relationship perspective assumes interaction between buyers and sellers, and between other actors in the international marketing context. In international marketing terms, therefore, this perspective looks at the context in terms of distances which may hinder relationship development, and studies different types of international marketing relationships and how value may be added in these.

The network perspective looks at the complex interplay of the web of relationships surrounding the firm. Distinctive characteristics of networks in different international and industry contexts are studied, as are the challenges of international marketing activities, such as determining international marketing strategies, prices and promotions.

THEORETICAL BACKGROUND: A REVIEW OF RELATIONSHIP AND NETWORK PERSPECTIVES OF MARKETING

INTRODUCTION

Gummesson (1999) suggests that relationship marketing is a pair of 'eyeglasses' a reader might use to study marketing issues. Once the reader puts on these eyeglasses, the same issues look different. New angles are revealed, greater clarity and valuable insights can be gained. Building on this analogy, this book uses three different pairs of eyeglasses to study international marketing: traditional, relationship and network eyeglasses. Through the lenses of each of these pairs of eyeglasses the reader can study each topic of international marketing.

This opening chapter offers an initial review of the theory surrounding relationship and network perspectives of marketing. From this, the reader can gain an understanding of the ways in which these perspectives differ from traditional marketing and build an awareness of the ways in which these can offer insights into international marketing.

RELATIONSHIP PERSPECTIVES ON MARKETING

A number of different strands have contributed to the development of the relationship perspective on marketing. Here two strands, interaction studies of business-to-business (B2B) markets and relationship marketing literature are explored.

Interaction Studies

Definitions and Origins

Interaction studies are based on the belief that firms do not market to passive customers, but that *customers interact with marketers*. Imagine the scene: your firm is on the point of launching a carefully researched new product into the market. All of the market research is good, everyone likes 'Acme Paperclips'. You visit the buyer of your largest industrial customer to persuade him or her to buy the product. Despite your positive expectations and carefully honed negotiation skills, the customer is not interested in your new product. You leave wondering what went wrong...

Interaction studies identify a number of characteristics of business-to-business marketing that may help you to understand. First, business-to-business buyers are very different to final consumers. They tend to be large, professional buyers and have specific requirements for paperclips or any other product or service. The financial controller of your customer may have introduced a policy of cutting down on the number of paperclip suppliers. Acme may have short delivered on your last product, Acme drawing pins, just before your meeting. Although you have been successful in the past, the customer may just have appointed a new buyer who wishes to review the choices of her predecessor and remain with the suppliers she used in her last firm. Moreover, when first you met you were delayed in traffic and arrived late for the meeting.

In sum, business-to-business marketing involves a dynamic interaction between suppliers and their buyers. Developing marketing plans is good and useful, but the success of these will depend on the relationship you have with a small number of sophisticated buyers.

This interaction view of marketing is principally associated with the work of the Industrial Marketing and Purchasing Group (IMP) and its affiliates. The beginnings of the IMP work can be traced back to research in the areas of industrial marketing (Håkansson and Östberg 1975; Håkansson and

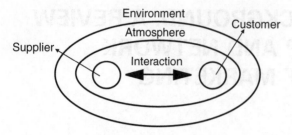

Figure 1.1   Understanding business-to-business
relationships
Source: Turnbull and Valla (1986). Reprinted with
permission of Routledge Publishers

Wootz 1975) and internationalization (Johanson
and Wiedersheim-Paul 1975; Johanson and Vahlne
1977). From these beginnings, the work of the IMP
group and its associates has developed to represent
a considerable and ongoing contribution to relationship and network marketing.

The interaction approach to business-to-business
marketing was originally defined in a pan-European IMP project (Håkansson 1982). A valuable
overview of the development of this area can be
found in Ford (1990).

Four types of variables play a role. Variables
which:

- describe the parties involved, both as organizations and individuals;
- describe the elements and process of interaction;
- describe the environment within which the
  interaction takes place;
- describe the atmosphere (conflict or co-operation)in which the interaction takes place.

These are shown visually by Turnbull and Valla
(1986) (see Figure 1.1).

Marketing increasingly recognizes the importance of relationships. Möller and Wilson (1995)
integrate the IMP interaction model with other
strands of relationship literature from the areas
of marketing channels, strategy and organizational behaviour to provide a comprehensive
checklist of these relationships (Figure 1.2).

Returning to the previous example, the decision to buy a new paperclip is not just the

---

Buyer–Seller Characteristics and Environmental Influences
1. Environmental context
    - Context of the buying organization
    - Context of the selling organization
    - Common context

2. Supplier characteristics
    - Organizational level
    - Departmental level
    - Group level
    - Individual level

3. Buyer characteristics
    - Organizational level
    - Departmental level
    - Group level
    - Individual level

Interaction
4. Interaction processes
    - Exchange processes
    - Adaptation processes
    - Co-ordination processes

Relationship Development
5. Outcome factors
    - Changes in the state of buyer–seller factors
    - Changes in the states of interaction process
      factors
    - Dynamic patterns in processes and organizational
      factors
    - Changes in the environmental context

Figure 1.2   Checklist of IMP relationships
Source: Adapted from Möller and Wilson
(1995)

decision of the buyer, but is influenced by
broader organizational decisions. These *buyer
characteristics* will influence your chances of
success. At an individual level, the new buyer
is less familiar with your firm and has a preference for a previous supplier. The relationship between individuals on each side may
develop bonds of trust and familiarity. Furthermore, the exchanges your firm has had with the
customer on other products have not always
been good. If drawing pins were short delivered, will you do the same on paper clips? The
interaction processes influence the successful
development of the relationship. The relationship has clearly changed with the arrival of the
new buyer so that it has developed positively
or negatively.

This following section explores further some of the above features of interaction.

Interaction Processes

Every contact between a buyer and seller, through a sale, phone call, delivery or social meeting represents an *episode in the relationship*. These episodes may be positive, if both buyer and supplier are happy, or negative, if one or the other is unhappy with the experience. Episodes build up into a relationship between the buyer and supplier. The relationship, therefore, is:

> built out of the history of the companies' dealings with each other and can be described in terms of adaptations, commitments, trust and conflict. (Ford 1984)

Types of Distance between Suppliers and Buyers

Ford (1984) identifies five types of distance between buyers and sellers:

- Social
- Cultural
- Technological
- Time
- Geography.

Imagine, for example, that the buyer is in the USA and the seller in Japan. Each partner may have different cultural expectations of good business practice. They may not understand each other's languages. One may use different software versions to the other and be unable to read electronic communications. All of these may hinder development of business relationships. As a result developing relationships may take a long time from first contact to first sale. This may be extended if travelling to meetings involves a significant geographic distance:

- *Social distance* is the unfamiliarity with the way the other works
- *Cultural distance* is the result of diverse national characteristics

- *Technological distance* is a gap in product or process technologies
- *Time distance* is the elapsed time between establishing contact and the final transfer of the good or service
- *Geographic distance* is the extent to which firms are physically separated.

Many of these distances reduce in longer-established relationships. While geographic and cultural distance cannot be reduced, other than by relocation and employing more local nationals, their impact may be reduced the more individuals and organizations become accustomed to dealing with each other. Social distance is similarly overcome by familiarity with counterparts. The time taken for each transaction to take place reduces with repeat purchases. Technological differences may reduce with convergence towards a norm over time. This may involve one or other firm making adaptations.

Developing Relationships

Trust

The obstacles to relationships reduce as firms get to know each other. The two firms develop trust in each other. Moorman, Zaltman and Deshpandé (1992, p. 315) define trust as:

> a willingness to rely on an exchange partner in whom one has confidence. A willingness to accept the partner's judgement, advice and behaviour.

Håkansson (1982) argues that successful relationships tend to be based upon trust rather than formal commitment. In other words, trust which develops through social interaction between individuals in the firms (Cunningham and Roberts 1974; Turnbull 1979; Webster 1979), is more important than legally binding contracts. Often, when building relationships, social bonds develop long before there is any economic exchange. The two parties may have met at industry trade shows, sales pitches and other events and have made judgements on whether they could work together.

Trust plays a vital role in overcoming the potential for conflict. In situations where small sellers deal with large buyers, there is an imbalance of power. Consider the growing globalization and concentration of the retail sector. Wal Mart ranked as number 2 in an *FT 500* list of the world's largest Fast Moving Consumer Goods (FMCG) firms in 2000. With this size and the roll out of its Every Day Low Pricing strategy, Wal Mart is clearly developing a position of power over its suppliers. Whether this power results in co-operation or conflict depends largely on whether Wal Mart and its suppliers see mutual benefits and can both achieve their goals.

In the 1970s, studies of marketing channels focused on power imbalance as resulting in conflict (Lusch 1976; Etgar 1978; Hardy and Magrath 1989). More recent studies have shown, however, that trust and mutual focus on co-operation can overcome the negative effects of power imbalance (Jackson 1985; Narus and Anderson 1986; Young and Wilkinson 1989). Initiatives such as Category Management and Efficient Consumer Response help to switch the emphasis onto creating co-operative 'win–win' relationships.

Trust and Commitment

Research also suggests that trust may result in commitment between two partners. The question of why some firms become committed to each other and develop long-term relationships is central to interaction literature. Both Anderson and Weitz (1992) and Morgan and Hunt (1994) suggest that if a buyer can rely on its seller it is less inclined to terminate the agreement and may increase its commitment.

Commitment is defined by Morgan and Hunt (1994, p. 23) as:

> an exchange partner believing that an ongoing relationship with another is so important as to warrant maximum efforts at maintaining it.

Anderson and Weitz (1992, p. 19) offer the alternative definition that commitment is:

> a desire to develop a stable relationship, a willingness to make short-term sacrifices to maintain the relationship, and a confidence in the stability of the relationship.

While Moorman, Zaltman and Deshpandé (1992, p. 316) define commitment as:

an enduring desire to maintain a valued relationship.

It should be noted that the above definitions of commitment suggest that firms may need to make sacrifices, maximum efforts and so forth to maintain the relationship. In order to do this, one or both firms may need to adapt the way in which they operate. A seller might, for example, need to reduce its production lead times, buy new machinery or alter its salesforce structure to improve interaction with a particular buyer. The buyer may also need to make adaptations, such as learning more about the manufacturing process, changing its warehousing or training its buyers to handle a particular type of product.

Adaptation, then, may be necessary by one or both firms to allow the relationship to prosper (Håkansson and Östberg 1975; Håkansson and Wootz 1975).

In summary, research suggests that successful relationship development is based on:

- Marketing mix variables such as quality, product, price and delivery
- Adaptability
- Overcoming distance between the firms
- Creating commitment to the relationship (Ford 1984).

Are Long-Term Relationships Beneficial?

Long-term relationships result in cost reductions and increased revenues (Ford 1990). They may also offer a number of other benefits including free exchange of information which may stimulate innovation and effective use of available resources.

Yet long-term relationships are not always considered desirable. Some firms remain in unhealthy relationships through inertia (Young and Denize 1994). These disadvantages are more apparent in some industry sectors than others. In advertising agency–client relationships, long-term relationships may reduce the level of creativity. Agencies may have a house style and produce similar ideas over a period of time (see Chapter 10). In sum, some authors argue that there is a 'dark side' to long-term relationships (Grayson and Ambler 1999) and that these do not, necessarily, lead to commitment.

Relationship Marketing

Definitions and Origins

Relationship marketing goes back to the basics of determining what customers *need and want* (De-Bruicker and Summe 1985; Christopher, Payne and Ballantyne 1991a; Narus and Anderson 1995) but goes beyond the traditional (relationship marketing refers to this as 'transactional') approach to look at the development of ongoing relationships with these customers.

Relationship marketing, then, is: 'as much about keeping customers as it is about getting them in the first place' (Christopher, Payne and Ballantyne 1991a, p. 1). Berry (1983) describes 'relationship marketing' as the development, maintenance and enhancement of customer relationships. In this respect it is a reinforcement of the central importance to marketing of building ongoing customer relationships.

Gummesson (1999, p. 11) explains of transactional marketing:

> In transaction marketing, the fact that a customer has bought a product does not forecast the probability of a new purchase, not even if a series of purchases have been made. A customer may repeatedly use the same supplier because of high switching costs, but without feeling committed to the supplier or wanting to enter a closer relationship. Transactions lack history and memory and they don't get sentimental.

Relationship marketing is similar to interaction in that it looks at interaction between buyers and sellers, but broadens the focus from business-to-business into services and also consumer markets. It has its roots in services marketing (Berry 1983; Gummesson 1994) as well as the interaction studies discussed in the previous section.

Relationship marketing began with a focus on *direct contact* with *sophisticated buyers* who required *high levels of service quality*.

Its central theme is that of building loyal customer relationships. It aims to persuade customers to climb a 'loyalty ladder' (Christopher, Payne and Ballantyne 1991a) from being a prospect, to a customer (first purchase), to a client (recurrent purchases). Once a long-standing relationship is established, the client may become a supporter and finally an advocate for the supplier.

Given the links with services marketing, it is not surprising that loyal relationships are often connected with superior service. Narus and Anderson (1995) see service as comprising:

> programs that help customers to design their products or reduce their costs as well as rebates or bonuses that influence how customers do business with a supplier.

They emphasize that services can be used to 'meet customer requirements, get more of their business and enhance profits' (Narus and Anderson 1995, p. 76). Existing services should be assessed as to their value and cost. The basic package should be limited to only those services which are valued highly by the customers in a particular segment. Others may be offered as options. In this way, firms may reduce the number and cost of services by providing flexible service offerings.

Gronroos (1990) suggests that excellent service may be different at each stage of the relationship. Establishing relationships involves making promises, maintaining them involves fulfilling promises, while enhancing a relationship involves making a new set of promises based on fulfilment of earlier promises.

The Broader Application of Relationship Marketing

A common feature of interaction and services marketing was that of building direct, face-to-face relationships with customers. One of the barriers to relationship building in consumer marketing is the number of consumers involved. This barrier has been partially overcome by developments in information technology that have made it possible to build relationships not only in sectors with a few buyers, but also, virtually, via E business, with large numbers of consumers (Everett 1994; Mitchell 1995).

Retailer loyalty cards and databases of buyer behaviour have made it possible for firms to know enough about large numbers of consumers to interact with them. These developments have prompted a growing body of theoretical and practitioner studies of relationship 'value' (Gould 1995; Mitchell 1995; Prus and Brandt 1995).

A series of practical steps are recommended. These include:

- Prioritizing the customer portfolio on some basis to identify those who are most loyal (Prus and Brandt 1995)
- Creating communities of loyal customers – for example, through development of loyal customer clubs (Mitchell 1995)
- Providing rewards for loyalty (O'Brien and Jones 1995).

An important distinction exists, however, between database and relationship marketing. Shani and Chalasani (1993) (summarized in Figure 1.3) identify a number of key distinctions between the two. These can be summarized by the fact that database marketing uses the same technology but still takes the transactional marketing view that consumers are passive, whereas relationship marketing uses the same technology to interact with consumers and to adapt and tailor its offer to them. Increasing domestic proliferation of the Internet brings increased possibilities of interaction.

The basic premise is that technology can make it possible to develop direct and long-standing

Database marketing	Relationship Marketing
Transaction-driven	Relationship-driven
Single addressable message	One-to-one communication
Short-term interest in customer	Long-term interest
Keeps traditional information	Requires a larger information base
One-way communication channel	Interactive Communication
Emphasis on reaching customer efficiently	Emphasis on making the customer an equal partner

Figure 1.3   Database marketing contrasted with relationship marketing

relationships with consumers in a way that was previously possible only in situations with few buyers. Mitchell (1995) expresses this as follows: 'it is cheaper and easier to keep existing customers than to try and woo new ones.'

Mitchell cites an average increase in profits of double or triple the increase in customer retention. Hepworth and Mateus (1994) propose steps to measure how great is the contribution to the bottom line of customer loyalty. These include calculating the revenue at risk from poor customer service and establishing a base line knowledge of customer satisfaction rates so that any reduction in satisfaction can quickly be established. However, Reichheld (1993, p. 64) suggests that, despite this:

> flurry of activities aimed at serving customers better, only a few companies have achieved meaningful, measurable improvements in customer loyalty.

A key contribution to the field of relationship marketing is the focus on value creation. Christopher, Payne and Ballantyne (1991a, p. 1) describe the aim of relationship marketing as being: 'to provide unique value in chosen markets, sustainable over time.' They see this value as being provided by bringing together quality and customer service and requiring provision of critical service support and internal marketing.

O'Brien and Jones conclude (1995, p. 75) that providing rewards for customer loyalty does add value: 'If the company understands how to share value.' Normann and Ramirez (1993, p. 66) describe firms as co-operating in a network of economic actors: 'suppliers, business partners, allies, customers' which all work together to co-produce value. They see this co-production of value as signalling a move from Porter's value chain (1990) to a 'value constellation'.

The idea of a constellation of relationships contributing to value creation mirrors the work of Christopher, Payne and Ballantyne (1991a, 1991b) which views the firm as existing in a set of relationships with customers and other stakeholders.

Further explanation of these relationships is provided in Figure 1.4.

The focus on a number of different relationships might suggest that relationship marketing is similar to network studies of marketing. A distinction drawn by Easton and Håkansson (1996), however,

1. **Customer markets** (new and existing)
The goal is not only to get customers but to *keep them*. Sustained growth in business usually depends upon the same customer coming back again and again. Existing relationships with customers cost less to sustain than new ones.

2. **Supplier markets**
Establishing *long-term relations with suppliers* is a departure from traditional adversarial buyer–supplier positions. This development means that suppliers are seen as collaborators or partners in improving quality and managing costs.

3. **Referral markets**
Developing relationships in referral markets means linking up with those people or institutions that have the *power to direct business to the company*. Key existing customers are often referral sources, and so are intermediaries, third-party buyers, agencies and business networks.

4. **Employee markets**
Managing staff intakes and induction processes for new employees means an improvement in the reliability of staff and a direct opportunity for the inculcation of *company culture*.

5. **Influencer markets**
The opportunity exists to develop relationships with people and organizations whose goodwill or activities can directly or indirectly influence success in customer markets. There is overlap here with the activities and means of Public Relations, except that the underpinning orientation is success in *customer markets*.

6. **Internal markets**
Internal marketing means developing strategic plans and actions to identify and collaborate in the management of any *internal* activity which has as its goal the enhancement or success of the *external* marketing plans.

Figure 1.4 The six markets model: a broader view of marketing relationships
Source: Christopher, Payne and Ballantyne (1991a), p. 8

is that relationship marketing looks at many different relationships in parallel rather than as a totality. While some overlap is shown between the different types of relationship, relationship marketing does not explore the broader web of relationships surrounding the firm.

Relationship marketing does, however, highlight the importance of relationships in consumer as well as industrial marketing. Furthermore, it focuses not only on buyer–seller relationships, but also on relationships with other actors in the environment. To this extent, it demonstrates the importance of exploring the relationship concepts of interaction and services marketing for the broader field of marketing.

NETWORK STUDIES OF MARKETING

Markets as Networks

The last section identified the existence of many different types of relationships that may surround a firm. It is this 'network' of relationships that forms the basis of the 'markets as networks' literature.

The importance of networks in management is increasingly recognized. The concept of networks is, however, used to cover a number of different phenomena. Among others, 'networking' is used to describe the process of building relationships with buyers and other stakeholders, leveraging contacts to improve business possibilities; 'network marketing' is even used as another way of describing pyramid selling.

Some consider that the popularity of networks threatens its credibility as an area of study:

> Anyone reading through what purports to be network literature will readily perceive the analogy between it and a 'terminological jungle' in which any newcomer may plant a tree. This indiscriminate proliferation of the network concept threatens to relegate it to the status of an evocative metaphor, applied so loosely that it ceases to mean anything. (Nohria 1992, p. 3)

The first task of any review of networks in marketing must, therefore, be to define what is understood by a network. While there are a broad number of different views within management as whole, marketing and strategy focus on two different strands of literature:

■ Networks are a type of organization that a firm may choose to use.
■ Markets are made up of webs of relationships.

Networks as an organizational choice

Thorelli (1986, p. 37) argued that networks are a type of organization between free markets and hierarchical organizations:

> at one end of the spectrum is what we would call the open market. At the other we find the firm which is relatively self-sufficient in terms of vertical of functional integration. In some ways these distinctions are analogous to Williamson's (1975) markets and hierarchies, although he would likely include as part of 'markets' a number of in-between forms where we would rather apply the generic term networks.

By this definition, the network is similar to other forms of co-operation such as strategic alliances. In other words, the network is a type of co-operative arrangement that can be used if appropriate. Miles and Snow (1986) suggest that the networks offer flexibility in turbulent environments. Lorenzoni and Ornati (1988) describe the benefits which networks (described in their words as constellations) provide for small firms in the Italian textile industry in furthering innovation.

Markets as Networks

The 'markets as networks' view is most closely associated with the work of the IMP group. It builds on the interaction studies described earlier in this chapter. From this perspective, markets are made up of a complex web of interactive relationships:

> The markets are characterised by interaction between firms in relationships where the parties have some control over each other and the organisations are not 'pure' hierarchies. To us the legal frameworks of the transactions are less important and the boundaries of the networks are unclear. (Johanson and Mattsson 1987, p. 12)

Different levels of relationship exist in the network. A variety of different terminologies have been used to describe these different levels. Blankenburg (1995) distinguishes between relationships in the broader marketing environment, relationships between organizations and relationships within the firm. The work of the IMP group commonly describes these as macro-, inter-organizational and intra-organizational relationships respectively. In his synthesis of interaction, networks and relationship marketing, Gummesson (1999) categorizes these as 'mega' (macro environmental), 'market' (competitor, supplier and customer relationships) and 'nano' (relationships within the firm).

These categories of relationship are summarised in Figure 1.5.

The Network Perspective in this Book

In this book, the network sections use the 'markets as networks' view. The distinction between the relationship and network sections of each chapter are:

■ **Relationships** – look at the nature and development of international marketing relationships.
■ **Networks** – look at the impact of operation within a complex web of relationships.

This book uses the IMP terminology of macro-, inter- and intra-organizational relationships.

Blankenburg	IMP	Gummesson
Macro-environment	Macro	Mega
Between organizations	Inter-organizational	Market
Within organizations	Intra-organizational	Nano

Figure 1.5   Network levels

Key Themes in the Markets as Networks Literature

What is a Network?

At the broadest level, the markets as networks literature considers all firms to be connected directly or indirectly (Easton 1995). The level of complexity is immense. Pragmatism, and the need to achieve insights rather than just describing this complexity, lead researchers to different conclusions over the level at which networks should be studied.

For some purposes, the network is broken down into its smallest component, the single relationship (Ford, Håkansson and Johanson 1986, Easton and Araujo 1992). This is commonly referred to as a *'dyad'*. Others move beyond this to study the links between three actors (Smith and Laage-Hellman 1992) (known as a *'triad'*).

Breaking down the network in this way has certain key limitations.

1. **It oversimplifies the nature of a network**. The interaction within a network is more complex than can be shown in a single relationship. Firms may be influenced by others to whom they are only indirectly connected. A firm which alters its computers system to match the needs of one customer may, for example, then wish to use different systems in its dealings with another customer.

2. **Relationships cannot be added back together to represent a network**. The learning from single relationships cannot be put together to represent the whole network. Network researchers have taken different views on this issue over time. Johanson and Mattsson's earlier work (1986) argues that this is possible but later this view was revised. Interaction within a network may be affected by changes anywhere in the network, which would not be captured if the first approach were taken. For example, a change in Wal Mart's computer systems may ripple back through its supply chain to affect suppliers and their suppliers. These may also influence the decisions made by competitor retailers and cause the same impact on their suppliers.

An alternative approach to network study, then, looks at the network as a whole. Deo Sharma (1989) looks at network operation in the technical consultancy industry, while Lee (1991) looks at networks in market entry into Korea. Although these studies capture the richness of the network, their level of complexity makes it difficult to see how this approach can be developed other than in relation to specific industries or situations, without becoming unwieldy.

For practical purposes, therefore, studies tend to break down the network on market, technology or other grounds, into subsections or 'nets'. Cunningham and Culligan (1991, p. 254) suggest the use of 'focal nets,' which consist of:

> relations above a certain minimum degree of closeness to a focal or 'hub' firm. The focal net defines the set of the most important relationships for that focal firm at any one point of time.

Networks are Dynamic

A particular feature of networks is that they are dynamic. Understanding networks of relationships, therefore, involves exploration of the nature and processes of change. The development of long-term relationships remains an issue, but this tends to be viewed with greater ambivalence.

Studies of network stability stress the importance of building lasting relationships. Relationships are seen to become stronger over time, often involving an increasing number of exchanges: 'The strength of the relationship might also increase in terms of social and knowledge-based bonds' (Mattsson 1989).

Stable 'structured' networks function more effectively as they show a 'clear division of labour between firms, [well defined] technologies and strong bonds between firms' (Mattsson 1989). An example of a stable network is that in a mature industry, such as the car industry, in which there are relatively few new entrants and all the players have developed clear 'positions' in the market.

In contrast, the frequent changes of membership in loosely structured networks are viewed as both time-consuming and costly. This type of network might be found in the emerging dot.com sector where there are many new entrants and an increasing number of firms who fail to survive.

But is stability in networks good? Håkansson (1992) suggests a downside of stability in networks. 'Structuring' or deepening and elaborating existing ways of doing things develops systems and norms within the network. Once these exist, the network can become similar to a firm which has established 'recipes' for how it behaves. The creation of norms, recipes, etc. reduces flexibility, innovation and other characteristics frequently associated with networks.

Change, more especially innovative adaptation, is the lifeblood of the network. A key feature of the network is that relationships can easily be dissolved and, when the network reforms, it can metamorphose to meet any given market situation. An example of this metamorphosis is seen in Håkansson and Waluszewski (1997). The recycled fibre network surrounding SCA in Sweden changed in composition and priorities to meet growing demand for environmentally friendly processes. A number of characteristics of innovation process in networks can be identified from this example:

1. Elements of old solutions may be intertwined with the new
2. This is an ongoing process, where development of relationships may result in changes to the way activities and resources are combined
3. No single actor controls the innovation process.

As well as stability, then, the network literature stresses the benefits of networks as dynamic structures that change. Håkansson (1992) identifies the need for 'heterogeneity', or the ability to find new ways of combining activities and resources. Lundgren (1992) distinguishes between 'co-ordination' or continuous change, and 'mobilization' or discontinuous change to create new resource structures and access routes.

Taking a Dynamic View of International Marketing

An important contribution of the network perspective when applied to international marketing

is its ability to look at phenomena over time. International markets are subject to rapid, and increasingly unpredictable, change. Trade embargoes imposed by governments – such as that imposed by the Malaysian government in the Pergau Dam (see Box 4.2) incident – may alter the dynamics of international marketing overnight. The ability of large retailers, such as Wal Mart and Carrefour, to acquire other large retail chains means that their international expansion is not gradual, but rapid and stepwise.

Studying international marketing as a dynamic area where firms are surrounded by webs of relationships can capture complex phenomena such as the transitory nature of competition and co-operation. The fact that today's competitor may be tomorrow's partner in co-operation, or even part of the same firm is seen in examples such as the network surrounding the Big Six accounting firms. In one instance, two competitor Big Six firms used complementary skills to collaborate informally on an aid agency contract in Ukraine. Later the same firms merged. A growing focus of network studies is on change in networks (Easton, Wilkinson and Georgieva 1997; Håkansson and Waluszewski (1997); Fu, Spencer, Wilkinson and Young 1999; Wilkinson and Wiley 1999).

COMPARING THE INTERACTION, RELATIONSHIP AND NETWORK LITERATURE

The above review of interaction, relationship and network approaches to marketing illustrates the fact that while these are similar in some respects, there are still fundamental differences in others.

A number of authors have attempted to classify and identify the similarities and differences between these evolving streams of research (Wilson and Möller 1995; Easton and Håkansson 1996; Mattsson 1997). Mattsson (1997, p. 448) points to the fact that, given their common interest in relationships, it is surprising that the network and relationship marketing schools 'do not overlap and interact very much'. A major reason for this might be that these are parallel streams, which take different perspectives on relationships.

Game theorists have referred to the assumptions of traditional marketing as those of a 'zero-sum' game. A firm can gain only (+1) at the expense of a competitor (−1) resulting in zero in sum. All relationship literature, however, focuses on the fact that firms are engaged in relationships where it is possible for two or more actors to gain. This is known as a 'win–win' situation.

Traditional marketing also makes assumptions about the nature of the interface between the firm and its environment. Firms are discrete entities, operating in a 'faceless' environment (Axelsson 1992). Macro-environmental trends may present opportunities or threats and must be monitored, but are beyond the control of the firm. In contrast, relationship approaches all consider that there is some interaction between the firm and its environment. It is here, however, that differences begin to be seen between different strands of relationship literature.

Traditional marketing sees the macro-environment, competitors and other stakeholders as uncontrollable, or at best semi-controllable, forces in a 'faceless' environment (Axelsson 1992; Nohria 1992). In relationship marketing, the six markets model (Christopher, Payne and Ballantyne 1991) proposes interaction not only with customers, but with other organizations via referrals and influencers. The concept of interaction with macro-level actors is introduced by Gummesson (1999) as 'mega-relationships'. Previously relationship marketing had predominantly focused on inter- and intra-organizational relationships.

Interaction models go further, seeing relationships as embedded in both a surrounding atmosphere of conflict or co-operation and an outer macro-environment. 'Markets as networks' takes the concept of 'embeddedness' further. Firms are engaged in 'full-faced' interaction with other firms and actors at the macro-, inter- and intra-organizational levels Network studies see firms as embedded in a web of interdependent relationships with other firms and in the broader environment.

Easton and Håkansson (1996) highlight further distinctions between interaction studies, relationship marketing and networks as existing in their unit of analysis, prescriptive or descriptive nature and as to whether they are structural or dynamic.

Unit of Analysis

The unit of analysis of traditional, transaction-based marketing is that of the firm as a discrete entity. In relationship studies, the minimum unit of analysis is the single relationship, usually involving interaction between a buyer and seller. Relationship marketing moves beyond the buyer–seller relationship to take into account relationships with other stakeholders (see Figure 1.2). These, however, are largely viewed as a set of parallel relationships. The relationships between the 'six markets' are not explored. In consequence, this should rightly be viewed as a 'multiple dyadic' rather than a network approach. In contrast, while the 'markets as networks' literature sometimes breaks down the network to its subparts for the purposes of study, arguments that this cannot be built up to represent the total network favour study of the totality of the network (Easton 1992).

Description or Prescription?

Both interaction and network studies tend towards description. While interaction studies highlight the value of stable long-term relationships (Jackson 1985; Narus and Anderson 1986; Young and Wilkinson 1989), these are not prescribed. Indeed some interaction and network literature argues against stability if it results in stagnation (Håkansson 1992; Young and Denize 1994). In contrast, however, relationship marketing prescribes co-operative relationships and makes clear reference to the increases in profit which can be gained by adopting activities such as database, services or internal marketing.

Network studies, particularly those looking at complex webs of relationships, tend to describe. Networks are not seen as a type of operation which can be adopted where it confers benefits, as with networks as a hybrid organizational forms (Miles and Snow 1986; Thorelli 1986; Lorenzoni and Ornati 1988). Rather, they are the context in which the firm exists (Johanson and Mattsson 1987; Axelsson and Easton 1992). A first distinction, then, between the approaches might be that interaction and networks describe, while relationship marketing prescribes.

Static or Dynamic?

While traditional, transaction-based marketing studies static snapshots of the decisions which customers make, all relationship approaches take a dynamic view of marketing. Within interaction and relationship marketing this is reflected in a focus on relationship development, enhancement and maintenance. Markets as networks, however, look at evolution in network positions, which may involve both building new relationships and breaking existing ones.

The similarities and differences between traditional, interaction, relationship and network perspectives on marketing are summarized in Figure 1.6.

It is clear that relationship perspectives differ substantially from traditional marketing. Relationship perspectives are win–win and tend to study the evolution of relationships over time. Combining interaction, relationship and network studies into one perspective is complicated by differences in the unit of analysis and the interface between the firm and its environment. To present all four perspectives separately in studying international marketing might duplicate points.

This book, therefore, takes the pragmatic approach of using three perspectives: the traditional, or transaction-based, perspective, the relationship perspective and the network perspective. The characteristics of these perspectives are shown in Figure 1.6. It should be noted that the combination of interaction and relationship perspectives is not intended to denigrate the contribution of either to the understanding of marketing. Rather, it is a recognition of commonalities in their contribution to understanding relationships

and an attempt to communicate the value of their contribution to a wider audience.

In this book the distinction between the perspectives can be summarized as in Figure 1.7.

RELATIONSHIP AND NETWORK PERSPECTIVES ON INTERNATIONAL MARKETING

Marketing practitioners and academics alike face a set of challenges in international marketing. The economy is globalizing. The reasons for this globalization are presented more fully in Chapter 4 and in terms of the implications for international marketing strategy (Chapter 5). In their every day operation, businesses are increasingly competing and co-operating with firms of various nationalities. It is not uncommon for firms to be engaged in multiple transnational relationships at any point in time. As Johanson and Mattsson (1988, p. 315) put it:

> A Swedish firm might increase its penetration in a South American market because of its relationship in Japan with an internationalising Japanese firm.

Some of these relationships are collaborative (Easton 1990) rather than co-operative. The 1980s and 1990s have witnessed significant growth in the use of joint ventures and strategic alliances in international markets (Contractor and Lorange 1988). Zero-sum analyses stress the benefits of co-operation where this affords access to scarce resources (Porter and Fuller 1986; Jarillo 1988; Hamel, Prahalad and Doz 1989). Together with pressure from host governments (Schlegelmilch,

Dimension	Traditional	Relationship marketing	Interaction studies	Markets as networks
Unit of analysis	Transaction	Multiple relationships	Single relationship	Network of relationships
View of markets:	Zero-sum	Win–Win	Win–Win	Win–Win
Interface with environment	Faceless	Interactive	Interactive	Full-faced
Prescriptive or descriptive	Prescriptive	Prescriptive	Descriptive	Descriptive
Temporal perspective	Static	Dynamic	Dynamic	Dynamic
Predominant view of relationships	Focus on buyers and sellers separately	Long-term relationships add value	Long-term relationships add value	Long-term relationships add value, but flexibility is important

Figure 1.6   Traditional relationship and network perspectives on marketing: similarities and differences

Traditional perspective	Reviews the key challenges for international marketers from a traditional perspective
Relationship perspective	Identifies types of international marketing relationships and the successful development
Network perspective	Studies networks of relationships – at different levels, in different places or engaged in different types of marketing activities – over time

Figure 1.7   The perspectives on marketing distinguished in this book

Diamantopoulos and Petersen 1991), this may account for the dominance of joint ventures for entry into regions such as East and Central Europe (Shama 1995) and China (Johnston 1991). This view of co-operation is neatly captured by Hamel, Prahalad and Doz in the title of their 1989 article 'Collaborate with your Competitors and Win'.

Even within this zero-sum approach to relationships, however, there is a growing recognition that relationships are not easy. As Harrigan (1987) explains:

> Even sceptical managers are being swept up by the contagious belief that joint ventures and other forms of corporate marriage will solve their firms' problems with a handshake and a stroke of a pen.

A dominant proportion of relationship studies in international marketing, therefore, are based on the assumptions of traditional marketing, maybe with a recognition of the importance of relationships which bring this closer to the relationship marketing perspective. In this book, it is hoped to review the types of international marketing relationships which play a role, and to apply learning from both relationship and interaction literature to understand the challenges of developing these successfully. As interaction and relationship marketing literature suggest (Håkansson 1982; Christopher, Payne and Ballantyne 1991), they must be analyzed and managed.

Relationship development across international borders is complicated by a number of different types of distance (Turnbull 1979; Ford 1980). The book begins (Part II) by exploring in greater detail the Cultural Environment (Chapter 2), the Technological Context (Chapter 3) and the Economic and Political Context (Chapter 4) of relationships.

As previously discussed, the extent to which firms can influence this context varies between the perspectives:

■ Traditional marketing sees the international context as uncontrollable
■ The relationship perspective focuses on building relationships with actors in these contexts
■ The network perspective takes the broadest view, focusing on complex patterns of interaction between firms and their international context.

Following the context section, the book moves on to consideration of international marketing strategy and relationships (Part III). In this section, inter- and intra-organizational relationships of the firm become a focus. Chapter 5 looks at international marketing strategy from traditional, relationship and network perspectives.

From a traditional perspective, international marketing strategy is a global chess game where firms jockey to win global market share at each other's expense. From a relationship perspective, international marketing strategy revolves around adding value in international relationships. From a network perspective, firms are building positions in global networks. Chapter 6 applies the different perspectives to the issue of market attractiveness, reviewing traditional tools, looking at the nature of knowledge in relationships and considering firms as part of a knowledge economy.

Chapters 7 and 8 look at the types of international organization that firms might use. Chapter 7 reviews economic-based theories of international organization, looks at joint ventures and alliances in international markets and considers, at this point in the book, what might be learned from viewing the network as a hybrid organizational mode (Thorelli 1986). Chapter 8 takes the dynamic perspective, reviewing the process of internationalization from each perspective.

Part IV identifies some of the challenges in the international marketing mix. Issues relating to international pricing (Chapter 9) and international promotion (Chapter 10) are reviewed.

Having explored international marketing contexts and strategies, Part V identifies challenges of marketing in different geographic regions, such as the Triad (Chapters 11–13), Emerging (or Mega-) Markets (Chapter 14) and Less Developed Markets (Chapter 15). Finally, the book concludes in Chapter 16 with a discussion of the issue of international marketing organization from each of the different perspectives. From a traditional perspective, the links between marketing orientation and different organizational forms are explored for a range of countries. From a relationship perspective, the organizational implications of decoupling the value chain are examined. Lastly, the network perspective of intra-organizational relationships is considered.

BIBLIOGRAPHY

Anderson, E. and Weitz, B. (1992) 'The Use of Pledges to Build and Sustain Commitment in Distribution Channels', *Journal of Marketing Research*, 29: 18–34.

Axelsson, B. (1992) 'Network Positions and Strategic Action – An Analytical Framework', in Axelsson, B. and Easton, G. (eds), *Industrial Networks: A New View of Reality*, Routledge.

Axelsson, B. and Easton, G. (eds) (1992) *Industrial Networks: A New View of Reality*, Routledge.

Berry, L. L. (1983) 'Relationship Marketing', in Berry, L. L., Shostack, G. L. and Upah, G. D. (eds), *Emerging Perspectives on Services Marketing*, Chicago: American Marketing Association, 25–8.

Berry, L. L. and Gresham, L. G. (1986) 'Relationship Retailing: Transforming Customers into Clients', *Business Horizons*, November–December: 43–7.

Blankenburg, D. (1995) 'A Network Approach to Foreign Market Entry', in Möller, K. and Wilson, D. (eds), *Business Marketing: An Interaction and Network Perspective*, Kluwer: 375–410.

Christopher, M., Payne, A. and Ballantyne, D. (1991a) 'Relationship Marketing: Bringing Quality, Customer Service and Marketing Together', Cranfield School of Management, *Working paper*.

Christopher, M., Payne, A. and Ballantyne, D. (1991b) *Relationship Marketing*, Heinemann.

Contractor, F. and Lorange, P. (1988) (eds) *Co-operative Strategies in International Business*, Lexington Books.

Cunningham, M. and Culligan, D. (1991) 'Competitiveness through Networks of Relationships in Information Technology Product Markets', in Paliwoda, S. J. (ed.), *New Perspectives in International Marketing*, Routledge.

Cunningham, M. and Roberts, D. (1974) 'The Role of Customer Service in Industrial Marketing', *European Journal of Marketing*, 8, 1: 15–28.

Debruicke, F. S. and Summe, G. (1985) 'Make Sure your Customers Keep Coming Back', *Harvard Business Review*, January–February: 92–8.

Deo Sharma, D. (1989) 'Technical Consultancy as a Network of Relationships', in Cavusgil, S. T. (ed.), *Advances in International Marketing*, 3: 57–74.

Dibb, C. S. and Meadows, M. (1998), *Journal of Marketing Management*.

Easton, G. 1990 'Relationships Among Competitors', in Day, G., Weitz, B. and Wensley, R. (eds), *The Interface of Marketing and Strategy: Strategic Management, Policy and Planning*, JAI Press.

Easton, G. (1992) 'Industrial Networks: A Review', in Axelsson, B. and Easton, G. (eds), *Industrial Networks: A New View of Reality*, Routledge.

Easton, G. (1995) 'Methodology and Industrial Networks', in Wilson D. T. and Möller, K. (eds), *Business Marketing: An Interaction and Network Perspective*, Kluwer.

Easton, G. and Araujo, L. (1992) 'Non-Economic Exchange in Industrial Networks', in Axelsson, B. and Easton, G. (eds), *Industrial Networks: A New View of Reality*, Routledge.

Easton, G. and Håkansson, H. (1996) 'Markets as Networks: Editorial Introduction', *International Journal of Research in Marketing, Special Issue on Markets as Networks*, 13, 5: 407–13.

Easton, G., Wilkinson, I. F. and Georgieva, C. (1997) 'Towards Evolutionary Models of Industrial Networks: A Research Programme', in Gemünden, H.-G., Ritter, T. and Walter, A. (eds), *Relationships and Networks in International Markets*, Pergamon Press.

Etgar, M. (1978) 'Selection of an Effective Channel Control Mix', *Journal of Marketing Research*, 15: 53–8.

Everett, M. (1994) 'Database Marketing: Know Why they Buy', *Sales and Marketing Management*, December: 66–71.

Ford, D. (1980) 'The Development of Buyer–Seller Relations in Industrial Markets', *European Journal of Marketing*, 14, 5–6: 339–53.

Ford, D. (1984) 'Buyer–Seller Relationships in International Industrial Marketing', *Industrial Marketing Management*, 13, 2: 101–13.

Ford, D. (ed.) (1990) *Understanding Business Markets: Interaction, Relationships, Networks*, Harcourt Brace.

Ford, D., Håkansson, H. and Johanson, J. (1986) 'How do Companies Interact?', *Industrial Marketing and Purchasing*, 1, 1: 26–42.

Fu, H., Spencer, R., Wilkinson, I. F. and Young, L. (1999) 'The Recent Evolution of Business Networks in China: Two Case Studies', *EMAC Proceedings*, Berlin.

Gouillart, F. J. and Sturdivant, F. D. (1994) 'Spend a Day in the Life of Your Customers', *Harvard Business Review*, January–February: 116–25.

Gould, G. (1995) 'Why is it Customer Loyalty that Counts (and How to Measure it), *Managing Service Quality*, 5, 1: 15–19.

Grayson, K. and Ambler, T. (1999) 'The Dark Side of Long-Term Relationships in Marketing Services', *Journal of Marketing Research*, 36, February: 132–41.

Gronroos, C. (1990) 'Relationship Approach to Marketing in Service Contexts: The Marketing and Organizational Behaviour Interface', *Journal of Business Research*, 20: 3–11.

Gummesson, E. (1994) 'Making Relationship Marketing Operational', *Service Industry Management*, 5, 5: 5–20.

Gummesson, E. (1999) *Total Relationship Marketing: Rethinking Marketing Management: From 4Ps to 30Rs*, Butterworth–Heinemann.

Håkansson, H. (1982) *Industrial Marketing and Purchasing of Industrial Goods: An Interaction Approach*, Croom Helm.

Håkansson, H. (1992) 'Evolution Processes in Industrial Networks', in Easton, G. and Axelsson, B. (eds), *Industrial Networks: A New View of Reality*, Routledge.

Håkansson, H. and Östberg, K. (1975) 'Industrial Marketing – An Organisational Problem?', *Industrial Marketing Management*, 4, 1: 113–23.

Håkansson, H. and Walusewski, A. (1997) 'Recycled Fibre Turning Green', in Gemünden, H.-G., Ritter, T. and Walter, A. (eds), *Relationships and Networks in International Markets*, Pergamon Press.

Håkansson, H. and Wootz, B. (1975) 'Supplier Selection in an International Environment: An Experimental Study', *Journal of Marketing Research*, 12, February.

Hamel, G., Prahalad, C. K. and Doz, Y. (1989) 'Collaborate with your Competitors and Win', *Harvard Business Review*, January–February: 133–9.

Hardy, K. G. and Magrath, A. J. (1989) 'Dealing with Cheating in Distribution', *European Journal of Marketing*, 23, 2: 123–9.

Harrigan, K. R. (1987) 'Why Joint Ventures Fail', *East-Asia Business Review*, July.

Hepworth, M. and Mateus, P. (1994) 'Connecting Customer Loyalty to the Bottom Line', *Canadian Business Review*, 21, 4: 40–3.

Hertz, S. (1992) 'Towards more Integrated Industrial Systems', in Axelsson, B. and Easton, G. (eds), *Industrial Networks: A New View of Reality*, Routledge.

Jackson, B. B. (1985) 'Build Customer Relationships that Last', *Harvard Business Review*, November–December: 120–8.

Jarillo, J.-C. (1988) 'On Strategic Networks', *Strategic Management Review*, 11: 479–99.

Johanson, J. and Mattsson, L.-G. (1986) 'Interorganisational Relations in Industrial Systems: A Network Approach Compared with a Transaction Cost Approach', University of Uppsala, *Working Paper*.

Johanson, J. and Mattsson, L.-G. (1987) 'Interorganisational Relations in Industrial Systems: A Network Approach Compared with a Transaction Cost Approach', *International Studies of Management Organisation*, 17, 1: 34–48.

Johanson, J. and Mattsson, L.-G. (1988) 'Internationalisation in Industrial Systems – A Network Approach', in Hood, N. and Vahlne, J.-E. (eds), *Strategies in Global Competition*, Croom Helm.

Johanson, J. and Vahlne, J.-E. (1977) 'The Internationalisation Process of the Firm: A Model of Knowledge Development and Increasing Foreign Market Commitments', *Journal of International Business Studies*, 8, 1: 23–32.

Johanson, J. and Wiedersheim-Paul, F. (1975) 'The Internationalisation of the Firm – Four Swedish Cases', *Journal of Management Studies*, October: 305–22.

Johnston, W. J. (1991) 'Alternative Approach Strategies for Buyer–Seller Relations with the People's Republic of China', in Paliwoda, S. J. (ed.), *New Perspectives on International Marketing*, Routledge.

Lee, J.-W. (1993) 'The Development of Strategic Position in the Korean Industrial Turbines Market', *Uppsala Working Paper Series*, 1993/8.

Lorenzoni, G. and Ornati, O. A. (1988) 'Constellations of Firms and New Ventures', *Journal of
Business Venturing*, 4, 2: 133–47.

Lundgren, A. (1992) 'Co-ordination and Mobilisation
Processes in Industrial Networks', in Axelsson,
B. and Easton, G. (eds), *Industrial Networks: A
New View of Reality*, Routledge.

Lusch, R. (1976) 'Sources of Power: Their Impact on
Intra-Channel Conflict', *Journal of Marketing
Research*, 13: 382–90.

Mattsson, L.-G. (1984) 'An Application of a Network
Approach to Marketing: Defending and Chang-
ing Market Positions', in Dholakia, N. and
Arndt, J. (eds), *Changing the Course of Marketing.
Alternative Paradigms for Widening Marketing
Theory*, JAI Press.

Mattsson, L.-G. (1989) 'Development of Firms in Net-
works: Positions and Investments', in Cavusgil,
S. T. (ed.), *Advances in International Marketing*, 3,
JAI Press: 121–39.

Mattsson, L.-G. (1997) ' "Relationship Marketing" and
the "Markets as Networks Approach" – A Comparative Analysis of Two Evolving Streams of
Research', *Journal of Marketing Management*, 13:
447–61.

Miles, R. E. and Snow, C. (1986) 'Organisations: New
Concepts for New Forms', *California Management Review*, 28: 62–73.

Mitchell, A. (1995) 'The Ties that Bind', *Marketing
Today*, June: 60–4.

Möller, K. and Wilson, D. T. (1995) 'Business Relation-
ships – An Interaction Perspective' in Möller,
K. and Wilson, D. T. (eds), *Business Marketing:
An Interaction and Network Perspective*, Kluwer
Academic.

Moorman, C., Zaltman, G. and Deshpandé, R. (1992)
'Relationships between Providers and Users of
Market Research: The Dynamics of Trust
within and Between Organizations', *Journal of
Marketing Research*, 29: 314–28.

Morgan, R. M. and Hunt, S. (1994) 'The Commitment–Trust Theory of Relationship Marketing',
Journal of Marketing, 58: 20–38.

Narus, A. J. and Anderson, C. J. (1990) 'A Model of
Distributor Firm and Manufacturing Firm
Working Partnerships', *Journal of Marketing*,
54: 42–58.

Narus, J. A. and Anderson, J. C. (1995) 'Capturing the
Value of Supplementary Services', *Harvard
Business Review*, January–February: 75–83.

Nohria, N. (1992) 'Is a Network Perspective a Useful Way of Studying Organisations', in Nohria, N. and Eccles, R. G. (eds), *Networks and
Organizations*, Harvard Business School Press:
1–22.

Normann, R. and Ramirez, R. (1993) 'From Value
Chain to Value Constellation: Designing Inter-
active Strategy', *Harvard Business Review*,
July–August: 65–77.

O'Brien, L. and Jones, C. (1995) 'Do Rewards really
Create Loyalty?', *Harvard Business Review*,
May–June: 75–82.

Porter, M. E. (1990) *Competitive Advantage of Nations*,
Macmillan.

Porter, M. E. and Fuller, M. B. (1986) 'Coalitions and
Global Strategy', in Portes, M. E. and Fuller, M.
B., *Competition in Global Industries*, Harvard
Business School Press.

Prus, A. and Brandt, D. R. (1995) 'Understanding
your Customers: What you can Learn from a
Customer Loyalty Index', *Marketing Tools*, July–
August: 10–14.

Rackham, N., Friedman, L. and Ruff, R. (1996) *Getting
Partnering Right: How Market Leaders are Creat-
ing Long-term Competitive Advantage*, McGraw-
Hill.

Reichheld, F. F. (1993) 'Loyalty-Based Management',
Harvard Business Review, March–April: 64–73.

Schlegelmilch, B. B., Diamantopoulos, A. and Petersen, M. (1991) 'Conquering the Chinese Market: A Study of Danish Firms' Experiences in
the People's Republic of China', in Paliwoda, S.
J. (ed.), *New Perspectives on International Marketing*, Routledge.

Schurr, P. H. and Ozanne, J. L. (1985) 'Influences
on Exchange Processes: Buyers' Preconceptions
of a Sellers' Trustworthiness and Bargaining
Toughness', *Journal of Consumer Research*, 11:
939–53.

Shama, A. (1995) 'Entry Strategies of US Firms to the
Newly Independent States, Baltic States and
Eastern European Countries', *California Man-
agement Review*, 37, 3: 90–108.

Shani, D. and Chalasani, S. (1993) 'Exploiting Niches
using Relationship Marketing', *The Journal of
Business and Industrial Marketing*, 8, 4: 56–65.

Smith, P. C. and Laage-Hellman, J. (1992) 'Small
Group Analysis in Industrial Networks', in
Axelsson, B. and Easton, G. (eds), *Industrial
Networks: A New View of Reality*, Routledge.

Thorelli, H. B. (1986) 'Networks: Between Markets
and Hierarchies', *Strategic Management Journal*,
7: 37–51.

Turnbull, P. W. (1979) 'Roles of Personal Contacts
in Industrial Export Marketing', *Scandinavian
Journal of Management*: 325–37.

Turnbull, P. W. and Valla, J.-P. (1986) *Strategies for
International Industrial Marketing*, Routledge.

Webster, F. E. (1979) *Industrial Marketing Strategy*,
John Wiley.

Wilkinson, I. F. and Wiley, J. (1999) 'Simulating Industrial Relationships with Evolutionary Models', *EMAC Proceedings*, Berlin.

Williamson, O. E. (1975) *Markets and Hierarchies: Analysis and Antitrust Implications*, Macmillan.

Wilson, D. T. and Möller, K. (1995) 'Introduction: Interaction and Networks in Perspective', *Business Marketing: An Interaction and Network Perspective*, Kluwer Academic Publishers.

Wilson, D. T. and Mummalaneni, D. V. (1986) 'Bonding and Commitment in Buyer–Seller Relationships: A Preliminary Conceptualization', *Industrial Marketing and Purchasing*, 1, 3: 44–58.

Young, L. and Denize, S. (1994) 'Super-Glued Relationships: The Nature of Bonds between Professional Service Suppliers and Buyers', *Working Paper* presented at the 10th IMP Conference, Groningen, Netherlands, September.

Young, L. and Wilkinson, I. F. (1989) 'The Role of Trust and Co-Operation in Marketing Channels: A Preliminary Study', *European Journal of Marketing*, 23: 109–22.

PART II

MACRO-LEVEL CONTEXT

In traditional 'competitive' analyses of the uncertainties that pose opportunities and threats for international marketers, the environment is represented as a series of tiers surrounding the firm (see Figure II.1). The outer tier, known as the macro-environment, is traditionally considered to be uncontrollable by the firm. Trends in the political, economic or other areas of the environment must be monitored and 'strategic windows' of opportunity seized. The middle tier is considered semi-controllable. A firm interacts with its competitors to the extent that it might pre-empt or react to a competitor's actions. Similarly public relations might be targeted at publics who could influence the firm's success. Chemical firms might, for example, produce literature designed to show their customers and environmental groups, such as Greenpeace, that they are involved in environmental clean-up. A firm might manage the way it announces its financial performance to shareholders, who are stakeholders in the business, to minimize the impact on share price. The inner tier of the firm and its channel to market are shown as the only bodies over which the firm has 'control' and even then, channels literature has tended to emphasize the possibilities for conflict within channels.

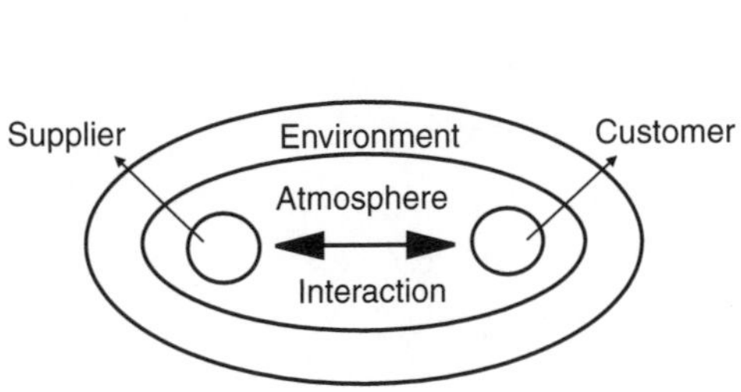

In contrast, the relationship perspective sees the firm interacting with its suppliers, buyers, publics and other stakeholders to form long-term stable relationships. The nature of these relationships forms an atmosphere of conflict or co-operation, which may affect the relationship's success. The relationship and its atmosphere are both embedded within a macro-environmental context, which impact upon the relationship.

The network perspective builds on the relationship concept that the firm is embedded in its environment. This is taken further, so that now the firm is seen as connected by a web of direct or indirect relationships to every other player across the levels of the competitive and macro-environment.

It is first apparent that the resulting interface between firms and other actors in the environment is a complex web. In fact it is arguable that, from this perspective, no boundary exists between macro-level context, atmosphere and actors engaged in buyer–seller relationships. These have been left in here only to demonstrate the similarities and differences between the relationship and network views of the firm's interface with its environment. From a network perspective, this has been described as 'full-faced', in that the firm is aware of and interacting with actors at all levels. This is contrasted with the 'faceless' traditional model.

Figure II.1 Understanding Relationships
Source: Turnbull and Valla (1986). Reprinted with permission of Routledge Publishers

BIBLIOGRAPHY

Turnbull, P. W. and Valla, J.-P. (1986) *Strategies for International Industrial Marketing*, Routledge.

chapter
2

THE CULTURAL ENVIRONMENT

Objectives

The issues to be addressed in Chapter 2 include:

1. The concept of *culture* as a complex blend of values and norms
2. The role of *national and regional cultures* in international marketing
3. The frameworks that have been developed to *classify culture*, their advantages and their limitations
4. How measures of *cultural difference* can impact on international marketing strategies
5. How cultural differences can be a barrier to the creation of *cross-national relationships*, and their implications for the creation of trust
6. How network structures vary in *different cultural contexts*.

After reading Chapter 3 you will be able to:

1. Define the concept of culture
2. Demonstrate how such aspects of culture as time, space, objects, friendships/family, language, religion, ethnicity, education system and symbols impact on international marketers' strategies
3. Show how cultural stereotypes can inhibit marketers' expectations of customers' needs and wants
4. Distinguish low context cultures (where the 'how' is less important than written words) from high context cultures (where the way business is transacted is more important)
5. Classify national cultures into Hofstede's five dimensions of power distance, uncertainty avoidance, masculinity–femininity, individualism–collectivism and long-term/short-term orientation
6. Recognize and overcome stereotypical country-of-origin perceptions
7. Develop an awareness of the role of individuals in international business-to-business marketing, and an appreciation that only individuals can make relationships work
8. Assess the perceived psychic distance and the cultural distance within and between two cultures or networks, and how they can be operationalized
9. Show how the former belief in the marketing literature that national cultures are stable over time has been undermined by globalization/cultural convergence
10. Show how a network context is unique to each firm's set of relationships and distinctive in different countries, and how this impacts on marketers' network-building strategies.

INTRODUCTION

The word 'culture' was used as early as the eighteenth century to refer to civilisation and the social norms on which civilized societies are based. Child and Kieser (1977, p. 2) define the modern conception of culture as: 'patterns of thought and manners which are widely shared.'

Hofstede (1980, p. 13) describes culture as a 'collective programming of the mind.' He believes that cultural patterns are: 'rooted in value systems of major groups in the population and ... are stabilized over long periods in history.'

In international marketing, national and regional cultures play an important role in determining whether groups of customers will perceive benefits in the same products and services, understand the same communications and make the same associations for cultural symbols such as colours, smells and objects.

Attempts to classify cultures have tended to be at the national level. This chapter reviews the frameworks that have been proposed for the study of culture and identifies their advantages and limitations. From a relationship perspective, cultural differences represent one of the most significant barriers to the creation of cross-national relationships. This chapter identifies the types of difficulties that occur and considers the implications of these for the creation of trust. *Measures of cultural difference*, including cultural and psychic distance are explored. The network section of the chapter examines the extent to which network structures vary in different cultural contexts.

THE TRADITIONAL PERSPECTIVE

Influences on National Culture

Culture is the collective term for a complex blend of values and norms. Research suggests a number of aspects of culture that impinge on the actions of international marketers.

Hall (1960) proposes that societies may vary with respect to their conception of:

- **Time**. There are a number of norms surrounding the timescale in which international marketing actions should be taken. Hall (1960) contrasts the example of the USA, where delaying the answer to a request until an urgent deadline passes is acceptable. This type of delay would be interpreted differently in other cultures because of differing norms. In Ethiopia, for example, the amount of time before answering is seen to be proportional to the importance of the decision. If something is important, an Ethiopian takes, and may expect others to take, a long time in making a decision. Answering quickly may be an insult! In some Arab countries, important people get faster service than less important ones. In this case, a delay would be an insult. Therefore, if the US respondent were dealing with a customer in Ethiopia, the slow response would be positive, but if the customer were an Arab it would be viewed as negative.

- **Space**. The symbolic meaning of space is also open to different cultural interpretation. While a large office in the UK may symbolize importance, the French are more likely to create a network of points. The supervisor may occupy a middle position to symbolize his control. The Japanese might locate furniture in a room towards the centre, whereas in the UK it would tend to be placed round the edges. The location of precise objects may have symbolic importance. The Chinese art of Feng Shui has seen an upsurge of interest globally; Feng Shui believes that where objects are placed creates different atmospheres.

- **Objects**. Objects may also assume different types and level of importance. Conspicuous consumption, which involves signalling success through expensive possessions such as status cars, designer clothes or the latest technology gadget, is found to varying extents around Europe (Paitra 1992) and in other countries such as the USA. These objects may be less significant in other countries. Aspirational effects, however, seem to be causing this trend to spread. Market research on the car market in the emerging Czech economy in the early 1990s showed that while there was no middle market, there was a thriving market for luxury cars.

  In different cultures, objects may prompt traditional or cultural associations. In Britain, a bulldog may signify tenacity, an oak tree solidity and a cucumber coolness. International marketers cannot assume that these associations are, necessarily, transferable.

- **Friendship and family**. The concept of friends and family also has a number of meanings. One dimension of difference is the size of the family unit. The typical British family unit is defined as parent(s) and children. Family in France or Italy might involve closer links with an extended number of grandparents, cousins, aunts and uncles.

  Another difference is what is implied by 'friendship'. Friendships may imply different types of reciprocation and indebtedness in different cultures. For example, friendships are struck quickly in the USA, involve some concept of reciprocity but no real obligations. 'Being a friend' in other countries may take longer and have greater ramifications. In Latin America, your 'friends' will not let you down in adversity; they may even give you what they cannot really afford. In India, friendship is acting in the interests of others for the good of one's own psyche rather than in anticipation of a return.

The valuable cultural briefing sessions at Farnham Castle (Hutton 1988) propose that international marketers should also take into account cultural variation on the basis of:

- **Language**. Cultural differences are often exacerbated by difficulties in understanding the language of another country. A particular problem is posed by 'false friends', words in two languages that sound as though they mean the same thing when they actually have different meanings. Imagine the possible confusion between English 'terrible' (meaning awful or dreadful) and French 'terrible' which can, colloquially, mean great or wonderful.

  The use of idioms, such as 'kettle of fish' or 'to laugh one's head off', may not translate literally into another language and be an additional cause of confusion.

- **Religion**. Most wars have resulted from religious differences. Prejudice on the basis of religion is still widespread and can occur within as well as between nations, witness the catastrophic events in the former Yugoslavia, or the persecution of Jews in the Second World War. In less dramatic ways, religions are a cause of cultural differences as each religion has its own customs and beliefs. Worshippers of different religions celebrate different festivals, may have different eating habits and perceive different taboos.

- **Ethnicity**. The 1990s witnessed an unprecedented level of fragmentation on ethnic grounds. Ethnic groups may also have different religions and languages (see previous section). Tensions may be resolved peacefully (the Velvet Divorce between the Czech and Slovak Republics in 1990 and the claims for the secession of Crimea in Ukraine, for example) or result in bloody civil wars (Kosovo, Bosnia, Rwanda and Chechnya, for example). At the very least, the ethnic composition of a nation may complicate attempts to identify one national culture.

- **Education system**. The age at which education begins and ends differs considerably between countries. In Germany, for example, children do not tend to begin school until aged six and, if they repeat years, might still be at school aged twenty. Their UK equivalents start school at four or five and finish aged eighteen. Moreover, the breadth and depth of education varies. If the same German and British pupils continue beyond their first set of secondary exams, the German teenager will study a broad curriculum including mathematics, a language and sport. The English teenager is likely to specialize in three or four subjects at sixteen.

  Levels of literacy and numeracy tend to relate to the economic wealth of the country, although this is not always the case. In 1999, Less Developed Countries (LDCs) featured largely amongst those with low literacy rates. African countries account for half of the bottom twenty literacy rates. Figures for the highest enrolment in tertiary education, however, show Russia and Ukraine among the top twenty. Economic wealth alone is not an explanation of differences in educational systems.

- **Symbols**. Colours, smells and even numbers can convey different meanings to different cultures. White symbolizes purity in the UK, but signifies death in Japan and some other parts of Asia: McDonald's use of Ronald McDonald, a white-faced clown, would not work as a promotion to children in Japan! Green is often used to signal freshness in Europe and North America, but represents danger or disease in Malaysia (Ricks 1984). Black is not universally used for mourning. Copeland and Griggs (1986) identify the fact that: 'in many Asian countries [the colour of mourning] is white; in Brazil it is purple, yellow in Mexico and dark red in the Ivory Coast.'

  Red means danger or stop in the UK. It means good fortune in China, but in Turkey it signifies death. Red is a masculine colour in the UK, but blue is considered the more masculine in the USA. Mint flavour is denoted by a green wrapper in the UK, but a red wrapper in Africa (Copeland and Griggs 1986).

  Given the diverse associations of colours, smells and other symbols, international marketers may unwittingly communicate the wrong message. The use of purple for luxury (e.g. Cadbury's use of purple for chocolate wrappers in the UK), would not transfer to the USA where purple means inexpensive (Usunier 1993). Showing a picture of smiling babies on the wrapper of baby food did not work in Africa, where locals assumed this to mean that the jar contained babies (Ricks 1984). Choosing the right symbols and colours for a global brand requires rigorous verification that the cultural assumptions of the brand owner are those of the target market.

Cultural Stereotypes

England is a Nation of Shopkeepers. (Napoleon, 1 1810)

The French will only be united under the threat of danger. Nobody can simply bring together a country that has 265 kinds of cheese. (De Gaulle 1951)

America is the only nation in history which miraculously has gone directly from barbarism to degeneration without the usual interval of civilisation. (Attributed to Clemenceau, 1841–1929)

This type of generalization about national characteristics exemplifies the phenomenon of cultural stereotypes. Cultural stereotypes are an additional complication to understanding cultures of other countries. Popular myth holds that people from a country exhibit particular characteristics. Stereotypes would have us believe that Americans are loud, British are reserved, Germans are humourless and French are flamboyant. First encounters may be coloured by this type of stereotypical expectations and this may stand in the way of seeing people as they really are. In marketing terms, stereotypes may lead to incorrect assumption of the needs and wants of customers in a particular country.

Classifying National Culture

A number of classifications of national cultures have been proposed. The variables identified by these differ. One of the earlier classifications comes from the work of Edward Hall (1960). Hall differentiates between national cultures on the basis of the 'con-text' surrounding international marketing. By 'context', Hall means the non-verbal cues and procedures that may play a role in international exchanges.

Low context cultures, therefore, are those where the 'how' is less important than written words. Contracts, letters of confirmation and other documentation are of key significance. Low context cultures include Anglo-Saxon countries and the USA. High context countries, such as China, Korea and Japan, accord greater importance to the way in which business is transacted. Failure to approach a customer in the correct way or otherwise offending local custom is more significant in a high context culture.

The most frequently used classification of national cultures is that created by Hofstede (1980). Hofstede used factor analysis to identify four underlying dimensions of national culture for individuals within national subsidiaries of IBM. These dimensions are used to explain differences in their relationship to the firm they work for.

Hofstede's four dimensions are:

- Power Distance
- Uncertainty Avoidance
- Masculinity–Femininity
- Individualism–Collectivism.

Power Distance

Hofstede (1994) defines power distance as the extent to which a culture accepts unequal distribution of power. Cultures with a high power distance might favour strong, hierarchical structure with autocratic control mechanisms. Low power distance might, in contrast, be associated with more democratic and consensus-building structures with greater delegation of responsibility.

Individualism–Collectivism

This dimension measures the extent to which a culture accepts self-interest. Individualist societies adopt an 'every person for themselves' approach. Individuals are motivated by the idea that rewards can be gained by their own efforts. Popular icons in individualist societies are successful entrepreneurs and sporting heroes. Collectivist societies show greater concern for the good of the group. This may be expressed by the existence of extended families or communities. Individuals may accept constraints, even if these act against their own interests, if this is best for the group.

Masculinity–Femininity

This factor refers to the 'distribution of roles between the sexes'. Hofstede refers to the two extremes as 'masculine' and 'feminine' (1980, 1994). Values associated with masculine cultures are assertiveness, competitiveness and maximal gender differences. Values of feminine cultures include modesty, caring and equality between the genders.

Uncertainty Avoidance

Uncertainty avoidance is defined (Hofstede 1994) as the extent to which a culture tolerates uncertainty and ambiguity. High uncertainty avoidance may express itself in a preference for structure and is associated with minimizing risks. Low uncertainty avoidance cultures are happier to take risks as they can accept uncertainty more readily.

Long-Term versus Short-Term Orientation (LTO)

Following criticism that his measures were biased towards Western values, Hofstede proposed a fifth dimension of 'Confucian Dynamism' (Hofstede and Bond, 1988). This is later referred to as 'long-term versus short-term orientation' (Hofstede 1994). This fifth dimension is most concerned with Eastern Cultures, which may exhibit either orientation. Long-term oriented cultures are those that value persistence, ordered relationships, thrift and a sense of shame. Short-term oriented cultures value personal steadiness and stability, protection of one's 'face', respect for tradition and reciprocation of gifts and greetings. All of these values devolve from the teachings of Confucius, but long-term orientation is distinguishable by its consideration of the future. Short-term orientation is about the here and now.

Country-of-Origin Effects

One of the impacts of stereotypical perceptions of different nationalities is that goods or services are assumed to be high or low quality on the basis of national origin. So, if Germans are heralded as good engineers, a customer may prefer German cars to those from other countries. Many of the commonly held 'strengths' associated with different nationalities are based on some element of truth. Table 2.1 gives examples of product and service strengths commonly associated with different nationalities.

If countries are perceived as strong providers of a product or service there is a positive 'country-of-origin' effect. Customers might, then, be expected to prefer French perfume, Czech beer or Italian shoes. A 'positive halo' favours producers of these. In contrast, a Japanese brewer, such as Kirin, or a German fashion house, such as Lagerfeld, may have to overcome a negative country-of-origin effect. In this case customers may have negative expectations that international marketers need to alter.

Research into country-of-origin effects (Roth and Romeo 1992) identifies a number of reasons why such effects may affect purchase preferences. These include product involvement, patriotism and knowledge of a particular country. Country-of-origin effects are important for international marketers who must know when to promote and when to downplay nationality.

At a basic level, country-of-origin effects relate to perceived quality (Hong and Wyer 1989). The 'Made in...' tag is an intangible attribute as distinct from tangible features of the product or service. This does not lessen its potential impact on the product's success in the market. Despite its importance, there is little agreement on what is meant by country-of-origin effect. Johansson, Ronkainen and Czinkota propose (1994) that country-of-origin effects may have a number of facets:

- **Familiarity**. Lack of familiarity with a product or service might result in unwillingness to include it in the consideration set.
- **Risk-taking attitude**. Consumers who are prepared to take risks might be more inclined to try new, or more risky, products or services.
- **Ethnocentric attitude**. Consumers might be patriotic and prefer to buy products or services from their own country where possible.
- **Political influences**. Operation within a trading bloc or other trading agreement might favour purchase of goods or services from

Table 2.1 What countries are believed to be good at

Country	Perceived strengths
France	Perfume, fashion
Russia	Vodka
Japan	Electronics
Germany	Engineering, cars
Switzerland	Watches and clocks
Czech Republic	Beer
Italy	Shoes
Ireland	Crystal
Scotland	Whisky

within this region. In contrast, past or present political tensions might inhibit trade with a particular nationality.

It can be seen that country-of-origin effects are not only cultural but may be influenced by other macro-environmental factors.

Peterson and Jolibert (1995) have studied a range of papers in this area and found that 26 per cent of consumers changed their purchase decision positively or negatively as a result of the country-of-origin of the product. Studies tend to focus on negative country-of-origin effects. The example in Box 2.1 below shows negative country-of-origin effects hampering Russian marketers.

THE RELATIONSHIP PERSPECTIVE

The critical link between culture and international marketing relationships is in the acceptance that individuals are important in making relationships work. Hallén and Sandström (1991, p. 108) describe the role of individuals in international business-to-business marketing:

> Personal interaction is required. This both causes difficulties and opens up possibilities, as it increases the role of human differences, similarities, antipathies, sympathies, etc. In international industrial business this becomes still more pronounced as it involves personal interaction between people with different cultural backgrounds and different expectations and interpretations of performance, behaviour, practices, rules, etc....Thus, in international business personal interaction becomes still more important and also more sensitive, as personal interaction is necessary to neutralize possible cultural barriers to business exchange.

Box 2.1   Country-of-Origin Effects: The Case of the New Russia

The need to market products and services successfully to industrialized countries is of vital importance to the ongoing political and economic development of post-liberalization Russia. A key question for Russian marketers, though, is the extent to which consumers put off buying Russian products because of poor perceived, rather than actual, quality.

In studying the introduction of the Soviet 'Belarus' tractor into the world market, Johansson, Ronkainen and Czinkota (1994) focus on a new product introduction, which might be expected to encounter significant negative country-of-origin effects. Studies show more positive country-of-origin effects for products from advanced industrial economies compared with newly industrializing or Less Developed Countries (Gaedeke 1973; Bannister and Saunders 1978). Indeed Russian products not only ranked lowest in a study of Finnish consumers' perceptions of country of origin but, over the period of the study, Russia's image worsened

year on year (Darling 1990). Russia was also ranked lowest in expected quality as a producer of tractors (Johansson, Ronkainen and Czinkota 1994).

The fortunes of the 'Belarus' tractor were studied alongside those of tractors from the USA, Canada, Germany, Italy and Japan. Familiarity with the tractor brand seemed to be an important influence for farmers buying a tractor. The 'Belarus' rated lower than other brands partly because it was not a familiar brand but also because of the poor image of Russia as a quality producer. Johansson, Ronkainen and Czinkota conclude:

The image of anything marked 'made in a developing country' is usually low. Therefore, it may not be wise to emphasize such a country of origin and run the risk of being rejected before the actual quality of the product can be demonstrated.

Sources: Based on Gaedeke (1973); Bannister and Saunders (1978); Darling (1990); Johansson, Ronkainen and Czinkota (1994).

What Hallén and Sandström (1991) call 'personal interaction' is an important precursor to the development of trust. Development of trust in relationships is hampered by cultural or geographic distance between the actors (Hallén 1982). The actors' feelings in the process of interaction have been described as the 'atmosphere' of the relationship. Cultural misunderstandings have a negative impact on the 'atmosphere' of a relationship.

The Impact of Culture in International Relationships

Assessing Cultural Differences

From a relationship perspective, classifying cultures is less useful than examining the extent to which partners from different cultures might expect to differ. The two most commonly used measures of difference between national cultures are *psychic distance* and *cultural distance*. The concepts underlying each of these and how they might be operationalized are discussed more fully below.

Psychic Distance

In recent decades, the extent of the cultural distance between one country and another has often been referred to as 'psychic distance'. Psychic distance is defined (Beckermann 1956) as: 'the factors preventing or disturbing the flows of information between firms and markets.'

Psychic distance may not only be cultural, but may comprise other factors such as political systems, level of development or geographic distance. In their valuable evaluation of psychic distance as a measure, Vahlne and Nordström (1992) redefine psychic distance as: 'factors disturbing firms' learning about and understanding a foreign environment'. This revised definition emphasizes the fact that understanding a different culture is an ongoing process.

Beckermann's earlier work notwithstanding, the Nordic studies of Johanson and Wiedersheim-Paul (1975) and Johanson and Vahlne (1977) are often seen as the catalyst for increased interest in psychic distance in recent decades. These Nordic studies described a process whereby firms tended to expand international operations from countries with lower towards countries with higher levels of psychic distance (see Chapter 8 for a fuller discussion of the internationalization process).

Operationalizing Psychic Distance

In order to look at its impact on firms, Nordic researchers faced the challenge of operationalizing psychic distance. A number of different attempts have been made. The variables used vary. One such operationalization (Vahlne and Wiedersheim-Paul 1973) uses the following seven variables:

- Level of economic development of the country in question
- Difference in the level of economic development between the home and foreign country
- Level of education of the country
- Business language
- Cultural distance
- Everyday language
- Existing relationships between the home and host country.

Rankings were based on 'hard' economic and other published statistical data and on 'soft' subjective judgements. A ranking based on these variables was produced by Hörnell and Vahlne (1973) and is still the most common operationalization of psychic distance. Being developed by Swedish researchers, it measures psychic distance from a Swedish perspective (see Table 2.2).

Attempts to measure psychic distance have been subject to criticism (Langhoff 1997). First, the subjective adjustments may result in inaccuracy or, at least, a lack of clarity as to the method of calculation. Secondly, psychic distance is measured using macro-economic and other published data, which uses the country as the unit of analysis. Yet Hörnell and Vahlne's psychic distance ranking has been used for a number of purposes. One use is to infer the impact of psychic distance on relationships between firms from different countries. Yet relationships exist between individuals within each firm and the assumption that these individuals perceive similar levels of psychic distance seems at best an oversimplification, at worst misleading. The following section explores in greater detail the difficulties faced in using psychic

Table 2.2 Ranking of countries by psychic distance from Sweden

Country	Rank (from psychically closest (1) to psychically most distant (20) from Sweden)
Denmark	1
Norway	2
Finland	3
West Germany	4
Great Britain	5
The Netherlands	6
Belgium	7
USA	8
Switzerland	9
Canada	10
Austria	11
France	12
Italy	13
Spain	14
Portugal	15
Japan	16
Brazil	17
South Africa	18
Argentina	19
Australia	20

distance as a measure of cultural differences between relationship partners.

Psychic Distance is a Perception

The most important feature of psychic distance is that it is a perception. Research suggests that *perceived* psychic distance influences managerial decisions. Individuals from the same country, or even the same firm within the country, may not perceive the same level of psychic distance in marketing to a country. In reviewing the impact of psychic distance on the internationalization of Australian firms, Fletcher and Bohn (1998) list a range of factors that may alter the level of perceived psychic distance (see Figure 2.1).

Given these different perceptions of psychic distance, individuals within a firm may have different attitudes towards a particular cross-cultural relationship. A US firm might, for example, employ a marketing manager of Chinese origin who perceives lower levels of psychic distance in entering China. Similarly, graduates of an international business degree might be expected to perceive lower levels of psychic distance than the general population.

An implication of this kind of difference is that international marketing decisions may be viewed as higher or lower risk, depending on the background of the individual manager. A situation might exist where tensions result from one manager feeling that a decision is low risk, while another perceives higher risks. This type of situation is particularly prevalent in multinational corporations where the Headquarters and international subsidiaries are located in different countries. An example is given in Box 2.2.

As is seen in the ChemCo case, a positive or negatively 'charged' atmosphere can favour or inhibit business development (Hallén and Sandström 1991). Differences in 'attitudes, beliefs and values' may exist, though, within as well as

Demographic characteristics
Research shows a relationship between the *age and level of education of managers* and their perception of psychic distance. Older and less educated managers perceive higher levels of psychic distance than do younger and more educated managers (Barrett 1986; Fletcher 1996).

International exposure
Links have been shown between psychic distance and exposure to other international markets. Marketers of the same nationality, but with different ethnic backgrounds or country of birth, may perceive greater or lesser psychic distance than their fellows (Barrett 1986; Fletcher 1998). Likewise, time spent overseas and frequent international travel may reduce perceived psychic distance.

Knowledge of international business
Understanding the complexities of doing business internationally and of different cultures also reduce, perceived psychic distance (Shoham and Albaum 1995; Fletcher 1996).

Managerial approach
Managers who plan international activities (Cavusgil 1984) and those with a strategic or proactive approach are more likely to internationalize (Diamantopoulos and Inglis 1988).

Figure 2.1 Perceptions of psychic distance
Source: Based on Fletcher and Bohn (1998)

Box 2.2 Diaspora and Distance

As part of the former Soviet Union, Ukraine had been culturally and economically divorced from other nations since the Russian revolution in the early twentieth century. After liberalization in late 1991, and the subsequent creation of a nation state, few international marketers had any cultural knowledge of Ukraine. Some firms did, however, have recent experience in other parts of liberalized East and Central Europe upon which they could draw, although these tended to be further into the process of economic transition. Among a number of other distinctions between Ukraine and other countries within the region is the fact that it was a former Soviet Union state. Central European countries had been independent within the living memory of the older generation. In Ukraine 'nobody's grandfather was a merchant' (Rajan and Graham 1991).

A vital untapped resource lay, however, within some international firms. For generations, citizens of the Soviet Union had migrated to other parts of the globe. National languages and cultures had been preserved amongst this 'Diaspora'. Now, firms were finding employees with a national heritage, which was to prove invaluable in understanding these newly re-created countries. When it entered Ukraine, ChemCo appointed as country manager an existing employee whose parents were Ukrainian. While he had never lived in the country he did speak the language and readily adapted to life in the country.

Given his background, the local Ukrainian manager perceived relatively low psychic distance in the country. Although the market was uncertain he had begun to develop promising relationships with potential customers and distributors. Managers in the Head Office of ChemCo though took a more pessimistic view. Viewed from a distance, the prospects in Ukraine seemed much bleaker. Quite simply, ChemCo bosses saw the risks as much higher. This was to complicate a number of international marketing decisions, such as the best type of operation to use and the speed at which ChemCo should aim to penetrate the emerging Ukrainian market.

---

between organizations (the complexities of psychic distance are studied more fully in the Network section of this chapter).

Cultural Distance

The second commonly used measure of differences in culture is cultural distance. Classifications of cultural distance (see Arnott, Grey and Yadav 1995; Fletcher and Bohn 1998; Kogut and Singh 1988 as examples) use Hofstede's cultural classification (1980) as a base for measurement of cultural distance.

Cultural distance is sometimes used as a proxy for psychic distance as it can be calculated more readily. The two measures differ in scope, however. It has been argued that psychic distance is made up of cultural distance plus a number of other dimensions including:

- Structural dimensions. These include issues such as the legal and administrative systems of a country (Nordström and Vahlne 1992).
- Language differences (Nordström and Vahlne 1992).

- Industry structure (O'Grady and Lane 1996).
- Competitive environment (O'Grady and Lane 1996).

Kogut and Singh's formula for measurement of cultural distance (1988) has been used in a number of studies. On the basis of this formula cultural distance has been calculated from Australia (see Fletcher and Bohn 1998).

The resulting cultural distance ranking is shown in Table 2.3. High index numbers are countries with greater levels of cultural distance.

Similarly, Arnott, Grey and Yadav (1995) use the Kogut and Singh formula (1988) to calculate cultural distance from the UK for a range of countries (Table 2.4. reprinted with permission from Haworth Press, Inc.).

According to this calculation, the USA is culturally closest to the UK, while Japan is the most distant of this range of countries. Note that within Europe, the UK is culturally similar to Switzerland and Germany, but relatively less so to France, Netherlands and Sweden.

Table 2.3   Cultural distance measured from Australia outwards

Country	Index	Country	Index
USA	0.1	Turkey	13.6
Great Britain	0.6	Japan	15.2
Canada	0.6	Philippines	15.7
New Zealand	0.7	Russia	16.0
Switzerland	1.5	Nigeria	16.3
Germany	1.7	Ghana	16.3
Ireland	1.7	Uruguay	16.4
South Africa	2.0	Thailand	16.5
Italy	2.2	Pakistan	17.3
Finland	4.7	Mexico	17.6
Netherlands	5.5	Greece	18.0
Belgium	6.1	Indonesia	18.3
France	6.1	Singapore	19.3
Austria	6.3	Korea	20.3
Israel	7.1	Taiwan	20.4
Denmark	7.3	Hong Kong	20.5
Norway	7.4	Chile	20.7
Spain	8.6	Portugal	21.2
Sweden	8.8	Yugoslavia	21.9
Argentina	9.2	Peru	23.3
Iran	9.3	Colombia	23.5
India	9.7	Malaysia	23.6
Kenya	12.2	Costa Rica	25.0
Zimbabwe	12.2	Venezuela	26.2
Tanzania	12.1	Ecuador	27.4
Rwanda	12.2	China	29.2
Brazil	12.3	Panama	31.4

Source: Fletcher and Bohn (1998) *Journal of Global Marketing*, 12, 2: 47–68. Reprinted with permission from Haworth Press Inc.

Table 2.4   Cultural distance measured from the UK

Country	PD	IND	MAS	UA	LTO	Country distance from the UK
CH	34	68	70	58		0.45
DK	18	74	16	23		1.80
FR	68	71	43	86		2.21
GE	35	67	66	65	31	0.65
JP	54	46	95	92	80	4.83
NL	38	80	14	53	44	2.01
SW	31	71	5	29	33	2.41
US	40	91	62	46	29	0.09

Notes: CH = Switzerland; DK = Denmark; FR = France; GE = Germany; JP = Japan; NL = Netherlands; SW = Sweden; US = USA; PD = Power Distance; IND = Individualism/Collectivism; MAS = Masculinity/Femininity; UA = Uncertainty Avoidance; LTO = Long Term Orientation

Criticisms of Cultural and Psychic Distance

National Culture Remains Stable Over Time

Hofstede (1980, 1994) assumes that national cultures remain stable over long periods of time:

> culture patterns are rooted in value systems of major groups of the population and ... they remain stable over long periods of time. (Hofstede 1980, p. 13).

Critics, however, argue that national cultures can change such that historic data can no longer give any insights. Obvious examples of dramatic changes are found in regions such as Eastern Europe where liberalization has had a significant impact on individual aspirations, or in Hong Kong, where Chinese influence from 1997 may bring in a different set of values.

Cray and Mallory (1998) show that within the two waves of Hofstede's own research in 1968 and 1972 shifts were in power distance and uncertainty avoidance in some countries. This seems to confirm the fact that national cultures *do* change. An implication of this is that culture is not a stable influence but must be monitored over time.

Cultural and Psychic Distance Assumes One Cohesive National Culture

The data used in measurement of psychic and cultural distance are at the national level. As most countries contain regional, ethnic or other subcultures this is an oversimplification. An example of the difficulties of this aggregation of data is that Yugoslavia is shown in older studies as having one national culture. The recent catastrophic escalation of ethnic tensions shows both the changes that can occur in national culture and suggests that the country may never have had one cohesive culture.

Is Cultural Distance Decreasing?

In his argument for global standardization, Levitt (1983) bases his case primarily on the fact that advances in travel and technology have broken down cultural distance. Levitt argues for the existence of a homogenization of tastes across cultures. Critics suggest a less dramatic shift. Some segments, such as youth culture, conspicuous consumption and technological innovation, exist across markets (see Chapter 5 for a fuller discussion of global convergence).

From this evidence one might expect a reduction in differences between cultures over time. Cray and Mallory (1998) suggest that this is one interpretation of the shift in Hofstede's data over time. In fact, Hofstede suggests the opposite trend of divergence of national cultures. A useful conclusion, drawn by Usunier (1993, p. 174), is that competition is becoming more global, but consumer preferences are not: 'Consumers always "construct" the identity of brands, even for "global products," and they do so on a local culture and identity base.'

Culture is Studied at the National Level

As discussed in the section on psychic distance above, individual managers of the same nationality may perceive different levels of psychic distance. This suggests another limitation of many attempts to assess cultural difference. Culture is often studied at the national level. Determining an average culture for a nation is necessarily simplistic and may overlook significant differences between cultural subgroups and individuals with different experiences and characteristics.

Critics suggest that measures such as psychic and cultural distance should actually study the *perceptions of individual managers*. By inference, seeking universal recipes may lead international marketers to make dangerous generalizations.

Assessing Cultural Perceptions at the Individual Level

Criticisms of psychic and cultural distance for taking a national view of culture suggest that a more accurate assessment might be achieved by studying culture at the level of the individual. Some attempts have been made at this complex task. Langhoff (1997, p. 146) draws upon the study of semiotics or symbols:

> The significance of culture on human life cannot be explained and understood by reducing cultural studies to [Hofstede's] variables. Common to all cultures, however, is the assignment of meaning, i.e. humans' creation of meaning of the world... Human beings use and need culture as a 'mechanism' to organise a coherent meaning of the world around themselves and they do so by developing and applying symbols.

Individuals allocate specific meanings to particular objects. As each individual has had a different history and set of experiences they may make different associations. At a simple level, one person may associate water with a happy seaside holiday, while another, who fell in the swimming pool as a child, may make an unhappy association. If these two come from the same culture, it is clear that an international marketer would fail by assuming that each makes the same associations.

While this type of individual level analysis reveals the richness and diversity existing within cultures, its application in a large market is likely to be complex and time-consuming. Marketers need to identify groups of customers with relatively homogeneous needs and wants. They may, however, need to exercise caution before making generalizations about segmentation on the basis of cultural grouping.

From a relationship perspective, individuals play a key role in the success or failure of a relationship. Particularly in cross-cultural relationships it is essential to gain an understanding of the values and perceptions of those involved.

THE NETWORK PERSPECTIVE

Are There Culturally Different Network Structures?

A network has been defined as the 'set of directly and indirectly connected relationships [that] form the network context' (Håkansson and Snehota 1989). Network context is unique to each firm as it is made up of their own particular set of relationships. Moreover, each national subsidiary of a firm may have its own relationships and, therefore, context. This network context is complex and difficult to understand.

In addition to understanding the number and type of relationships within each national network context, the question arises whether nets are distinctively different in different countries. If so, is this a function of different national cultures or of other environmental influences? Insights into this question may be gained by studying network structures in different markets. The example of China is examined below.

Guanxi Networks in China

One thing that anyone doing business in China has to come to terms with is paradox – a philosophy that eludes linear thinking Westerners. Another is Guanxi, or business connections, a widely misunderstood concept which is at the foundation of Chinese business. (Ambler 1995, p. 23)

A number of authors have argued the importance of 'relationship-building' in doing business with China (Tung 1982; Bond 1986; Hofstede and Bond 1988). As transition to market economy in China progresses, the Chinese 'net' might be expected to become economically similar to those found in Western countries. To what extent, though, is it culturally different? Ambler argues that the central role of relationship-building in China is 'based on culture, history, education, and a mass of other subtle influencers'.

Contrary to popular belief, Guanxi, defined by Leung, Wong and Tam (1995) as the 'old friend' approach and by Chen (1995) as 'friendship with implications of a continual exchange of favours', is not unique to China. Similar influences exist in, amongst others, Japan, Korea and India and the former Soviet Union (FSU). Guanxi involves using personal relationships with family and friends to enhance business. This goes further than the 'old school tie'; it is the preserve of a privileged few, but permeates all levels of society

Relationship Development in China

An important feature of Guanxi is that it is *reciprocal*. While the West might rely on contract law to make sure that firms honour their obligations, this is not needed in China. The relationship is more valuable than each episode within it, so it is unlikely that a firm would act in a way that would damage the relationship.

The importance of reciprocity for a Chinese partner is reinforced by Leung, Wong and Tam (1995), who identify three factors that explain the degree of understanding between Hong Kong and Chinese firms: relationship-building, mutual expectation and information exchanges:

- **Relationship-building** includes keeping in touch with the counterpart, frequent co-operation and attempting to understand cultural norms
- **Mutual expectation** refers to the level of understanding and consensus within the relationship
- **Information exchanges** are of market, economic and organizational information.

Ironically, conscious attempts to build relationships and understand the Chinese culture do not work. It is explained that these tend to be one-sided attempts by Hong Kong firms to understand Chinese partners. Reciprocal actions, such as consensus-building and exchanges are far more effective in relationship development.

Are Guanxi Networks Different?

A key distinction between the way relationships are viewed in China and the West is found in the process of relationship development. Western marketers expect that transactions occur and, if these work well, a relationship develops. From a Chinese perspective, the relationship is built and, if this is successful, transactions follow (Ambler 1995). In other words, relationship development is essential to business activity.

Wong (1995) gives a Chinese perspective on some of the constructs underlying Western studies of network development:

- **Trust**. Five constant virtues for the Chinese are benevolence, righteousness, propriety, wisdom and fidelity. The last of these means the payment of debts of gratitude and honesty. It is expected that repayment should be greater than the original value of the debt. The expectation that firms will adhere to these virtues creates trust in Chinese networks.

■ **Exchange**. In the Chinese culture, repayment of a debt involves more than economic exchange. There is also a considerable social obligation and the value of personal relationships in Guanxi means that social exchanges will be especially important.

■ **Dependence**. Preserving internal harmony is important to Chinese culture. In the interests of harmony, or social conformity, individual interests may be compromised. Sources of dependence are complex. If one firm wishes to do business with another it may involve a third party to arrange a formal introduction. The third party might also exert pressure to win business for the 'petitioner,' or firm seeking business (Chen 1995).

■ **Building network positions**. Another cultural influence described by Ambler (1995, p. 25) is the 'dominant philosophy' of China compared to Western cultures. While Western cultures perceive 'dualism' between contradictory forces, such as good and evil, Chinese culture retains influences of Taoism:

> In China, yin and yang are not so much opposites, as complementary. Red meat and brandy are yang, for example, whereas fish and white spirits tend to be yin. A meal should be balanced in many dimensions, including yang and yin.

In building network positions, a Western manager may fail in negotiations because he has given insufficient attention to building relationships before moving on to conclude a transaction. Moreover, Western marketers may assume that two options are alternatives, while from a Chinese perspective it seems quite possible that both can exist together. Ambler uses the classic example of Japan's demonstration in the 1970s that high quality and low costs need not be opposites, but that both could be achieved simultaneously.

Psychic Distance in Networks

At network level, the effects of psychic distance are complex. Psychic distance may exist within as well as between firms (see the ChemCo example).

Similarly, if a US multinational corporation (MNC) enters China, Head Office may perceive higher psychic distance than an existing Singaporean subsidiary. Of course this example is oversimplistic. The US Head Office may employ people of Chinese origin. Others may have worked in China or in other parts of East Asia. Some may have been closely involved in the decision to enter China and have become comfortable with the idea. Any of these categories of employees may have a clear view and acceptance of the decision to enter China. In contrast, individuals within the Singaporean subsidiary may be worried at the political power of their neighbour or, for a variety of reasons, may not feel happy about the decision to establish a subsidiary in China.

Network literature refers to differing levels of 'visibility' within networks. 'Opacity', or poor visibility, exists when individuals feel greater psychic distance (Axelsson and Johanson 1992; Blankenburg 1992). The level of visibility or opacity experienced is specific to the individual because of differences in their experiences or role in the network. Forsgren (1989) argues that the existence of psychic distance, or poor visibility, within a firm is a feature of decentralized multinational corporations.

This 'poor visibility' may mean that some individuals do not support or understand the international marketing strategies of the firm:

> In a network actors have fairly clear views of their own relations with, and dependencies on, other actors and some relations of these actors to third actors although these are generally much vaguer. The views of more distant parts of the network are, however, rather unclear. Furthermore, the views of different actors may differ considerably. (Axelsson and Johanson 1992, p. 231)

Pahlberg (1997) argues that cultural differences between individuals within an organization are a major source of conflict. Individuals may also react differently to conflict. Should it be confronted or ignored? Should they deal with a situation personally or escalate it up the hierarchy?

Yet, despite the complexity it creates, cultural diversity is one of the most valuable assets of multinational corporations (Pahlberg 1997). Organizations should not strive to create a common culture, but accept that different cultures make different contributions to the whole. The strengths of different subsidiaries in developing particular relationships should be encouraged.

SUMMARY

In Chapter 2 we have attempted to establish the nature and scope of cultural distance and show how cultural stereotypes can impact on the marketer's strategy. After classifying and measuring the factors creating psychic and cultural distance we have developed strategies to show how such problems can be analyzed and overcome.

BIBLIOGRAPHY

Ambler, T. (1995) 'Reflections on China: Re-orienting Images of Marketing', *Marketing Management*, 4, 1: 23–30.

Arnott, D. C., Grey, S. and Yadav, S. (1995) *Working Paper*, Academy of International Business UK Conference, City University.

Axelsson, B. and Johanson, J. (1992) 'Foreign Market Entry – the Textbook Versus the Network View', in Axelsson, B. and Easton, G. (eds), *Industrial Networks: A New View of Reality*, Routledge.

Bannister, J. P. and Saunders, J. A. (1978) 'UK Consumers' Attitudes Towards Imports: The Measurement of National Stereotype Image', *European Journal of Marketing*, 12, 8: 562–570.

Barrett, N. J. (1986) 'A Study of the Internationalisation of Australian Manufacturing Firms', University of New South Wales, PhD Thesis.

Beckermann, W. (1956) 'Distance and the Pattern of Intra-European Trade', *Review of Economics and Statistics*, 28.

Benito, G. R. G. and Gripsrud, G. (1992) 'The Expansion of Foreign Direct Investments: Discrete Rational Locational Choices or a Cultural Learning Process', *Journal of International Business Studies*, 23, 3: 461–76.

Blankenburg, D. (1995) 'A Network Approach to Foreign Market Entry' in Möller, K. and Wilson, D. (eds), *Business Marketing: An Interaction and Network Perspective*, Kluwer: 375–410.

Bond, M. H. (1986) *The Psychology of the Chinese Mind*, Oxford University Press.

Cavusgil, S. T. (1984) 'Differences between Exporting Firms Based on their Degree of Internationalisation', *Journal of Business Research*, 12: 195–208.

Chen, M. (1995) *The Asian Management System: Chinese, Japanese and Korean Styles of Doing Business*, Routledge: 52–66.

Child, J. and Kieser, A. (1977) 'A Contrast in British and West German Management Practices: Are Recipes of Success Culture Bound?' paper presented at the Conference on Cross-Cultural Studies, Hawaii.

Copeland, L. and Griggs, L. (1986) *Going International*, Plume Books.

Cray, D. and Mallory, G. R. (1998) *Making Sense of Managing Culture*, International Thompson Business Press.

Darling, J. R. (1990) 'A Study of Changes in Finnish Consumer Attitudes towards the Products and Associated Marketing Practices of Selected Countries', *Finnish Journal of Business Economics*, Fall: 175–87.

Diamantopoulos, A. and Inglis, K. (1988) 'Identifying Differences between High and Low Involvement Exporters', *International Marketing Review*, 5, Summer: 52–60.

Fletcher, R. (1996) 'The Role of Countertrade in the Internationalisation of the Australian Firm', University of Technology, Sydney, PhD thesis.

Fletcher, R. and Bohn, J. (1998) 'The Impact of Psychic Distance on the Internationalisation of the Australian Firm', *Journal of Global Marketing*, 12, 2: 47–68.

Forsgren, M. (1989) *Managing the Internationalisation Process: The Swedish Case*, Routledge.

Gaedeke, R. (1973) 'Consumer Attitudes towards Products "Made In" developing countries', *Journal of Retailing*, 11, Fall: 694–99.

Håkansson, H. and Snehota, I. (1989) 'No Business is an Island: The Network Concept of Business Strategy', *Scandinavian Journal of Management*, 5, 3: 187–200.

Hall, E. T. (1960) 'The Silent Language of International Business', *Harvard Business Review*, May–June: 87–96.

Hallén, L. (1982) *International Industrial Purchasing: Channels, Interaction and Governance Structures*, Acta Universitatis Upsaliensis, Stockholm.

Hallén, L. and Sandström, M. (1991) 'Relationship Atmosphere in International Business', in Paliwoda, S. (ed.), *New Perspectives in International Marketing*, Routledge.

Hofstede, G. (1980) *Culture's Consequences: International Differences in Work-Related Values*, Sage.

Hofstede, G. (1994) *Cultures and Organizations: Intercultural Co-operation and its Importance for Survival*, HarperCollins.

Hofstede, G. and Bond, M. H. (1988) 'Confucius and Economic Growth: New Trends in Culture's Consequences', *Organizational Dynamics*, 16, 4: 4–21.

Hong, S. T. and Wyer, R. S. Jr. (1989) 'Effects of Country-of-Origin and Product Attribute Information', *Journal of Consumer Research*, 16, 2: 175–88.

Hörnell, E., Vahlne, J.-E. and Wiedersheim-Paul, F. (1973) 'Export och Utlands-Etableringar (Export and Foreign Establishment) Stockholm' cited in Johanson, J. and Wiedersheim-Paul, F. (1975) 'The Internationalisation of the Firm – Four Swedish Cases' *Journal of Management Studies*, October: 305–22.

Hutton, J. (1988) *The World of the International Manager*, Philip Allan.

Johanson, J. and Wiedersheim-Paul, F. (1975) 'The Internationalisation of the Firm – Four Swedish Cases', *Journal of Management Studies*, October: 305–22.

Johanson, J. and Vahlne, J.-E. (1977) 'The Internationalisation of the Firm: A Model of Knowledge Development and Increasing Foreign Market Commitments', *Journal of International Business Studies*, 8, 1: 23–32.

Johansson, J. K., Douglas, S. P. and Nonaka, I. (1985) 'Assessing the Impact of Country-of-Origin on Product Evaluations: A New Methodological Perspective', *Journal of Marketing Research*, 22, November: 388–96.

Johansson, J. K., Ronkainen, I. A. and Czinkota, M. R. (1994) 'Negative Country-of-Origin Effects: The Case of the New Russia', *Journal of International Business Studies*, 1: 157–76.

Kogut, B. and Singh, H. (1988) 'The Effect of National Culture on the Choice of Entry Mode', *Journal of International Business Studies*, 19, 3: 411–32.

Langhoff, T. (1997) 'The Influence of Cultural Differences on Internationalisation Processes of Firms: An Introduction to Semiotic and Intercultural Perspective', in Björkman, I. and Forsgren, M. (eds), *The Nature of the International Firm*, Copenhagen Business School Press.

Leung, T. K. P., Wong, Y. H. and Tam, J. L. M. (1995) 'Adaptation and the Relationship Building Process in the People's Republic of China (PRC)', *Journal of International Consumer Marketing*, 8, 2: 7–26.

Levitt, T. (1983) 'The Globalization of Markets', *Harvard Business Review*, May–June: 92–102.

Mascarenhas, O. A. J. and Kujawa, D. (1998) 'American Consumer Attitudes toward Foreign Direct Investments and their Products', *Multinational Business Review*, Fall: 1–9.

O'Grady, S. and Lane, H. W. (1996) 'The Psychic Distance Paradox', *Journal of International Business Studies*, 2: 309–33.

Pahlberg, C. (1997) 'Cultural Differences and Problems in HQ-Subsidiary Relationships in MNCs', in Björkman, I. and Forsgren, M. (eds), *The Nature of the International Firm*, Copenhagen Business School Press.

Paitra, J. (1991) 'The Euro-Consumer: Myth or Reality?', *Futuribles*, 150: 25–35, reprinted in Halliburton, C. and Hünerberg, R. (1993) *European Marketing: Readings and Cases*, Addison-Wesley.

Petersen, B. and Pedersen, T. (1997) 'Twenty Years After – Support and Critique of the Uppsala Internationalisation Model', in Björkman, I. and Forsgren, M. (eds), *The Nature of the International Firm*, Copenhagen Business School Press.

Peterson, R. A. and Jolibert, A. J. P. (1995) 'A Meta-Analysis of Country-of-Origin Effects', *Journal of International Business Studies*, 4: 883–900.

Rajan, M. N. and Graham, J. L. (1991) 'Nobody's Grandfather was a Merchant: Understanding the Soviet Commercial Negotiation Process and Style', *California Management Review*, Spring: 40–56.

Reardon, K. K. (1984) 'It's the Thought that Counts', *Harvard Business Review*, September–October: 136–41.

Ricks, D. A. (1984) 'How to Avoid Business Blunders Abroad', *Business*, April.

Roth, M. S. and Romeo, J. B. (1992) 'Matching Product Category and Country Image Perceptions: A Framework for Managing Country-of-Origin Effects', *Journal of International Business Studies*, 23, 3: 477–97.

Shoham, A. and Albaum, G. S. (1995) 'Reducing the Impact of Barriers to Export: A Management Perspective', University of Oregon, *Working Paper*.

Törnroos, J.-A. (1991) 'Relations between the Concept of Distance and International Industrial Marketing', in Paliwoda, S. (ed.), *New Perspectives in International Marketing*, Routledge.

Tung, R. L. (1982) 'US–China Trade Negotiations: Practices, Procedures and Outcomes', *Journal of International Business Studies*, 13: 25–38.

Usunier, J.-C. (1993) *International Marketing: A Cultural Approach*, Prentice-Hall.

Vahlne, J.-E. and Nordström, K. (1992) 'Is the Globe Shrinking? Psychic Distance and the Establishment of Swedish Sales Subsidiaries During the Last 100 Years', Stockholm School of Economics Institute of International Business, *Working Paper*, RP 92/3.

Wong, Y. H. (1998) 'The Dynamics of Guanxi in China', *Singapore Management Review*, 20, 2: 25–42.

THE TECHNOLOGICAL CONTEXT

Objectives

The issues to be addressed in Chapter 3 include:

1. The role of innovation in successful international marketing
2. The real impact of the Internet on international marketing
3. The challenges of creating technology relationships
4. The distinctive characteristics of these relationships
5. What happens when these relationships are international
6. Examining 'virtual' or E marketing relationships
7. Networks and technology industries.

After reading Chapter 3 you will be able to:

1. Understand the innovation imperative in international marketing
2. Distinguish the characteristics of relationships via the Internet
3. Understand the dynamics of international technology relationships
4. Assess the issues facing international marketers when operating in technology networks
5. Understand the difference between database marketing and virtual relationship building.

INTRODUCTION

Human ingenuity has continued to turn out new technologies changing the technological landscape (Lindquist 1987). Where our grandparents were bewildered with typewriters, telephones and horn gramophones, we pride ourselves on personal computers, cellular phones, and portable CD players. Continuous streams of technological innovations have unfolded alongside the progress of society. The history of technology runs like a common thread through human history, always capturing our attention. (Håkansson and Lundgren, 1995, p. 292)

In today's rapidly changing environment a firm needs to innovate to become and remain successful. Unless a firm can introduce new products that meet market needs, competition will inevitably erode its margins and reduce its profits. A common confusion exists between 'invention', developing clever products and services, and 'innovation', which involves new or effective response to changes in market conditions.

This chapter examines the role of innovation in successful international marketing. It explores the impact of specific technological advances, such as the Internet, from traditional, relationship and network perspectives. From a relationship perspective, technology creates possibilities for new types of 'virtual' interaction on a global scale. These 'virtual' relationships, however, are remote and creation of trust is complex. The network section of this chapter explores the extent to which innovation is favoured by interconnection with other firms in nets.

THE TRADITIONAL PERSPECTIVE

The Innovation Imperative

Customer needs change rapidly with tastes, fashions and new technological developments. To prosper, businesses must maintain a fit with these changes in the market environment. Doyle and Bridgewater (1998) identify five challenges for marketing innovation:

1. **Global scope**. Competition exists on a global scale. Customers now choose from suppliers around the globe and the standards they demand have become higher with global choice. Motorola reduced their number of suppliers for a range of components from 2000 globally to just four in 2000. Advances in information technology, fewer trade restrictions and lower transportation costs mean that more and more companies now face global competition.

2. **Eroding boundaries**. The boundaries between industries are crumbling. The technological separation of industries is disappearing. While cars were once considered to be in the mechanical engineering sector, now they contain more and more electronics. The burgeoning Internet market is contested by telephone operators, computer and electronics firms.

3. **All industries are becoming high-tech**. High technology is a pre-requisite of survival for firms today. Firms are reliant on technology. Even if not in products and services, technology may play a role in manufacturing processes or channels to market.

4. **Mass customization**. Sophisticated global customers increasingly demand tailored solutions rather than imperfectly fitting mass-market answers. To cope with the demands for more variety, manufacturers are using flexible manufacturing systems and CAD–CAM to create variety at lowest cost.

5. **Shortening product lifecycles**. Customers are also demanding a continual stream of new and improved products and services. As a result, firms must engage in a continual process of innovation. A single good idea is no longer sufficient to create sustainable competitive advantage. The lifecycle of Dell's notebook computer screen is around 9–12 months.

Technology and Changing Markets

Technological advances have fuelled many of the market changes since the 1980s. Miniaturized microchips, the development of computers and software applications have all found a myriad of business applications. Drucker (1999) suggests, however, that it the impact of IT lies not so much in the T, for technology, but in the I, for information.

In the late twentieth century, a new information revolution got under way. This revolution was based on the emergence of electronic data about customers and their preferences, databases and Internet. Drucker further suggests that, while data has been collected and stored for some fifty years, this revolution relates to more effective analysis of the *purpose and meaning of this data*.

New concepts for today's marketers included Efficient Consumer Response (ECR) whereby retailers could analyze sophisticated data from Electronic Point of Sale (EPOS) terminals to map consumer purchase behaviour and preferences. The related concept of category management allows suppliers and retailers to work together with this data to identify new purchase opportunities. Management information systems (MIS) are in the process of revolution with the introduction of standardized computerized reporting, using systems such as SAP. In sum, the potential learning about international customer behaviour from these, and other, sources of information cannot be underestimated.

The Real Impact of the Internet

Early studies of the Internet focused on whether it would penetrate households globally. Up to the present, statistics cite 90 million Internet users in the USA and Canada and 35 million in Europe. Estimates suggested that 550 million people (10 per cent of the global population) would be using Internet by the year 2000 (Dutta and Segev 1999).

Given the rapid growth in popularity of the Internet, it is commonly accepted that it does offer a new route to market that will change the face of global competition. Amongst the predicted impacts of E-Commerce are a reduction in the barriers of time, geography and cost:

- **Time**: Firms can communicate with customers regardless of time zone

- **Geography**: The interface with the customer is on their desk wherever in the world they are physically located
- **Cost**: Costs associated with setting up agents, subsidiaries or other types of operation to reach international customers are significantly reduced.

This reduction in barriers is predicted to have a more significant impact on small than on large firms. Quelch and Klein (1996) suggest that existing multinational corporations will use the Internet as an on-line brochure rather than to trade on-line with international customers.

The failure to capitalize on potential may be attributable to a number of causes. Some of these concern a lack of time or resources to devote to an alternative channel when costs have been incurred for existing international operations. Perhaps more significantly, firms are facing a number of challenges as a result of global connectivity (Bridgewater and Arnott 2002). Firms may not, for example, wish to engage with the potential consequences of the Internet's price transparency. If Levi Jeans retail in a San Francisco store for US$45 but sell in a London boutique at £45 (US$70), the firm may not wish to post its US prices on the Internet!

Indeed Dutta and Segev (1999) suggest that, to date, few firms are utilizing the Internet's potential to interact with customers remotely. While more than 80 per cent of Internet firms supply an on-line brochure, only 12 per cent allow customers to participate in customizing products to their requirements. More than 80 per cent offer on-line ordering, but only 30 per cent allow on-line payment and less than 10 per cent on-line delivery. (The challenges of building interactive on-line relationships are discussed further in the Relationship section of this chapter.)

The literature also prophesies that Internet will have profound impacts on international marketing. These include:

- **Increased visibility** (Sterne 1995). The ability to make the corporate image known increases with the availability of low cost Internet space. Commentators suggest that the costs of registering domain names and of Internet space via the main providers will increase as a result of mar-

ket forces so that this benefit may be short-lived. Already firms must decide whether there is greater kudos in an @aol rather than an @freeserve, or other low cost provider, address. The relative costs of these may diverge over time.

- **Reduction in resources required for internationalization** (Quelch and Klein 1996). Initial barriers based on advertising costs and scale economies may reduce, although costs of logistical infrastructure remain. Firms may attract orders from China but can they physically supply these customers, and at what cost?
- **Adoption of global niche strategies** (Quelch and Klein 1996). A number of smaller firms have come into existence as a result of the Internet. These firms are more likely to begin by selling on the Internet, rather than providing information, as they need to generate profits. Moreover they are not constrained by the impacts of Internet strategy on existing international operations. The limited resources of smaller firms favour the use of global niche strategists (see the relationship section of this chapter for a fuller discussion of Quelch and Klein's work).
- **Performance improvement**. Research is coy about suggesting performance improvements as a result of the Internet. While the arguments for costs reduction are clear, the extent to which new customers will be found and repeat sales achieved is still subject to debate. Cronin (1994, 1996) remains one of the few who predict performance improvements.
- **Reduction in barriers** (Hamill and Gregory 1998) such as:

- *Psychological*. Access to data via the Internet can increase the confidence of international markets. Participation in global network communities may create links with potential customers.
- *Operational*. The export procedure itself may be simplified electronically. Hamill and Gregory (1998) suggest the use of electronic payments and electronic data transfer.
- *Organizational*. Traditionally entry into international markets required investment in export or use of agents or distributors. On-line sales and (hot) links with other firms reduce the costs and complexity of traditional routes to market.

– *Product/Market.* On-line market research, possibilities for customer feedback and global niche strategies should also facilitate successful international marketing.

Despite these potential benefits of the Internet, a number of obstacles remain to its use. It is not clear that information provision will necessarily reduce the perception of psychic and other

---

Box 3.1   The Real Impacts of the Internet on International Marketing

Much has been made of the ways in which Internet will revolutionize international marketing. Much of the research to date, however, is conceptual. Where there is data, this is often based on North American respondents, as the Internet has achieved greater penetration to date in the USA. Arnott and Bridgewater (2002) test the extent to which international managers actually feel that Internet delivers the proposed benefits (Table 3.1) and the principal barriers (Table 3.2) that remain.

Table 3.1   Potential benefits of international marketing via the Internet

Variables	Mean score[1]	Standard deviation
1. Increased profits	4.8	0.42
2. Increased sales	4.7	0.47
3. Visibility	4.7	0.47
4. Corporate Image	4.6	0.5
5. Ease of access to international markets	4.4	0.68
6. Interaction with customers	4.0	0.82
7. Speed of business	3.6	1.34
8. Low resource market entry	3.4	1.26
9. Global niche strategies	3.0	1.56
10. Ability to tailor products/services	2.9	1.37

Note: 1. Where 5 = extremely important and 1 = not at all important

Table 3.2   Barriers to international marketing via the Internet

Variables	Mean score[1]	Standard deviation
1. Low penetration of Internet	3.8	1.03
2. Competition	3.4	1.26
3. Price transparency	3.4	1.17
4. Need to build awareness of web site	3.4	1.07
5. Logistics of serving international markets	3.4	1.17
6. Legal complexity	3.3	1.09
7. Cultural barriers	3.1	0.74
8. Need to alter market offering	3.1	1.29
9. Language barriers	3.0	0.94
10. Costs of serving international markets	2.9	1.05

The highest ranking barriers to international marketing via the Internet relate to market structure. Low penetration of the Internet in some international markets is the most significant barrier, while competition via the Internet also represents a major barrier. Marketing mix issues, such as price transparency, promoting the web site's existence and physical distribution are also rated as barriers.
Note: 1. Where 5 = extremely important and 1 = not at all important
Source: Based on Arnott and Bridgewater (2002)

barriers. The Internet may, in fact, result in information overload. Existing small firms (other than Internet start-ups) may be too resource constrained to explore the potential offered by the new technology. All firms need to increase the level of interaction with customers to ensure that Internet sales translate into ongoing Internet business. The example in Box 3.1, based on the work of Arnott and Bridgewater (2002), identifies some of the major benefits and obstacles to the Internet in international marketing.

Respondents perceive the main benefits to be those of visibility, building corporate image and ease of access to international markets. The possibilities to interact with customers and design tailored offerings are recognized.

THE RELATIONSHIP PERSPECTIVE

Distinctive Characteristics of Technological Assets

Kogut and Singh (1988) suggest that relationships involving technology face particular problems because of technology's distinctive characteristics. Technological knowledge is considered to be 'fragile' and tacit. That is to say the value of a particular piece of knowledge can often only be guessed at. Contractor and Lorange (1988) explain this concept using the example of Western Electric licensing its transistor technology to Sony. Sony gained the necessary product technology to launch a massive assault on the US market. This example raises a number of issues. Did Western Electric gain adequate recompense given the ultimate profit gained by Sony from this technology? Given that Sony might have failed to launch the product, considerable risk attaches to paying a high price for the technology. A large proportion of the ultimate value of the technology lies in successful marketing rather than in the invention itself.

Technology Relationships

Technology development is seen as the keystone of competitive edge and the need for technolo-

gical development is accordingly stressed whenever the competitive power of a company is discussed (Porter 1983). The underlying reason for this interest in technological development is its effect not only on a company's way of functioning in a technical sense, but, at least as important, on the company's relations to customers and suppliers, and thereby also to competitors. (Håkansson and Henders 1992, p. 32)

The rising costs of technological development are frequently mentioned as a driver of globalization. These costs might be reduced by technology co-operation with a partner (Hladik 1990; Thomas and Ford 1995). In combination firms may have sufficient research resources to compete at the leading edge, whereas singly the costs may be prohibitive. Once such example of the benefits gained by both partners is given in Box 3.2.

As can be seen in Box 3.2, technological co-operation can improve technical and, ultimately, economic success (Håkansson 1989; Gemünden, Ritter and Heydebreck 1996). The importance of technology co-operation for international marketing success is clear.

There are, however, a number of difficulties in this type of co-operation:

- **Complexity**. Håkansson and Henders (1992) point to the complexity of combining technologies within or between firms. Systems may not be compatible and time loss and friction may result.
- **Diffusion**. Gemünden and Heydebreck (1996) suggest a danger that sharing technological knowledge may result in one or other partner losing control of the technology. For example, a larger partner with greater ability to commercialize the technology may become so associated with it that the smaller partner loses credit for its technology.
- **Timeliness**. As relationships become more international the 'urgency of maintaining up-to-date awareness of technological developments around the world' increases (Håkansson and Henders 1992).

These and other obstacles must be overcome for the co-operation to be successful.

Box 3.2   Apple and IBM

When Apple launched its first machine it 'offered individuals the possibility of decentralized computer power with a convenience and cost that was on a completely different level from that provided by centralized mainframes' creating what Streber (*Financial Times* 1 March 1996) describes as a 'breakpoint.' A breakpoint occurs when a new offering to the market is distinctively better than its competitors.

Although large computer manufacturers paid little attention to Apple, its machines offered users a simple first computer system. Apple's user-friendliness and graphics capability were core strengths of the brand. Large mainframe manufacturers may not have been threatened, but smaller entrants into the personal computer (PC) market saw the success of Apple as good reason to enter. These new entrants refined their machines until they began to resemble each other. At this point IBM entered the market with a product offer that matched consumer expectations of the optimal PC. This second breakpoint saw the introduction of what became the industry standard PC.

By early 1996, competition in the PC market had escalated to the point of global shakeout. The PC market had seen the growth of Compaq to market leader with 36 per cent and new entrants such as Dell gaining share with its direct sales strategy. Now the development of networked desktops PCs had created a new breakpoint. By February 1996, the PC market was locked in a price war. IBM lowered its prices in response to weak sales in North America and triggered responses from a number to its competitors. On March 5 1996, leading US personal computer firms announced price cuts of up to 20 per cent. Digital Equipment lowered prices of its US desktop by 26 per cent and Hewlett Packard its personal computers by 21 per cent in all markets (Kehoe, *Financial Times* 5 March 1996). Profit margins were 'razor thin' (Taylor, *Financial Times*, April 3 1996).

One major casualty of this escalating competition was Apple. Severe pressure on sales resulted in management changes and a loss of profitability. IBM-compatible machines and Microsoft's Windows operating system now dominated the market. The created a vicious circle for Apple; it lost market share, which pushed up prices and meant that software producers did not write applications for Macintosh machines. Despite its technological superiority, new Apple Chief Executive Officer, Gilbert Amelio, struggled with the challenge of developing a new strategy that would revive the company's fortunes. In April 1996, Apple announced that it has licensed its technology to IBM. By the conditions of this technological co-operation, Apple would license its operating software to other manufacturers. Apple had resisted this move for ten years, fearing the creation of Macintosh clones (Lex Column, May 8 1996). At this point, however, the co-operation would allow Apple to gain royalties on wider sales of its system and encourage software producers to retain an interest in creating new applications. IBM would gain access to an operating system with technological capabilities superior to the dominant Windows.

Sources: Kehoe, L. (1996) 'Computer Price Battle Escalates: Digital and Hewlett-Packard Announce Cuts of over 20 per cent', *Financial Times*, March; Lex Column (1996) 'Apple/IBM', *Financial Times*, 8 May; Strebel, P. (1996) 'Mastering Management – Part 17 (13): Breakpoint – How to Stay in the Game', *Financial Times*, 1 March; Taylor, P. (1996) 'Survey – Information Technology: Dynamic Forces at Work', *Financial Times*, 3 April.

Gemünden and Heydebreck (1996) identify four problems in identifying a technology partner:

1. **No knowledge of each other**. In this case the partners are willing to co-operate but have not found, or maybe even looked for appropriate partners.
2. **No ability to co-operate**. These firms are willing, but do not have appropriate skills to be able to co-operate. The social and technological distances between partners must be overcome (Ford 1980, 1984). The partners must also 'learn' a common language in order that they can understand each other. They must agree on a definition of the problem, objectives for the co-operation and gain appropriate financial support.
3. **No wish to co-operate**. There may be either active or passive resistance to co-operation in

one or both organizations. This may come from factions within organizations and may not always prevent co-operation from taking place.

4. **No permission to co-operate**. This may be prohibited because of the political, cultural or legal context (Macdonald 1993).

Issues for Consideration in Technology Relationships

The following section identifies a number of issues for consideration in technology relationships.

Scope of the Co-operation

As with other types of co-operative relationship (see, for example, Chapter 7 for further discussion of strategic alliances) a clear definition of both the *objectives* and *scope* of the co-operation is important. Both partners should know which technologies they must contribute to the relationship (Hladik 1988; Thomas and Ford 1995) and the precise nature of the agreement.

Characteristics of the Partners

On entering into the relationship both partners will have a set of characteristics. Each partner will, for example, have an initial level of technological skill. Research suggests (Thomas and Ford 1995) that firms with similar levels of technological skill are more likely to work well together. Each will also have a set of resources, financial, human resources, etc. which may be deployed in the relationship.

Differences (referred to in the literature as 'asymmetry') in size or level of technological skills may create tensions in the relationship. Indeed Doz (1988) points to fact that acquisitions of smaller firms by larger ones are seldom a success. The anticipated synergies seldom materialize. Acquisition of smaller, entrepreneurial firms by larger, established firms might seem to offer an exchange of ideas for resources to commercialize them. Both in the microelectronics and pharmaceutical sectors, there have, however, been well-publicized failures (e.g. Honeywell – Synertek, GE – Intersil, Schlumberger – Fairchild, Thorn – EMI – Inmos). As a result, split equity or 'strategic alliance' agree-

ments tend to be preferred as lower risk forms of co-operation.

In cases of asymmetry, however, problems still arise:

- **Consistency of purpose**. The strengths of the firms may be complementary, but differences in power result in potential conflict over the objectives of co-operation. The larger firm is often attempting to capture the technology of the smaller partner (Doz 1988). Conversely, the smaller firm may be nervous and attempt to retain control over its technologies whatever the intentions of its partner.

- **Consistency of position**. The existence of subunits or coalitions of interest (Cyert and March 1966) within larger firms may bring political influences to bear on the relationship. While co-operative objectives may have been agreed and supported at one level, these may not be supported elsewhere in the organization.

Learning and Adaptation

Håkansson and Henders (1992, p. 35) point to strengthening of relationships through a process of learning and social exchange:

> Learning brings the parties closer together in multiple ways, helps avoid conflict, and creates opportunities for co-operation. Social exchange is equally important as it implies that a certain degree of mutuality based on trust will develop. This means that over time the two parties realize that they are not just counterparts, but at least partial partners in many areas – including technological development.

Learning in the relationship is argued to favour technological development in a number of ways. The firms may adapt their technologies to each other which may, in turn, increase efficiency. Also, attempts to understand and resolve differences in the bodies of knowledge of each partner may result in innovation. Remaining as two separate partners, however, may be beneficial. Occasional differences in opinion may spark debate (see Håkansson's discussion of the value of friction in Chapter 1). Moreover, retaining a separate identity may facilitate optimal differentiation and specialization of the partners.

Boundary Spanning Roles

Given the importance of the interface between the partners, it is not, then, surprising that a recurrent theme of the technological co-operation literature is that of individuals who play a 'boundary spanning' role (Box 3.3). These individuals interface with another organization.

Even within an organization, the interface between technology developing teams and others in the organization can pose challenges. As innovation literature increasingly proposes cross-functional teams for radical innovation, the acceptance of their ideas is affected by the nature of their interface with the rest of the organization (Ancona 1992). In this situation boundary roles involve lateral communication with other functions, as well as vertical communication with management. In an average innovation team, each individual has been found to spend 48 per cent of their time working alone, 38 per cent working with other team members and only 14 per cent working with others outside the team.

When the boundaries are with other organizations, the problems intensify.

Doz (1988) suggests that partnerships are often decided by top management, but implemented by middle management or technical specialists. These individuals may be more or less committed to making the relationship work. The literature has identified a number of *boundary roles* which may exist:

■ **Technological gatekeeper**. The gatekeeper controls the flow of information. He or she promotes technology internally and across boundaries. This role lacks the control over resources and does not have authority. It is essentially an influencing role. The gatekeeper may be an individual who has developed an interest in new technologies and remains at the forefront out of interest. Interface with other organizations occurs because, in the words of Persson (1981) 'well-informed people preferably look for dialogue partners who are well-informed themselves'. The gatekeeper can, however, communicate or guard and retain information.

■ **Salesperson and purchasing agent**. In buyer – seller relationships the interface is often considered to take place through repeated transactions and negotiations. Although buyers

---

Box 3.3   Supplying Marks and Spencer: Boundary Spanning Roles

In the late 1980s, Marks and Spencer dominated high street retail sales of food and clothes. Given the difficulty of gaining additional market share in a mature market, Marks and Spencer had made a number of attempts to diversify. Since the early 1970s, Marks and Spencer had been attempting to enter new international markets, but had gained a niche rather than mass market position in these. It had also attempted to enter the premium clothes market with limited success.

The firm had also expanded its operation to target its existing mainstream customers with new product categories, such as home furnishings. Given its premium positioning the firm were keen to achieve high quality products. They were also keen to create co-ordinated ranges of fabrics, wallpapers, crockery and other items. These were, however, frequently sourced from different firms.

Successful Marks and Spencer suppliers needed, therefore, to interface with the customer but also

with a range of other suppliers. This co-operation involved different types of individuals from each of the firms. Among the areas involving the highest level of communication between the suppliers were Research and Development and Manufacturing. Some of the products were technically complex with plain backgrounds that caused problems with shade variation. Production of each type of product posed its own distinctive sets of issues, yet the final range had to be as near as possible co-ordinated in colour and finish. Sales and marketing personnel were involved in many of the discussions, but did not always understand the finer technical points. Ultimately, direct contact was established between technical representatives from each of the firms to resolve difficulties. These individuals performed 'boundary spanning roles' in the launch of new ranges into Marks and Spencer.

have been seen as the least important function in the new product development process (Atuahene-Gima 1995), they may become involved. Personal characteristics of those becoming involved include propensity to take risks, level of education and confidence. Organizational factors include whether purchasing is viewed as an operational or strategic function in the organization.

- **Relationship promoter**. As can be seen above, the technological gatekeeper may choose to promote a relationship or may act against the interests of a technological co-operation. Other types of relationship promoter are proposed by Gemünden and Walter (1997) these may be based either on personal or structural sources of power. Personal sources include expertise, knowledge of partner, social competency or charisma. Structural sources rely on position within the organization or position in the broader network surrounding the firm (see a further discussion of this last issue under Network perspective in this chapter).

International Technology Co-operation

When technology co-operation involves international partners the benefits must be weighed against barriers that may hinder learning:

Håkansson and Henders (1992) pose three questions:

1. **How common is international technology co-operation?** In a study of Swedish technology firms, 60 per cent of all such co-operation involved international partners. This proportion seems likely to increase in line with the importance of innovation in global competition. As the costs of technological development increase, co-operative relationships with large international players may become essential to being at the forefront of technology.

2. **What are the characteristics of these relationships?** Relationships may be international in different ways. Information may also be transferred between two firms within a market and then transferred across borders by one or other firm. For example, Dell asked one of its suppliers in the USA to produce components for a computer. A condition of the business was that global coverage could be achieved with the component in question. When the supplier began producing the component in a European plant, it used the learning gained within its own US facility. Technology co-operation may also exist between technical experts in one firm and their opposite numbers in the other firm wherever they are located. For example, one global firm may have a technology centre in Japan while another bases its expertise in USA and a third has specialists in each country.

3. **How do these differ from domestic technology development relationships?** Additional challenges relate to the existence of distances within the relationships. As well as personal characteristics, cultural, geographic, economic and other distances may inhibit the process of learning and social exchange. These tend to be higher in international relationships of all types. In technology relationships, the technology may provide a common language for boundary spanning experts. This may minimize distances between some individuals in each firm. In contrast, the technical complexity of the co-operation may increase the negative consequences of miscommunication. If one party, for example, adds the wrong proportion of sulphuric acid to a product, or wrongly passes a product as microbiologically safe the resulting hazards can be imagined.

Virtual Relationships

Database Marketing Alone does not Build Relationships

Advances in technology allow marketers to identify customers using sophisticated databases and to maintain contact via technological advances such as the Internet. These technological advances have opened up the possibility of building and maintaining interactive relationships with a far greater number of partners than would previously have been possible (McKenna 1991; Everett 1994).

(See Chapter 1 for a fuller discussion of the roots of relationship marketing.)

At the root of the growing popularity of database marketing is the belief that knowing more about customers can help a firm to target them more effectively. The knowledge that a family has just had a baby, for example, allows baby goods' producers to target them with appropriate offers. Given pressures on time, and the amount of choice facing consumers, timely and well targeted direct mail serves a useful purpose.

The possibilities to interact with customers on a larger scale than would be possible face-to-face exists largely as a result of database technology. There are, however, a number of popular misconceptions about database marketing:

- **Database marketing is all about choosing the right database technology**. Successful database marketing requires more than just a technology. At the very least, integration of all systems is needed to allow one point of contact with the customer. This presents the full picture and may require organizational restructuring.
- **If we know a lot about our customers we can target them effectively**. Databases contain large volumes of customer data and details about their purchase behaviour that allow firms to predict their behaviour in the future. The value of this information is only as great as its accuracy. The Telesales manager of one small firm using a database of possible prospects commented that company and contact information was often wrong and even those for whom details were correct weren't necessarily in the company's target market. It is common practice to buy mailing lists. One firm cites the case of buying a mailing list of customers who take weekend breaks in prestige country hotels because it was assumed that they might also buy fine wines. Many of the mailing list were discovered, however, not to drink alcohol on health or other grounds. The underlying assumptions of database marketing are reminiscent of segmentation strategies more generally. As Haley points out in his classic article (1968), demographic, geographic and other descriptions of customers do not ask the question 'why' a customer buys a product or service and whether they are likely to in the future.

- **If we know a lot about our target customers we can identify prospects that will buy our products or services**. Unless a firm interacts with its customers to ask questions about 'why' they would buy or not buy a product or service, the information is only the firm's view. Database marketing may provide sophisticated information, but it is assumes the active marketer/passive buyer model of traditional marketing (see Chapter 1). Yet the possibilities exist through the Internet to interact with the customers to build 'virtual' relationships.

Building Virtual Relationships

The range of channels to market has increased dramatically with the advent of new technologies. Services such as telephone sales, the Internet and home shopping via television have fundamentally changed the channel options for customers and providers. These new channels to market raise associated issues of relationship management:

> Customers once expected low prices and good service. Today, they demand low prices and outstanding service. But finding the right technologies to let you get closer to your customer while remaining competitive isn't so simple. Such challenges force companies to rethink their supply chains and redefine customer ties. (Stahl 1999)

Virtual relationships pose a number of distinctive challenges.

Building Trust

The benefits of technological advances are much vaunted. We reputedly exist in a 'republic of technology' (Levitt 1983) where technology will break down the barriers between countries. Oviatt and McDougall (1918) claim that:

> An internationally experienced person who can attract a moderate amount of capital can conduct business anywhere in the time it takes to press the buttons of a telephone, and, when required, he or she can travel virtually anywhere on the globe in less than a day.

Locke (1999) believes that technological advances, such as telecommuting (use of videoconferencing and other technologies) rather than making a visit in person will limit direct contact as it will be increasingly difficult to justify the time and cost involved in business travel.

In industrial markets, social exchange has long been seen as essential to the development of trust in relationships (see Chapter 1 for a fuller discussion of the fundamentals of interaction). Although technology allows firms to replace direct personal contact, firms will still need to overcome the difficulties resulting from a lack of face-to-face contact:

> A certain amount of security comes from face-to-face interactions. Now you have to trust in the medium, not any one person you can see... It is difficult to identify with a system, so on-line retailers have to try to have a pseudo-relationship with the customer. (*Marketing News*, November 1998)

One of the most common concerns of customer entering relationships on-line (virtual relationships) is that of security. Well-publicized episodes of hacking into apparently secure computer systems, such as the jamming of the Yahoo Internet search engine in 2000 suggest that the new technology is open to abuse. To shop on-line, customer must often provide personal and financial information, so fears over unauthorized use of data are not surprising.

As the number of people on-line increases, so does the number of customers disenchanted because they cannot find the products and services they want. The Internet research firm Zona Research in the USA, indicates that 20 per cent of consumers try unsuccessfully to buy on-line three times before succeeding, while 39 per cent end up not buying on-line (*Target Magazine*, January 1999). The more concerned customers are at the security of their financial information, the more likely they are to be dissatisfied with their shopping experience. David Szymanski, of Texas A and M University says:

> There has to be something to tell the consumer that this is not a risky purchase... consumers are thinking 'I've given you my credit card number and now its out there and its gone.' (*Marketing News*, November 1998, p. 2)

Anything marketers can do to reduce that perceived risk helps. Firms often offer on-line acknowledgement of orders and helpline numbers to contact in case of problems. Szymanski also believes, however, that marketers should not overdo the reassurance. If too much emphasis is placed on security risks, consumers may suspect there have been problems with security in the past.

The relatively low level of repeat purchase in Internet relationships (Balabanis and Vassileiou 1999) seems also to suggest an underlying dissatisfaction or lack of trust in the virtual relationship. Trust may be difficult to develop in virtual relationships for a number of reasons. As Locke notes (1999):

> Good old fashioned conversation has enormous social and psychological benefits, but certain attitudes and technologies are eliminating the leisurely face-to-face chat, even among family and friends... If people are not careful, this 'de-voicing' may cause both Westerners and Easterners to become more isolated, distrustful and unhappy.

So is lack of trust an inherent feature of the technology? Some argue that the lack of trust in virtual relationships stems from the marketer's attitude towards the technology: 'Despite the rhetoric, many marketers still think of consumers as an alien entity' (Mitchell 1999).

Others contend that an active marketer – passive consumer ethos prevails in Internet marketing. Yet interactive relationships are possible. For example the Ford Motor Co. has launched a web-based initiative in which owners receive regular one-on-one interaction designed to build their loyalty to the brand. (*Brandweek*, January 1999). In exchange for time (to fill in details) and hard data, which it can disseminate to dealers, Ford offers perks such as sports memorabilia, extra car rental or upgrades. The 'exchange' must be sufficient to 'lure consumers past the privacy issues that still loom over Internet marketing in general'. It is not sufficient to create a 'brochure environment'. *Brandweek* argues that it is action, using corporate assets, that will overcome consumer doubts. Ford is 'dangling its corporate assets' to bring consumers aboard, with their data, voluntarily. Dell.com provides not only cheaper systems but also advanced features such as the ability to tailor products and work out prices or the resulting machine.

According to research, customers also prefer simple sites, which load quickly, and allow them to find what they are looking for with the minimum number of clicks. These are the sites to which they are most likely to return and, in consequence, build an affinity. Experiences that may create relationships also include details such as 'remembering' customers' ordering and payment details to avoid them filling them out again. The challenge is to make it personal. Szymanski says: 'That personal component feeds into satisfaction.'

■ **Time and virtual relationships**. One of the vaunted benefits of virtual relationships is that they eliminate the obstacles of geography, time zones and location (see the Traditional Perspective Section of Chapter 4 for a fuller review of the proposed benefits of the Internet). Products that can be digitized, such as music, software or video can be purchased on-line and downloaded instantly whatever the time difference between the customer's and supplier's markets. Other orders can be held in the system and handled at an appropriate time.

The Internet also offers the possibility of 'real time' interaction:

> Did you ever wish you could market on the fly – taking advantage of opportunities of smart cross-selling, upselling and customer retention – that would otherwise be missed by waiting on direct mail campaigns? Now you can. (*Target Magazine*, March 1999)

Until the advent of the Internet, 'real time' communication and feedback was possible only in face-to-face relationships. Now, however, marketers can interact with their customers in real time. Real time communication, however, poses a number of challenges:

– **Higher expectations**. As customers know that 'real time' response is possible, they will expect instant, or at least speedy, response. In web sites, the topicality of the information will be subject to scrutiny. Customers will expect regular updates. Moreover, customers will

increasingly expect any products or services bought on the Internet to be available instantaneously. As the possible of 'real time' interaction becomes feasible, it will increasingly be the expectation. If instant delivery is not possible, for example as a result of time zone differences, lead times or delivery times, international marketers may have to make clear the timescale involved.

– **Timing of entry?** Despite the high levels of attention to the Internet and E-Commerce the profit gains are not yet clear (see Part IV). Even the most famous Internet ventures such as Amazon.com are not yet profitable and profits from electronic commerce also remain, for the majority of firms, a long way off:

> Electronic commerce will play an increasing role in business, but even the best-known startups aren't profitable yet and only a few Fortune 100 companies have profitable Internet commerce operations. (*Business Communications Review* February 1999, p. 8)

The high market valuations of '.com' startups are based on arguments of future potential. So, too, for many firms comes the question of whether and when to engage in the Internet. Involvement may be a case of putting a toe in the water. Quelch and Klein (1996) suggest that a majority of firms are using the technology to provide an on-line brochure. This minimum level of involvement is often viewed as taking an option on the future of the technology.

■ **Cross-border virtual relationships**. As highlighted earlier in the chapter, virtual relationships are also proposed as a means of circumventing tariff and non-tariff barriers (NTBs) to international markets. Both experienced international firms and those not previously engaged in international marketing should benefit. The initial set-up costs are low and products and services need to be offered within a restricted market, but can reach global customers across cyberspace (Sterrett and Shah 1998):

> It costs about \$200 per month to reach the entire world on-line compared with thousands a month to rent space for a single store in a shopping mall.

In addition, all the technical support you need is available off-the-shelf, or from companies that design Web home pages. p. 43

Lower barriers should open up the possibility of international marketing to a broader range of firms, including smaller firms whose resource constraints might previously have preventing this scope of operation:

> The Net enables them to go global virtually overnight. In the past, small businesses operated primarily within a local area, even relying on local suppliers for many of their needs. In the Internet market, small businesses have access to a customer base numbering in the millions as well as a global population of suppliers. (Sherrett and Shah 1998, p. 45)

This potential to expand comes, however, with its own challenges. As firms post on-line brochures, sales enquiries may be generated from markets as geographically remote as China, Russia and Greenland. Unless the service can be delivered on-line, firms may not be able, or may not choose, to serve all these markets. The open access provided by the technology has been referred to as *connectivity*. Global connectivity has a set of implications that will be explored more fully in the Network section of this chapter.

THE NETWORK PERSPECTIVE

In their discussion of the Internet and international marketing, Dutta and Segev (1999) propose a revised view of the context in which firms determine marketing strategies. According to this view, they see firms as operating against a context of technological capability (the possibility of Internet access) and connectivity (how should firms handle the global scope and open nature of their connections?).

One can imagine a number of potential consequences of connectivity:

1. International marketers may need to develop a protocol for handling sales enquiries they do not wish to accept without causing offence.
2. International marketers may need to keep in mind the fact that prices and other information posted on the net are accessible by customers in all markets.

3. Where different offers and prices exist, net design may need to allow customers to choose the appropriate market. An example of this type of net design can be seen at <www.dell.com>. Customers may access the parent site, but are then directed towards the appropriate national site. Sales support, prices in appropriate currency and local delivery leadtimes reinforce the need to deal with the appropriate market. Where differences in feature or prices exist, these clearly require explanation and justification.
4. Relationships with local agents or physical delivery specialists may be used to provide service to markets outside the scope of the advertizing firm.

In addition to the connectivity identified by Dutta and Segev (1999), the global Internet network has a number of other distinctive features:

Rapidly Changing Network Structures

As barriers to entry for firms and individuals are low, the actors and relationships in an Internet network may change rapidly. Low barriers mean that new competitors can easily build positions in the network.

The impact of one firm's actions on others will be communicated throughout the network. As competitive offerings of firms are visible and comparisons can be made rapidly, firms will face demands to deliver low costs and high quality service.

The requirement to do business in 'real time' may fuel the pace of change in technology-based networks.

Types of Exchange

Although firms wish to build ongoing relationships, the Internet may attract many browsers. Many consumers may be looking for information only.

From a firm's perspective, Quelch and Klein (1996) identify two types of Internet users: existing multinational corporations (MNCs) and small business start-ups created to do business solely on the Internet. The types of exchanges in which each engage differ:

- **MNCs who use the Internet**. These firms are seen to begin by offering information to address the needs of existing customers. Quelch and Klein (1996) use the example of Federal Express whose initial site was 'a relatively small twelve-page site focusing on the package-tracking service previously only available to business customers'. Enthusiastic customer reaction led to rapid expansion of the site to include other delivery, billing and pick-up options. 3M similarly began by product information. This 'brochure' approach is a typical early Internet use by existing firms.

  The process then for existing multinational corporations moves from information provision to information collection to customer service and ultimately to transactions via the net.

- **Internet Start-ups**. In contrast, start-ups based on the idea of using the Internet as a channel to market begin with transactions in order to cover costs. The medium is then used to achieve other goals such as building brands, offer customer service and, thus, build relationships with customers. In other words, Internet start-ups go through a process from transaction, to customer service and information.

Quelch and Klein (1996) identify two types of Internet usage: the use of the Internet by existing multinational corporations and the small business start-ups created to do business solely on the Internet. These latter they see as automatically becoming an multinational corporation, whatever their size.

One of the principal challenges is that firms must be able to physically supply products or services if these cannot be delivered on-line. Some product or service categories are suited to on-line delivery. The compression software Winzip can, for example, be bought and downloaded instantaneously on entry of a credit card number. Dell computers, who now do 40 per cent of computer sales on-line must, in contrast, arrange speedy and efficient delivery of computer hardware to wherever in the world the on-line customer is based. While information exchange via the Internet is easy, physical exchange of goods or services may be less easy.

Host Government Intervention

The Internet is seen as a particular boon for consumers in emerging and less developed markets, who will now gain access to a broad range of previously inaccessible goods and services. The extent to which this access will really be possible depends, however, on levels of technological development and wealth and on the intervention from other stakeholders, such as the government of the country.

Some emerging markets have espoused the new technology willingly. In the mid-1990s, China launched 'ChinaWeb', a web site whose stated aim was: 'To help China in her rapid transformation to an information society, and to promote business and commerce with China through the bridge of Internet' (Quelch and Klein 1996, p. 61). The authors also suggest, though, that governments may try to limit their population's access to the Internet as they may fear the impacts of the free flow of ideas and increased import of goods.

Legal Restrictions

Legal restrictions currently restrict cross-border sales in some product categories. Software packages, for example, are sometimes prohibited if they include encryption technologies. Exports of alcohol to some countries are prohibited via the Internet as through other channels. Although it is early days for Internet law, it seems that a range of tariff and non-tariff restrictions will be introduced, which will increase the barriers to global Internet access.

The Internet and Cultural Differences

Although the trend towards English as a business language tends to be reinforced by the Internet, international marketers may gain significant advantages from remembering that cultural differences persist. Research shows that, in Japan, firms whose sites are on a local web provider are much more successful than those on an international provider. If posted on a local provider, sites can be more readily translated and tailored to local market needs.

Changing Channel Roles

As the Internet offers direct access to consumers it seems to obviate the need for channel intermediaries. Yet opinions on the extent to which retailers will be by-passed vary. Procter and Gamble (P&G) has announced an intention to start sponsoring the creation of its distributors' web sites in an attempt to direct efforts to 'where the customer is':

> The practical use of driving people to the P&G site is not obvious . . . It's more important to drive them to points of sale. If there are no points of sale-on-line that will hamper P&G's ability to perform. (*Marketing News*, 28 November 1998, p. 17)

Thus, contrary to expectation, retailers seem to be among the more active users of the Internet. In the UK, Tesco, W. H. Smith and others offer their own network software; 41 per cent of 'traditional' retailers in the USA now sell on-line and a further 22 per cent intend to do so soon (*Marketing News* 28 November 1998). The interest of retailers may be defensive as they stand to lose if direct consumer access is established by manufacturing firms.

The value of retailers serving customers via the Internet is contested by some, however, as they have already incurred the costs of a retail network. If manufacturers can reach customers directly, then they may cut out the costs of trading via channels. Retailers adopting the Internet add this onto the cost of existing channel formats.

Building Positions in New National Nets

While connectivity increases the ease of international sales, creating relationships to allow physical distribution of goods in a constantly changing set of international markets is less easy. Consumers may be attracted from all parts of the globe. Some of these will be from markets to which goods have not previously been supplied. Creating a distribution infrastructure for each of these markets in the required timescale may become one of the major challenges of the Internet. To meet relationship expectations, delivery must be speedy and efficient even if it is the first

time the distributor has been used. One solution may be to form a relationship with a global carrier, such as FedEx, who is able to provide coverage of all global markets. This type of international relationship may become increasingly important to firms using the Internet as a sales channel.

Intra-Firm Impacts

> When researchers work with their colleagues on the Internet, they may generate more ideas. But some aspects of collaboration – such as trust – are hard to develop electronically. (Ross-Flanigan 1998)

The words of Ross-Flanigan raise an issue previously addressed under 'virtual relationships'. This lack of trust is not only an issue in building relationships with potential customers, but may increasingly become a challenge within organizations. How often in your organization does someone two desks away send you an e-mail rather than coming to have a conversation in person? Do you feel more free to express anger, sorrow and other emotions remotely than you would face-to-face? Sociologists fear that these are all symptoms of technology-driven changes in interaction between individuals.

Technology makes it possible for individuals within organizations to work together without being physically in the same place:

> In some kinds of work, electronic links foster interdisciplinary co-operation, provide access to a wider range of instruments and information, . . . But something is lost, too, when people interact with instruments and peers from afar. Sitting in front of a computer is no match for travelling to interesting parts of the world, and it's hard to develop trust in people you've only met through electronic channels. What is immediately apparent is that as the future unfolds, ever more people will collaborate electronically. (Ross-Flanigan 1998)

The above description of electronic co-operation by space physicists electronically in a 'centre without walls' raises issues which may have to be addressed by organizations more broadly, as: 'even the best collaborative technologies seem to be poor substitutes for a handshake and eye contact' (Ross-Flanigan 1998, p. 58).

For multinational corporations electronic interaction between colleagues may offer cost saving benefits. It may, however, exacerbate the levels of psychic distance experienced within the organization (Forsgren 1989, Forsgren, Holm and Thilenius 1997). (See the discussion in Chapter 2 of the impact of psychic distance in networks for fuller coverage of this issue.)

Networks in Technology Industries

Technology most certainly has the power to shape society, but it is not autonomous, and it has no value except in relation to the social pressure that fosters it. (Håkansson and Lundgren 1995)

A number of concepts underpin discussion of technology from a network perspective:

1. Technological solutions may be developed in *several locations simultaneously* by sets of people working independently on the same problems. As a result a number of technologically similar products or services may be created.
2. *All of these developments will not be able to prosper.* They may not be equally applicable and some firms are more technologically skilled than others. Some 'paths' will remain open for exploration while others will close. An interesting debate surrounds the question of why one technology rather than another becomes the industry standard. In video technology, both Betamax and Philips were technologically superior to the eventual industry standard, VHS. The success of VHS seems to be result from it having gained rights to convert the major Hollywood movies to this format.
3. *Technologies exist in a changing context.* Some developing technologies will be favoured and others disadvantaged by changes in context. The example of IBM and Apple (see Box 3.2, p. 43) shows that changes in the market favoured both firms' technologies at different points. Both firms lost ground to new entrants, such as Dell and Compaq, as networked computers and Microsoft's Windows technology gained a hold on the market.

4. The technologies adopted as standards will be *integrated into the structure of networks* and may continue long after other technological developments make them obsolete. Håkansson and Lundgren (1995) use the example of the QWERTY keyboard developed for typewriters, which remains a standard for computer keyboards.
5. Prevailing technologies may not be those supported by the most powerful firms. Both *political and social forces* may also determine which succeed. In some cases firms have become natural monopolies as a result of their technology becoming standard, e.g. Sun Microsystems.

From these points it can be seen that, from a network perspective:

- Technological development is seen as a **parallel, rather than sequential, process**. It may involve many actions and reactions. It may also change gears at different points in time. Some changes will occur fast, while others stand still for long periods of time.
- **Technological development is relative**. Technologies depend upon and interact with each other. Håkansson (1987, p. 286) argues that:

  an innovation, therefore, should not be seen as the product of only one actor, but as the result of an interplay between two or more actors; in other words as a product of a 'network' of actors.

The value of a given technology may depend upon how it relates to other technologies. Concern over the future of the Internet in the UK, for example, is expressed because of relatively high local telephone call charges. Critics suggest that changes in telephony will be needed before the Internet can grow on the scale seen in the USA. Technologies are also affected by social and other influences. Technology to produce electric cars exists, albeit with limitations on range of travel. It may take consumer demand for greener transport solutions before automotive manufacturers are forced to commit seriously to developing this technology. A converse relationship between societal and technological developments can also be seen. Håkansson and Lundgren (1995) point to fact that the inefficiency of frontal lobotomy as a technological solution for treating mental disorders could have been shown when it was first discovered. However, it remained a socially acceptable treatment for many years. Håkansson and Lundgren (1995, p. 286) conclude:

> Technological innovation is one specific such sequence of actions perpetuated in networks and it is affected by the existing structure of networks: the involved actors, their interorganizational relationships, and the specific combinations of activities and resources.

■ **The network perspective takes a dynamic view of technology**. Change in innovative and technological networks is a predominant theme of research in the area. Technological change has a number of facets:

– Technological change will come about through routine as well as through innovative behaviour.

> Changes in one part or dimension of the network will call for responses in others, producing sequences of changes each working on the other in complicated and unforeseen ways. Small, everyday events can thus produce surprising outcomes. (Håkansson and Lundgren 1995, p. 297)

Thus the magnitude of technological change may far exceed expectations.

– Technological change may be planned or occur by chance. It may result from purposeful or unconscious actions. The outcomes of very uncertain projects may ultimately depend on the particular characteristics of the firms and individuals involved.

– Major technological changes may, therefore, be difficult to predict. The pattern and nature of changes involved may be complex. To benefit from a technological development, changes may be required elsewhere in the network.

International Technology Networks

In the late 1990s, the increased convergence of different streams of technology development – computers, mobile communications, telephony etc. – seemed to have increased transferability of skills between relationships and even sectors. Yet, technological advances have fuelled consumer demands for increasingly sophisticated and customized products and services.

These contradictory trends impact on international technology networks. Firms may use network positions to access technologies. If the leading supplier of leading edge computer chips is, say, located in Korea or the USA, a firm might use existing network connections in the market to develop a relationship with a supplier or to establish a co-operative link.

One of the issues discussed in relation to technology networks is that of transferability, the extent to which technological development of one relationship can be transferred to another. This may be a function of the similarity between the partner firms in each relationship. The network in which the firms are embedded may also exercise an influence. Transferability is complicated by the existence of cultural and other distances within the network. Although Doz (1988) argues that these are less significant than organizational differences, they may still result in misunderstandings and uncertainty (see the discussion of the impact of psychic distance on networks in Chapter 2).

SUMMARY

In Chapter 3 we have explored the importance of technology in international marketing. After examining the Internet and high-technology partnerships, we have identified strategic challenges for international marketers in successfully creating and managing this type of relationship.

BIBLIOGRAPHY

Ancona, D. (1992) 'Bridging the Boundaries: External Activity and Performance', *Administrative Science Quarterly*, 37, 4: 634–66.

Arnott, D. C. and Bridgewater, S. (2002) 'Internet, Interaction and Implications', *Market Intelligence and Planning* (forthcoming).

Atuahene-Gima, K. (1995) 'Involving Organizational Buyers in New Product Development', *Industrial Marketing Management*, 24: 215–26.

Balabanis, G. and Vassileiou, G. (1999) 'Some Attitudinal Predictors of Home Shopping through the Internet', *Journal of Marketing Management*, 15: 361–85.

Biemans, W. G. (1992) *Managing Innovations within Networks*, Routledge.

Briones, M. G. (1998) 'Customer Service the Key to On-Line Relationships', *Marketing News*, 23 November, p. 2.

Brzezinski, C. (1999) 'Database Marketing: Separating Fact from Fiction', *Executive Journal*, July–August: 20–6.

Contractor, F. and Lorange, P. (eds) (1988) *Co-operative Strategies in International Business*, Lexington Books.

Cronin, M. J. (1994) *Doing Business on the Internet*, Van Nostrand Reinhold.

Cronin, M. J. (1996) *Global Advantage on the Internet*, Van Nostrand Reinhold.

Cunningham, M. T. (1995) 'Competitive Strategies and Organizational Networks in New-Technology Markets', in Wilson, D. T. and Möller, K. (eds) *Business Marketing: An Interaction and Network Perspective*, Kluwer Academic.

Cyert, R. M. and March, J. G. (1963) *A Behavioural Theory of the Firm*, Prentice-Hall.

Doyle, P. and Bridgewater, S. (1998) *Innovation in Marketing*, Butterworth–Heinemann.

Doz, Y. (1988) 'Technology Partnerships between Larger and Smaller Firms: Some Critical Issues', *International Studies of Management and Organisation*, 17, 4: 31–57.

Drucker, P. (1999) *Management Challenges for the twenty-first Century*, Butterworth–Heinemann.

Dutta, S. and Segev, A. (1999) 'Business Transformation on the Internet', *European Management Journal*, 17, 5: 466–76.

Ford, I. D. (1980) 'The Development of Buyer–Seller Relationships in Industrial Markets', *European Journal of Marketing*,

Ford, I. D. (1984) 'Buyer-Seller Relationships in Industrial Markets', *European Journal of Marketing*, 14: 339–53.

Forsgren, M. (1989) *Managing the Internationalisation Process: The Swedish Case*, Routledge.

Forsgren, M., Holm, P. and Thilennius, P. (1997) 'Network Infusion in the Multinational Corporation', in Björkaan, I. and Forsgren, M. (eds), *The Nature of the International Firm*, Copenhagen Business School Press.

Gemünden, H.-G. and Heydebreck, P. (1994) 'Matching Business Strategy and Technological Network Activities – The Impact on Success', in Biemans, W. G. and Ghauri, P. N. (eds), *Proceedings of the 10th IMP Conference*, Groningen.

Gemünden, H.-G. and Walter, A. (1997) 'The Relationship Promoter – Motivator and Co-ordinator for Inter-Organisational Innovation Co-operation', in Gemünden, H.-G., Ritter, T. and Walter, A. (eds), *Relationships and Networks in International Markets*, Pergamon International Business and Management.

Gemünden, H.-G., Ritter, T. and Heydebreck, P. (1996) 'Network Configuration and Innovation Success – An Empirical Analysis in German High-Tech Industries', *International Journal of Research in Marketing*, 13: 449–62.

Hagedoorn, J. and Schakenraad, J. (1994) 'The Effect of Strategic Technology Alliances on Company Performance', *Strategic Management Journal*, 15: 247–66.

Håkansson, H. (1987) 'Product Development in Networks', in Håkansson, H. (ed.), *Industrial Technological Development – A Network Approach*, Croom Helm.

Håkansson, H. and Henders, B. (1992) 'International Co-Operative Relationships in Technology Development', in Forsgren, M. and Johanson, J. (eds), *Managing Networks in International Business*, Gordon & Breach: 32–46.

Håkansson, H. and Lundgren, A. (1995) 'Industrial Networks and Technological Innovation', in Wilson, D. T. and Möller, K. (eds), *Business Marketing: An Interaction and Network Perspective*, Kluwer Academic.

Haley, R. I. (1968) 'Benefit Segmentation: A Decision-Oriented Research Tool', *Journal of Marketing*, 32: 30–5.

Hamill, J. (1997) 'International Marketing and the Internet', *International Marketing Review*.

Hamill, J. and Gregory, K. (1998) 'Internet Marketing and the Internationalisation of UK SMEs', *Journal of Marketing Management*, 14.

Hladik, K. J. (1990) 'R&D and International Joint Ventures', in Contractor, F. and Lorange, P. (eds), *Co-operative Strategies in International Business*, Lexington Books.

Kogut, B. and Singh, H. (1988) 'The Effect of National Culture on the Choice of Entry Mode', *Journal of International Business Studies*, 19, 3: 411–32.

Kozinets, R. V. (1999) 'E-Tribalized Marketing: The Strategic Implications?', *European Management Journal*, 17, 3: 252–64.

Lindquist, M. (1997) 'Infant Multinationals: The Internationalization of Young, Technology–Based Swedish Firms', in Jones-Evans, D. and Klofsten, M. (eds), *Technology, Innovation and Enterprise: The European Experience*, Macmillan: 303–24.

Locke, J. (1999) 'The Decline of Conversation', *The Futurist*, February: 18.

Lorge, S. (1999) 'Database Marketing for the Little Guys', *Direct Marketing News*.

Macdonald, S. (1993) 'Nothing Either Good or Bad: Industrial Espionage and Technology Transfer', *Journal of Technology Transfer*, 8: 217–42.

Mehr, P. R. (1994) 'Focusing on Large Prospective Customers in High-Tech and Industrial Markets', *Industrial Marketing Management*, 23: 265–72.

Mitchell, A. (1999) 'Ad Agencies Hit Back at Customer Loyalty', *Marketing*, 8 July, 22–4.

O'Sullivan, O. (1999) 'The Darker Side of Database Marketing' *USBanker*, May, p. 32.

Oviatt, B. M. and McDougall, P. P. (1994) 'Toward a Theory of International New Ventures', *Journal of International Business Studies*, Spring 45–64.

Quelch, J. A. and Klein, L. R. (1996) 'The Internet and International Marketing', *Sloan Management Review*, Spring: 60–75.

Ross-Flanigan, N. (1998) 'The Virtues and Vices of Virtual Colleagues', *Technology Review*, March–April: 52–9.

Rugullies, E. (1999) 'E Commerce Profits Still a Way Off', *Business Communications Review*, February: 8.

Stahl, S. (1999) 'Cost-Effective Customer Service', *Information Week*, 8 February: p. 14.

Sterne, J. (1995) *World Wide Web Marketing: Integrating The Internet Into Your Marketing Budget*, John Wiley.

Sterrett, C. and Shah, A. (1998) 'Going Global on the Information Super Highway', *SAM Advanced Management Journal*, Winter: 43–8.

Thomas, R. and Ford, D. (1995) 'Technology and Networks', in Wilson, D. T. and Möller, K. (eds), *Business Marketing: An Interaction and Network Perspective*, Kluwer Academic.

Turnbull, P. W. and Valla, J.-P. (1986) *Strategies for International Industrial Marketing*, Routledge.

Wilder, C. (1998) 'E-Business Defines Relationships', *Information Week*, November: 23–24.

Yoegel, R. (1999) 'Building Relationships on the Net', *Target Magazine*, January: 17.

THE ECONOMIC AND POLITICAL CONTEXT

Objectives

The issues to be addressed in Chapter 4 include:

1. The economic and political influences on international marketing
2. The increased interlinkage of the world's economies
3. A network view of the interface between international marketers and the economic and political context in which they operate.
4. The impact of direct and indirect relationships in this context.

After reading Chapter 4 you will be able to:

1. Understand classic economic theories that underlie international marketing
2. Critique the value of Porter's Competitive Advantage of Nations and the 'Double-Diamond' model that extends this framework
3. Recognize the challenges of operation in a globally interlinked economy
4. Identify the potential impact of the Euro on international marketing
5. Understand 'supranational' policy issues that affect international marketers
6. Recognize the distinctive characteristics of network structures in countries with different political systems and at different levels of economic development.

INTRODUCTION

Performance standards for products and services are now set in the global marketplace. Firms no longer compete solely against rivals in their own country, but have to add value to customers in the face of global competition. Similarly, the trends creating opportunities and threats for international marketers may stem from both changes in local market conditions and from broader global trends.

This chapter identifies a number of economic and political influences on international marketers. These include the grouping of countries into new free trade zones, the introduction of common currencies, such as the Euro, and the pressures for global price harmonization resulting from operation in the global economy.

Despite the pressures to adopt global marketing strategies, firms compete on the basis of different local cost regimes. Thus raw material and labour costs, tax regimes, exchange and inflation rates provide firms with different economic starting points. In consequence, economic pressures have fuelled the relocation of manufacturing operations to the best value locations: witness the shift of automotive manufacturing in Mexico and the fact that 80 per cent of the world's computer chips are made in Taiwan.

In addition to identifying global and local economic and political influences on firms, the chapter highlights the increased interlinkage of the world's economies. The economic crises in Brazil and Russia in the late 1990s both had their roots in the East Asian Crisis. While the ripples of impact lessened moving away from the epicentre of the crisis these still sent a chill through stock exchanges globally. This interlinkage, or interrelationship, between national economies is explored in the Relationship section of this chapter.

The Network section of this chapter adopts a contrasting view of the interface between global economic and political context and the firms it surrounds. Firms do not compete in a 'faceless' and, often, hostile competitive environment, but may build relationships in this context. Macro-trends still represent opportunities and threats. From a network perspective, however, international marketers interact with players in the political and economic realm and exert some influence over their own fate. Conversely, operation within a web of other actors means that firms are influenced by the actions of others with whom they are only indirectly connected. The Pergau Dam in Box 4.2 and case study on Bofors in India (p. 73) give a fuller exposition of this phenomenon.

THE TRADITIONAL PERSPECTIVE

Classical Economic Theories

Many of the phenomena highlighted in the introduction to this chapter could have been predicted from classical economic trade theories. Since Adam Smith's theories of absolute costs (1776), it has been recognized that each country has natural and acquired advantages. *Natural* advantages include the availability of land and labour. Ukraine, for example, benefits from a large land mass and relatively high population. It also has good agricultural soils. This combination of natural attributes resulted in its former role as the 'bread basket of the Soviet Union'. Japan, in contrast, has a small land mass but a relatively high population size. Porter (1990) suggests that Japan's strength in miniaturization (shown particularly in its development of computer chips and other electronic components) developed in compensation for its relative lack of land. Smith predicted that countries would trade internationally to benefit from each other's strengths.

David Ricardo's theory of comparative costs (1817) builds on the theory of absolute advantage. The question posed by Ricardo is: What happens

if one nation builds absolute advantage in all (or even most) products? Will other nations still trade with this country? Ricardo argues that they will because of cost differences. Based on the examples in the previous paragraph, it might be expected that Ukraine would have a cost advantage in agricultural produce and Japan in micro-electronics. If other countries could replicate the abilities of Ukraine or Japan in these areas, it is likely that they would do so only at greater cost.

Neither Smith nor Ricardo, however, explored the reasons why one country might be more *cost effective* in production than another. Researchers argue that such cost differences are based on differences in endowments of labour, land and capital. A clear and concise explanation of this and other classical economic principles underlying internationalization is provided by McKiernan (1992).

Heckscher and Ohlin (see Ohlin 1933) argue that firms should base their specialization on their country's endowments. McKiernan cites a number of combinations of these endowments:

- **High labour/low land**. Countries in this category include Japan, Taiwan or the Netherlands. These countries might best specialize in high labour industries, such as electronics or other types of secondary production. The type of production depends on the level of technological development.
- **High land/low labour**. Countries in this category include New Zealand and Australia. These countries might specialize in sectors using large amounts of land, such as agriculture.
- **High labour/low capital**. Countries might include India, China or Russia. These countries might specialize in labour intensive production in less advanced technologies such as basic cars Morris Oxford cars in India, cotton in China and basic chemicals in Russia.

It might be assumed that these examples could be extended to include other possible permutations, for example:

- **High capital/low labour**. More advanced economies of the first category. These might include

Canada and Australia, highly automated technology-based sectors.

■ **High capital/low land**. Countries such as Japan, using capital intensive and miniaturized technologies.

■ **High capital/high land**. Countries such as the USA, using capital intensive production of any type.

In the categories involving high capital, however, the Heckscher–Ohlin theory runs aground. All countries with high levels of capital might be predicted to export capital intensive products. In 1954, however, Leontief identified the fact that exports from Japan, the USA and Canada were in fact largely in labour intensive sectors. This anomaly, known as the 'Leontief paradox', has been explained by differences in skill levels of labour force. The ability to 'work smarter' seems to confer labour advantages to countries that do not have large amounts of available labour. Further research suggests that if the costs of creating skilled labour in these countries are accounted for then exports are indeed capital intensive (Branson and Monoyios 1977).

Competitive Advantage of Nations

Among the best known contributions to microeconomic theory in the 1980s and 1990s are those of Michael Porter of the Harvard Business School. Porter's work on the competitive advantage of nations (1990b) provides a useful synthesis of influences in the economic context of international marketing.

Porter's Competitive Advantage of Nations

Differences in national values, culture, economic structures, institutions, and histories all contribute to competitive success. There are striking differences in the patterns of competitiveness in every country; no nation can or will be competitive in every, or even most, industries. Ultimately, nations succeed in particular industries because their home environment is the most forward-looking, dynamic and challenging. (Porter 1990, p. 74)

Porter identifies four attributes, which individually and in conjunction with each other influence the ability of a firm, industry or nation to succeed:

■ Factor conditions
■ Demand conditions
■ Firm strategy, structure and rivalry
■ Related and supporting industries.

Each of these attributes is explored in greater detail below.

Factor Conditions

These are the endowments with land, labour and capital identified by Adam Smith (1776) and explored further by later classical economic trade theories. A fuller examination of these can be found in the previous discussion. For example, Ukraine has a relatively large land mass and good agricultural soils and has developed an advantage based on land. Mexico has developed a reputation as a low cost manufacturer of automobiles based on its labour advantages, while Kazakhstan increasingly attracts the attention of international investors because of its rich endowment of oil and gas.

Porter is keen to point out that a firm can also develop abilities from not having, as well as having, a particular natural attribute. These are referred to as 'factor disadvantages'. For example, Japan does not have much land and has developed miniaturization skills as a result of having to produce products small enough to fit into small Japanese homes:

> When there is an ample supply of cheap materials or abundant labor, companies can simply rest on these advantages and often deploy them inefficiently. But when companies face a selective disadvantage, like high land costs, labor shortages, or the lack of local raw materials, they must innovate or upgrade to compete. (Porter 1990b, p. 78)

Similarly, factor advantages are not based only on natural attributes but can result from economic wealth. With economic wealth, a country can educate a workforce or invest in leading edge technologies. These are advantages based on capital.

With capital, advantages can be created or perpetuated:

> In sophisticated industries that form the backbone of any advanced economy, a nation does not inherit but instead creates the most important factors of production – such as skilled human resources or a scientific base. Moreover, the stock of factors that a nation enjoys at a particular time is less important than the rate and efficiency with which it creates, upgrades, and deploys them in particular industries. (Porter 1990b, p. 78)

Demand Conditions

Once countries have developed strong local demand for a particular product or service, Porter argues that the consumers become sophisticated in their knowledge and demands. In Japan, the availability of advanced micro-electronic products has created knowledgeable consumers, who are accustomed to high quality standards. The challenge of offering benefits to these discerning consumers forces firms to remain innovative. The resulting innovative products and services, in turn, create competitive advantages that can be exploited in global markets:

> Instead of upgrading their sources of advantage, [US firms] settled for labor cost parity. On the other hand, Japanese rivals, confronted with intense domestic competition and a mature home market chose to eliminate labor through automation. This led to lower assembly costs, to products with fewer components and to improved quality and reliability. Soon Japanese companies were building assembly plants in the United States – the place the US companies had fled. (Porter 1990b, p. 79)

Firm Strategy, Structure and Rivalry

This category is based on the way firms are managed and the competitive context in which they operate. Within the same industry sector, or while

---

Box 4.1   Strategy, Structure and Rivalry?

In the early 1990s, both SC Johnson of the USA and Rothmans Cigarettes of the UK were looking at the prospects of expansion within the East and Central European (CEE) region. In 1993, SC Johnson had operated a manufacturing joint venture in Ukraine for five years, while Rothmans were exporting and prospecting the market from a 'representative office'. This latter was the lowest level of investment possible in Ukraine and did not allow the firm to trade. A number of factors may explain the different approaches to international markets of the two firms. Both were in consumer goods sectors and facing the same, relatively large international market. Both operated in mature markets, in which consolidation through Mergers and Acquisitions (M&As) had resulted in domination by a few strong international rivals.

Why, then, the difference in international marketing strategy? Some of the differences might be ascribed to organizational structure, size and international experience. The two firms differed in size. In the early 1990s, when both firms were contemplating expansion in East and Central Europe, SC Johnson's sales were more than twice those of Rothmans. Higher levels of resources might lessen the level of risk perceived in each international investment decision. Perhaps more significantly, SC Johnson operated in 71 countries compared to 17 for Rothmans and had operated internationally for more than twice as long (50 years compared to 23 years). SC Johnson could potentially draw on a greater level of previous international experience in making decisions about operation in this region. East and Central European countries were at various stages in the process of transition to market economy and represented relatively high risk market opportunities at the time.

Maybe the most significant explanation of the different decisions of the two firms was, however, in managerial approach to international operations. SC Johnson sees itself as a pioneer, always entering international markets ahead of rivals to gain first mover advantages. Rothmans Cigarettes, in contrast, describes itself as relatively cautious. While it is difficult to disentangle the impacts of strategy, structure and rivalry, it is clear that differences in marketing strategy and willingness to bear risk play a major role in determining the extent of their international operations.

operating in the same country, different firms can achieve differing levels of success. Levels of success may relate to management and marketing decisions, to structural influences such as size, resources and international experience or to the competitive dynamics of a particular industry sector.

One need only look at the contrasting fortunes of IBM and Dell in the early 1990s, or Marks and Spencer and Tesco in the late 1990s to appreciate the way in which one firm can fail to appreciate emerging trends and another ride the crest of a wave (see Box 4.1).

Porter also emphasizes the fact that different organizational structures and strategies work better in some industries than others:

> In industries where Italian companies are world leaders – such as lighting, furniture, footwear, woollen fabrics, and packaging machines – a company strategy that emphasizes focus, customized products, niche marketing, rapid change and breathtaking flexibility fits both the dynamics of the industry and the character of the Italian management system. The German management system, in contrast, works well in technical or engineering oriented industries – optics, chemicals, complicated machinery – where complex products demand precision manufacturing, a careful development process, after-sale service, and thus a highly disciplined management structure. (Porter 1990b, p. 81)

The intensity of rivalry, particularly in mature, oligopolistic industries (those with a few strong players) may prompt firms to remain innovative and develop strong brands in order to survive. In turn, innovative products and processes and strong brands may enhance global competitiveness.

Related and Supporting Industries

Industries with sophisticated consumers and strong industry rivals tend also to have strong suppliers and other supporting firms. Consider the close, just-in-time (JIT) partnerships in the automotive industry or the precision plastic and metal cast components required by mobile telecommunications firms. Strong suppliers and other firms in clusters around industries may

also fuel competitive success. These firms are themselves sophisticated and innovative and may be the source of ideas which keep the buying firm successful in global markets. As Porter (1990, p. 80) puts it: 'they deliver the most cost-effective inputs in an efficient, early, rapid, and sometimes preferential way.'

This focus on 'clusters' of relationships between firms in an industry links to the growth in attention to partnering or 'win–win' relationships. These are discussed more fully in the Relationship section of Chapter 5 on international marketing strategy. The distinctions between this and the network perspective on relationships is explored in the Relationship and Network section of Chapter 7.

Critique of Porter's 'Diamond Framework'

Porter attributes competitive advantage to possession of strengths in all four elements of his 'diamond framework'. He argues that strength in only one part of the diamond – for example factor conditions without strong consumer demand – is insufficient to result in competitive advantage.

In addition to the four elements of the 'diamond framework', Porter identifies two other influences on success: the role of government and chance. It would be difficult, for example, to assess the development of the Czech brewing industry without considering the role of the Soviet Union in the country's history, or to contemplate the future prospects of this industry without analyzing the reform process instituted by the government of the Czech Republic. Similarly, the development of automotive manufacturing in Mexico has been strongly influenced by the government's foreign investment policy.

Similarly, some aspects of international competitiveness are clearly affected by chance. What would have been the development of the Czech Republic had it been, as originally planned, in the British Zone after the Second World War, rather than in the Russian zone? What might the fortunes of Mexico have been if it had not had the USA as a near neighbour?

Porter's Contribution

Porter's 'diamond framework' makes a number of valuable contributions:

- Viewing the success of firms and industries in its national context offers a rich analysis that incorporates a broad range of potential influences on international competitiveness.
- The competitive advantage of nations framework brings together concepts from classical economic and micro-economic theory to provide a comprehensive framework for the study of international competitiveness. To this extent it provides a useful, and infrequently created, bridge between corporate strategy and international trade theories.
- It is also dynamic, looking at the development of advantages over time.
- It is based on data drawn from ten countries, so it is also comprehensively researched.

Critics of Porter

Critics have, however, challenged Porter's claims that the framework can explain national, industry and firm-level success:

> The breadth and relevance of Porter's theory do not come costlessly. The ambitious theoretical and empirical sweep of the analysis has been achieved at the expense of precision and determinancy. Lack of precision is apparent in the woolly definitions of some of the key concepts in the book and in the specification of relationships between them. (Grant 1991, p. 541)

- In support of his criticism, Grant (1991) points out that the concept of 'upgrading' competitive advantages seems to change from increasing sustainability to moving into high productivity segments of the market.
- A second criticism relates to Porter's claim that success is dependent on all aspects of the framework. Despite claims that strength in all parts of the diamond are needed for success, an oil rich nation, such as Saudi Arabia, seems to have sustainable advantage based on possession of raw materials alone. Indeed, Grant (1991) highlights the fact that many countries at

the 'factor-driven' development stage are among the world's most prosperous. When Porter's *Competitive Advantage of Nations* (1990b) was published, 15 of the top 25 industries in terms of world export share were based on natural resource endowments.

- A further criticism is that the four categories identified by Porter may overlap or be interrelated. The role of supporting firms is suggested as a means of improving innovation but, in turn, this may create cost savings. In other words, the effect of the 'supporting firm' variable is on the 'factor conditions' variable.
- Grant (1991) suggests that firm strategy, structure and rivalry is a 'catch-all' including a number of different aspects and levels of analysis. Such are the differences that these may be better treated separately. At least, more detailed analysis of strategy, structure and rivalry may be required. At worst, the validity of combining so many diverse variables in one category is questionable.
- It is not always clear what Porter means by 'success'. Porter bases his book on data explaining the success of certain industries within certain countries, for example ceramic tiles in Italy or micro-electronics in Japan. At the same time, Porter makes broader claims that the 'diamond framework' explains national-, industry- and firm-level success. The framework has not been tested on national- and firm-level data.
- Following from the question of empirical evidence for all levels of analysis, Grant (1991) argues that Porter presumes 'the existence of some invisible hand whereby firms' pursuit of competitive advantage translates into increasing national productivity and prosperity' (Grant 1991, p. 541). Yet this is not necessarily the case. Success in several industry sectors in the USA did not translate into rises in US productivity and living standards. If this link is not proven, then use of the framework at a national level may be questionable. Nor is it clear that the creation of a successful industry sector in a country means that every firm will be equally successful. Consequently, the framework may be inappropriate for the study of firm-level success.

Global Interlinkage of Economies

An Isle is emerging that is bigger than a continent – the interlinked economy (ILE) of the Triad (the United States, Europe and Japan) joined by aggressive economies such as Taiwan, Hong Kong and Singapore. (Ohmae 1989, p. xi)

One of the principal challenges to frameworks that study economic and competitive forces at national level is that of the growing *interdependence* of the world's economies. In the previous section, Porter proposed influences on national competitive advantage. Yet, theorists studying the growing trade links between nations suggests that the advantages created by firms may deliver benefits in the global arena.

According to Ohmae (1989), for example, a successful firm may grow, but the jobs it creates may be in cost effective production centres such as Taiwan or Mexico. Or else they may be located in regions where the firm wishes to expand its customer base next. Altering national interest rates may result in firms sourcing funds from other countries. Currencies, stock markets and other economic institutions are increasingly linked together in a global reality that transcends national borders.

Since Ohmae published his *'Borderless World'* in 1990, the concept of the Triad (Asia Pacific, Europe and North America) and the existence of globally interlinked economies has become part of the accepted wisdom of management. By the early 1990s, around 60 per cent of global trade took place between members of the Triad. In the later 1990s, trade between the Triad and emerging markets witnessed significant growth. Trade between the USA, Japan and the EU and emerging markets more than doubled between 1991 and 1998 (IMF, *Direction of Trade Figures* 1998). Global trade is not solely a characteristic of Triad nations but increasingly involves a broad raft of developing nations.

Despite such compelling evidence of global competition, McKinsey consultants have suggested that only 20 per cent of world output (around $28 trillion) is open to global competition in products, service or ownership (*The Economist, The World in 2000*, p. 108). In other words, barriers still exist in some industry sectors and in some countries. Within 30 years, however, it is predicted that the liberalization of China and India and globalization of industry sectors such as financial services and retailing will increase this to around 80 per cent.

In his opening prophesies for the year 2000, Dudley Fishburn, editor of *The World in 2000*, predicted (*The Economist* 2000, p. 9):

> 2000 will be a year in which the world shifts its balance. America's magnificent economy will slow; Europe and Asia will pick up the slack. Overall, the world will increase its wealth by 3.5 per cent. For the world that lives in China and India, prosperity will grow at twice the speed of the rich world, to all our benefit. It will be the first year in which the majority of the people on the Internet do not speak English.

So globalization will widen its grip and global competition will dominate a greater number of industry sectors. What are the potential implications for international marketers? As global players strengthen their hold on a broader range of countries, the pressures will intensify on weaker national and regional players. This may fuel a shakeout in mature industry sectors and result in further mergers and acquisitions.

These forces can be seen in play in the global automotive industry. At the mature stage, the industry is experiencing global overcapacity. With overcapacity comes a spate of mergers: Daimler and Renault, Renault and Nissan, Ford's purchase of Britain's Jaguar then Sweden's Volvo. Together with global consolidation comes shakeout. Those who do not become part of one of the few, large global players will fail. Commentators are already questioning the future of firms such as Daiwoo, Fiat and Peugeot…

Operation in a Globally Interlinked Economy

Operation in the global economy of Y2K sets a number of challenges at the top of the strategic agenda.

Common Currency – The Euro

4 January 1999 may count as an epic moment in the saga of global interlinkage. This was the date on which the first common currency, the Euro, was introduced. Currencies have in the past been tied together. Argentina's peso is currently tied to the US dollar. Indeed, Argentina's President Menem has spoken of adopting the US dollar as Argentina's currency (*The Economist* 13 February 1999). He further proposed the notion of a common currency for the Latin American free trade area Mercosur; some say he would also prefer this to be the dollar. Given its global popularity some may argue that the US dollar has already been an informal common currency for some time.

The introduction of the Euro, however, heralds a new stage in integration within Europe. Its progress is watched anxiously from within the European Euro zone, the European non-Euro zone and also by interested outsiders. Some suggest that the Euro should be adopted by Monaco, Liechtenstein and even parts of West Africa, such as Congo-Brazzaville whose currency (the CFA Franc) is tied to the French Franc, not to mention French territories such as Martinique and Guadeloupe (*The Economist* 9 January 1999).

The question of fixed or floating currencies divides economists (*The Economist* 30 January 1999). *Floating currencies*:

- Allow countries to adjust to external shocks through the exchange rate
- Control economic policies at national level
- Maintain flexibility
- Force companies to be prepared and hedge against exchange rate fluctuations
- Make banks more cautious about lending.

As a downside floating currencies:

- Might become unstable
- Might reduce investors' faith in a currency
- Might make it harder to fight inflation.

Particularly if the country is vulnerable to external shocks, such as a sudden shift in commodity prices (as in the case of emerging markets), some form of currency fixing is often suggested because this:

- Provides confidence and stability
- Ties emerging markets to more stable economies
- Provides benefits of currency 'size'
- Encourages foreign investment.

Introduction of a common currency is a dramatic step in the 'fixing' process. This was the step taken by Europe in early 1999. Potential entrants into the European Union (EU), such as Poland, the Czech Republic and Hungary may also adopt the Euro at some stage.

Sceptics still point to the potential drawbacks of a common currency. Critics of the Euro suggest that the European Central Bank (ECB) is secretive, opaque and lacking a consistent voice (*The Economist* 26 June 1999). This has resulted in a lack of confidence in the Euro, which has fallen (against the dollar) by around 12 per cent from its launch. Nonetheless, many argue that the omens for the Euro in the longterm are good.

The issue of a common currency is especially topical in the UK, which is still debating entry into the Euro zone. This debate highlights some key advantages and disadvantages of monetary union. In a survey of Britain's top economists (*The Economist* 17 April 1999) almost two-thirds of respondents suggested that Britain should adopt the Euro within five years.

In many countries, the issue of the Euro brings a blurring of economic and political decisions. The Euro is an economic means to a political end (even closer European integration). In the UK, Prime Minister Tony Blair suggests that the decision should be made on purely economic grounds: adopt the Euro if it is economically sensible. The *The Economist*'s survey suggests that a majority of economists believe that the Euro:

- Would bring a more stable exchange rate, although the Euro is still vulnerable to changes in the value of the yen, dollar etc.
- Would bring closer links with the Euro zone, which currently represents around 50 per cent of Britain's exports
- Would favour foreign investment, which might otherwise move towards the larger Euro zone within the EU – around 40 per cent of foreign investment in the EU currently comes to UK

- Whatever the formal arrangements some firms will want to use Euros in any case: this may become a signal of 'European' orientation
- An independent monetary policy will become increasingly difficult
- Britain will lose its say in the region's monetary and financial institutions.

Yet despite these compelling arguments, those of the 'no' camp are also striking:

- The European Central Bank (ECB) has a bias against being tough on inflation
- The ECB lacks democratic accountability
- The ECB introduces a 'one-size-fits-all' approach to monetary policy; booming Ireland, slumping Germany and any potential entrants, including the Central European economies, may be linked together to the detriment of some and benefit of others.
- The same interest rate may have different impacts on different markets. Britain's housing market is dominated by variable rate debt making Britain sensitive to interest rates. German companies favour debt rather than equity, so its firms are interest rate sensitive.
- If exchange rates, interest rates and taxation cannot absorb external shocks, then wages and prices will have to do so. This may increase unemployment. In the USA, this type of shock is countered by the existence of a mobile labour force. Critics doubt the mobility of labour around Europe.
- If anything European labour markets are becoming less, not more, flexible.

In summary, most agree that most obstacles to the Euro in Britain will gradually disappear, but different sides take optimistic and pessimistic views of how long this will take.

Impacts of the Euro on International Marketing

There are several predicted impacts of the Euro on international marketing.

Changing Market Structure

The introduction of the Euro and the relative stability of the European economy are seen as drivers of increased concentration of the members states of the EU (Gautier 1999). This concentration may result from further internationalization of both manufacturing and retail firms within Europe. Currently, only four European retailers earn more than 50 per cent of revenue from outside the home country, but the pace of internationalization will only increase with the entry into the UK of Wal Mart of the USA. Increased international competition is likely to result in further shakeout. Press reports on Vodaphone's bid for German competitor Mannesmann and UK retailer Kingfisher's search for a new acquisition after its failure to acquire Asda both suggest that acquisitions are fuelled by fears of 'eat or be eaten'.

Price Harmonization in Europe

Prior to the Euro, prices across Europe were already converging as a result of deregulation, the removal of formal trade barriers and the reduced ability of manufacturers to influence retailers' prices. Introduction of the Euro is expected to accelerate the process of price harmonization.

In some industry sectors the range of variation within Europe was considerable. Price differences in the automobile industry were as high as 40–50 per cent, CDs up to 80 per cent, computer hardware (such as printer) up to 40 per cent and pharmaceuticals around 50 per cent (Ahlberg, Garemo and Nauclér 1999).

A number of factors underlie the rate at which prices will converge around Europe. These include the nature of the product (*Business Europe* 5 May 1999), price sensitivity of customers, their buying power and the impact of electronic commerce (e-commerce) on the industry sector. Ahlberg, Garemo and Nauclér predict that the rate of harmonization will be greater in pharmaceuticals because of government regulations. Similarly, harmonization may be rapid in sectors using the Internet to reach customers, or accessing customers via pan-European retailers.

Consistency of International Marketing Strategy

The example of the Euro given above illustrates pressures from the economic environment for firms to achieve maximum consistency in their international marketing strategy. Variations in pricing policy for different markets may need to be explained by differences in other parts of the marketing mix. For example, different features, quality or service levels may be a justification of premium pricing in a particular market.

Supranational Economic and Political Challenges

We have previously illustrated the impact of macro-level economic decisions on the day-to-day international marketing activities of firms within Europe. Economic and political decisions form the context for international marketing. As policies change, new challenges emerge for international marketers. The global context is not only shaped by national policies, but by a growing cadre of 'supranational' bodies, such as the World Bank, International Monetary Fund (IMF) and the World Trade Organization (WTO).

Entering the new millennium, a number of issues have been identified by supranational policymakers. Resolution of these is believed to be vital to maximize economic growth in the twenty-first century. In its *World Development Report* (World Bank 2000), the World Bank lists these as:

Foreign Trade

Encouraging foreign trade remains a priority. In recent years, foreign trade has grown as a proportion of the world economy and is predicted to grow further. Foreign trade brings a number of benefits to host markets. Successful international entrants raise the level of consumer choice and competition. As a result, consumers in the market become more sophisticated and demand this standard from local firms (see the parallels with Porter's 1990 concept of demand conditions). Local firms can use international firms as benchmarks of

good practice and improve their own competitiveness. This, in turn, allows them to compete internationally.

Free Trade

The WTO was created in 1995 out of the previous General Agreement on Tariffs and Trade (GATT) movement. Successive rounds of GATT talks successfully removed a number of barriers to free trade. The World Bank suggests that financial flows across borders afford a number of benefits. Inflows of foreign capital improve national wealth and offer associated benefits, such as management expertise, training, links to suppliers and contact with other international markets. Outflows of foreign investment diversify risks outside the home market and offer access to profitable markets globally.

Much was promised of the Millennium Round of free trade talks, under the auspices of the new WTO, held in Seattle in November 1999. Challenges to be addressed by the Millennium round included:

- **Creating a forward-looking agenda for broader trade liberalization**. Priority areas were services and agriculture. The emphasis on services was a priority because of the explosive growth of services driven by advances in information and communications technology. The World Bank cited a 25 per cent growth between the years 1994 and 1997.
- **Encouraging countries to make greater use of WTO mechanisms**. The WTO wanted to encourage countries to see its mechanisms as a set of rules within which national goals could be achieved rather than as 'obstacles to self-determination' (World Bank 2000).
- **Creating policies to help displaced workers**. Many workers blame foreign trade for job losses and wage cuts resulting from increased foreign competition in markets. Supportive labour market policies were considered a means to counter calls for protectionist responses.
- **Changing policies that hinder rather than promote free trade**. For example the WTO currently allows anti-dumping laws to prevent

products being sold below a 'fair' price in international markets. This was intended to protect domestic firms but turned into a barrier to imports.

The public stalling of the Seattle talks in the face of local and international protests raises questions over the future of the process.

Global Environmental Challenges

Industrial countries are responsible for the majority of global environmental problems, such as greenhouse gases. Developing countries are, however, increasingly implicated, too. Individual governments, or even regional organizations, cannot respond effectively, and the World Bank suggests that these problems should be tackled at global level. A precedent for global resolution of problems was seen in the 1987 Montreal Protocol on control of chlorofluorocarbon (CFC) emissions, which may potentially create holes in the ozone layer of the upper atmosphere.

THE NETWORK PERSPECTIVE

The Interface Between an Organization and its Macro-Context

The principal distinction between network and other views of context lies in the perception of how firms, and other actors, interface with the environment in which they operate. As Nohria (1992, pp. 5–6) explains:

> From a network perspective, then, the environment consists of a field of relationships that bind organizations together...To those familiar with Michael Porter's framework for analyzing industries, this conception of the environment might appear remarkably similar. In many respects it is, except that greater attention is paid in the network perspective to the overall pattern of relationships among the firms in the industry.

Axelsson and Johanson (1992) refer to this as operation in a 'full-faced' environment. The macro-environment is not made up of uncontrollable trends but is a context that firms can see and understand. From a network perspective, firms can interact with other actors in this context.

Interaction may not only be economic, but may also involve social, technological and information exchange (Araujo and Easton 1996). For example, firms might exchange information with environmental regulators about their emissions standards and seek technical advice to improve performance against standards.

Forsgren and Johanson (1992, p. 2) argue that if firms are seen to interact with a 'full-faced' environment, the ensuing agenda for international marketing is different to that traditionally accepted:

> Rather than viewing the environment as a set of separate anonymous forces – political, competitive, legal, cultural, economic, etc. – all the actors are considered bearers of diverse interests, power and characteristics. It is in the meetings in the international business arena that such factors impinge on the development of business.

In summary, the macro-level context is full of complex actors. Each of these is made up of many individuals with different interests and characteristics. It is within the power of international marketers to influence their success through the relationships they develop with these actors.

The network literature does not, however, take a unified stance on the macro-context. In describing macro-level differences, Forsgren and Johanson (1992, p. 14) argue that:

> the greater the differences between the countries concerning institutional, social, cultural, legal and other conditions the greater are the difficulties in understanding each other, and this is a factor inhibiting exchange between the countries.

Implicit in this quote is the view that macro-level context is seen through the lens of the firm. A somewhat different conclusion may, however, be drawn from Barley, Freeman and Hybels (1992, p. 5) who state:

> Not only are organizations suspended in multiple, complex and overlapping webs of relationships, the webs are likely to exhibit structural patterns that are invisible from the standpoint of a single organization caught in the tangle. To detect overarching structures, one has to rise above the individual firm and analyze the system as a whole.

The inference here is still that the firm's perspective is important but that a higher level view is required. This is similar to the concept of 'helicopter vision'. Only by rising above the level of the firm and its day-to-day international marketing operations can a full picture of the issues be achieved.

Whatever the nature of the interface, then, looking down on the challenges facing international marketers from the broader macro-environment enriches understanding.

A Network View of the Economic Context

This overview of the position of the firm in its 'macro-context' is presented in the Network sections of chapters 2 (Cultural Environment), Chapter 3 (Technological context) and Chapter 4 (Economic and Political context) of this book.

Four key characteristics of the economic and cultural context are now examined.

Global Scope

As already identified, world trade in goods and services (including invisibles) is larger than ever before and continues to grow. Different cost structures and exchange rates have become determinants of a firm's ability to compete internationally. These may prompt firms to locate operations in countries where they can benefit from low raw material and labour costs or favourable exchange rates.

The global scope of trade means that the firm's network will also move towards being global. This increases the complexity of the interrelationships. The complications which firms may face from cultural distances in networks are explored further in Chapter 2. An opportunity arising from this global scope of networks is that each network position in each country may lead to the development of relationships that provide opportunities for further expansion.

This type of situation is typified by the example of one of the 'Big Six' Accounting firms to enter Ukraine because of pressures from existing rela-

tionships between its Brussels subsidiary and the EU and its Washington office and the World Bank. Similarly, Johanson and Mattsson (1988, p. 315) describe global networks as creating the sort of situation whereby, for example:

> a Swedish firm might increase its penetration in a South American market because of its relationship in Japan with an internationalizing Japanese firm.

Building Positions in Triad 'Nets'

Over 50 per cent of world GNP, over 85 per cent of competitors in consumer electronics and the bulk of the world's converging global consumers are in the Triad of Asia-Pacific, Europe and North America. Ohmae (1990) originally argued that globalization would force companies to launch the same products, at the same time, into each corner of the 'Triad'.

The 'Triad' is full of sophisticated consumers, with similar tastes, lifestyles and disposable incomes. Penetration of the Triad, then, allows international marketers to gain scale and scope economies that provide cost efficiencies and rapid capital payback from large Research and Development (R&D) outlays. In practice the notion of parallel penetration has proved difficult to implement despite Ohmae's claims of a borderless world (1989).

Nevertheless, the Triad is clearly a crucial market for any serious global player. While customers are relatively wealthy and sophisticated, the countries of the Triad are characterized by high levels of competition and restrictive regulations.

Were parallel penetration a realistic possibility then, from a network perspective, international marketers would be faced with building positions in 'nets' in each part of the Triad simultaneously. This would be complicated by the fact that the nature of the macro-network structures in Japan, the USA and Europe differ. Consider, for example, the diversity between 'tightly structured' US networks (Kinch 1995) and the *Keiretsu*-like relationships in Japan. The specific characteristics of network structures in North America, Europe and Asia-Pacific are discussed in the Network sections of Chapters 11, 12 and 13, respectively.

It seems unlikely that Ohmae's claim (1990) that positions in different markets should be built simultaneously is unlikely to become a reality. The impact of building a position in one national net on international marketing activities in other national nets does, however, have significant ramifications for firms opting for global scope.

'Net' Structures and Level of Development

In addition to serving Triad markets, international marketers are increasingly focusing on emerging markets. While 'mega-markets' such as China, India and the former Soviet Union (FSU) are less advanced in economic terms (that is they have substantially lower rates of GDP *per capita*), they still hold the majority of the world's population (see Chapter 14 for a fuller discussion of Emerging mega-markets). While the customers in these markets may not be quite so sophisticated, they have serious needs, wants and demands that require servicing. The requirement for less sophisticated products creates opportunities for international marketers. Long after it ceased to be produced in the UK, the Morris Oxford is still produced in the Indian market. Similarly, clockwork technology has recently found new applications in radios designed for regions without mains electricity. These do not require expensive consumables such as batteries and therefore offer additional benefits.

The structures facing firms entering these 'nets' seem substantially different from those in the Triad. In describing Volvo's entry into the USA in the 1950s, Kinch (1992, p. 206) says:

> The American market for cars in the 1950s can be characterized as a rather tight network. The companies dealing with American cars had fixed, well defined roles in relation to each other. The way the business was handled followed well established rules. The big three – GM, Ford and Chrysler – dominated, and accounted for more than 90 per cent of the sales.

Contrast this situation with that to be found in former Soviet networks:

> One of the several important differences between Ukraine today and Ukraine as it was six and twelve months ago is that Ukraine is now far deeper into

the transition process than it was then. Old governmental command-control structures and institutional relationships have disintegrated to a far greater degree now than they had then, creating confusion and disorder. (Manninen and Snelbecker 1993)

Ukrainian firms often do not know the identity of their previous customers and suppliers, or where they are located. Creation of new national boundaries and the withdrawal of central planning have left actors trying to re-establish previous indirect relationships, or else with an urgent need to establish new supplier and customer relationships. A myriad of new regulatory actors have also entered Ukraine to help in the transition process.

It is dangerous to generalize over the nature of net structures in different markets. Each is unique (as is discussed in greater detail in the network section of Chapter 2 on Cultural context). All the same, some patterns are evident. The degree of structuring differs between advanced industrial economies where a few well established global competitors operate to a clear set of rules, and emerging economies where net structures are subject to far more rapid change.

Mega-markets may seem easier in that firms can capitalize on existing technologies. International marketers should not, however, underestimate the challenges of identifying the actors in 'loosely structured' networks and of building relationships in very dynamic nets.

Kinch (1992, pp. 206–7) says of 'tightly structured nets':

> If the new entrant can somehow complete the existing structure it may be integrated into the net. However, another reason more relevant to this case is that a highly structured situation often creates discontent by actors disfavoured by the way the network is handled. There is no alternative offered by the established actors for groups wanting a different solution. This may make them leave the traditional outlets once they are given an alternative.

In contrast, in mega-markets there are many new actors, their positions are likely to be fluid and the structures may be extremely difficult to understand. This 'opacity' is often attributed to cultural distances within the network (Axelsson and Johanson 1992;

Blankenburg 1995) but may also be a feature of loosely structured mega market nets.

Political Relationships

Relationships with political actors may also play a significant role in net structures. In his discussion of entry into 'blocked' mega markets, Kotler (1983) does not depict passive marketers, but advocates that firms add the 'Ps' of Politics and Public relations to the activities in which they engage.

The impact of relationships in the political sphere on relationships is nowhere more apparent than in Hådjikhani and Håkansson's analysis (1996) of the impact of government-level interactions on individual firms operating in India.

The Bofors scandal (see Case Study 4.1) does not only impact on the Bofors firm, but on a range of other Swedish firms operating in India. These firms have previously operated successfully in India but are now caught up in the scandal.

Hådjikhani and Håkansson (1996) conclude that the Bofors case shows the impact of 'non-business actors', such as the media or political actors, on a business relationship. A major implication of network studies of political relationships is the understanding that political actors may comprise diverse interests, can interpret their remit in different, and sometimes contradictory, ways and that their actions affect businesses operating in their country.

A second contribution is the realization that, in the face of political actions such as those in the Bofors case, firms are affected to different extents, depending on the nature of their relationships. These may be relationships with political actors and with a number of other agencies such as local partners, customers and the workforce.

Box 4.2   The Pergau Dam Incident

In 1989, UK Prime Minister Margaret Thatcher agreed to finance a £300 million hydro-electric station on the banks of Malaysia's Pergau river. This agreement was reached a few months after the Thatcher government had signed a £1 billion military sales agreement. The Foreign Office consistently denied that the two deals were connected (government policy prevented overseas aid being used to buy arms). The Pergau Dam deal was ratified by Margaret Thatcher's successor, John Major and Foreign Secretary, Douglas Hurd. Mr Major and Mr Hurd claimed to have taken advice from government lawyers that the deal did not involve a breach of the 1980 Overseas Development and Co-Operation act.

In January 1994, however, it emerged that, while the denials of a link between the two projects were strictly accurate, in 1988 the government had tied the offer of an aid package to the prospective arms deal. Although the Pergau Dam scheme was not specifically mentioned at this time, it was ultimately funded from this money. Letters confirming this were signed by Lord Younger, then UK Defence Secretary. Amid mounting criticism, the House of Commons All Party Foreign Affairs Committee launched an investigation. Several departments of the UK government were called to account, including the Ministry of Defence and the Department of Trade and Industry. Both the size of the British subsidy and the fact that the offer was made against the advice of Timothy Lancaster, then Permanent Secretary of the administration, were unusual.

One businessman closely involved in UK–Malaysian Trade Relations alleged: 'you know and I know that there is a connection between winning arms sales in Malaysia and offers of aid – but the question is whether anyone was stupid enough to leave explicit evidence' (*Financial Times* 3 February 1994). As the dispute escalated, another allegation emerged that the government had suppressed evidence in a case against a Malaysian banker to prevent embarrassment to the Malaysian government. Despite government statements deploring the handling of the deal and promised changes in the future, the Malaysian government declared the exclusion of all British companies from government contracts in February 1994. The ban seems primarily to have resulted from anger at the press' suggestions that the Malaysian government was corrupt.

British business leaders expressed concern at the potential loss of business. Lord Weinstock of GEC, supplier of defence equipment to Malaysia, wrote to John Smith, Labour Party leader, implying that the Conservative party's political opponents were behind media criticism of the government:

> It cannot be worth exploiting inaccurate media comment for the sake of a temporary embarrassment to your opponents...when the consequences is to help bring about job losses in UK employment and business.

Other firms were equally angry over the impact on British business. Some claimed the potential losses for UK firms might be as much as $4 billion pounds worth of business. John Laing, the British engineering and construction firm was involved in several large construction projects, but feared it would lose a multi-million-pound contract to build an army barracks and University complex in Kuala Lumpur, on which negotiations had been taking place for four years. Trafalgar House, part of an Anglo-Japanese consortium who had been assured the bulk of the work on the £3 billion construction of a new airport south of Kuala Lumpur, were subsequently told by Dr Mathahir Mohamed and his government that no further work would be awarded to UK firms.

The main threat seemed to be confined to three industries: construction, defence and power generation. While the ban only officially covered government contracts, some firms were worried that it might spread to the private sector and affect firms in other industry sectors.

Possible resolution of the dispute was promised if the press ceased to print 'lies' about the Pergau Dam issue. In fact, one hint of a thaw came after a successful Malaysian search for five missing British soldiers in Borneo. The failure of the OECD to publish a report thought critical to resolution of the dispute prolonged the agony. By September 1994 the ban had been lifted. The long-term loss of business had been lower than some expected. Many firms had continued to negotiate for work in the anticipation of a resolution.

Sources: Stephens, P. and Blitz, J. (1994) 'Aid for Malaysia was Linked to Arms Sale', *Financial Times*, 19 January, p. 8; Blitz, J. and Burns, J. (1994) 'Hurd to Explain Aid for Malaysia', *Financial Times*, 3 February, p. 4; Peston, R. and Burns, J. (1994) 'Build up of Allegations behind the Malaysian Dam', *Financial Times*, 5 February, p. 21; Peston, R. and Blitz, J. (1994) 'Malaysia Rejects UK Appeal on Trade Ban', *Financial Times*, 26 February, p. 17; Cooke, K. (1994) 'The Malaysian Trade Ban: Honey Pot of as much as £4 Billion Down the Drain', *Financial Times*, 26 February, p. 4; Jackson, T. and Taylor, A. (1994) 'The Malaysian Trade Ban: Companies Fear Losing a Shop Window', *Financial Times*, 26 February, p. 5; Brown, K. (1994) 'Rescue Prompts Hope of a Thaw with Malaysia', *Financial Times*, 26 March, p. 24; Taylor, A. and Baxter, A. (1994) 'Boycott was no Big Deal', *Financial Times*, 8 September, p. 12.

A parallel can be drawn between the Bofors case and the impact on British firms of the Pergau Dam incident in Malaysia (see Box 4.2).

In the Pergau Dam case, firms in some sectors suffered more than others (see Figure 4.1). Firms serving end consumers or customers other than the Malaysian government were more distant from the disputed sectors. The complexity and number of the political players involved in the incident, the role of the opposition party and the media all provide illustration of the 'human' face of the political context.

If the relationship between firms B and C were to break down such that either government intervened (or else if either government intervened for any political motive) a situation might arise in which either firms A or D might lose business. Neither is directly involved with the actions of firms B and C.

Protectionism is another type of political activity that impacts on networks. Job losses and protection of natural factor endowments (e.g. oil) provide strong incentives for governments and firms to act according to national, rather than international, interests.

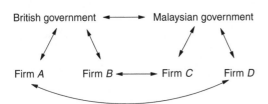

Figure 4.1   Simplified network at the time of the Pergau Dam incident

Protectionist activity favours some relationships within the network at the expense of others. Firms who have previously built successful relationships (e.g. European banana producers serving cus-tomers in America) may find these activities are restricted by political activities (see Case Study 11.1 Banana Wars, for a fuller description of one such instance of protectionism).

CASE STUDY 4.1   BOFORS IN INDIA

Reprinted from *International Journal of Research in Marketing* (1996) 13: 431–47, Hådjikhani, A. and Håkansson, H., 'Political Actions in Business Networks: A Swedish Case'

BACKGROUND

In 1986, a contract between the Swedish firm Bofors and the Indian Defence Ministry became a major issue in the Indian political and social system. The media and opposition accused the government of corruption in connection with a large order given to the Swedish firm. For several years, this question headed the political agenda in India. There were demonstrations in the streets and the newspapers were full of articles about the 'affair' and its handling by Rajiv Gandhi's government and state departments. This case does not analyze the affair in itself but investigates how it affected the operation of other Swedish firms in India, describing the process leading up to the scandal, the different stages in the scandal and its effects.

Bofors is a Swedish company well known for its military products. In February 1986, Bofors signed one of its biggest contracts with the Indian army for M410 artillery pieces of 155 mm FH 77 howitzers. The contract also included ammunition and traction vehicles. The total amount of the deal was over US$1 billion. The negotiations had started in 1981, and before the contract was signed there had thus been several years of hard discussions. The strongest competitor was the French artillery producer PIAT. The Swedish prime Minister, Olof Palme, played an important role in assisting Bofors; the contract was seen as important for Swedish industry, and Olof Palme had a very close personal relationship with Rajiv Gandhi.

It is not surprising that the negotiations between Bofors and the Indian Army also involved the governments of the two countries, as is normal in such a deal. The negotiation was carried out at a high level and the parties agreed not to engage agents in order to reduce the cost of the project. In 1985, the process had reached the point at which the Indian government had to choose between PIAT and Bofors. In the same year, Rajiv Gandhi informed Olof Palme that the contract could be signed with Bofors, given some minor price changes and removal of the provision for agents. (Since 1970, Bofors had two such agents, one in Switzerland and the other in Panama.) Accordingly, Bofors informed the Indian government that the agents were not to be included in the project. In 1986, when Bofors reduced the project costs, all the demands from the Indian government were fulfilled and, soon after, the contract was signed.

In November 1986, the Central Bank in Sweden discovered that Bofors had paid US $30 million to the agent in Panama. An investigation was started, and Bofors declared that the Panamanian firm had always been an agent and that the transfer of money was therefore legal. The Swedish Central Bank accepted the declaration, but the acceptance meant that Bofors had not followed the demands of the Indian government. The result was a strong reaction from the media and from various people in India. Rajiv Gandhi had earlier declared that he was going to fight against corruption and now he himself was accused of being involved in corruption by possibly receiving money through the agents for the contract.

The media, together with the opposition, began to focus on the affair and declared that Gandhi, 'Mr Clean', was deeply involved in the Bofors deal. Several powerful ministers and parliament members suggested to Gandhi that he annul the contract. Bofors was asked to disclose the names of the agents who had received money, otherwise the contract would be annulled. Bofors refused and stated that the information was a business secret. In 1987, Gandhi, together with the defence minister and a few others, declared that they were going to investigate the accusations. Legal proceedings were started and for a period it seemed that the problem was solved. However, in 1988, an Indian newspaper printed an article about the secret payment made by Bofors to the agents. The figure named was now US $60 million. This article led to more new articles, and demonstrations against Gandhi began. The Gandhi administration tried in many ways to maintain a distance from the problem, but it was impossible. The opposition took up the affair in Parliament, and Gandhi had difficulty in maintaining his innocence. In the 1989 elections, which were dominated by the corruption charges against the Gandhi administration, the opposition took advantage of the accusations and succeeded in defeating the Congress Party.

Bofors had naturally been the focus of the political opposition and the media was regarded as responsible for the scandal and, since 1989, has been on a black list. The name 'Bofors' has been adopted as a neologism in the Indian vocabulary to mean scum, or corruption at a high level.

The manager responsible for the delivery of the project to the Indian army tried not to make any comments about the impact of the scandal on the positioning of the firm in the market. The manager stated that the most important concern for Bofors was to have a satisfied customer. He explained that in this project, in contrast to other situations in which the customer had been dissatisfied, Bofors had made all possible efforts to fulfil the demands of the Indian Army. He proclaimed, therefore, that there had been no problems with the buyer. The Indian Army wanted the product and still wished to buy it. Despite the scandal, co-operation had gone well between the different ministries and between the personnel of the Indian Army. All the Indian partners were familiar with the situation and noted that the question had become a non-business (political) issue. Bofors has since withdrawn from the market, and it has consequently become difficult for the Indian Army to procure M410 pieces of artillery. The army wished to fulfil the contract, but no one dared approach Bofors.

EFFECTS ON OTHER SWEDISH FIRMS

This section is devoted to a description of how the Bofors scandal caused disturbances in the business relationships that other Swedish companies had with Indian buyers, based on both primary and secondary data. The primary data was collected through personal interviews in India. More than 20 interviews were carried out in New Delhi – the centre for Swedish companies in India. Interviews were conducted with the General Managers of the subsidiaries or, in two of the cases, with the Swedish managers of large projects in India; state departments and other buyers in India who were connected with the Swedish companies; representatives of the Chamber of Commerce in the Swedish embassy in India; ASSOCHAM (Associate Chambers of Commerce), FICCI (Federation of Indian Chambers of Commerce), a research institute, and an English economic journal.

The seven related firms can be grouped into three categories, depending on how they were influenced by the Bofors scandal. The first group consists of the three firms Sandvik, Tetra Pak and Elof Hansson, which were influenced only marginally by the scandal. The second group includes the three firms Ericsson, ABB and Uri Civil, which all faced serious problems for a certain time. Finally, the third group includes only one firm, Kockums, which was seriously damaged for a long time.

Sandvik Asia W

Sandvik is a very old and very Swedish multinational corporation (MNC), producing steel, carbide tools, saws and hand tools. Sandvik Asia is its subsidiary in India. The company, besides being engaged in import activity, also has a local joint venture partner. It has a dominant position in the market and produces and imports a large percentage of domestic steel products. The Indian market is covered by eight sales offices located in different parts of the country. The Bofors scandal did not have any noticeable impact on their business, one of the major reasons being that Sandvik Asia was not identified by the Indian authorities or by Indian buyers as being a foreign firm. The firm had been in the market since 1960 and had succeeded in expanding to a leading position in the market long before the scandal. During the period of the scandal, it even managed to establish several production units in the country. Sandvik Asia has more than 1200 local employees working in administrative and production units. All the recruitment, except for top management, is local. It is thus easy to understand why buyers and others saw Sandvik Asia as being mainly an Indian company and therefore having nothing, or at least very little, to do with Sweden.

Another reason was its unique position as a market leader selling an important and advanced assortment of special metals and tools to the steel and mining industries in India. The mining industry is recognized as a prioritized sector by politicians in India. As a consequence, Sandvik Asia succeeded in maintaining a strong relationship with public buyers, despite the Bofors affair. A third reason was that private buyers never even discussed the Bofors affair with Sandvik's manager. They saw the whole scandal as a non-business affair (political issue) and did not mix it with their business concerns.

Tetra Pak India Ltd

Tetra Pak, engaged in selling packaging of milk products, is heavily involved in the agricultural sector, which is important in India's socio-economical system. Despite the important influence of government in food and milk production, Tetra Pak faced few problems in India as a result of scandal. The scandal was viewed as similar to other, almost daily, incidents in India. However some buyers had tried to connect Tetra Pak, as a Swedish company, to Bofors.

Why, then, did Tetra Pak face so few problems, even though it had been established in India in 1988 when the scandal was at its peak? One reason might be that Tetra Pak has its headquarters in Switzerland and therefore was seen by the majority as a Swiss company. It is not uncommon for people to have difficulty differentiating between these two countries. It may even be the case that when such a misunderstanding took place, and it was seen as beneficial for the company, there were no efforts made to correct it. Another reason was probably that Tetra Pak was linked to the Ministry of Agriculture, which was not the focus of the media. Finally, compared to Bofors, the firm has a completely different customer structure, all products being sold to a large number of local producers.

Elof Hansson India Pvt Ltd

Elof Hansson India is a trading company owned by the Elof Hansson Trading Group in Sweden. The firm entered the Indian market in 1977 and had at that time four sales subsidiaries in the country. The firm is engaged in both selling and buying in the Indian market. It sells products to the paper and textile industries and buys textile and agriculture products. The firm is involved with a large number of private local Indian firms, and the contacts are handled by the branch staff, who are all from India.

When the scandal started, none of the Indian buyers or sellers brought up the matter. Even the Indian managers within Elof Hansson failed to bring up the issue with their Swedish colleagues. When the furore increased during 1987, the matter became a joke. It was treated as an external question and was seen as involving mainly Bofors and the media. There was no sign from the Indian partners that they were connecting the issue to their business and no attempt was made to use the scandal to improve their negotiation power.

There are three main reasons that explain why Elof Hansson was not affected. First, the firm itself has no connections to Bofors or to the Indian government. Secondly, their Indian customers and suppliers had no contacts with either of parties involved in the Bofors affair. They were private companies with little or no relationship with the government. Thirdly, the relationships were handled mainly by the local branch managers who were all from India, which certainly increased their distance from the Swedish 'affair'.

Ericsson India Ltd

Ericsson is a well-known Swedish MNC operating in the telecommunications industry. Ericsson India is a wholly owned sales subsidiary responsible for selling Ericsson's products in India. The buyer is usually the Indian Telecommunication Department (DOT). The Bofors scandal had severe effects on the business because Ericsson was negotiating for several contracts at the relevant time. The negotiations were about the sales of switchboards for which some parts would be produced in a local unit on a licensed basis and others would be delivered from Sweden. Before the scandal, the negotiations had gone well and the firm was very optimistic about getting the contracts. However, when the Bofors scandal began to dominate the media, problems arose in the negotiations. The project group from the DOT became more aggressive and very concerned about small details. This caused delays and extended the negotiation process, which in turn increased costs. One consequence was that Ericsson felt it impossible to predict the outcome. Competitors from Germany and France become much more active and tried to take over and finalize the main contract. Immediately before the elections in 1989, the DOT interrupted all negotiations and informed Ericsson that there would be no further orders. For about 8–9 months there were very few contacts. There seemed to be an implicit understanding among the managers at the DOT that they did not want to be connected with a Swedish firm during the election period. There were even individuals in the DOT who recommended that Ericsson keep a low profile during this time. The advice was given in a very informal way, and it seemed to be a friendly way of informing Ericsson of the delicacy of DOT's own position.

Ericsson was influenced by the scandal to such an extent that the managers considered it a catastrophe. Ericsson India had been established in India since 1971; however, despite its long involvemnent in India, Ericsson could be easily connected to Sweden and thus to Bofors. One reason for this was that the company is highly associated with foreign high technology. Ericsson India had only 150 employees and was mainly responsible for marketing. Only a few low tech-

nology parts were produced in India. Another important reason was that the DOT, the big state buyer, was in many ways very similar to the buyer of Bofors products. The DOT people were afraid that the media could easily connect Ericsson to Bofors. Ericsson also had some special projects with Bofors in Sweden. Consequently there was a clear effort by both the DOT and the India State Department of Communications to keep its distance from Ericsson and all Swedish firms in order to avoid being connected with the Bofors affair.

As soon as the elections were over, business life became much more normal again. The new government had no political reasons for maintaining a negative attitude towards Swedish firms in general, and the whole issue was presented as a mistake made by the earlier government. The DOT began to negotiate with Ericsson again but was still very cautious about all details until Ericsson and the DOT finally signed the contract. Ericsson estimated that the scandal had caused delays of several years in the project and also an unnecessary repetition of negotiations. Both of these consequences had caused not only a substantial increase in costs but also a very problematic strategic situation as Ericsson had to keep personnel on a project for which the outcome was very uncertain.

ABB Ltd–Rihand–Delhi project

ABB has two different headquarters in India and several regional offices engaged in selling ABB products. ABB also has several production units in Bangalore, Mysore and Nasik. The Rihand-Delhi project is a very large power station project with total costs of over US $200 Million. The most obvious effect of the scandal was an increased and more complicated project bureaucracy. It was not a question of decreased trust of the firm's products or of the management but that the Indian bureaucrats and politicians had become frightened of doing business with Swedish firms. The manager described how the scandal had made the Indian decision makers follow the bureaucratic rules to the letter. Relationships with Swedish firms were in sharp focus and any mistake would easily be discovered by the media; by following the rules strictly, the bureaucrats could protect themselves from any accusations of impropriety.

One consequence of this was a change in the way decisions were made. As decision makers became afraid of accusations of corruption and all connections to Swedish firms were seen as a potential risk, decisions were referred to higher hierarchical levels. The problems became successively larger as there were changes in the project plans and other commitments. All decisions, even small and unimportant ones, were sent to the decision board. The consequences were delays, costly negotiations and uncertainty about the future. The uncertainty became so high that it was considered whether or not it was worthwhile to continue the negotiations. After the elections, when the new government saw no further use for the scandal, the behaviour of the bureaucrats became normal again. Consequently, state departments such as the Energy and Water Resources Department began to change their behaviour towards ABB. Project negotiations could begin in earnest, and in 1989, the contract with ABB was signed.

Despite the fact that the Rihand-Delhi project was recognized as an important project for the industrial development of the country, the Bofors affair caused severe problems. One important reason was the timing. The negotiations were conducted during the most intense period of the scandal. The importance of the project was, however, at such a level that the Indian buyer, NTPC (National Thermal Power Corporation), probably never ready wanted to end co-operation. NTPC therefore continued to co-operate, despite the fact that the managers felt negative pressure from other state departments. One way NTPC recognized this was that there were a lot of complications in the bureaucratic handling of the project in the other state departments. The main effect of the scandal on the project was, accordingly, to cause delays and increase administration and negotiations.

Uri Civil Contractor AB

Uri Civil AB is a Swedish–British consortium that was aiming for a large dam project in Uril, located in the north of India. The total project amounted to approximately US $1 billion. The group involved the Swedish companies Skanska, NCC, ABB Generator and Sweco and the British company Kvaerner-Boving. The counterpart in India was NHPC (National Hydro Power Corporation). The negotiations for the construction of the dam began in 1985, but when the Bofors scandal began, the buyer started to delay the negotiations. They began to change their demands and asked for additional information and also new bids. This was interpreted as an attempt by the Indian project group to use the scandal to strengthen their position in the negotiations. It was, of course, difficult to deny the Swedish origin of some of the firms in the consortium. The buyers told the Swedish manager that they were obliged to follow the written law and all rules, and the protocol and orders in the negotiations followed the rules to the letter. Details were checked and rechecked and thus all activities became complicated and time-consuming. During 1989 – the election year – the consortium did not know if it really would get the contract. However, in a similar way to the case of Ericsson, when the new government took over and state departments could behave normally again, negotiations proceeded and the contract was signed in 1990.

One important reason that the buyer continued the process was that the whole project was financed by Swedish and English aid agencies. The Indian government had a low level of input into the project, and the Indian buying side knew they would lose the whole project if they created too many problems. The project was not mentioned or discussed by the opposition or the media for the same reason. Everyone realized that there was a risk that the foreign financial support would be cancelled if the project was criticized. Thus, NHPC continued and finalized the contract.

Kockums AB

This firm performed extensive marketing activities selling submarines and shipping equipment during the period of the Bofors scandal. There was an understandable unwillingness on the part of this company to release information to us regarding the impact of the scandal on their business. However, there are third-party reports and published information that gives a very clear picture of the problems. Before the scandal, the negotiations had proceeded without complications and the chance of getting a contract was estimated to be high. Kockums already had a similar contract with the Australian government, but the project was too similar to the Bofors project to be unharmed by the scandal and Kockums has, to this day, failed to win a contract.

The reasons are clear. First, Kockums is as well known in the defence industry field as Bofors.

Secondly, the potential buyer was the Indian Navy, which in turn is close to the Indian Army which was buying Bofors' products. Both the army and navy were closely connected to the defence industry which had received most of the criticism and accusations and was under attack from the media, from the political opposition, and from lay people as well. Even several years after the scandal, there was scepticism from many quarters about the defence purchasing process in general but particularly in relation to Swedish firms. It was a general belief among Swedish firms that no one in the Indian defence ministry wanted to jeopardize his or her future by doing business with a Swedish firm.

SUMMARY

In Chapter 4 we have explored the economic and political theories and models that impact on international marketers. We have explored the implications of operation in a globally interlinked economy for international marketing. We then explored the distinctive characteristics of network structures in different types of economies.

BIBLIOGRAPHY

Ahlberg, J., Garemo, N. and Nauclér, T. (1999) 'The Euro: How to keep your Prices Up and your Competitors Down', *The Mclliney Quarterly*, 2: 211–18.

Araujo, L. and Easton, G. (1996) 'Networks in Socio-economic Systems: A critical Review' in Iaccobucci, D. (ed.), *Networks in Marketing*, Sage.

Axelsson, B. and Johanson, J. (1992) 'Foreign Market Entry – The Textbook versus the Network View', in Easton, G. and Axelsson, B. (eds), *Industrial Networks: A New View of Reality*, Routledge.

Barley, S. R., Freeman, J. and Hybels, R.C. (1992) 'Strategic Alliances in Biotechnology' in Nohria, N. and Eccles, R. G., *Networks and Organizations*, Harvard Business School Press: 311–47.

Blankenburg, D. (1995) 'A Network Approach to Foreign Market Entry', in Möller, K. and Wilson, D. (eds), *Business Marketing: An Interaction and Network Perspective*, Kluwer Academic: 375–410.

Business Europe (1999) 'Pricing for the Euro (2)', 5 May: 4.

Economist, The (1999a) 'The non-European Euro: The Euro Travels Outside the EU', 9 January.

Economist, The (1999b) 'A Survey of Global Finance: Fix or Float?: It all Depends', 30 January.

Economist, The (1999c) 'The Americas: Brazil Rocks the Mercosur Boat: Devaluation: The Collapse of Brazil's Currency has Shaken its Regional Trade Partners', 13 February.

Economist, The (1999d) 'Britain: Economists for EMU', 17 April.

Economist, The (1999e) 'Finance and Economics: Sailing in Choppy Waters', 26 June.

Economist, The (2000) *The World in 2000*.

Forsgren, M. and Johanson, J. (eds) (1992) *Managing Networks in International Business*, Gordon & Breach.

Gautier, P. H. (1999) 'The Impact of pan-European Retail Consolidation', *UK Venture Capital Journal*, 1 April 33.

Grant, R. M. (1991) 'Porter's Competitive Advantage of Nations: An Assessment', *Strategic Management Journal*, 12: 535–48.

Hådjikhani, A. and Håkansson, H. (1996) 'Political Actions in Business Networks: A Swedish Case', *International Journal of Research in Marketing*, 13: 431–47.

Håkansson, H. and Snehota, I. (1995) 'Economy of Business Relationships and Networks', in

Developing Relationships in Business Networks, Routledge: 382–97.

Johanson, J. and Mattsson, L.-G. (1988) 'Internationalisation in Industrial Systems – A Network Approach', in Hood, N. and Vahlne, J.-E. (eds), *Strategies in Global Competition*, Croom Helm; reproduced in Buckley, P. J. and Ghauri, P. (eds), *The Internationalisation of the Firm: A Reader*, Academic Press.

Kinch, N. (1992) 'Entering a Tightly Structured Network – Strategic Visions or Network Realities', in Forsgren, M. and Johanson, J. (eds), *Managing Networks in International Business*, Gordon & Breach.

Kotler, P. (1986) 'Mega-marketing', *Harvard Business Review*, March–April: 117–24.

Lee, J.-W. (1993) 'The Development of Strategic Position in the Korean Industrial Turbines Market', *Uppsala Working Paper Series*, 1993/8.

Leontief, W. (1954) 'Domestic Production and Foreign Trade: The American Capital Position Re-examined', *Proceedings of the American Philosophical Society*, 97: 331–49.

Manninen, K. and Snelbecker, D. (1993) 'Obstacles to Doing Business in Ukraine', *Working Paper*, Project for Economic Reform in Ukraine, Harvard University, April.

Mattsson, L.-G. (1985) 'An Application of a Network Approach to Marketing: Defending and Changing Market Positions', in Dholakia, N. and Arndt, J. (eds), *Alternative Paradigms for Widening Marketing Theory*, JAI Press.

McKiernan, P. (1992) *Strategies of Growth: Maturity, Recovery and Internationalization*, Routledge.

Nohria, N. (1992) 'Introduction: Is a Network Perspective a Useful Way of Studying Organizations', in Nohria, N. and Eccles, R. G. (eds), *Networks and Organizations: Structure, Form and Organizations*, Harvard Business School Press: 1–22.

Ohlin, B. (1933) *Interregional and International Trade*, Harvard University Press.

Ohmae, K. (1989) 'Managing in a Borderless World', *Harvard Business Review*, May–June, reprinted in Buzzell, R. B., Quelch, J. A. and Bartlett, C. A. (eds), *Global Marketing Management: Cases and Readings*, 53–68.

Porter, M. E. (1990a) 'The Competitive Advantage of Nations', *Harvard Business Review*, March–April: 73–86.

Porter, M. E. (1990b) *The Competitive Advantage of Nations*, Macmillan.

Ricardo, D. (1817) *Principles of Political Economy and Taxation*, J. M. Dent.

Salmi, A. (1996) 'Russian Networks in Transition: Implications for Managers', *Industrial Marketing Management*, 25, 1: 37–44.

Smith, A. (1776) *An Enquiry into the Nature and Causes of the Wealth of Nations*, The Modern Library (1937).

World Bank (2000) *Entering the twenty-first Century: World Development Report*, Oxford University Press for the World Bank.

PART III

INTERNATIONAL MARKETING STRATEGIES

Having decided to operate internationally, a firm must then formulate an international marketing strategy that is consistent with its corporate objectives and strategy. If the firm differentiates itself, for example, on high service quality, as does Hertz, or specialist knowledge, as does KPMG, then this will dictate the most appropriate type of international operation, the pricing strategy and other elements of the firm's international marketing strategy and mix.

A number of strategic issues must be resolved. What will be the scope of the firm's international operation? Does it wish to operate regionally or globally? Is the firm's differential advantage sustainable globally? What level of risk should it accept in entering new international markets and how best can it serve these?

Part III of this book addresses four strategic issues:

- Developing an international marketing strategy
- Assessing market attractiveness
- The mode of international operation
- The process of internationalization.

Chapter 5 considers the formulation of international marketing strategies. From a Traditional perspective, this includes choices on the scope of international marketing and the extent to which the firm's marketing strategy and mix are transferable across international markets. From a Relationship perspective, international marketing strategies focus on developing and managing international relationships. These relationships may be between subsidiaries of one firm, or between the

firm and its suppliers, partners and other stakeholders. From a Network perspective, international firms are connected to other firms via a complex web of direct and indirect relationships. This web may influence the strategic choices made by the firm. International marketing strategy, from a network perspective, is the process of building positions and strengthening ties in international networks. Chapter 5 explores the challenges of developing international marketing strategies from each of these perspectives.

The identification of attractive new international markets is complicated by rapid and unpredictable changes in world events. Few could have anticipated the speed at which the liberalization of East and Central Europe (CEE) took place, or the full ramifications of the East Asian crisis. Yet a majority of the tools and techniques proposed for assessment of international market attractiveness were developed in the more stable and incrementally changing climate of the 1960s and 1970s. Chapter 6 evaluates the advantages and disadvantages of a range of techniques. Scenario planning copes best with the type of discontinuous change that characterizes today's market environments as it projects forward to consider a range of possible futures.

From a relationship and network perspective, the selection of market attractiveness is not a rational process beginning with a blank piece of paper. Firms exchange information and develop the knowledge to formulate these decisions from their relationships. This chapter reviews the latest conclusions in the debate over the nature of knowledge and the extent to which it can be transferred between individuals and firms. From a network perspective, the implications of existence in a knowledge economy and of firms as knowledge communities are discussed.

Once a firm has selected the markets or markets which it wishes to target, it must decide upon the optimal type, or mode, of international operation to serve these markets. Chapter 7 reviews the broad range of economic and strategic literature that explains the influences on the mode of international operation. The chapter explores the growth in popularity of strategic alliances as a method of entry. Finally, the chapter identifies different understandings of 'network', ranging from a hybrid organizational form to a fundamental feature of operation in international markets.

Building on the discussion of international mode of operation in Chapter 7, Chapter 8 goes on the look at the total process of internationalization. A firm may make a series of different deci-

sions over time. These may involve either entry into additional markets or changing the mode used to serve existing markets. Each new decision is influenced by what has gone before. If, for example, a firm was unsuccessful in entering the USA, it might be more cautious about entry into Canada. Why did the operation fail? Should the firm enter another market in the region? Should it use a different mode? Likewise, positive experiences may result in firms taking higher levels of risk in subsequent decisions.

Chapter 8 looks at different models that have been proposed for the process of internationalization. In particular it explores the underpinning of incremental, or sequential, models that show gradual international expansion. These are contrasted with arguments that globalization results in more rapid, or even simultaneous, international expansion. The chapter concludes with a discussion of the network view of the internationalization process.

INTERNATIONAL MARKETING STRATEGY

Objectives

The issues to be addressed in Chapter 5 include:

1. The development of international marketing strategies
2. Assessing the extent to which international marketing strategy and mix are transferable across international markets
3. The development and management of international relationships
4. The strategic choices facing firms in a networks environment.

After reading Chapter 5 you will be able to:

1. Understand the assumptions of traditional marketing
2. Identify the strategic challenges facing international marketers from a traditional perspective
3. Assess the advantages and disadvantages of global standardization of international marketing strategy and mix
4. Understand the issues involved in managing international relationships
5. Understand the challenges of building positions in international markets.

INTRODUCTION

International marketing activities are inextricably linked to a firm's corporate goals and strategy. The overall goals and strategy of the firm influence international marketing decisions such as whether to enter uncertain markets, how great a risk the firm is prepared to accept or the level of control required over international operations. Traditional relationship and network perspectives on international marketing are based on different assumptions on the nature of markets and the strategic challenges facing firms. In turn, these differing assumptions raise a different strategic agenda for international marketers.

From a traditional perspective, firms strive to capitalize on distinctive capabilities, such as technologies, brands or service quality in a hostile global environment to gain advantages over rivals. Based on these assumptions, international marketing strategy decisions relate to the scope of international operation, how to benefit from distinctive competences and how to achieve the optimal balance between the global consistency and local responsiveness of the international marketing strategy.

From a relationship perspective, firms are engaged in developing and maintaining *interactive international relationships*. Some relationship literature is based on essentially the same worldview as traditional international marketing strategy. Within firms, value chains are reconfigured to gain cost advantages with low cost manufacturing hubs supplying global sales and marketing operations. Similarly, firms may outsource parts of their operation if the costs of doing so are less than those of performing the function internally. As a result, managing relationships within and between firms is a key competence of the firm.

Interaction and network studies, however, see firms as embedded in a web of relationships that influence strategic decisions. Further insights into international marketing relationships are gained from an interaction perspective. Interaction literature studies the ways in which relationships *differ in different national contexts* and when involving partners of different nationalities, and the features which are common.

From a network perspective, international marketing strategy involves a more complex web of relationships and is the process of building positions in international networks. This chapter reviews the challenges for international marketers of building these positions.

THE TRADITIONAL PERSPECTIVE

Traditional marketing is based on neoclassical microeconomics. Its worldview, typified by the work of Porter (1980, 1985, 1990), is of firms maximizing advantages resulting from technological innovations, brands and other distinctive capabilities in the face of zero-sum competition (see Chapter 1 for a full explanation of zero-sum and win–win strategies). In this zero-sum world, advantage can be gained only at the expense of a competitor. Thus marketers will attempt to gain market share from rivals, to introduce innovative products or services sooner and more effectively or offer higher levels of service quality. When competition is global in scope, one of the critical debates for international marketing strategy is that of how to gain maximum economies from global operation while remaining responsive to the needs of local customers.

Global competition, economies of scale and scope, creation of free trade agreements, liberalization of previously blocked markets, convergence of consumer tastes, advances in travel and communication technology have all intensified the pace of globalization of the world economy:

> Whether to globalize, and how to globalize, have become two of the most burning strategy issues for managers around the world. Many forces are driving companies around the world to globalize by expanding their participation in foreign markets. Almost every product market in the major world economies – computers, fast food, nuts and bolts – has

foreign competitors. Trade barriers are also falling. (Yip 1989)

That marketing takes place on an increasingly global scale is largely uncontested. The question for international marketing managers, then, is how to develop effective strategies for a global economy. Some international marketing strategy literature argues that operation on a global scale means that global standardization, serving all markets with the same products or services, is possible and desirable. Critics, however, highlight the loss of local responsiveness that may result from this 'one-size-fits-all' approach to international marketing.

International Marketing Strategies for a Global Economy

> Walk into a capital goods factory anywhere in the developed world, and you will find the same welding machines, the same robots, the same machine tools. When information flows with relative freedom, the old geographic barriers become irrelevant. Global needs lead to global products. For managers, this universal flow of information puts a high premium on learning how to build the strategies and the organizations capable of meeting the requirements of a borderless world. (Ohmae 1989)

Ohmae (1989), Yip (1989) and others present compelling arguments that the future lies in a global scope of operation. Only by operation across trading blocs can firms protect themselves against downturns in a globally interlinked economy (Ohmae 1985). Only by maximizing sales in global markets can firms offset the increasing costs of remaining innovative (Lorenz 1985). If a firm does not operate globally it may be vulnerable to the actions of global competitors with greater resources and ability to direct these to gaining market share in any specific country (Hamel and Prahalad 1985; Hout, Porter and Rudden 1985). Based on this evidence, few would argue against the concept that firms are increasingly driven to globalize their scope of operation. If anything, recent decades have seen the pace of globalization increase. Riesenbeck and Freeling (1991) show that the speed of international expansion of new brands has reduced from around 20 years for the traditional, sequential or 'waterfall' process to one–two years for simultaneous or 'sprinkler' launches. But does globalization of the economy dictate standardised products and services?

Arguments for Global Standardization

The global standardization debate began with the work of Buzzell (1968), which challenged the prevailing wisdom that standardized marketing strategies were not realistic because of the great differences between nations:

> The prevailing view, then, is that marketing strategy is a local problem. The best strategy for a company will differ from country to country, and the design of the strategy should be left to local management in each country. (Buzzell 1968)

Buzzell presented balanced arguments highlighting potential benefits and barriers to standardization. Benefits included:

- **Significant cost savings.** Although marketing argues in favour of offering products and services adapted to local tastes, income levels, etc. profitability depends both on sales and costs. Offering the same basic product (maybe with some variation in features or usage) might – depending on the nature of the production process – allow longer production runs. This would reduce variable costs and the larger volume of sales would amortize research and development and other fixed costs. Offering a standardized global product might also reduce marketing costs:

  > Still another area for cost savings is that of advertising. For some of the major packaged goods manufacturers, the production of art work, films and other advertising materials costs millions of dollars annually. Although differences in language limit the degree of standardization that can be imposed, some common elements can often be used. (Buzzell 1968)

- **Consistency of marketing strategy.** An additional benefit of standardization is that customers see a consistent marketing strategy. Use of a global brand, global identity and global product features may add value as customers travel across international borders. Exposure to the same messages strengthens brand identity. Conversely, inconsistency in marketing strategies might create dissatisfaction. For example, disparity in price levels is topical in the light of the late 1990s discussion of 'rip-off' Britain. The Internet, globalization of retail and other changes to international market structures serve to highlight this type of inconsistency. Similarly, improved travel possibilities mean that consumers will be exposed to a company's marketing messages around the world.

- **Improved planning and control.** Buzzell (1968) cites the example of Philips Lighting, who at one stage in its history found its German subsidiary undercutting prices charged by its Dutch subsidiary by 30 per cent. Examples of other such disparities abound in multinational corporations. At the very least the company may cannibalize sales in one market by actions in another. Worse, it may switch sales to a market with lower profit margins and cause an overall loss of profit. Multinational marketing strategies are complex. In the late 1980s, the Anglo-Dutch multinational, Unilever, had over 200 formulations of margarine within Europe alone. While some of these existed in response to different consumer preferences, others resulted from national subsidiaries unwittingly duplicating product development and other marketing efforts. Standardized global marketing strategies simplify the product or service offer and allow firms to make effective use of their resources.

- **Exploiting good ideas**. If there is a premium on innovative ideas, then those that work should be exploited to maximum effect. Buzzell (1968) argues against the use of average ideas if the firm has better ideas globally. Again this is an argument in favour of maximizing benefits from the firm's global marketing expertise.

The standardization debate continued over a number of years, but stepped up a gear with Levitt's controversial article on the subject in 1983. Rather than presenting the pros and cons of standardization, Levitt argued that technological advances and homogenization of global consumers would inevitably result in firms serving the world as a single market:

Starting from opposing sides, the high-tech and high-touch ends of the commercial spectrum gradually consume the undistributed middlemen in their cosmopolitan orbit. No one is exempt and nothing can stop the process. Everywhere everything gets more and more like everything else as the world's preference structure is relentlessly homogenized. (Levitt 1983)

Levitt's basic argument is that offering globally standard products and services offers economies of scale and scope, allowing firms to make profits while still reducing prices to consumers. Given this improved value for money, consumers would waive any remaining cultural preferences:

> The most effective world competitors incorporate superior quality and reliability into their cost structures. They sell in national markets the same kind of products sold at home or in their largest export market. They compete on the basis of appropriate value – the best combinations of price, quality, reliability, and delivery for products that are globally identical with respect to design, function and even fashion. That and little else, explains the surging success of Japanese companies dealing worldwide in a vast variety of products.

As an example, Levitt highlights the fact that the washing machine industry in the 1970s was highly fragmented. Customers in different markets expressed strong preferences. These included preferences for different sizes of machines, top loading or front loading and hot or cold rinse. In the face of these diverse preferences, the entry of Zanussi with a small, low cost washing machine might have been expected to fail. Such was the value represented by this washing machine, however, that it gained significant market share even in Germany, a market with strong preference for large, more highly engineered machines.

Arguments Against Global Standardization

Critics suggest that some of the promised advantages of global standardization are exaggerated. Indeed a number of barriers exist to total standardization, and few, except Levitt, have argued for such radical global standardization. Four barriers to global standardization can be noted:

- **A lack of evidence of homogenization** (Douglas and Wind 1987). While some argue the existence of global consumers, contradictory evidence suggests a trend towards greater fragmentation of markets. This might in fact suggest products tailored to individual needs (Toffler 1970). An application of this debate is found later in this book (Chapter 12) with reference to the feasibility of even pan-European marketing.
- **Market characteristics**. Even if arguments based on customer convergence are accepted, some national differences persist. Buzzell (1968) suggests that physical characteristics – climate, topography and resources – are particularly immutable. Coca Cola found that large 2 litre bottles were too large in some countries where soft drinks had to be refrigerated to remain cool, although this was no problem in colder climes. Unilever have margarines with different melting points for hotter and colder climates. Robust Lada cars may be necessary for the rough road surfaces in Russia that may be too much for standard cars. Legal requirements represent a further cause of adaptation. The need for health warnings on cigarettes, labelling requirements for food products, tariff structures and protection of intellectual property may all require firms to adapt to local conditions.

  Similarly, levels of economic wealth, cultural norms and other aspects of the context reviewed in Part II of this book may necessitate market-specific adjustments. Philip Morris, when trying to sell standardized packs of Marlboro cigarettes into Ukraine, were at a loss to understand why some sold without difficulty and others remained on the shelves. Eventually they discovered that the barcodes (not used in Ukraine but also not viewed as a disadvantage) were being interpreted as the production codes used to identify products in the Soviet regime. Some factories had a poor reputation for quality. Barcodes ressembling the numbers used for these factories were assumed to indicate poor quality!
- **Production not marketing orientation**. While globalization of the economy might favour a

global scale of operation, it does not necessarily require global standardization of products and services. Yip (1989) stresses the potential benefits of the 'multidomestic' model whereby: 'companies set up local subsidiaries that design, produce, and market products or services tailored to local needs.'

The suggestion that customers will accept product offerings that do not exactly match their requirements if these are good value for money is essentially a return to a Henry T Ford production orientation. From a market orientation, if global suppliers do not provide the products and services customers need and want, they ultimately expose themselves to those able to do so. Customers may be prepared to pay a premium for 'customized' offerings.

■ **Value of economies of scale?** While global standardization, within limits, may be efficient, the value of the economies to be gained may also have been overstated. Advances in production technology, such as flexible manufacturing systems, mass customization and computer aided design and manufacturing (CAD/CAM) may mean that variety can be achieved at lower cost. Similarly, marketing economies may be overstated. While Gillette Sensor may have made savings of $20 million from using a standardized advertizing message (Riesenbeck and Freeling 1991), this represents a small proportion of their total advertising budget ($175 million for two years) and product development costs ($200 million). Also, although some aspects of marketing expenditure may be reduced by standardization, others remain the same whatever the advertizing campaign. Media space, for example, represents a significant proportion of the cost of advertizing campaigns and will not be reduced even if a standardized message is used.

Globalization

Nonetheless, a number of authors (Quelch and Hoff 1986; Douglas and Wind 1987; Ohmae 1989; Riesenbeck and Freeling 1991) suggest standardization where possible to afford savings, without going to the extremes proposed by Levitt (1983).

Quelch and Hoff (1986) suggest that the extent of standardization of products and services depends on both their nature and the cultural similarity of the markets. Industrial products and commodities are the easiest to standardize globally. Products and services consumed in the home, such as food, are more culturally sensitive. While questioning the applicability of global standardization, Douglas and Wind (1987) accept that it may be more possible to find global segments in 'high-technology' and 'high-touch,' or luxury niches. Yip (1989) suggests that the extent to which a firms customers, channels and competitors are global may dictate the extent to which consistency is both desirable and necessary.

THE RELATIONSHIP PERSPECTIVE

With global scope of operation, a number of different type of relationships become important for international marketers.

Decoupling the Value Chain

In some industries, globalization means that the firm's value chain has been reconfigured. Global overcapacity in the automotive industry, for example, means that firms must achieve efficiency in their production processes to remain competitive. As a result, a number of competitors in the automotive sector have relocated their production to countries with low labour, raw material and other costs. Mexico is preferred by a number of producers. Within Europe, Ford opted for production in Portugal for its relative factor advantages. Firms may not, then, perform all the parts of the value chain in each country of operation, but may decouple production from sales and marketing activity. This means that firms must manage international relationships between different subsidiaries and functions of the business.

Value Constellations

Literature in the 'New Economics of Information' area argues that advances in information technology (IT) alter the value chain still further. The previous section has explained that a firm's value chain may be split between different geographic locations. Advances in IT mean that some links in the value chain can be performed by other firms (Normann and Ramirez 1993; Evans and Wurster 1997; McGee 2000).

The New Economics of Information begins with the premise that firms typically possess *tacit knowledge* that makes it beneficial for them to perform activities within the firm. Tacit knowledge may take many forms. A European manufacturer of wallpaper experienced major production problems on one of its machines on the retirement of one of its production supervisors. Scrap levels rose from an acceptable 5 to an unacceptable 30 per cent. On enquiring why, other workers in the area said 'Oh, the gauge on that machine hasn't worked for years, but Bob could judge by eye how to line up the paper.' This type of knowledge, often resulting from experience, meant that firms may have distinctive corporate knowledge whose value is difficult to quantify.

IT has made it easier to *codify* some types of knowledge. Codified knowledge is more readily transferable to other parties outside the firm. For example, advances in CAD/CAM mean that once a component is specified in a computer system, it can easily be produced by an outside firm. As a result of codification the value chain can be split between a number of different actors. The New Economics of Information literature suggests that the changes in knowledge transfer capability are sufficiently radical to require a revision of the standard models of corporate strategy. In place of the value chain, a *value constellation* is proposed (Normann and Ramirez 1993). In the value constellation, a firm may have only a few distinctive competences at its core. These are surrounded by tiers of relationships with primary-and secondary-level suppliers who perform many of the traditional functions of the business.

The costs of performing an activity outside the firm have often been described in terms of transaction costs (Williamson 1975; Jarillo 1988). Jarillo (1988) argues that an activity should be performed externally when the costs of doing so are less than the costs of performing the activity within the firm. The New Economics of Information literature argues that transaction costs of performing operations are reduced by technological advances, and may ultimately reduce to zero.

This argument is based on a number of assumptions. The first assumption is that the availability of information increases knowledge. This is based on the concept of codified data as explained above. Yet, while codification is possible for technical data via computer systems, some types of knowledge, such as understanding of an international market, or the history of a particular relationship, may be less easy to codify. The counter argument then, is that some transaction costs are likely to remain, particularly in 'softer' areas such as understanding relationships, different national cultures and different market conditions.

Accordingly, the argument seems to emerge that areas relying on technical skills (such as production, distribution and IT strategy) may be prime candidates for outsourcing. The ability to manage relationships and to understand the complexities of relationships conducted in and across a range of international markets remains, however, among the distinctive competences at the core of the company.

Branding

As brands are among the core competences at the centre of the value constellation, their strategic importance is set to endure. According to Doyle (2000, p. 242):

> Successful brand names convey powerful images to customers that make them more desirable than competitive products. Owners of strong brands possess assets that attract customers, often earn premium prices and can be enduring generators of cash.

It is such brands that prevent products or services from becoming commodities. Successful brands encapsulate the distinctive characteristics of a product or service in a specific name or symbol allows customers to differentiate and esteem the distinctive characteristics of a particular firm's products or services. Such is the strategic importance of brands, that firms with strong brands can not only use these to build wealth and loyalty, but they become powerful assets of the organisation. Doyle (1994) cites statistics showing that, while the average British and American company is valued at twice its balance sheet assets, firms with port-folios of strong brands are valued by the stock market at four times net assets. When Nestlé acquired the UK firm Rowntree, it paid six times net assets in recognition of the firm's confection-ary brands – including globally recognized brands such as KitKat and Milky Bar.

Given the financial importance of strong brands, the topic of *brand valuation* has become central to the marketing field. Although a number of different valuation methods are proposed (See Perrier 1997; Aaker 1999; Doyle 2000 for valuable summaries of the contributions in this area), the brand valuation studies of Young and Rubicam's brand valuation division are popularly cited. The dimensions of this brand valuation framework are described in Box 5.1.

Managing International Relationships

Within interaction studies, developing and man-aging international relationships is a dominant theme (Turnbull 1979; Ford 1984). One focus of these studies is on the distances that may hinder and the factors that may favour development of international relationships. These are discussed more fully in part IV, The Context of International Marketing.

The original IMP study (Håkansson 1982; Turn-bull and Valla 1986) provides insights into inter-national business-to-business (B2B) relationships in France, Germany, Sweden and the UK. Focusing on the management of buyer–supplier relationships within and between these countries, the study gives valuable insights into international marketing strategy from an interaction perspective.

Interaction studies focus predominantly on industrial markets and, as explained more fully in Chapter 1, these have distinctive features. They are characterized by:

- Complex products with high purchase value
- High levels of investment to enter new inter-national markets
- High risk of entry into new markets

- Risk reduction via relationship building result-ing in:
  - Stability
  - Loyalty to suppliers/buyers
  - Interaction and mutual dependence. (Turn-bull and Valla 1986, p. 3)

Given these characteristics, marketing strategy from an interaction perspective can be defined as:

> [planning] a balanced portfolio of profitable and stable supplier–customer relationships and [ensuring] that the marketing organisation is sufficiently flexible and that appropriate resources are available in order that the company can respond and adapt to specific customer needs. (Turnbull and Valla 1986, p. 9)

An important finding from the cross-national study of these issues is that country-specific differ-ences, such as market size, market potential, expectations and perceived risks result in firms adopting different market positions and that rela-tionships developed in each have specific traits (Turnbull and Valla 1986, pp. 53–4).

Valla (Turnbull and Valla 1986, p. 52) attributes these differences to:

- **Differences in relationship cost.** Relationships may demand differing levels of investment, depending on product type, country of part-ner, etc. If, for example, a technologically advanced product is involved, or the market is one in which the firm has not previously been present, the investment, or 'relationship' costs will be higher. One inference of different relationship costs is that higher relationship costs result in greater commitment to making the relationship succeed.
- **Different managerial perceptions of each market.** These may be stereotypical or based on previous experiences in the country. Based on these differences, the manager may approach the relationship differently.
- **Different customer attitudes and behaviour.** Valla gives the example that, in Sweden, cus-tomers are inclined to look for close co-opera-tion with suppliers. Significant differences are seen in customer expectations of relationship closeness and willingness to make adaptations to further the relationship.

Box 5.1   Young and Rubicam's Brand Asset Valuator Framework©

Young and Rubicam's corporate mission is to be an 'indispensible partner in creating profitable growth by building, leveraging, protecting and managing their brand assets both in the long and short-term – everywhere in the world.'

To provide this service the company works in 76 countries across 6 continents and provides a full portfolio of marketing communications, brand valuation and brand futures services. Within Europe, the firm had almost 5000 staff and billings of $5.9 bn in 1998, the largest for a single agency in the world.

The Brand Asset valuation studies form an ongoing part of the Young and Rubicam portfolio. The firm's brand database spans 32 countries and covers 9200 brands, 450 of which are global.

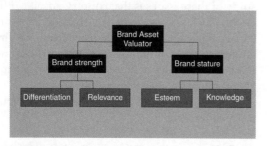

Figure 5.1   Young and Rubicam's Brand Asset Valuator. Reprinted with permission from Young and Rubicam

In Figure 5.1, the two dimensions of brand strength and brand esteem are considered separately. It is possible for a brand with a good basis of differentiation and relevance to its target audience to fail to thrive if there is insufficient esteem and knowledge. The poor performance of Marks and Spencer since 2000 is ascribed by experts to a loss in relevance of the brand. This has resulted in a loss of brand strength. A brand may also lack strength if it does not have differential advantages that are valued by its target audience as was the case with the Skoda Estelle in the 1970s. The engineering and

features of the new Skoda Octavia – in contrast – are much stronger in terms of differentiation based on solid performance at a value for money price.

In contrast, a new brand with insufficient marketing support to communicate its existence and benefits to a target audience might fail to thrive because its target market has insufficient knowledge of the brand and does not esteem it.

Young and Rubicam describe these different positions as the Brand Power Grid (Figure 5.2).

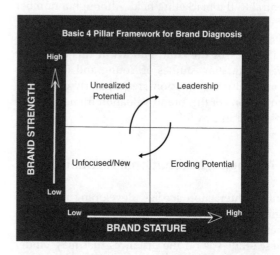

Figure 5.2   The Brand Power Grid. Reprinted with permission from Young and Rubicam

Mercedes is valued as one of the leading brands; many of the dot.com brands remain in the unfocused/new sector. Brands with unrealized potential – such as Yahoo – require better communication of the brand's strength to improve stature and those with eroding potential a re-evaluation of their relevance and the sustainability of their differential advantage.

Source: Reprinted with permission from Young and Rubicam.

■ **Differences in chosen organizational structure.** Chapter 7 discusses more fully the choice of organizational type to serve different international markets. In addition to investment,

control and other economic implications of the chosen organizational type, interaction suggests that the firm's choices impact on the nature of co-operation and interaction. A firm using an agent to enter a market may not, for example, develop close relationships with its customers as it does not have direct contact. Social exchange and trust are important in relationship development and these processes may not take place with customers if marketing effort is channelled via an intermediary.

Despite the differences, relationship development shows some common features across markets:

- A high level of commitment
- The need for counterparts to adapt to each other
- The importance of the technical dimension: understanding each other's products/services and processes
- The existence of transaction, or relationship costs.

These characteristics reinforce the findings of the original interaction model (Ford 1980; Håkansson 1982) and result in the conclusion that international marketing strategy, from an interaction perspective, can be defined as *the process of adding value by building long-term, stable international relationships*.

Many of these characteristics would also be included in a definition of international marketing strategy from a relationship marketing perspective. Gummesson (1999) identifies four fundamental values of relationship marketing:

- Long-term collaboration
- Win–win relationships
- All parties should be active
- Importance of relationship and service values, not bureaucratic/legal values.

It is important to note that this focus would be adopted in all markets, not only business-to-business markets.

The principal differences in creating successful relationship strategies in international markets, then, relate to understanding the extent to which the different national contexts impact on relationships (see Chapters 2, 3 and 4). It is also important to review the relationship implications of the type of international organization (see Chapter 7), the process of international expansion (Chapter 8) and marketing mix issues such as price and promotional decisions (Chapters 9 and 10).

THE NETWORK PERSPECTIVE

International marketing strategy, from a network perspective, is the process of building positions in international networks. The concept of a network position comprises a two key elements:

- **Mutual control of resources.** The network approach assumes that firms do not have total control over their resources but are mutually interdependent with other firms via their relationships. If two firms collaborate to develop a new technology, for example, neither can make the decision to invest further or enter a new market without consulting the other.
- **Both direct and indirect relationships play a role.** For example, if two firms supply components to the same automotive manufacturer and one develops a cost saving new technology, the customer may demand that the second firm also reduces the costs of its components. Seyed-Mohamed and Bolte (1992, p. 215) express this as follows:

> The position of a firm, in a network, is directly dependent upon its relationship with counterparts, but indirectly dependent upon the counterpart's relationships with others.

The process of building network position involves relationships at macro-level, relationships between organizations (inter-organizational) and relationships within the organization (intra-organizational level) (Nohria 1992; Lee 1993, Blankenburg 1995). The strategic issues of relationships at each of these levels are neatly summarized by Lee (1993) (see Figure 5.3).

Lee's framework is now used to discuss the issues at each of these levels.

Macro-Level Network Relationships

The features of the macro-level network are described more fully in the Network section of this book. The network view is that 'full-faced' relationships can be developed in the macro-environment. An implication of international

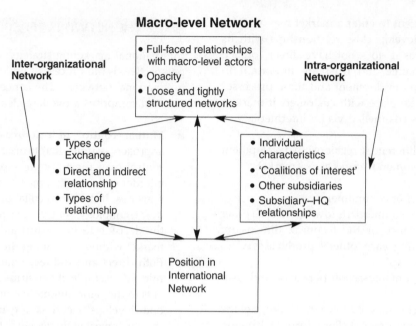

Figure 5.3   Building positions in international markets

marketing strategy, then, is that marketers should inform themselves about the nature and interests of these actors. It should be noted that network theory does not prescribe lobbying or other attempts to build macro-level relationships as suggested both by Kotler's mega-marketing (1986) or even the communication and relationship building of Gummesson's mega relationship marketing (1999). Rather, from a markets as networks perspective, the firm is directly and indirectly connected to a web of macro-level actors. As a result, both macro-level actors and those with whom they have relationships will influence a firm. Box 4.2 describes the impacts rippling out from the epicentre of the Pergau Dam incident in Malaysia to a web of other British firms in related sectors.

Inter-Organizational Network Relationships

Types of Exchange

In his seminal article, Thorelli (1986) highlights the flow of power, information, money and utilities within the network. He stresses that flows of goods and money may be less important than those of information and power. Mattsson (1984) also distinguishes between technical, knowledge, economic or social exchanges.

From both of these network descriptions, it is clear that networks involve exchanges of different types. At different times a relationship may involve some, or all, of these types of exchange. Some authors argue that while economic exchange is the underlying motivation behind business networks, non-economic factors such as information or social exchanges, may play a valuable role in strengthening relationships (Thorelli 1986; Håkansson 1992).

It may be noted that this may especially apply to international marketing. If firms face macro-environmental and other uncertainties in international markets, then flows of information in networks may be invaluable in increasing knowledge of other markets. Social exchanges are an important means of building trust. As discussed in Chapter 2 on Cultural Environment however, cultural and other distances may hinder the development of trust in international relationships.

Types of Relationship

A number of different types of relationship have been identified. These can be classified by whom they are with – for example, channel relationships, buyer–supplier links, other stakeholders. Also, relationships can be classified, as here, by their competitive or co-operative nature.

Competitive relationships have been the focus of a number of studies. An important contribution to understanding these from a network perspective lies in the realization that there is not a simple connection between traditional strategy and competition and networks and co-operation. In fact, each perspective identifies a spectrum of behaviour from zero-sum to win–win.

Easton (1990) identifies five types of relationships between competitors:

1. **Conflict**, in which a firm can attain a goal only at the other's expense
2. **Competition**, where firms strive to attain the same goal
3. **Co-existence**, where firms have goals which are not linked
4. **Co-operation**, where firms work together to achieve the same goal
5. **Collusion**, where firms co-operate at the expense of a third party.

Interesting insights into the interplay between these are gained from the network perspective. Consider, for example, the situation in the accountancy industry in the later 1980s (Box 5.2).

This example shows the complex interplay of competitive and co-operative forces existing between two actors. As a final note, the two firms were later subject to speculation of a merger. Had this occurred as part of the same organization, two previous competitors would have become co-operators with a high level of mutual interdependence.

In summary, Box 5.2 shows a complex interweaving of co-operative and competitive relationships. Moreover, the dominant force in a relationship may change over time.

Network Structures

The number of relationships, their 'quality' or intensity, and their 'type' or closeness to the core activities of the firm, are defined by Thorelli (1986) as determining whether a network is *tight* or *loose* in its structure. In the Regional section of this book (Part V), examples of tightly structured and loosely structured networks are provided.

Tightly structured networks have a stable membership and actors are clear as to the rules and objectives of doing business. Loosely structured networks, in contrast, have changing membership

---

Box 5.2   The 'Big Six' Accounting Firms in Eastern Europe

The late 1980s saw a number of mega-mergers between the global players in the accounting and financial services sector. By late 1989, the global industry had shaken out to a 'Big Six' firms: Coopers and Lybrand, Arthur Andersen, Price Waterhouse, Ernst and Young, KPMG and Deloitte, Ross, Tohmatsu.

On the liberalization of Eastern Europe, these already internationally diversified companies were early entrants into the region. A primary motivation was the entry of major multinational customers, although the firms were also influenced by the availability of contracts funded by regulatory sector agencies, such as the World Bank, IMF and EU among others.

Focusing on the relationship between two of the 'Big Six' accountants, referred to here as firms *A* and *B*, in Eastern Europe, we see first that the two are *competitors* seeking profits from a finite set of international customers and regulatory agencies. For the purposes of some regulatory sector contracts, the two must work together. In these contracts, the two firms *collaborate*. Indeed, the two firms have different specialisms and in pursuing these may *co-exist*. Both can prosper with the same customers and this is not at the expense of the other. Both firms also have a local partner with whom they *collaborate* to gain local knowledge. This enhances the ability of each firm to *compete*.

and rules and procedures may be evolving. Structuring clearly plays a role in determining the international marketing strategies that are appropriate. Tightly structured networks may be associated with advanced industrial economies, such as the USA (see the work of Kinch, 1992, in Chapter 11). Rather than being associated with levels of economic development in markets, however, tight structures may relate to the lifecycle stage of the industry. The market for Digital Video Discs (DVDs) is still in the introductory, or perhaps early growth phase. The structure of networks in this industry may still be rapidly evolving, as new technologies, new entrants and new industry standards emerge. The market for automobiles is mature, with a small number of established players globally. The identity and positioning of the players, the rules and procedures may be more stable as a result.

Intra-Firm Relationships

Intra-firm relationships are the subject of Chapter 16 of this book, International Marketing Organization. In terms of international marketing strategy, it should be noted that relationships within the firm may be as influential as other types of relationships in determining network positions.

The role of individuals with particular characteristics and experience is identified both in Chapter 1 on Theoretical Background and in Chapter 2 on Cultural Environment, as vitally important in developing social relationships and trust. Individuals might, for example, perceive different levels of cultural distance in a market, depending on the extent to which they have worked or travelled abroad.

Internal marketing literature (Gronroos 1990; Varey 1995) focuses on the importance of shared goals and communication within companies. Some of these concepts are shared by network literature. In the words of Gummesson (1999): 'If a company does not consider the links between all functions, there will be "broken chains", which are one of the "invisible competitors."'

Network literature identifies the existence of relationships between individuals within and between organizations. These may play a valuable role in building relationships, but internal politics,

the goals of different profit centres or subsidiaries and headquarter–subsidiary tensions may all create obstacles to relationship development.

Building Positions in International Markets

Macro-, inter- and intra-organizational relationships all play a role in building network positions. Positions have been defined as a 'location of power to create and/or influence networks.' Positions are seen to be important for the development of the firm. A key implication of the network perspective is that the firm must invest in developing its position in the network:

> On entering a network the new member faces the strategic challenge of positioning himself among the pre-existing members of the network...The established members may have to do some repositioning to accommodate the new member...positioning of the firm in the network becomes a matter of as great strategic significance as positioning its product in the marketplace. (Thorelli 1986, p. 42)

While this might not immediately seem apparent, it may be easire to build a position in a tightly rather than loosely structured market. Although competition may be intense in stable, tightly structured nets, the players and their positions are clearly defined. If customers have dissatisfaction with the product or service offering of these players, it may be relatively easy to identify value creating new positions. Entry into loosely structured nets may be complicated by opacity, changing composition and uncertainty about which positions will be appropriate in the longer-term. These issues are discussed more fully in relation to emerging mega-markets in Chapter 14.

Positions can be built by investments in both internal development and within the external market. Mattsson (1989) refers to these as Marketing and Market investments respectively. In making investment decisions, firms may be influenced by others with whom they are directly and indirectly linked. This interdependency is shown diagrammatically by Johanson and Vahlne (1990) to illustrate the issue of entering a new international market (see Figure 5.4).

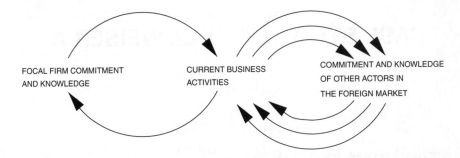

Figure 5.4   Firm interdependency
Source: Johanson and Vahlne (1990). Reprinted with permission from *International Marketing Review*, MCB Press.

Håkansson and Snehota (1989) also identify the imperative of studying the firm in relation to other firms in their article 'No Business is an Island', concluding that, from a network perspective, the strategy and identity of an organization are created in interaction with its major counterparts.

CASE STUDY 5.1   BUDWEISER A

Background to the Dispute

Use of the *Budweiser* name in connection with beer dates back to as early as 1531. In that year, the German king Ferdinand, whose royal court was in the town of Ceske Budejovice (then called Budweis), gave the city the right to brew beer for his court. This beer was identified as *Budweiser*, literally meaning beer 'from the town of Budweis'. *Budweiser* beer became known as the 'Beer of Kings' owing to its link with Ferdinand's court.[1]

Several centuries later, in the mid-1860s, a German immigrant named Adolphus Busch established a small brewery in St Louis, USA called the Bavarian Brewery. In 1876, in searching for a name for a new beer which would appeal to the many German immigrants living in and around St Louis, Busch appropriated the name '*Budweiser*' from the beer long-produced in the Bohemian town of Budweis. Busch also borrowed upon the old slogan of the *Budweiser* beer, 'Beer of Kings', but inverted it, calling American *Budweiser* the 'King of Beers'.[2] In 1879 Busch's brewery merged with another brewery and changed its name to Anheuser-Busch (AB).

Two decades later, in 1895, a group of Czech investors founded Budejovicky Budvar (also called Budweiser Budvar) and also laid claim to the name *Budweiser*. The Czechs cited the historical precedent for using the name, dating back to the early sixteenth century. Moreover, they claimed the right to the name as it properly identified the origin of their beer.

1911 Agreement

As Budvar and Anheuser-Busch grew, it was inevitable that they would eventually run into conflict over use of the *Budweiser* name. By the early twentieth century, the two breweries were warring over the right to the *Budweiser* name. In 1911, the two breweries came together and signed an agreement which they hoped would end the dispute. The agreement recognized AB's right to the name *Budweiser*, as it was a registered trademark of AB in the USA. However, the agreement also acknowledged Budvar's legal right to the *Budweiser* name. AB was thus given the right to *Budweiser* in the USA and all other non-European countries. AB could use the *Budweiser* name in any way they chose, however, they had to stop using the words 'original' in combination with their product, in order to avoid giving the impression to the consumer that their product was the first beer to be known as *Budweiser*.

In exchange, Budvar was given the exclusive right to use the *Budweiser* name in the European market. In addition, recognizing that *Budweiser* was the name which identified the origin of their product, Budvar could still market its beer as *Budweiser* in *any* country of the world, including the USA.[3]

Over the next several decades, AB grew from a provincial brewery to the largest brewery in the world. Perhaps predictably, AB began to chafe under the 1911 agreement, which allowed Budvar to sell as *Budweiser* in AB's home market.

1939 Agreement

By the late 1930s, Budvar was selling significant quantities of Czech *Budweiser* in the USA. AB clearly felt that Budvar was overstepping its bounds in AB's home market. AB charged that the US public associated the *Budweiser* and *Bud* names with AB products. Since Budvar was exporting its beer to the USA under the name *Budweiser*, Budvar was confusing the customer, and unfairly using the brand name that AB had built.[4]

AB went to Budvar with an agreement which blocked Budvar's access to the North American market. In the settlement proposed by AB, Budvar agreed to surrender all rights to the *Budweiser*, *Budweis* and *Bud* names, and all other names containing 'Bud', in all territories north of Panama, as well as all US colonies and territories. In addition, Budvar could not market other beer brands in these market using the word 'manufactured in Budweis'. Instead, they had to use the words 'manufactured in Ceske Budejovice.' In return, AB agreed to pay $50 000, to Budvar and $15 000 to Budvar's American distributor, provided Budvar's *Budweiser* was removed from the North American markets within six months.[5]

Although the agreement seemed rather slanted against Budvar, AB managed to convince Budvar to sign it. The conditions under which Budvar agreed to sign the agreement are not altogether clear, but what is known is that the agreement was signed several days before the Nazis invaded what remained of Czechoslovakia in 1939. The Czechs later claimed that the 1939 agreement was signed under duress and declared it invalid.

AB's Attempt to Buy Rights to Budweiser

The period after 1939 saw the start of the second World War and then the imposition of Communism in Czechoslovakia. During this time, Budvar's exports went primarily to Western Europe and Budvar was not in any position to threaten AB. Therefore, the two restraint arrangements between Budvar and AB endured until 1970.

That year, AB was striving for further international expansion. However, the terms of the restraint agreements effectively locked them out of the countries of Western Europe, some of the most attractive beer markets in the world at that time. Attempting to settle the trademark dispute once and for all, AB offered the Communist Czechoslovak government $1 million for the European rights to the *Budweiser* trademark.[6]

Perhaps AB underestimated the degree of national pride Czechs held in their small but inter-nationally known brewer. Perhaps the ideology at the time, which viewed Americans as 'capitalist imperialists', predominated in the Czechs' decision. Whatever the motivation, the offer by AB to purchase the rights to the *Budweiser* name in Europe was categorically refused.

Legal Battles

After failing to buy the right to the *Budweiser* name in Europe, AB attempted an attack from a different angle. AB launched legal challenges to Budvar's right to the *Budweiser* name in 15 countries throughout Europe.[7] In 1984 AB won a decisive victory in its battle to enter the European market when a UK court judged that AB's *Budweiser* should be allowed to co-exist with Budvar's *Budweiser* brand. The court ruled that the co-existence should be reinforced by the two firms using their respective names in different ways.[8] In Finland and Sweden AB also succeeded in legal battles, and were able to market *Budweiser*. However, in France, Italy, Portugal and a number of other markets AB's legal offensives failed. In these markets, AB was able, however, to sell its beer under the name '*Bud*'.

The Appellation of Origin Issue

AB's legal defeat in the 1980s in a number of European countries was ultimately the result of the development of a new concept in intellectual property law called the 'appellation of origin'. An appellation of origin is a name which serves to identify the geographic origin of a product. If registered, the appellation of origin cannot be used by a producer from outside that town or region. The names Champagne, Cognac and Bordeaux are three of the best-known names which are protected appellations of origin. Over the past several decades, the appellation of origin has emerged as a strongly protected element of intellectual property in many Europeans countries, as well as in a group of non-European countries which have signed to a special multilateral convention on intellectual property called the Lisbon Agreement.[9]

Budvar had registered and uses a number of appellations of origin. Most importantly, 'Budweiser' is a registered appellation of origin, designating Budvar's beer as a product of Budweis. For the European countries which recognized the appellation of origin, it was an infringement of Budvar's rights for AB to use the name Budweiser.

In 1989, the end of communist rule of Czechoslovakia, and the formation of the independent Czech Republic seemed finally to offer potential for a solution to the ongoing dispute. In need of capital to increase production capacity and for international expansion, Budvar seemed a likely privatization prospect. AB saw investment in the company as a final solution to gaining rights to the brand name in Europe.

AB'S PERSPECTIVE ON THE TRADEMARK DISPUTE

Company Background

AB is the biggest brewer not only in America, but in the world. Its 14 brands account for approximately 45 per cent of the total US beer market, and this translates into a 9 per cent share of the total world beer sales.[10] AB's flagship brand, Budweiser is the number one selling brand in the USA, with 21.8 per cent market share. In addition, Bud Light is the best-selling light beer in America and claims an 8.2 per cent share of the total beer market. Brand extensions such as Bud Dry and Bud Light Dry account for an additional 5 per cent or so of the US market.[11]

AB produced 88.5 million barrels (104 million hectolitres) of beer in 1994.[12] This is almost four times the volume of AB's closest competitor, Heineken. But while AB certainly dominates its home market, the US beer market is quickly becoming saturated. This is not good news for AB, which still has 95 per cent of its sales in America.

The Budweiser Brand

AB stress the different brand images of the two Budweiser beers. Budvar's European-style lager is a super premium product aimed at older beer drinkers that appreciate its heavier and more robust character. Its American cousin is lighter and less alcoholic and aimed at a younger market segment.[13]

The core market for AB's Budweiser are 18 to 24-year-old blue-collar males. There is strong association between the brand and its American origins. Brand analysts describe Budweiser as the 'safe back-up buy for hosts uncertain what guests will want, but its long term positioning as the brand for everybody...clashes with the popularity of distinct tastes and marketing niches. It is sort of a victim of its own success – a brand that is institutionalized, established, difficult to move.' There is strong identification of the classic brown bottle and busy label 'Our customers say, whatever you do, don't change that'. However, such is the tradition that Budweiser may be viewed by today's youngsters as 'Dad's beer'.[14]

Budweiser has a dominant 44 per cent share of the US market. The brand has declined over the past five years because of recession, higher taxes and a price war in California. Rival brands Coors and Miller High Life have faced dramatic loss of brand share. Anheuser-Busch's Bob Lachky comments 'We are not overly concerned at Bud's leakage...The 'family' is up 4 per cent and flagship brands Budweiser and Bud Light are outperforming competitors'.[15] Still, AB's move from long-standing agency D'Arcy Masius Benton and Bowles to DDB Needham suggests concern that the brand image needs refreshing.

Philip Kotler questions Budweiser's sponsorship of concert tours by the Rolling Stones as the group is less popular with younger drinkers than with their parents. He sees the beer market as depending on a continual inflow of drinkers in their early 20s. More in line with the interests of this age group is Budweiser's sponsorship of basketball. The interests of the younger age group are also targeted by an extension of the brand into the clothing market with the launch of a jeans and clothing range in February 1997:

The US Beer Market

The US beer market had undergone an upheaval recently. For the past 10 years, the size of the market has been relatively flat, with a small decline in the total market in 1992 and 1993. At the same time, established beer brands have been under attack from all sides. Imports have risen significantly and now comprise almost 5 per cent of the market. The regional and microbrewing segment of the market is also becoming a significant force, claiming 4.6 per cent of the market in 1994.[16] In addition, niche products like ice beer, dry beer and red beer, and a host of new non-alcoholic beverages, are all growing at the expense of large, established beer brands. Sales of *Budweiser* actually declined 16 per cent in volume terms from 1991 to 1993, from 50 million barrels to 42 million barrels. At the same time, however, sales of *Bud Light* rose 49 per cent from 10.6 million barrels to 15.8 million barrels.[17]

AB has employed several strategies to deal with the current situation in the domestic market. First, it has pursued new, innovative products. This has led to the launch of its own ice beer and dry beer products. However, innovation in the brewing industry can go only so far. AB has therefore also begun to acquire equity stakes in microbreweries and regional breweries to tap into the surge in consumer interest for these beers. Finally, and most importantly, AB has begun to focus intensively on new markets abroad.[18]

AB's International Sales

AB first launched itself seriously onto the international scene in 1981, with the formation of its international division. Since 1981, international sales have climbed from a paltry 900 000 barrels to 4.5 million barrels in 1994.[19] This growth in sales was achieved through a combination of exporting, licensing and contracting out production of AB's beer. While AB does sell some *Michelob* and *Busch* brands of beer abroad, *Budweiser* is its primary international brand. Interestingly, while domestically *Budweiser* is positioned as a mainstream, and to some extent working man's beer, internationally *Budweiser* is positioned as a premium product with a premium price attached.

Figure 5.5 charts AB's growth in international sales from 1981 to 1994. While AB initially concentrated on developing a foothold in established beer markets like Canada and Europe, AB now sees greater profits in equity stakes and acquisitions in developing markets.[20] This has led AB to aggressively pursue partnerships in China, other Asian markets and in Latin America. In the past five years AB has concluded an 80 per cent stake in a joint venture with Kirin brewery in Japan, an 80 per cent interest in a joint venture with the Zhongde brewery in Wuhan China, a 5 per cent

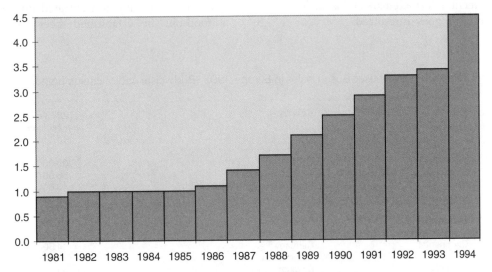

Figure 5.5   Anheuser-Busch, international sales[1], 1981–94 (million barrels)
Note: International sales include export, contract- and licence-brewing volume
Source: Anheuser-Busch, public relations materials

stake in the Chinese Tsingtao Brewery and a partnership with a brewery in India, to name only a few of its international deals.[21]

AB's Activities in Europe

While AB appears to be focused on the fast-growing beer markets of the developing world, it has not put Europe on the back burner. Table 5.1 shows AB's European sales of the *Budweiser* and *Michelob* brands in 1993.

Despite significant sales volumes in Europe, AB's marketing is seriously constrained by the trademark dispute with Budvar. AB can sell under the *Budweiser* name in Cyprus, Denmark, Finland, Iceland, Ireland, Malta, Sweden and the UK, having won law suits against Budvar in these countries.

However, AB is restricted to using the *Bud* name in Belgium, France, Greece, Italy, Luxembourg, the Netherlands, Portugal, Spain and Switzerland, the Canary Islands and Gibraltar owing to the trademark dispute. Currently AB cannot sell under the name *Budweiser* or *Bud* in Germany, Austria, or Norway. Moreover, they are technically prevented from entering the newly opened beer markets of Central and Eastern Europe. AB recently began selling as *Bud* in Russia, but Budvar considers this an infringement of its trademark and is likely to sue AB if the dispute goes unresolved.

Building the Global Brand

AB's drive to globalize the *Budweiser* brand is partly influenced by what the competition is doing. While AB now has sales in approximately 65 countries,[22] it is still well behind the competition in establishing a beer that is recognized and consumed around the world. The other major international brewers have been busy far longer building an international presence. The Dutch brewer Heineken has been very active internationally since the 1920s and now sells in approximately 160 countries. Similarly, Carlsberg, currently sells in over 140 countries, and has 80 per cent of sales outside its home market of Denmark.[23] Guinness also has successfully been building a global presence in the past decade.

While industry analysts once thought that the brewing industry would remain dominated by regional and national brewing companies, Carlsberg, Heineken and Guinness have proven that beer has global branding potential. Resolution of the trademark dispute with Budvar is crucial for AB's effort to build a global beer brand out of *Budweiser*. Without unrestricted access to the European market, AB will not be able to utilise a unified branding strategy, and will not be able to freely pursue new opportunities for *Budweiser*.

While AB initially concentrated on developing a foothold in established beer markets like

Table 5.1   Anheuser-Busch, sales in Europe, 1993 (Budweiser and Michelob brands)

Region	Country	1993 AB brand volume (hl)
British Isles	UK, Ireland	700 000
Scandinavia	Finland, Sweden	56 000
	Spain, Canaries and Gibraltar	43 000
Continental	France	15 000
wine	Italy	13 500
countries	Greece	11 000
	Switzerland	9 600
Continental	Germany [a]	4 500
beer	Netherlands	4 500
countries	Belgium	1 400

Note: a. Michelob only
Source: Anheuser-Busch, *Annual Report*, 1994

Canada and Europe, AB now sees greater profits in equity stakes and acquisitions in developing markets.[24] This has led AB to aggressively pursue partnerships in China, other Asian markets and in Latin America. Since 1995 AB has concluded an 80 per cent stake in a joint venture with Kirin brewery in Japan, an 80 per cent interest in a joint venture with the Zhongde brewery in Wuhan China, a 5 per cent stake in the Chinese Tsingtao Brewery and a partnership with a brewery in India, to name only a few of its international deals.[25]

Attempts to Resolve the Trademark Dispute

The end of Communism had opened a new chapter in the relations between AB and Budvar. AB saw its golden opportunity to settle the dispute once and for all when privatization of Czech industries got under-way in 1991. AB approached Budvar, and the two firms agreed to a moratorium on legal actions, under the assumption that they would attempt to resolve the dispute. However, AB refused to discuss the trademark dispute until talks got under-way regarding the purchase of a stake in Budvar. This was the ideal opportunity to end the dispute forever.

Stephen J. Burrows, Vice President of Anheuser-Busch International, was quoted as implying that AB would employ a carrot and stick approach with Budvar. He suggested that if AB could invest in Budvar, resolution of the dispute could be quick and painless, but that if Budvar were sold to another party, settling the dispute might be far more difficult.[26] In early 1993, AB suggested a 'strategic alliance', which would ensure co-existence in the world market between Budvar's and AB's *Budweiser* brands. AB's proposal included providing Budvar access to AB's formidable marketing and distribution network and gave guarantees of continuous investment in the Budejovice brewery. AB also promised that they would not tamper with Budvar's taste, production process or ingredients. The only changes which would be necessary, according to AB were 'appropriate name and label modifications to avoid confusion wherever necessary.'[27]

Full-Scale Public Relations Campaign

AB recognized that their proposal would be greeted with suspicion by the Czech public. In early 1993 AB started a massive public relations campaign explaining why they wanted to buy a stake in Budvar. AB took out full-page advertisements in several national daily newspapers discussing their intentions and giving promises to maintain the distinctive quality of the beer and the centuries-old brewing traditions.

AB also spent over $1 million to build the 'St Louis Cultural Centre' in Ceske Budejovice. The centre offers English language classes and a library, and sponsors events. Some residents of Ceske Budejovice believe the centre serves as a thinly veiled public relations arm for AB in Budvar's home-town, and the centre has been compared to a Trojan horse.[28]

Despite its extensive public relations campaign, the Czech government made it clear that AB would need to follow the normal procedures of the Czech privatization process, and would not receive special treatment. AB would need to put in its bid along with any other interested parties when, and if, the government decided that a stake in Budvar should be sold to a foreign investor.

International Attention to AB's Bid

The ongoing controversy over the right to the *Budweiser* name and the possibility of Budejovicky Budvar being acquired by AB received considerable international attention. The British pressure group Campaign for Real Ale (CAMRA) took an interest in the Budvar case. CAMRA, which boasts 37 000 members in the UK, has been active in trying to stem the growing number of acquisitions of small local breweries by large multinationals. CAMRA believes that consolidation in the brewing industry is resulting in the loss of the distinctive character and quality of small brewers. CAMRA was thus a natural advocate for Budvar.

When CAMRA President Iain Dobson found out about the possible acquisition by AB of a stake in Budvar he flew to the Czech Republic to meet with Budvar management. Dobson reportedly warned the management, 'Budvar is about

300 times smaller than Anheuser-Busch, but right now it represents a problem for Anheuser-Busch's international marketing plans. As soon as you offer an initial 30 per cent share, Anheuser-Busch will swallow you, regardless of your tradition.'[29]

Back to the Negotiating Table

The government's indecision over the Budvar privatization situation endured until July 1995, when the Prime Minister suddenly announced publicly that privatization would definitely not proceed until the trademark dispute with AB was resolved. AB had little choice but to agree to meet Budvar for a fresh attempt at negotiations to resolve the trademark dispute.

AB's final offer included a 10-year agreement to purchase of Czech hops worth $76 million and a down payment of $20 million on the future purchase of shares in Budvar by AB. But Budvar General Manager, Jiri Bocek, was concerned that the final offer

> would [leave] his company playing second fiddle to US Budweiser in European markets...Mr Bocek said the offer was unacceptable to Budvar and the government. 'I believe the decision was rational and based on pragmatic considerations. Budvar is capable of developing itself without becoming a vassal of Anheuser-Busch'.[30]

Budvar's uncertain future was hindering other privatizations. Bass of the UK, Denmark's Carls-

berg and AB were bidding for a minority stake in Jihoceske Pivovary (South Bohemian Breweries), a regional Czech brewery. As there was a simultaneous plan to merge SBB with Budvar, this plan was suspended by the Czech government until the outcome of the SBB privatization was clear: 'If SBB selected Anheuser-Busch, any merger with Budvar would be abandoned.[31] Finally, in September 1996, AB pulled out of the talks when the Czech government finally decided to privatize Budvar, but indicated that it would remain in domestic hands.[32]

AB recently won court rulings allowing it to use the *Budweiser* name in Spain, and the *Bud* name in Norway. It has had nine wins in European countries – five in the past year – and has 27 underway.[33] AB believes that it has achieved 'undisputed access' to Europe, with sales of 2.2 hectolitres of beer in Europe, an increase of 25 per cent. However, each legal battle involves both time and expense and hinders its expansion strategy. AB recently pulled out of a $145 million Vietnamese brewing joint venture because *Budvar* registered the name there in 1960.

QUESTIONS

1. What are the advantages and potential dangers to Anheuser-Busch of developing a global brand?
2. What potential dangers for the Budweiser brand are posed by the trademark dispute with Budejovicky Budvar?

SUMMARY

In Chapter 5 we assessed the advantages and disadvantages of standardized international marketing strategies. We explored the issues involved in managing international relationships. We examined the challenges of building positions in international markets.

NOTES

1. Masek, I. 'Jiri Bocek: Anheuser-Busch je pouze jednim ze zajemcu!', *Magazin Uspech*, September, 1993, p. 19
2. Masek, 'Jiri Bocek', p. 19.
3. Original mutual restraint agreement between Budvar and Anheuser-Busch, 19 August 1911.
4. Original mutual restraint agreement between Budvar and AB, 7 March 1939.
5. 1939 mutual restraint agreement.
6. Masek, 'Jiri Bocek', p. 19.

7. Masek, 'Jiri Bocek', p. 20.
8. Gever, F., Trademark attorney, 'Conflict between appellation of origin and trademark, preliminary answers', June 1995.
9. A very prominent legal case involving appellations of origin concerned the champagne-makers of the Champagne region of France. French champagne-makers were able to force producers from outside the Champagne region to cease calling their product 'Champagne', as this word had been a registered appellation of origin and served to identify the origin of the product. Producers outside the Champagne region must now call their product 'sparkling wine'.
10. Anheuser-Busch, *Annual Report*, 1994.
11. Tenowitz, I. 'Bud Tops Turnaround of Premium-Priced Beers', *Advertising Age*, 28 September 1994, p. 13.
12. Anheuser-Busch, *Annual Report*, 1994.
13. Masek, I., 'Jiri Bocek', p. 20.
14. Gibson, R. and Charlier, M., 'Corporate Focus: Fresher Bud Image Requires Light Touch', *Wall Street Journal*, November 25, 1994, p. 1.
15. Gibson and Charles 'Corporate Focus'.
16. Gibson and Charles 'Corporate Focus'.
17. Lubove, S. 'Get 'Em before they Get You', *Forbes*, July 31, 1995, p. 93; 1 barrel = 1.18 hectolitres.
18. Anheuser-Busch, *Annual Reports*, 1993 and 1994.
19. Anheuser-Busch, *Public Relations Materials*, July 1995.
20. Anheuser-Busch, *Annual Report*, 1994.
21. Anheuser-Busch, *Public Relations Materials*, July 1995.
22. Anheuser-Busch, *Public Relations Materials*, July 1995.
23. Guttman, R. J., 'Danish Business Goes Global', *Europe*, 17 May 1995, p. 10.
24. Anheuser-Busch, *Annual Report*, 1994.
25. Anheuser-Busch, *Public Relations Materials*, July 1995.
26. Guyon, J. 'Row Over Budweiser Brand Name Highlights the Value of Brands', *Wall Street Journal Europe*, September 16, 1993, p. no. unknown.
27. Newton, J. S., 'Stalking Budvar, Disregarding Heritage', *Prognosis*, 14–27 May, 1993, p. 11.
28. Newton, 'Stalking Budvar'.
29. Masek, I., 'Jiri Bocek', p. 23.
30. Boland, V., 'Companies and Finance: International: Budvar takes lid off US Rival's Offer', *Financial Times*, 20 December.
31. Boland, V., 'International Company News: Brewing Bid Battle May affect Budvar', *Financial Times*, 5 March.
32. Boland, V., 'Back Page – First Section: Anheuser-Busch pulls out of Budweiser Name Talks', *Financial Times*, 23 September.
33. Boland, V. and Oram O., 'Companies and Finance: Europe: US Brewer leaves Budvar Fighting for Identity: Czech Group Faces Marketing Challenge after Collapse of Brand Right Talks with Anheuser-Busch', *Financial Times*, 1 November.

BIBLIOGRAPHY

Aaker, D. (1998) 'Measuring Brand Equity Across Products and Markets', *California Management Review*.

Blankenburg, D. (1995) 'A Network Approach to Foreign Market Entry', in Möller, K. and Wilson, D. (eds) *Business Marketing: An Interaction and Network Perspective*, Kluwer Academic, pp. 375–410

Buzzell, R. D. (1968) 'Can you Standardize Multinational Marketing?', *Harvard Business Review*, November–December: 102–13.

Douglas, S. and Wind, Y. (1987) 'The Myth of Globalization', *Columbia Journal of World Business*, Winter: 19–29.

Doyle, P. (1994) 'Marketing in the New Millennium', *European Journal of Marketing*.

Doyle, P. (2000) 'Valuing Marketing's Contribution', *European Management Journal*, 18, 3: 232–45.

Easton, G. (1990) 'Relationships Among Competitors', in Day, G. F. and Wensley, J. R. (eds), *The Interface of Marketing and Strategy: Strategic Management, Policy and Planning*, 4, JAI Press.

Evans, P. B. and Wurster, T. S. (1997) 'Strategy and the New Economics of Information', *Harvard Business Review*, September–October: 71–82.

Ford, D. (1980) 'The Development of Buyer–Seller Relations in Industrial Markets', *European Journal of Marketing*, 14, 5–6: 339–53.

Ford, D. (1984) 'Buyer–Seller Relationships in International Industrial Marketing', *Industrial Marketing Management*, 13, 2: 101–13.

Grönroos, C. (1990) *Service Management and Marketing*, Macmillan and Lexington Books.

Gummesson, E. (1999) *Total Relationship Marketing: Rethinking Marketing Management: From 4Ps to 30Rs*, Butterworth–Heinemann.

Håkansson, H. (1982) *Industrial Marketing and Purchasing of Industrial Goods: An Interaction Approach*, Croom Helm.

Håkansson, H. (1992) 'Evolution Processes in Industrial Networks', in Axelsson, B. and Easton, G. (eds), *Industrial Networks: A New View of Reality*, Routledge: 129–42.

Håkansson, H. and Snehota, I. (1989) 'No Business is an Island: The Network Concept of Business Strategy', *Scandinavian Journal of Management*, 4, 3: 187–200.

Hamel, G. and Prahalad, C. K. (1985) 'Do you really have a Global Strategy?', *Harvard Business Review*, July–August: 139–48.

Hout, T., Porter, M. E. and Rudden, E. (1982) 'How Global Companies Win Out', *Harvard Business Review*, September–October: 98–108.

Jarillo, J.-C. (1988) 'On Strategic Networks', *Strategic Management Review*, 11: 479–99.

Johanson, J. and Vahlne, J.-E. (1990) 'The Mechanism of Internationalization', *International Marketing Review*, 7, 4: 11–24.

Kinch, N. (1992) 'Entering a Tightly Structured Network – Strategic Visions or Network Realities?', in Forsgren, M. and Johanson, J. (eds), *Managing Networks in International Business*, Gordon & Breach: 194–214.

Kotler, P. (1986) 'Mega-Marketing', *Harvard Business Review*, March–April: 117–24.

Lee, J.-W. (1993) 'The Development of Strategic Position in the Korean Industrial Turbines Market', *Uppsala Working Paper Series*, 1993/8.

Levitt, T. (1983) 'The Globalization of Markets', *Harvard Business Review*, May–June: 92–102.

Lorenz, C. (1985) 'The Birth of a Transnational', *The McKinsey Quarterly*, Autumn: 72–93.

Mattsson, L.-G. (1984) 'An Application of a Network Approach to Marketing: Defending and Changing Market Positions', in Dholakia, N. and Arndt, J. (eds), *Changing the Course of Marketing. Alternative Paradigms for Widening Marketing Theory*, JAI Press.

Mattsson, L.-G. (1989) 'Development of Firms in Networks: Positions and Investments', in Cavusgil, S. T. (ed.), *Advances in International Marketing*, 3 JAI Press: 121–39.

McGee, J. (1999) *Working paper*, University of Cadiz, Spain.

Nohria, N. (1992) 'Is a Network Perspective a Useful Way of Studying Organisations', in Nohria, N. and Eccles, R. G. (eds), *Networks and Organizations*, Harvard Business School Press: 1–22.

Normann, R. and Ramirez, R. (1993) 'From Value Chain to Value Constellation: Designing Inter-

active Strategy', *Harvard Business Review*, July–August: 65–77.

Ohmae, K. (1985) *The Borderless World*, Collins.

Ohmae, K. (1989) 'Managing in a Borderless World', *Harvard Business Review*, May–June.

Perrier, R. (1997) (ed.) *Brand Valuation*, London, Interbrand and Premier Books.

Porter, M. E. (1980) *Competitive Strategy: Techniques for Analysing Industries and Competitors*, Free Press and Macmillan.

Porter, M. E. (1985) *Competitive Advantage: Creating and Sustaining Superior Performance*, Free Press and Macmillan.

Porter, M. E. (1990) *Competitive Advantage of Nations*, Macmillan.

Porter, M. E. (ed.) (1986) *Competition in Global Industries*, Harvard Business School Press.

Quelch, J. A. and Hoff, E. J. (1986) 'Customising Global Marketing', *Harvard Business Review*, May–June: 59–68.

Riesenbeck, H. and Freeling, A. (1991) 'How Global are Global Brands?', *The McKinsey Quarterly*, 4: 3–18.

Seyed-Mohamed, N. and Bolte, M. (1995) 'Taking a Position in a Structured Business Network', in Forsgren, M. and Johanson, J. (eds), *Managing Networks in International Business*, Gordon & Breach.

Thorelli, H. B. (1986) 'Networks: Between Markets and Hierarchies', *Strategic Management Journal*, 7: 37–51.

Toffler, A. (1970) *Future Shock*, Bantam Books.

Turnbull, P. W. (1979) 'Roles of Personal Contacts in Industrial Export Marketing', *Scandinavian Journal of Management*, 16, 5: 325–37.

Turnbull, P. W. and Valla, J.-P. (ed.) (1986) *Strategies for International Industrial Marketing*, Routledge.

Varey, R. J. (1995) 'Internal Marketing: A Review and Some Inter-disciplinary Research Challenges', *Service Industry Management*, 6, 1.

Williamson, O. E. (1975) *Between Markets and Hierarchies: Analysis and Antitrust Implications*, Macmillan.

Yip, G. (1989) 'Global Strategy...In a World of Nations?', *Sloan Management Review*, Fall: 29–41.

6

ASSESSING MARKET ATTRACTIVENESS

Objectives

The issues to be addressed in Chapter 6 include:

1. The nature and value of risk indicators, Delphi models and matrices for assessing market attractiveness
2. The applicability of these tools to the current turbulent international marketing environment
3. The use of scenario planning to consider a range of possible futures
4. The role of knowledge and learning in understanding international markets
5. Operation of the knowledge economy.

After reading Chapter 6 you will be able to:

1. Apply risk assessment techniques and understand their limitations
2. Use scenario planning to understand a range of possible futures in international markets
3. Assess the impact of knowledge and learning in international marketing
4. Identify the challenges of operation in a knowledge economy.

INTRODUCTION

Traditional tools for assessing market attractiveness, such as risk indicators, Delphi models and matrices, have been subject to a number of criticisms. They may only offer a snapshot at one point in time (matrices and Delphi models), they may be simplistic, or be open to criticism over the variables used to measure attractiveness and risk. More fundamentally, these techniques assume we can say something about the future based on what has happened in the past. This assumption may not be true in the current rapidly changing market conditions – known as *discontinuous change*. If the future is uncertain, can history help us predict what might happen? Alternative techniques that consider attractiveness have been proposed as more appropriate tools for market planning in the new millennium. One such technique, *scenario planning*, is explored in this chapter.

From a relationship perspective, one of the important debates is that over the type of knowledge needed to overcome uncertainty in international markets. Opinions vary between those arguing for direct, market-specific international experience and those who believe that this knowledge can be acquired from new staff or previous experiences. Interaction literature argues that information and knowledge can be exchanged in relationships. This chapter looks at the types of relationships and types of information that may be exchanged. The network perspective shows that the flows of knowledge may be complex and involve direct, as well as indirect relationships of the firm.

THE TRADITIONAL PERSPECTIVE

Uncertainty and Risk

When assessing market attractiveness, an important distinction is that between *uncertainty* and *risk*.

Uncertainty arises because we cannot know everything:

> We do not perceive the present as it is, and in its totality, nor do we infer the future from the present with any high degree of dependability, nor yet do we accurately know the consequences of our actions. In addition...we do not execute our actions in the precise form in which they are imagined and willed. (Knight 1921, 203)

In a marketing sense, uncertainties stem from not anticipating changes in the macro- or competitive context or not predicting the consequences these might have for the firm. It is uncertain what the future may hold for transitional economies: will they move forward to market economies or revert to central planning? It is uncertain whether the Euro will hold its value against other currencies. It is unclear what impact Vladimir Putin will have on Russia's market reforms. It is uncertain to what extent the East Asian Crisis will have an impact on new entrants into the region.

Risk is the measurable consequence for the firm of this uncertainty.

If international market environments are uncertain, then a firm takes a certain risk if it makes an investment. The risk, in this case, is the financial cost of the investment and other expenses such as training, facilities, etc. that the firm incurs.

In operating internationally, firms must overcome high levels of uncertainty. Mascarenhas (1982) indicates that there are higher levels of uncertainty in international markets than in domestic operation:

> If the domestic business environment can be labelled uncertain, the international business environment is doubly so. In going overseas, firms face, in addition to domestic sources of uncertainty, foreign exchange and political risk. Unfamiliarity with operating in a new environment, aggravated by labour restrictions, different cultures and infrastructural difficulties contributes to the uncertainty of the international environment.

Chapters 2, 3 and 4 of this book explore the different types of uncertainty that may affect firms in international markets.

Within the literature, most attention has been paid to macro-level environmental uncertainty.

There is also a tendency to concentrate on particular types of uncertainty, such as political uncertainty (Smith 1971; Rummel and Heenan 1978) or psychic distance (Klein and Roth 1990). However, Miller (1992) sees limited value in research, which stresses the impact on firms of one, or a limited subset, of the influences in the international environment. He feels that these studied may overlook important causes of risk.

The literature proposes a number of frameworks that provide a more comprehensive overview of uncertainty. While a broad range of variables are proposed, these tend to be classified into categories. A recurrent classification is that which distinguishes between the external macro-level of market influences and strategic considerations, which emphasize the role of managerial discretion. Pettigrew (1985a, 1985b) refers to these as the 'outer' and 'inner' context of the firm. One of the most comprehensive classifications of 'uncertainty' comes from Miller's work (1992) (see Table 6.1).

Risk Assessment Techniques

A variety of methods have been proposed to assess the risks of international operation. These range in complexity from observation, entering the market and seeing what happens, through to quantification via Delphi techniques and multivariate analyses.

Risk analysis may have a range of different aims. It may be designed to measure the attractiveness of potential new international markets, assess the risks of investment or quantify the potential impacts for the firms of various environmental uncertainties. It may also take a variety of approaches to these tasks. The advantages and disadvantages of three of the more commonly used international marketing planning techniques are now discussed.

Risk Indices

Published risk indicators, such as those from Business Environment Risk Indicators (BERI) or The Economic Intelligence Unit (EIU), allow firms to use reliable and objective data, based on expert opinions. These indices tend to select a range of

Table 6.1   Classifications of 'uncertainty'

Environmental uncertainties	Industry uncertainties	Firm uncertainties
Political War Revolution Coup d'état Other political turmoil	**Input Market** Quality uncertainty Shifts in market supply Changes in quantity used	**Operating Uncertainties** Labour uncertainties Labour unrest Employee safety Input supply uncertainties Raw materials shortages

Governmental Policy
Fiscal and monetary
Price controls
Trade restrictions
Price controls
Nationalization
Trade restrictions
Government regulation
Barriers to earnings
  repatriation
Inadequate provision of
  Public Services
		Product Market
		Quality changes
		Changes in consumer tastes
		Spare parts restrictions
		Availability of substitutes
		Production uncertainties
		Scarcity of complementary goods
		Machine failure

Macroeconomic Inflation Changes in relative price Exchange rates Foreign exchange rates Interest rates	**Competitive** Rivalry among competition New entrants Technology uncertainty Innovation	**Liability** Product liability Emission of foreign pollutants
R&D Terms of trade Uncertain results	**Credit** Problems with collectibles	
Social Changing social concerns Social unrest Riots Demonstrations Small-scale terrorist movements	**Natural Uncertainties** Variations in rainfall Hurricanes Earthquakes Other natural disasters	
Behavioural Managerial of employee self-interest		

Source: Miller (1992)

variables covering a range of political, economic and financial or operational aspects of the country. The variables will be weighted. Not all may be of equal importance, so some may be given a higher weighting than others. In the BERI system, weights range between 0.5 and 3. The weighting makes some variables count more strongly than others in measuring overall attractiveness.

An expert panel gives each country a score for each variable. Scoring systems vary. Again in the BERI index, scores range between 0 (unacceptable risk) and 4 (superior conditions). The score and its weight are multiplied for each variable to reach a total 'risk' score for each country. The maximum country score is 100.

Broadly speaking, a score of over 80 is very attractive and less than 50 unattractive. Other systems may use letters, A = very attractive...E = unattractive, or a range from 'hot' or attractive countries, through to 'cold' or unattractive (Litvak and Banting 1968; Goodnow and Hansz 1972).

Risk indices are updated frequently and are now commonly available on-line. As can be seen above, more sophisticated indices include a forecasting option.

One danger of risk analysis, however, is that of assigning numbers or scores. This may mask complex phenomena, as simplification of the issues is required to arrive at a score. This may lead to premature screening out of countries in which profitable opportunities exist. In contrast, though a country may score as 'attractive' it does not necessarily follow that the firm will prosper there. Stable, advanced industrial economies, which tend to score highly, may also have large numbers of existing competitors. Very uncertain emerging markets may offer boundless opportunities to firms who can find ways to overcome the uncertain environment.

Another limitation is the difficulty of incorporating 'soft' factors, such as cultural and social differences, which may be critical to success or failure of market entry. Finally, such simplistic classification does not take into account the nature of the decision, nor the characteristics of the firm making the decision.

In summary, risk indices give initial insights, but are macro-level and are not tailored to specific decisions. It is possible that a country rating as unattractive may be the best choice for a particular firm depending on its circumstances. If, for example, a multinational corporation already operates in a large number of countries, it may be choosing between remaining investment targets that are all high risk. Similarly, markets that appear attractive may be subject to intense international competition, whereas in a market with difficult conditions, a firm that masters these may achieve high levels of success.

Delphi Models

At a practical level, the growing use of structured analyses for assessing country risks can be seen as a natural reaction to the increasingly difficult and complex problems facing those involved in international activities. Essentially, this type of systematic approach attempts to identify explicitly and to quantify the international risks arising from business operations. (Kern 1985)

The process of weighting and scoring described in the previous section is known as a Delphi technique. Delphi techniques also form the basis of some risk assessment models proposed by the literature. Risk assessment models allow for systematic appraisal of investment decisions and for comparison between investment opportunities. They build awareness in decision makers of the factors which may have an impact on the success or failure of investment decisions. Like risk indices, these models also simplify market attractiveness to a small subset of variables.

The range of variables that might play a role in international investment decisions is broad. Delphi techniques may allow firms to identify the variables that are most appropriate to a particular international marketing decision. If the decision, for example, is the most attractive international investment for an electricity generating firm, a key measure of attractiveness may be whether the electricity industry in the target country has been privatized. If not, then the country may be ruled out as an investment target. If the decision involves entry by a consumer goods firm, population and level of disposable income may be important variables. One example of this type of model is provided by Kern's risk model (1985). The model was designed by Kern in his role as Chief Economist at the National Westminster Bank in the UK to help governments decide whether to advance loans to particular countries. Not surprisingly, therefore, it focuses predominantly on macro-economic and financial variables.

A danger of risk models is that marketers may take a 'one-size-fits-all' approach and attempt to apply a model that was designed for a different purpose. Kern's model provides a valuable illustration of the genre but does not cover all the dimensions of attractiveness described in the electricity generation or consumer goods examples above. It does illustrate, however, that firms can design a model to measure attractiveness by their own definition and fine tune this by weighting more heavily the features of an international market that are most important to international marketing success.

Matrix Analysis

One technique that allows firms to combine assessment of macro-level market attractiveness and their own ability to compete in a market is matrix analysis (Wind and Douglas 1981; Perlitz 1985).

Matrix analysis can capture a snapshot of the business portfolio of a firm. One well-known matrix, or portfolio model, the Boston Consultancy Group (BCG) matrix, shows the resource implications of strategic business units at different stages of their lifecycle. Another popular model, the GE-Multifactor screen, matches the attractiveness of potential markets with the company's strengths.

These existing models have been extended into the international domain. Perlitz (1985), for example, extends the BCG matrix to international markets. Rather than the firm's growth in a particular market, he measures the growth of a country's gross domestic product (GDP). Market share is translated into the country's average share of world exports.

Immediately, however, this extension of the BCG highlights a potential limitation of matrices that use a single measure to assess attractiveness or growth. If only one measure is chosen, then the model is open to considerable criticism by those who do not believe that it is a valid measure (Day 1977; Wensley 1981). Strong growth in GDP may be found in emerging markets that have other problems to resolve in the process of development. Lower GDP growth may be found in stable, advanced economies that are actually more attractive targets. Critics of the BCG matrix suggest that it becomes compressed in mature industries where firms are unlikely to exhibit rapid growth. Similarly, advanced industrial economies are unlikely to ever count as 'stars' using Perlitz's measures.

The use of composite measures of attractiveness helps to minimize some of these problems. Indeed the GE-Multifactor used the variables from the BERI risk indicators at the time (Figure 6.1) to assess country attractiveness. As with the Delphi models described above, international marketers could define their own composite measure of attractiveness or competitive growth given the specifics of their particular situation. The GE-Multifactor allows firms to consider not only whether a country is attractive, but whether the firms have strengths that will allow them to succeed in the face of competitive challenges.

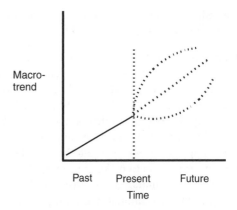

Figure 6.1   Scenario planning
Source: Leemhuis (1985). © with permission from Elsevier Science

Nonetheless, the dangers of portfolio analysis are well documented. Matrices may be subject to bias from managers (Wind and Mahajan 1981). Imagine that you are the international marketing manager charged with identifying whether the firm should enter China or India. If the most objective and accurate outcome of the model suggests that the firm should enter neither market the manager may feel uncomfortable. Will it be held as a failure not to enter a new international market? If the process produces an outcome that 'gut feel' says is the wrong decision, should the manager tweak the weighting, scoring or some other aspect of the model? Ghemawat (1991) suggests that errors may be either 'honest mistakes or deliberate distortions'. Furthermore, matrix analysis may limit the creativity of managers by prescribing preferred strategies (Wind and Mahajan 1981; McKiernan 1992).

Matrix analysis also requires simplification of complex problems.

McDonald and Leppard (1992, p. 3) argue that the reduction of complex problems to two-dimensional matrices is an acceptable and pragmatic approach:

> We accept that the purists among our readers might comment that the matrices we have included here are an oversimplification of complex problems. We would not argue with them on this issue, because intellectually, there is a lot of truth in what they say. Nevertheless, when practical decisions are required in a hard and competitive

world, any 'tools' which lead to higher quality outputs are not to be spurned lightly.

Indeed, nor should they be! However, reducing the assessment of market attractiveness to two-dimensional models is at best difficult, and, at worst, dangerous. In marketing literature, Greenley and Bayus (1993) conclude that tools such as the Product Lifecycle (PLC), portfolio analysis and perceptual mapping are perceived to be of little value in helping managers to make marketing decisions.

A particular limitation of all structured analysis techniques in international marketing is that they can be no more accurate than the data on which they are based. For some international markets data may be missing, or difficult to verify. In 1991, unemployment figures for Bulgaria from several sources read zero. This was presumably a legacy of the Soviet regime in which 'non-jobs' were created to conceal unemployment. This did not reflect reality and might have produced inaccurate assessment of the country's attractiveness relative to other countries with more accurate data.

International Marketing Planning in the New Millennium

The most fundamental challenge to matrices and other rational planning techniques is posed by the market conditions in the new millennium. Corporate planning gained credence in a period of relative stability. Paul, Donovan and Taylor (1978) contend that:

> With strategic planning's dependence on accurate forecasts, it probably was not accidental that such planning gained a wide acceptance during the 1960s, which were relatively stable and hence enabled forecasters to demonstrate sufficient accuracy.

Kami (1976) concurs:

> Corporate planning during the 1960s was relatively easy. Businesses could concentrate on international operations, because external assumptions were 'givens' with long-range predictability and few fluctuations...planning techniques of extrapolation and mathematical computation of future trends based on past history worked quite well.

He concludes, however, that these techniques are not suited to the additional demands of discontinuity:

> New conditions require new thinking, new techniques and new timing. It is time to proceed with a sweeping 'self-renewal' to cope with the era of unpredictability.

New thinking might include suggestions, such as that of Edwards and Harris (1977), that planning will cease to be a long-range process, but rather will be a 'series of discrete and sometimes unrelated steps'. Harrison (1976, p. 91) suggests that long-range plans will be hampered by uncertainty:

> At present it is very difficult and probably impossible to make a reliable 5 year forecast. Any plan based on such a forecast is unlikely to come to fruition, as anticipated.

As a result, plans are being seen as less of a 'blueprint for the firm's future' and more as 'a tentative aid to decision-making'. Flexibility is of increasing importance. Firms do not wish to be 'locked in' to a plan of action which may be inappropriate before its implementation.

In situations of discontinuous change, Leemhuis (1985) supports the use of scenario planning, a technique that considers a range of possible futures. Assessment of the worst and best case macro-environmental outcomes can incorporate both quantitative and qualitative data.

Scenario Planning

> There may be as many ways to think about the future as there are people. One common way is to look around, survey current trends and issues and to try to project the 'known' present on the 'unknown' face of the future. Another, richer, approach is to posit what a possible future or futures might look like, and then see if the tools exist in the present to bridge through to that future or those futures. (Mathews 1997, p. 24)

Scenario planning has its roots as a military intelligence tool used in the Second World War.

Despite some post-war usage, it did not achieve any level of popularity until the early 1970s when Royal Dutch/Shell set up a department of scenario planners to look at future corporate options. The popularity of planning techniques in oil companies may be linked to the size of the financial outlay required for international investments in this industry. Bigger outlay may require fuller analysis to justify the decision.

The essence of scenario planning lies in the fact that the future is uncertain and cannot be extrapolated from historical data. The major strength of the technique is that it allows firms to consider a range of *possible futures*, providing a disciplined planning framework (see Figure 6.1).

Scenarios are built around 'critical uncertainties in the business and critical uncertainties in the business environment' (Fein 1997). The wide range of what might affect any situation is reduced to a limited number of possibilities. The scenarios might represent three, five or more future scenarios spanning a spectrum from the most positive to most pessimistic outlook. If considering the future of Russia, for example, scenarios might include successful progression to a market economy as the most optimistic scenario, reversion of central planning as the most pessimistic and a range of scenarios in between.

These uncertainties can be classified using the PEST analysis framework. The key uncertainties may come from any aspect of market conditions. In the Russian example, a major source of uncertainty may be the political and economic situation. Other uncertainties, however, exist that a firm might consider important. The potential for unrest resulting from poor social conditions, the possibility that ethnic tensions may result in civil war, the rate at which technological advances will be made or infrastructure to rural areas improved might all be the basis of scenarios for the future of Russia.

A particular strength of the technique is that it can handle the possibility of complex, interrelated market changes. Imagine that political changes increase social unrest, or that political decisions increase spending on infrastructure. A change to one part of the environment may cause a web of other changes. Scenarios can capture this type of complexity.

Presenting Scenarios

Scenarios can be presented in a number of different ways. The literature suggests two key areas:

- **Construction of narratives**. Fein (1997, p. 74) and others suggest that one way of presenting scenarios is to create narrative accounts of different scenarios:

   The essence of the process lies in developing compelling stories that explore the connections and mutual implications of these uncertain driving forces.

Mathews (1997, p. 25) supports this use of stories suggesting:

   These possible futures are then expressed in the form of a story – sometimes complex, as in the scenario planning work of the Global Business Network and others, and sometimes in a series of vignettes, a technique used by The Institute for the Future. These stories are used to demonstrate how the combination of various critical uncertainties might express themselves across one or more futures.

One key constraint on such narratives is that they should be *plausible*. While Leemhuis (1985) suggests that best and worst case scenarios should represent the extreme ends of the spectrum of possibilities, Mathews (1997) argues that explanations should not be 'improbable, or frankly impossible', as this is detracts from consideration of more rational and probable scenarios.

An example of scenario planning narratives is given in Box 6.1 and Figure 6.2, using the key dimensions of Internet penetration (see Chapter 3 for a fuller discussion) and the extent to which consumer tastes converge globally (see Chapter 4 for a fuller discussion).

As can be seen from the four scenarios, a number of different and complex influences are combined in each scenario. In these complex narratives, however, international marketers may find it difficult to identify the driving influences.

- **X and Y grids**. Proponents of X and Y grids (Mathews 1997) such as that shown in Figure 6.2 argue that this technique is a way of simplifying diverse possibilities into 'clusters'

Box 6.1 Scenario Planning Narratives

SCENARIO 1 – CULT OF THE INDIVIDUAL

An increasing number of consumers are attracted to shopping via home computers. This is fuelled by greater government support for the Internet. Government intervention and competitive pressures force telephone companies to remove local call charges and this further increases Internet penetration. There is a reduction in barriers to Internet, even by governments currently averse to its usage. Advances in technology do not, however, reduce differences in consumer preferences globally. In fact, the opposite occurs. With the Internet, and the possibilities for customization on the basis of individual consumer preferences, retailers are increasingly expected to make home deliveries, alter pack sizes and tailor the marketing offer to each consumer. It is the norm that this should be done in the local language.

SCENARIO 2 – BRAVE NEW WORLD

An increasing number of consumers are attracted to shopping via their home computers. Technological advances make products and services widely available across all markets. Awareness of globally lowest prices puts pressure on margins. Global players with economies of scale and scope benefits are best able to cope with these pressures and global brands gain in strength. Media charges for Internet advertizing increase. The leading service providers raise charges for business users to compensate for free service to consumers. Many smaller competitors are forced out of Internet provision. Standar-

dized products and services become the norm. A new 'global consumer' emerges.

SCENARIO 3 – SPECIALIST SHOPPING

The Internet fails to have significant impact globally. The first enthusiasm fades as firms realize that there are few profits to be made. Moreover, there is a backlash as customers resist domination of the Internet by a small number of global players who can ride out the short-term lack of profits. This backlash fuels a return to local shopping in specialist stores where personal contact is the norm and customization to individual needs is possible.

SCENARIO 4 – GLOBAL STANDARDIZATION AND EXISTING CHANNELS

The Internet fails to have significant impact on global purchasing patterns. It does, however, build awareness of price levels for products in different global markets. Customers put pressure on governments to iron out differential pricing on cars, food and a range of other products. As prices drop and margins are squeezed, firms are forced to capitalize on economies of scale and scope. Through existing retail channels, standardized global products become the norm and customers accept that products may not be adapted to local market tastes. Free trade areas prosper, GATT breaks down barriers to global trade and global standardization becomes possible.

---

of uncertainties. The above narratives give richness, but are complex. The underlying forces can be shown much more simply on an X and Y grid. The contrast between the different scenarios becomes much more apparent, though much of the detail is lost. A combination of the two techniques may give the fullest picture.

Effective Scenario Planning

The literature recommends a number of steps to ensure effective scenario planning:

1. **Limit the area you wish to explore**. In Mathews' words: 'scenario planners don't sit around a crystal ball waiting for an "impression" of what the future might look like' (Mathews 1997, p. 25). An important first stage is to define the parameters of the problem.
2. Create a list of **driving forces, issues or trends that cause uncertainty**. These should then be condensed down to a set of key critical uncertainties, e.g. competitive or political. The ways in which this might be achieved range from gut feel to scientific. In other words, the process might be achieved by grouping trends in

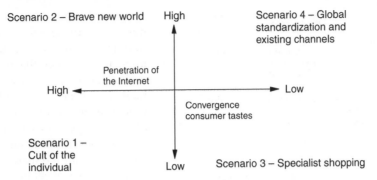

Figure 6.2   X and Y grid of scenarios for the future of retailing

a way that feels sensible. It could be achieved by listing and reaching a collective decision (by vote or creation of a scoring system) on the most important. It might also be achieved statistically using factor analysis or some other technique to identify related variables.

3. **Decide on a number of possible futures**. Planners argue (Leemhuis 1985) that at least three, if not more, scenarios should be created to represent a range of possibilities. If not, then planners may be making either/or decisions rather than viewing the full range. Too many scenarios may lead to difficulties in differentiating between these and complicate the process of making decisions.

4. Use **external advisors** to avoid company 'blind spots' (Elkington and Trisoglio 1996). Shell, together with other oil firms, is well known for its use of scenario planning. Despite this, however, Shell has run into environmental disputes both over Brent Spar and in Nigeria (see Case Study 15.1, Shell in Ogoni Land, p. 262). Identifying and anticipating reactions is complicated by difficulties in understanding the conflicting agendas of the various stakeholders. Shell might, for example, think it has anticipated the range of possible actions of environmental lobby groups. It may, however, not understand the strategic agenda of such groups. Elkington and Trisoglio (1996) suggest that selected external stakeholders be involved in developing scenarios to help avoid the possibility that the company has 'blind spots'.

5. Once scenarios are created, firms must decide what **strategies** they are seeking. Possibilities include maximizing returns, minimizing risks or mapping a course which is most favourable whichever outcome prevails.

6. A final, and complex, task is that of deciding whether or not a scenario is **happening**. There is a tendency to look for evidence to confirm scenarios rather than accepting that what is actually happening may not correspond exactly to any one scenario.

THE RELATIONSHIP PERSPECTIVE

Knowledge, Learning and International Markets

One of the ongoing debates in international marketing literature is over the type of knowledge which firms need to acquire to overcome the uncertainty of new international markets. The notion that firms begin with a blank sheet of paper and rationally evaluate the most attractive markets to enter is oversimplistic for three main reasons:

■ **'Pull' or 'push' triggers**. The influences which trigger the decision to enter international markets have been the subject of a wide body of literature. One of the most commonly suggested phenomena is that firms are influenced both by 'pull' and 'push' factors. Country-specific advantages, such as the availability of raw materials, skilled labour or large available

Strengths	Weaknesses
Size and military strength	Mind-set of colonial past
Strategic location	Borders with 7 countries
Political pluralism	Fragile institutions
Population and labour Force	Lack of political and administrative experience
Science and technology	Lack of private enterprise
Family and social infrastructure	
Physical and natural resources	
Industry and industrial infrastructure	
Opportunities	**Threats**
Rapid economic progress	Rise of the extreme right parties in Russia
Central role in European affairs	Ethnic divisions
Harmonizing East and West	Macro-economic instability

Figure 6.3   SWOT analysis: Ukraine
Source: Based on Srinivasan (1994)

population size may 'pull' firms into markets, as may competitive and other influences. Manninen and Snelbecker (1993) present this type of assessment of the attractiveness of Ukraine by a sample of foreign investors. High profit potential (48 per cent), local demand (37 per cent), the availability of cheap raw materials (30 per cent) and low labour costs (23 per cent) act as strong 'pull' factors. Similarly, Srinivasan (1994) lists the strengths, weaknesses, opportunities and threats (SWOT analysis) for entrants into the country (see Figure 6.3).

Alongside factors which 'pull' firms into markets, are those which may 'push' them to enter. Customers, suppliers, competitors and other stakeholders may all exert an influence on entry decisions. In the mobile telephony market, Motorola expects all suppliers to operate within a certain radius of any factory it builds to ensure Just-in-Time (JIT) deliveries. Failure to comply might, presumably, result in the loss of a global account. In this situation, the supplying firm is 'pulled' to enter the markets entered by Motorola.

■ **Entry and expansion**. The decision to enter a market may be made on the best knowledge available at the time. Aharoni (1966) points to the 'cost of knowledge'. Seeking perfect knowledge upon which to base decisions

may involve considerable costs in time and money. At the point where the costs of the information exceed the risks implied by investment in a market the firm should 'take an option' on entry. Further knowledge of the market may be gained after entry. This will influence the firm in subsequent decisions to expand its operations in the country, remain at the same level of investment or possibly even withdraw from the market in adverse circumstances. This is essentially the view of uncertainty which underlies incremental models of internationalization (see Chapter 8 for further discussion of the internationalization process). The nature of the knowledge which firms require to overcome uncertainly in international markets has exercised international marketers ever since Johanson and Vahlne (1977) first proposed the incremental model.

■ **The nature of knowledge required to overcome uncertainty**. In 1977, Johanson and Vahlne argued that only experiential and market-specific knowledge would allow firms to overcome uncertainty in new international markets. Based on the work of Penrose (1966 p. 53), objective knowledge can be taught or transferred. Experiential knowledge, however, can be learned only through personal experience: 'experience itself can never be transmitted, it produces a change – frequently a subtle change – in individuals and cannot be separated from them.' So knowledge cannot be passed from one firm, or even one individual to another. Moreover, according to Johanson and Vahlne, knowledge required to overcome uncertainty about a country must be specific to that country. Accordingly, they argue that a firm could not apply knowledge of working in one country to help in others. After considerable criticism of the incremental model (see Chapter 8), Johanson and Vahlne (1990) later accepted that knowledge might be transferred between similar countries. On this basis, a firm that has been operating in the Czech Republic and Poland may have learned valuable lessons which will help when it enters Russia.

Other authors contest even this revised view. Clark, Pugh and Mallory (1997) maintain that market-specific knowledge is not the only type available to the firm. As firms operate in markets they develop a knowledge of the process of internationalization. According to Millington and Bayliss (1990, p. 153) 'international experience, irrespective of the specific foreign market, represents transferable benefits.' In short, past experiences of entry into other markets feed into the decision making process of markets entered later. This supports the view of Aharoni (1966) that investment decisions should not be viewed in isolation but as series of interrelated episodes. It is on this last point that the 'relationship' view of assessing market attractiveness rests. In explaining higher risk entry decisions by firms with greater international experience, Clark, Pugh and Mallory (1997) say that:

> This is possibly due to the ability of the [firm] to utilize knowledge and experience of operating internationally from the group of which it is part.

Moreover, interdependencies between the international operations of a firm mean that relationships between the units and of each unit with other stakeholders also form part of the body of international knowledge informing decisions on a market's attractiveness.

Knowledge Interrelationships

Knowledge of international markets may be based on a wide variety of inter-relationships:

1. **Relationships with publics and stakeholders.** As suggested in the above discussion of scenario planning, companies may have subjective views of their own strengths and weaknesses. In completing a market attractiveness matrix or other planning exercise, firms tend to have clearer views of outside trends and influences than of their own strengths and weaknesses. Relationship marketing suggests that stakeholders are one of the six markets which should be managed. Stakeholders, such as shareholders, interest groups and involvement in industry conferences or professional bodies, may provide valuable information to see the firm as others see it.

2. **Relationships with customers.** Customer feedback provides a valuable source of feedback. As this relationship becomes more interactive, via the Internet and other media, the extent to which customers can give precise information about their needs and wants increases.

3. **Relationships with competitors.** Although traditional marketing does not show a direct link with competitors, relationship and network perspectives accept that firms do have such relationships. Common subscription to syndicated market research may provide one means by which firms share information with each other. Another interesting source of data on international market attractiveness seems to be the actions of other firms. Oligopolistic reaction theory (see Chapter 7) suggests that one reason why firms may be clustered in their market entry behaviour is that they revise upwards their opinion of a market's attractiveness if a competitor firm enters the market.

4. **Relationships within the firm.** As multinational firms operate across a number of markets, a large volume of relevant data and expertise may exist within the organization (see the discussion of 'knowledge organizations' in the Network section of this chapter.) Replication of data collection or analysis may occur within the organization. Technological advances to capture customer and market data on databases may help to overcome these problems.

5. **Relationships with market research agencies.** Market research agencies, together with other business-to-business service agencies, may form international, or even global, relationships with their customers. These may involve the market research agency in providing data across a range of countries.

6. **Co-operation with other firms.** The strategy literature contends that firms should enter collaborative relationships to gain access to scarce resources (Jarillo 1988; Hamel, Prahalad and Doz 1989). In uncertain international markets, one scarce asset may be knowledge of a market. Based on the belief that knowledge can be transferred, the growth in popularity of *strategic alliances* as an entry mode in emerging markets such as those in East and Central Europe (CEE) (Shama 1995, 1996) and in

China (Schlegelmilch *et al.* 1991) might be explained as attempts by foreign investors to access the local knowledge and network connections of a local partner.

THE NETWORK PERSPECTIVE

The Knowledge Economy

From a network perspective, knowledge as well as other assets are exchanged through network relationships. Understanding of the influences on an assessment of market attractiveness becomes yet more complex.

Recent literature suggests that, in the 1990s, firms operated in knowledge economies:

> New scientific discoveries, constant restructuring of whole industries, volatility in financial markets... To survive and prosper in this new environment, many firms have had to reorganise and become more responsive to change. They have had to build trust and responsibility. This has been achieved internally on the one hand, by flattening hierarchical structures and delegating responsibility in order to mobilise skills more effectively, and externally on the other, by building durable networks as a fundamental part of maximising value-added in output. (Vickery 1999)

Similarly, Drake (1998) argues that a 'new knowledge-based international economy of learning individuals, organisations and economies has evolved.'

In this 'knowledge economy', firms have become 'learning' organizations which exploit networks to gain access to the knowledge assets of other firms (Drake 1998). The network linkages are many and various. Vickery (1999) contends that small firms may present 'a conduit of ideas and innovations in the knowledge economy.' Drake suggests knowledge networks involving firms, suppliers, customers and universities.

Knowledge Flows and Networks

At the heart of the network view of organizations is the complex web of relationships. Given the overall increase in the flows of knowledge between organizations, it is clear that the way in which knowledge flows in networks is of central importance. Indeed, in their valuable analysis of this issue, Bångens and Araujo (1999) argue that organizational learning cannot be understood from within one organization, but 'must be understood as dependent on the types of links the firm develops with third parties e.g. suppliers, customers and distributors.'

This view differs from that commonly found in literature, as most studies either:

- study learning between two firms in a formal alliance (e.g. Larssen *et al.* 1998; Amelingmeyer and Specht 1999)
- focus on the firm as the centre of learning (e.g. Chandler 1990).

In attempting to understand the knowledge flows and types of knowledge required in complex network structures, the economics literature has differentiated between different types of activities that take place in organizations (Richardson 1972). Richardson argues that firms engage in activities that are:

- similar in that they use the same capability
- complementary in that they represent different stages of the value chain.

Richardson's classification forms the basis of studies of knowledge by Brown and Duguid (1998), Lundvall and Johnson (1994) and Loasby (1999). Loasby differentiates between 'knowledge how' and 'knowledge that'. 'Knowledge how' refers to skilled performance, experience and experts (Brown and Druid 1998). 'Knowledge that' is knowledge of facts and relationships that can be translated and codified. This latter form of knowledge has been broken down further by Lundvall and Johnson (1994) into 'know-what' and 'know-why'. 'Know-what' is information that can be codified and stored. This is the type of knowledge that forms the basis of the 'New Economics of Information' literature described in Chapter 5 (see Normann and Ramirez 1993 and McGee 1999 for a fuller description of this literature). 'Know-why' is more complex, as this refers to understanding the causes of something. If a market entry fails, 'know-why' would be understanding the reasons for this.

In summary then, the literature differentiates between:

- **Know what** – information that is easily stored, codified and transferred
- **Know why** – understanding the underlying reasons behind events and problems
- **Know how** – experience, expert and tacit knowledge.

This distinction has a number of implications for assessment of attractive international markets. First, the type of information provided by the Internet (see Chapter 3) and secondary market research data, risk indices, etc. (see Chapter 5, Traditional perspective) is *know what* knowledge. This can be transferred but will not provide answers to a number of critical difficulties that firms encounter in international markets.

The Relationship section of this chapter presents Aharoni's viewpoint (1966) that firms' knowledge of international market entry is *cumulative*. In other words, decisions about market attractiveness and entry are influenced by the failure or success of previous international operations. This phenomenon is based on *know why* knowledge. When reflecting on their lack of success in bids for privatized tobacco plants in the Czech Republic, one tobacco firm, for example, decided that they needed to be quicker in entering and assessing the attractiveness of other East and Central European investment opportunities. Rightly or wrongly, they had attributed failure to invest in the earlier markets to slow response.

To understand the full complexity of international markets, however, firms are likely to need *know-how* knowledge. This type of knowledge results from expertise gained from operation in the target or similar markets. As described in the Relationship section of this chapter there are a number of debates around knowledge and international markets. In the light of this classification of knowledge, these can now be revisited and summarized as follows:

- Is know-what knowledge sufficient to overcome uncertainty of international markets?
- Does know-why knowledge come from other network connections or only from the firm's own experiences?
- Does know-how knowledge reside in individuals or firms?
- Can know-how knowledge be transferred in collaborations or through networks?

Is Know-What Sufficient to Overcome Uncertainty of International Markets?

The type of market research described in the Traditional section of this chapter, and previously discussed in Chapter 4 with regard to the Internet is readily transferable. As it does not, however, explain either causes of success or failure (know-why knowledge) or confer expertise on the recipient (know-how knowledge), this should be viewed as providing a base level of knowledge of international markets rather than as sufficient for decision-making purposes.

Does Know-Why Knowledge Come from Other Network Connections or Only from the Firm's Own Experiences?

Aharoni's work (1966) suggests that firms gain valuable know-why knowledge from their own previous experiences. Can this knowledge, however, be gained through relationships with other firms? It is clear from Aharoni's argument that decisions are set in particular contexts that it is difficult to assume that the same outcome will result from a different entry decision. Based on the previous example, the tobacco firm blaming slow response for failure to enter the Czech market might conclude that early entry into Ukraine is likely to bring success. As this involves a different entry mode, different market conditions and likelihood of successful progression to free market economy this may not succeed. Attribution of causes is complex and may not even work within the firm, as each situation is unique.

Having said this, however, it is clear that firms can learn from previous actions. Moreover, the popularity of benchmarking, best practice and other techniques of comparison make it possible to look at features of other firms' successes. If this type of process involves studying the actions and reasons why competitor firms have succeeded or failed in entering a particular market this may provide useful knowledge.

Does Know-How Knowledge Reside in Individuals or Firms?

Having defined know-how knowledge as based on expertise and experience, it may seem most likely that this resides in individuals. Many firms make attempts, however, to create a *corporate memory* that remains with the organization even if a specific individual moves on. Processes such as mentoring and training may pass this type of knowledge down through organizations. Similarly, even capturing the details of previous decisions and outcomes in a database may allow a firm to revisit the history of activity in a particular market and the success of previous international marketing activities. The reasons for success or failure may not always be captured, infact as this knowledge cannot easily be codified.

Can Know-How Knowledge be Transferred in Collaborations or Through Networks?

Bångens and Araujo (1999) suggest that know-how knowledge can be shared rather than transferred. Individuals with such knowledge may be subject experts or specialists. These individuals may become members of broader communities that exist across firms (Wenger 1998). As a result knowledge-sharing may be common.

Based on these arguments, the transfer of know-how within networks may be feasible and provide benefits to international marketers. This is most likely to result from interaction with like-minded or similarly skilled individuals. Membership of trade associations, participation in embassy events, trade shows and other activities in the target market, for example, proved valuable as a source of knowledge and contacts to firms entering former Soviet markets. These types of links may not provide instant know-how, or expertise, but may help to overcome uncertainty, provide contacts in local market networks and hence improve the chances of successful market entry.

CASE STUDY 6.1 SCENARIOS FOR THE FUTURE OF CHINA

The death of Deng Xiaoping in 1997 heralded the end of an era. As China announced the news of his death, and the accession of his successor Jiang Zemin, simultaneously to minimize the risks of a leadership crisis, the world speculated over the possible impacts for the future of China as an investment target. Many of these uncertainties over the future of China as an investment target persist.

FOREIGN INVESTMENT IN CHINA

The fortunes of foreign investors in China to date have been mixed. Some firms have prospered. Reflecting on its intention to withdraw its expatriate managers and hand over the local operation to Chinese staff, Duncan Garrood, general manager of Wall's ice cream, a subsidiary of the Anglo-Dutch firm Unilever commented that, in the firm's view, this was a: 'matter of pride. This is the right process to have a Chinese business run by Chinese managers' (*Financial Times*, (27 August 1998).

The costs of expatriate managers, compared to local staff, are certainly considerable. According to a report from Arthur Andersen, expatriate managers tend to earn around US$200 000–US$ 300 000 per annum working in China. Living allowances and hardship allowances might add 30–40 per cent. In contrast, a highly paid local manager might earn around US$60 000. It is tempting to conclude that, despite Deng Xiaoping's death, control will soon be handed over to local managers.

At stake for multinational corporations, however, may be global brand names, product or service quality and protection of technological assets from lax local copyright and patent laws. Pirate goods are commonplace. handing over control too soon might result in a deterioration of 'financial discipline, quality control and corporate identity' (*Financial Times*, 28 August 1998).

Despite the argument that China is an emerging economic force that will 'become the world's largest economy early in the next century' (Kelley and Luo 1999), others are less certain about the future prospects for the Chinese market. Although China's own brand of market reforms, creating a market economy under the continuing communist regime, seemed to be progressing, Deng Xiaoping's death brought questions about the future.

THREATS TO THE FUTURE DEVELOPMENT OF CHINA?

A number of levels of threat exist. These range from the relatively mild issues relating to the future of China's political economy through to extreme possibilities, such as that that a new leader would close down the possibilities for foreign investors to enter China. Changes in foreign investment legislation, or surrounding repatriation of profits might make it an unattractive prospect for foreign firms. Similar problems occurred in the transition process of countries such as Ukraine. Agro-chemical firms entered Ukraine rapidly after liberalization on the strength of the country's good agricultural soils. In the face of a worsening economic crisis, the Ukrainian government changed legislation to ban exports of agricultural produce. This removed the possibility of a short-term return on investment for a number of foreign investors. Commentators feared the similar possibility of a return to central planning and a rejection of market values in China.

Even if this radical political step fails to materialize – Jiang Zemin appears a moderate leader who is conciliatory towards other nations – China may be impacted by the ripples of the East Asian Economic Crisis. China appears not to have suffered from the financial crisis that affected many of its neighbours. Commentators suggest

119

that this may be because it operates 'behind closed doors' (Song 1998). Commonly cited reasons for its avoiding the crisis were:

- The previous period of economic growth gave it resilience
- Balance of payment surpluses
- International reserves of US$140 billion by the end of 1997
- Moderate level of foreign debt (US$131 billion) by the end of 1997
- A stable currency since the reform of the exchange rate system in 1994.

Although it has remained unaffected to date, commentators suggest that China may need to commit to further market reforms to ensure ongoing economic growth. There are some risks to future market stability: there is weak market demand, excess supply in many industries and inefficiency of many state-owned enterprises (SOEs). There is also rising unemployment, which is widening the gap between the 'have's' and 'have not's' in China. Overall, China stands to

lose competitiveness compared to its East Asian rivals. As the currencies of the latter have weakened, China's products are relatively more expensive for international customers, and quality levels tend to be lower.

More fundamentally China, together with a number of other countries, possesses the technology to create weapons of mass destruction. Russia passed on nuclear and missile-related technologies to China and, in turn, China helped Pakistan with its nuclear programme, and transferred a medium-range missile system (the CSS-2) to Saudi Arabia and a mobile ballistic missile producing system to Pakistan.

Together with tensions over its relations, first with Hong Kong during the handover of the colony to China from Britain and also concerning its relations with Taiwan, China's possession of weapons technology represents the threatening face of the country as a world super power. The accidental bombing of the Chinese embassy in Serbia by NATO troops was one in a series of incidents which highlights the threat which China could pose on the world stage.

SUMMARY

In Chapter 6 we have explored the value and limitations of traditional risk assessment tools. The uncertainty of the current international environment suggests that scenario planning may be a useful tool. We have explored the role of knowledge and learning in international marketing relationships.

BIBLIOGRAPHY

Aharoni, Y. (1966) *The Foreign Direct Investment Process*, Harvard University Press.

Amelingmeyer, J. and Specht, G. (1999) 'Analysis and Structuring of Collaborations: The Knowledge Management Perspective', in McLoughlin, D. and Horan, C. (eds), *Proceedings of the IMP Conference*, Dublin.

Bångens, L. and Araujo, L. (1999) 'The Structures and Processes of Organisational Learning: A Case Study', in McLoughlin, D. and Horan, C. (eds), *Proceedings of the IMP Conference*, Dublin.

Brown, J. S. and Duguid, P. (1998) 'Organizing Knowledge', *California Management Review*, 40, 3: 90–111.

Chandler, A. Jr. (1990) *Scale and Scope: The Dynamics of Industrial Capitalism*, Belknap Press.

Clark, T., Pugh, D. S. and Mallory, G. (1997) 'The Process of Internationalization in the Operating Firm', *International Business Review*, 6, 6: 605–19

Day, G. S. (1977) 'Diagnosing the Product Portfolio', *Journal of Marketing*, April: 29–38.

Drake, K. (1998) 'Firms, Knowledge and Competitiveness', Organization for Economic Cooperation and Development, *The OECD Observer*, April/May: 24–7

Edwards, J. P. and Harris, D. J. (1977) 'Planning in a State of Turbulence', *Long Range Planning*, 10, June: 43–9.

Elkington, J. and Trisoglio, A. (1996) 'Developing Realistic Scenarios for the Environment:

Lessons from Brent Spar', *Long Range Planning*, 29, 6: 762–9.

Fein, A. J. (1997) 'Is Global Expansion your Future?', *Industrial Distribution*, 86, 11: 74–6.

Ghemawat, P. (1991) *Commitment: the Dynamic of Strategy*, Free Press and Macmillan.

Goodnow, J. D. and Hansz, J. E. (1972) 'Environmental Determinants of Overseas Entry Strategies', *Journal of International Business Studies*, 3, 4: 33–50.

Greenley, G. E. and Bayus, B. L. (1993) 'Marketing Planning Decision-Making in UK and US Companies: An Empirical Comparative Study', *Journal of Marketing Management*, 9: 155–72.

Hamel, G., Doz, Y. L. and Prahalad, C. K. (1989) 'Collaborate with your Competitors and Win', *Harvard Business Review*, January–February: 133–9.

Harding, J. (1998) 'When Expats Ought to Pack their Bags: Chinese Experience Points up the Dangers for Multinational Companies when they shed Expatriate Staff too Swiftly', *Financial Times*, 28 August 28: 8.

Harrison, F. L. (1976) 'How Corporate Planning Responds to Uncertainty', *Long Range Planning*, 9, 2: 88–93.

Jarillo, J.-C. (1988) 'On Strategic Networks', *Strategic Management Review*, 11: 479–99.

Johanson, J. and Vahlne, J.-E. (1977) 'The Internationalisation Process of the Firm – A Model of Knowledge Development and Increasing Foreign Market Commitments', *Journal of International Business Studies*, 8, 1: 23–32.

Johanson, J. and Vahlne, J.-E. (1990) 'The Mechanism of Internationalisation', *International Marketing Review*, 19: 11–24.

Kami, M. J. (1976) 'Planning in Times of Unpredictability', *Columbia Journal of World Business*, Summer: 26–34.

Kelley, L. and Luo, Y. (1999) 'An Introduction to Emerging Business Issues for China 2000', in Kelley, L. and Luo, Y. (eds), *China 2000*, Sage International Business Series.

Kern, D. (1985) 'The Evaluation of Country Risk and Economic Potential', *Long Range Planning*, 18, 3: 17–25.

Klein, S. and Roth, V. J. (1990) 'Determinants of Export Channel Structure: The Effects of Experience and Psychic Distance Reconsidered', *International Marketing Review*, 7, 5.

Knight, F. H. (1921) *Risk, Uncertainty and Profit*.

Larsson, R., Bengtsson, L., Henriksson, K. and Sparks, J. (1998) 'The Interorganizational Learning Dilemma: Collective Knowledge Development in Strategic Alliances', *Organization Science*, 9, 3: 285–305.

Leemhuis, J. P. (1985) 'Using Scenarios to Develop Strategies', *Long Range Planning*, 18, 2: 30–7.

Litvak, I. A. and Banting, P. M. (1968) 'A Conceptual Framework for International Business Arrangements', in King, R. L. (ed.), *Marketing and the New Science of Planning*, AMA Fall Conference Proceedings.

Loasby, B. J. (1999) *Knowledge, Institutions and Evolutions in Economics*, Routledge.

Lundvall, B.-A. and Johnson, B. (1994) 'The Learning Economy', *Journal of Industry Studies*, 1, 2: 23–42.

Manninen, K. and Snelbecker, D. (1993) 'Obstacles to Doing Business in Ukraine', Project for Economic Reform in Ukraine, *Working Paper*, April.

Mascarenhas, B. (1982) 'Coping with Uncertainty in International Business', *Journal of International Business*, Fall: 87–98.

Mathews, R. (1997) 'Food Distribution 2010: Four Futures', *Progressive Grocer*, 76, 9: 24–32.

McDonald, M. and Leppard, J. W. (1992) *Marketing by Matrix: 100 Practical Ways to Improve Your Strategic and Tactical Marketing*, Butterworth–Heinemann.

McGee, J. (1999) *Working Paper*, University of Warwick.

McKiernan, P. (1992) *Strategies of Growth; Maturity, Recovery and Internationalisation*, Routledge.

Miller, K. D. (1992) 'A Framework for Integrated Risk Management', *Journal of International Business*, Summer: 311–31.

Millington, A. I. and Bayliss, B. T. (1990) 'The Process of Internationalization: UK Companies in the EC', *Management International Review*, 30: 151–61.

Normann, R. and Ramirez, R. (1993) 'From Value Chain to Value Constellation: Designing Interactive Strategy', *Harvard Business Review*, July–August: 65–77.

Paul, R. N., Donovan, N. B. and Taylor, J. W. (1978) 'The Reality Gap in Strategic Planning', *Harvard Business Review*, May–June: 124–30.

Penrose, E. (1959) *The Theory of the Growth of the Firm*, Blackwell, Oxford.

Perlitz, M. (1985) 'Country Portfolio Analysis – Assessing Country Risk and Opportunity', *Long Range Planning* 18, 4: 11–26.

Pettigrew, A. M. (1985a) *The Awakening Giant: Continuity and Change in ICI*, Blackwell.

Pettigrew, A. M. (1985b) 'Contextualist Research: A Natural Way to Link Theory and Practice', in E. E. Lawler (ed.), *Doing Research that is Useful in Theory and Practice*, Jossey-Bass.

Richardson, G. B. (1972) 'The Organisation of Industry', *The Economic Journal*, 82: 883–96.

Rummel, R. J. and Heenan, D. A. (1978) 'How Multi-nationals Analyze Political Risk', *Harvard Business Review*, January–February: 67–76.

Schlegelmilch, B. B., Diamantopoulos, A. and Petersen, M. (1991) 'Conquering the Chinese Market: a study of Danish firms' experiences in the People's Republic of China', in Paliwoda, S. J. (ed.), *New Perspectives in International Marketing*: 174–201.

Schneider, W. (1998) 'Europe Comes into Range: The West must Recognise the Threat Posed by the Rapid Proliferation of Ballistic Missiles', *Financial Times*, 25 August.

Shama, A. (1995) 'Entry Strategies of US Firms to the Newly Independent States, Baltic States and Eastern European Countries', *California Management Review*, 37, 3: 90–108.

Shama, A. (1996) 'Cracking the Former Soviet Bloc Markets: An Empirical Study', *International Journal of Management*, 13, 2: 184–92.

Smith, C. N. (1971) 'Predicting the Political Environment of International Business', *Long Range Planning*, 5, 3: 7–14.

Song, L. (1998) 'China', in McLeod, R. H. and Garnaut, R. (eds), *East Asia in Crisis: From being a Miracle to Needing One?*, Routledge.

Srinivasan, T. S. (1994) 'Ukraine: Strengths, Weaknesses, Opportunities and Threats', *Unpublished working paper*, International Management Institute, Kiev.

Vickery, G. (1999) 'Business and Industry Policies for Knowledge-Based Economies', *The OECD Observer*, 215, January: 9–11.

Wenger, E. (1998) *Communities of Practice. Learning, Meaning and Identity*. Cambridge University Press.

Wensley, J. R. C. (1981) 'Strategic Marketing: Betas, Boxes or Basics', *Journal of Marketing*, 45: 173–82.

Wind, Y. and Douglas, S. P. (1981) 'International Portfolio Analysis and Strategy: The Challenge of the 1980s', *Journal of International Business*. Fall: 69–82.

Wind, Y. and Mahajan, V. (1981) 'Designing Product and Business Portfolios', *Harvard Business Review*, January–February: 155–65.

THE MODE OF INTERNATIONAL OPERATION

Objectives

The issues to be addressed in Chapter 7 include:

1. The type – or mode – of operation used in international markets
2. The economic assumption of theories of foreign direct investment as a type of international operation
3. The implications of joint ventures and alliances in international marketing
4. The interaction view of co-operation in international marketing
5. The value of networks as an organizational form.

After reading Chapter 7 you will be able to:

1. Assess the advantages and limitations of different modes of international operation
2. Understand the debate surrounding the benefits of foreign direct investment over other modes of international operation
3. Evaluate the implications of joint ventures and other co-operative modes of international operation
4. Assess the alternative view of networks as a mode of international operation.

INTRODUCTION

This chapter discusses the type, or mode, of organization used in international markets. Studies of mode of operation may have their roots in either economics or sociology. In the Traditional section, some of the contributions of economics literature are explored. The contribution of the widely used Dunning Eclectic Paradigm (1980) is examined. This section also discusses the reasons for a firm's decision to internalize, or take control of activities within the organization.

In the Relationship section, the chapter continues by reviewing some of the implications of using joint ventures and strategic alliances in international markets. In Easton's terms (1990) these are *collaborative ventures* rather than co-operation. Collaboration implies that the firms make complementary contributions but each

enter the agreement to further their own interests. Interaction and relationship studies, in contrast, see relationships as co-operative. Partners are mutually dependent and may even act against their own interests to further the relationship (see Chapter 1 for a fuller discussion of these contrasting views of relationships).

In international markets, joint ventures may offer benefits including access to scarce resources, such as technology, production facilities or local market knowledge. Yet many such venture fail. The chapter discusses reasons for failure and the creation of successful collaborative relationships.

The Network section of this chapter takes a different view of networks. Here, discussion centres on the value of networks as an organizational form. This view sees networks as a flexible and rapidly changing organizational form that may be well suited to operation in turbulent international markets. This view contrasts with the 'markets as networks' view of networks used in the rest of the book, but is consistent with this chapter's focus on types of international organization.

THE TRADITIONAL PERSPECTIVE

Economics-Based Theories

The type of operation that firms use in international markets has been a central topic in economics literature since the 1970s. In this chapter we refer, hereafter, to the type of operation – such as export, licensing or foreign direct investment (FDI) – as the 'mode' of international operation.

Monopolistic Advantage Theory

Early discussion of mode of international operation was triggered by the seminal work of Hymer (1960) and Kindelberger (1969). These authors proposed a theory of 'monopolistic advantage.' This theory argues that firms must possess some kind of advantage over and above that offered by local firms in order to succeed in a market. According to monopolistic advantage theory, for example, a new entrant into the USA's computer industry would need to offer faster processing speed, more innovative ideas or other advanced features to succeed against strong local competition.

Building on the theory of monopolistic advantage, a number of other authors (Caves 1971; Hirsch 1976) went on to identify particular types of advantages a foreign enterprise might possess. These advantages tended to be based on particular abilities of the firm, known as *firm-specific advantages*, or its organizational structure, known as *ownership advantages*.

In later studies the focus shifted to the influences a firm might encounter in particular countries that might encourage it to choose between different modes of operation. These are known as *location- or country-specific advantages*. Location-specific advantages include, for example, raw materials, skilled labour or a large land mass (for a fuller discussion of the advantages of particular countries, see the discussion in the Traditional section of Chapter 4 on Economic Context).

The three types of advantages identified in this section were integrated into one theory by Dunning's 'eclectic theory of international production' (1980).

Dunning's Eclectic Paradigm of International Production

In his eclectic paradigm, Dunning (1988) identifies three types of influences on the decision to locate manufacturing facilities in a country: location-specific advantages, internalization (firm-specific) advantages and ownership- (later referred to as internalisation) specific advantages.

- **Location-specific advantages**. These are advantages which the firm can gain from the availability of raw materials, labour, large population, geographic location or other advantages of a particular country.
- **Internalization advantages**. Literature has variously argued that firm-specific advantages accrue from the possession of superior marketing skills or management ability (Kindelberger 1969), the ability to differentiate products (Caves 1971), or continuous research and development (R&D) activity (Hirsch 1976). In 1976, Buckley and Casson applied the concept of internalization (making an operation part of, or internal, to the organization) to international business to show the benefits of internalizing these advantages to protect them against uncertain international markets. Dunning uses internalization rather than firm-specific advantages.
- **Ownership advantages**. Advantages can also be based on common governance, multinationality or intangible assets within the organization. Common governance, when there are a number of affiliates, may result in economies of scale and scope. The firm might, for example, be able to buy materials from its suppliers at a more favourable rate, or lower unit production costs with longer production runs. Multinationality might offer better knowledge of international markets, the ability to reduce risks by operation in countries with different currencies or political regimes, or the availability of a work force with appropriate cultural

and other skills to aid further international expansion. Intangible assets of the organization include softer skills, such as managerial know-how (see Chapter 6).

Dunning argues that the advantages in each category must be sufficient to outweigh the extra costs of operating in an international market.

Internalization

In revisions to the eclectic paradigm, Dunning (1988), increases the emphasis on internalization advantages. Given the uncertainty that firms face in international markets, performing an activity within the organization provides some kind of control. For example, intellectual property is difficult to protect given the high level of counterfeiting that takes place in China. In this situation, a firm whose advantage over its competitors lies in its technologies may be reluctant to disclose these to an agent or joint venture partner but may choose to produce within 100 per cent owned manufacturing facilities.

As Dunning expresses it:

> The greater the perceived costs of transactional market failure, the more MNEs [multinational enterprises] are likely to exploit their competitive advantages through international production rather than by contractual agreements with foreign firms.

As discussed in Chapter 6, firms face high levels of environmental uncertainty in international markets (Mascarenhas 1980; Miller 1992). In addition to political and economic uncertainty, high levels of psychic distance, or cultural dissimilarity may complicate the task of international marketers (see Chapters 2–4 for a fuller discussion of these different types of environmental uncertainty). Some markets are particularly uncertain. Emerging markets, markets in transition to free economy or those with poor legal enforcement of patents or other assets may prompt firms to take higher levels of control.

An example of a firm choosing high levels of control is that of McDonald's restaurants in Moscow. Although McDonald's franchises its brand and recipes to partners in most countries, on initial entry into Russia the firm chose to enter via investment in a joint venture agreement. While this required a higher level of investment, the McDonald's corporation chose this mode to enter new markets. In the case of Russia, this level of control was also taken for subsequent investments. In less turbulent markets, or where the firm attracts less public attention on entry, the firm tends to switch to franchise operations for further investments: in a franchise agreement the franchisee typically runs the operation as though it were their own business, but pays a royalty to McDonald's.

Klein and Roth (1990, p. 37) contend:

> firms should be wary of recommendations that they enter new and very unfamiliar markets with low degrees of commitment...When outside enforcement cannot be relied upon, a stronger earlier commitment to the market is necessary.

Oligopolistic Reaction Theory

Knickerbocker (1973) proposed oligopolistic reaction theory as an explanation of the FDI behaviour of multinational corporations. According to this theory, firms in the same industry tend to enter an international market at around the same time. Once the market leader has entered, other firms in the sector follow soon after. This 'clustering' of entry has been seen in a number of industries, examples include the rush into East and Central Europe (CEE) by the 'Big Six' accounting firms in the early 1990 (see Box 5.2) or into Mexico by automotive and computer manufacturers in the mid-1990s.

Buckley and Casson (1976, p. 78) say of Knickerbocker's theory:

> the timing of foreign investment is determined largely by reaction to competitors' investments... Once one firm invests in a region, the optimal strategy for other firms is to 'follow the leader', even if this confers no immediate advantage on the follower, but simply spoils the market for the leader.

The reasons why this 'clustering' takes place are not entirely clear. One suggestion is that industry rivals are watching each other's actions. Each firm's decisions may be triggered by a competitor's. This could be for fear of missing opportunities in a market. Alternatively, the lead firm might be assumed to have better market intelligence systems than its rivals and be first to enter a new market because of superior ability to assess its potential. The knowledge that a competitor views a market as attractive may increase its attractiveness in the eyes of competitor firms.

Knickerbocker did not specify the time period between entry of the first and last rivals. This might depend on the complexity of each firm's decision making process or the speed at which they assess market attractiveness. Hence Buckley and Casson (1976, p.79) stress:

> if there is a high degree of uncertainty or the initiating firm does not appear to be doing very well, then firms may defer their investment, so that they can benefit from the experience of the initiator. On the other hand, if there is little uncertainty, or the initiating firm is earning high profits, firms will tend to respond very quickly ... The theory, therefore, predicts that, across industries, bunching of foreign investment will be positively associated with profitability and with the stability and cohesion of the market concerned.

Vernon's Product Cycle Theory

The product cycle theory of Vernon (1966) identifies three phases in the life of a product: introduction, maturity and decline. These phases have different consequences for the production and marketing strategies of a firm:

- At the **early stage** of the product cycle, customers are relatively price insensitive so firms may charge high prices. Firms may need to devote resources to developing second-generation products, refining technologies or adding more sophisticated features.
- At the **second stage**, firms face increased competition, this reduces their ability to command premium prices and may mean that only smaller innovations are possible.
- At the **final stage**, competition may be based entirely on price and the product may become a commodity.

The notion of a *lifecycle*, when applied to the process of international expansion, also highlights different challenges, which the firm faces at the introduction, maturity and decline stages. Buckley and Casson (1976) describe these as follows:

- The **first phase** identifies criteria for where international production should be located. The firm is likely to be domestic at this stage and be beginning to look at international market opportunities.
- The **second phase** decides whether a market should be serviced by exports or by investment. Once a firm operates internationally, it faces decisions on when to increase its level of involvement in a market (this issue is discussed more fully in Chapter 8).
- The **final phase** looks at how the firm can best compete against local competition. This may involve relocating production to lower cost centres, or developing innovative products and services.

Vernon's model, however, is based on the stable market conditions of the 1960s. While this is accepted as an accurate description of the post-war expansion of US firms into Europe, it may be less applicable to current international marketing conditions. Looking at the entry of US firms into Europe today, we see that:

- labour costs in Europe have increased, therefore US firms are unlikely to enter the market in search of cheap production
- other markets may become attractive for cheap production, e.g. China and Mexico, but these have very different market conditions to stable, advanced economies
- US firms may make different choices depending on whether the target market is in the Single Market or not, Euro zone or non-Euro zone, etc.

Given the extent of the changes, critics question whether Vernon's model is applicable in the current turbulent environment. Furthermore, Hood and Young (1979) suggest that Vernon's theory may be more applicable to firms which are making their first international investment than to multi-national corporations.

Transaction Cost Analysis

Transaction costs have also been proposed (Williamson 1975, 1981) as a means of analyzing choices between different modes of international operation. Transaction costs are proposed by Williamson (1975) as a means of calculating the real costs of performing an activity within the firm (e.g. owning a manufacturing subsidiary) or having the activity performed by a partner (e.g. joint venture or licensed manufacture).

Williamson proposes a number of factors that may increase the transaction costs of carrying out an activity outside the firm:

- **Bounded rationality**. Managers do not have perfect knowledge. International marketing managers, when asked to identify a partner in a country whose culture, politics, economy or geography they do not understand, may not make the best decision.
- **Opportunistic behaviour**. Individuals or groups within an organization may make decisions for reasons of self-interest. If a firm producing under licence decides to replicate a technology for its own use, the costs of performing the activity outside the firm may be considerable.
- **Small numbers bargaining**. This is based on the premise of basic supply and demand. Choice may be restricted or prices may increase if there are few potential partners.

High levels of transaction costs of performing an activity externally may favour the firm performing the activity itself. The concept of transaction costs may be used in conjunction with internalization theory above to make choices of the optimal type of international operation. Jarillo (1988) argues that transaction costs are a useful way of deciding between external/internal options.

There are many criticisms of the transaction cost approach:

1. First, it assumes that opportunistic behaviour exists only in transactions *outside of the firm*.

There may, however, be costs of performing the activity internally that should be measured against these (see Jarillo 1988).

2. Secondly, transaction cost analysis focuses on relationships between *two parties*. This may overlook relevant actions of the broader network of firms (for the importance of the network view of international marketing, see Chapter 1 and the Network perspective throughout this book).

3. Finally, Buckley and Casson (1988) point to the difficulty of *operationalizing transaction cost analysis*. Although transaction costs have been classified as information costs, bargaining costs, enforcement costs and governance costs, there has been no estimate of how significant these are, in comparison to transport or marketing costs.

Balancing the Levels of Control and Risk

Despite these criticisms, transaction costs form the basis of a number of studies (Anderson and Gatignon 1986; Jarillo 1988; Klein and Roth 1989). Anderson and Gatignon (1986) use transaction costs to explore the relationship between control and risk. To gain control, for example by taking 100 per cent ownership or manufacturing goods themselves, firms may have to commit resources. This, in turn, creates risks for the firm. If a firm had to withdraw from a market through external causes such as civil war, earthquake or shortages of raw materials, or internal causes such as their ability to succeed in the market, the firm stands to lose this investment.

According to Anderson and Gatignon (1986), the optimal entry mode is a trade-off between the level of *control* that the firm wants to exercise, and the level of *risk* they must accept to achieve this. If a hotel positions itself on high levels of service quality, it might decide that it needs to protect service quality by running all the hotels itself. This involves higher levels of investment than, say, a franchise, and so increases risk. The decision is, however, consistent with its international marketing strategy.

Chapter 8 goes on to discuss the fact that firms may make different choices with respect to their mode of international operation at different stages of development. For example, in studying the level of control taken by service firms, Erramilli (1991), describes a 'U-shaped' relationship between experience and desired level of control. Firms with little international experience and those with significant levels both require a high level of control.

For firms with little international experience, the desire for control may be because international operations feel very risky to the firm. For firms with higher levels of international experience, as in the hotel example above, this may be because firms wish to protect advantages, such as superior service or brand reputation, which have taken considerable time and effort to build.

The complex trade-offs made by firms in choosing their mode of international operation is neatly summarized by Simyar and Argheyd (1987) (see Figure 7.1). The bottom axis shows four different types of international operation, export, license, joint venture and FDI. The levels of capital investment (equity participation) implied by each of these four modes are shown as a percentage on the top axis.

On the left-hand axis, the relationship between the mode and the perceived level of uncertainty is shown. In situations of high uncertainty, a firm may begin with low investment to reduce risks. As they overcome this uncertainty, by gaining greater understanding of the market, the firm may be more inclined to invest further.

This gradual increase in investment in a country is often referred to as an *incremental process of internationalization*. Most closely associated with the Uppsala model based on work by Johanson and Wiedersheim-Paul (1975) and Johanson and Vahlne (1977), incremental and other models of internationalization are debated more fully in Chapter 8.

The level of flexibility of the firm reduces as it moves towards investment in a subsidiary. If a firm exports to a country and then wishes to switch its attentions to a different country, the costs of doing so are relatively low. Had it invested in a manufacturing plant, the decision to change to a different location, a different market or different operation would have had far greater ramifications.

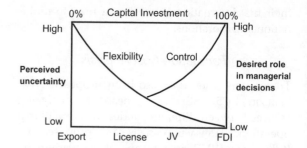

Figure 7.1   Trading off modes of market entry
Source: Simyar and Argheyd (1987). Reproduced with permission of Greenwood Publishing Group

On the right-hand side of Figure 7.1, Simyar and Argheyd (1987) show the desired role in managerial decisions. How much control does the firm wish to have? The control afforded by a wholly owned subsidiary is far greater than in a joint venture or licensing agreement where the interests of the partner must also be taken into account. Control here is seen as high for export and wholly owned operations and lower for co-operative relationships with a partner outside the firm.

THE RELATIONSHIP PERSPECTIVE

The previous section identifies lower control over international marketing strategy as a feature of joint ventures and other co-operative relationships. Nonetheless, the number of joint ventures and other types of co-operative relationship has increased dramatically since the late 1970s (Hergert and Morris 1988, Anderson 1990, Glaister, Husan and Buckley 1998). Moreover, the international scope of these relationships has broadened. It is now commonplace for this type of relationship to be between partners from different countries. More specifically, the number of co-operative relationships that involve firms from developed nations working with firms from advanced industrial nations has increased.

Glaister, Husan and Buckley (1998) have compiled a database of joint venture activity between firms in the UK and other parts of the Triad (North America, Western Europe and Japan) between 1990 and 1996. From this they present an updated picture of the nature and characteristics of joint venture activity in the 1990s. A number of features are identified:

- Joint venture activity increased dramatically in the late 1980s, but appears to have peaked. It should be noted, however, that this picture might look different if relationships with emerging market partners were included (Shama 1995, 1996).
- Research suggests that joint venture activity between developed and developing country partners increased during the 1990s.
- International joint venture activity between Triad partners does not appear to be strongly centred on particular industry sectors. For example, there is no support for arguments that joint ventures are more prevalent in high-technology industries, services or other groupings. Nor were these industry sector findings different for relationships with firms in different parts of the Triad.
- Relationships between UK firms showed similar patterns with firms in Western Europe, Japan and North America.

In sum, joint venture activity remains popular although its geographic focus may be shifting towards partners from developing nations. It is found across industry sectors. One reason for the decelerating growth of joint venture activity between partners in advanced nations is that firms are discovering that this type of co-operation does not provide easy gains.

In the 1980s, joint ventures seemed to be fashionable. As Harrigan (1987) expressed it:

> Joint ventures are in fashion again, and many firms throughout the world are rushing to find partners...Managers hope that by teaming up with partners that offer strengths that their own firms lack, the results will be a stronger competitive posture in the markets they hope to serve.

A number of factors combined to fuel this 'fashion'. In the 1980s, the cost of competing in global markets undoubtedly increased. Meeting the demands of information processing, technology, innovation and other competitive skills needed for international marketing is expensive and complex. As the costs and complexity were often beyond a single firm's capabilities, joint ventures appeared to offer a quick route to acquiring the skills to compete globally.

In her 1987 article, Harrigan cites both advantages and disadvantages of joint venture relationships. In a study conducted across 26 industries, Harrigan finds advantages to include:

- Easier access to expertise
- Easier access to distribution outlets
- Ability to gain market share more rapidly than if assets had to be developed by firm on its own
- Keeps initial costs low (until the firm generates sufficient sales to justify having their own plant, equipment and, salesforce).

In contrast, however:

- Learning to work together may initially slow down the speed of entry into markets
- Bureaucracy surrounding the agreement may be a hindrance, slowing down competitive actions
- In volatile or high-technology markets, this may result in missed opportunities.

The conclusion in the 1990s, then, was that joint ventures did not necessarily provide a universal panacea for the problems of expense and complexity in international marketing. These relationships may themselves be complex and difficult to manage. Nonetheless, joint ventures may offer a number of benefits for international marketers. The following section attempts to analyze further the joint venture phenomenon and to identify ways of increasing the success of joint venture activity.

Classifying Co-operative Ventures

A number of different labels have been used to describe co-operative relationships. These include international *coalitions* (Porter and Fuller 1986); *strategic networks* (Jarillo 1988); *hybrid organizational forms* (Thorelli 1986); *industrial systems constellations* (Perlmutter and Heenan 1986; Lorenzoni and Ornati 1988); *joint ventures* (Contractor and Lorange 1988); and *strategic alliances* (Hamel, Doz and Prahalad 1989; Doz 1992).

A common feature of all of these is that they involve two or more firms working together to *improve the competitive advantage of each partner*. The predominant focus of the literature in this area is on the extent to which alliances and other co-operative modes allow firms to compete more effectively by gaining access to scarce resources (Jarillo 1988). This is appositely expressed by Hamel, Doz and Prahalad up in the title of their 1989 article, 'Collaborate with your Competitors and Win'. Hence these might be referred to as 'collaborative' rather than 'co-operative' relationships.

How Can Joint Venture Effectiveness be Improved?

Academic literature classifies joint venture agreements according to industry type and stage, purpose, motivation and complexity. These may provide insights into the distinctive challenges of co-operation under different conditions:

- **What type of industry?** In newly developing industry sectors Harrigan (1987) proposes less formal joint venture agreements rather than more formal agreements (often characterized by equity swap). As it is not certain at early stages of industry development what will be the key success criteria, astute managers are those who do not enter binding agreements, which may later prove inappropriate. Handshakes are preferred to binding contracts. More formal agreements may, however, work in more mature industry sectors.
- **What stage of the industry lifecycle?** From the above, it appears that different types of joint venture agreement may be applicable to industries at different ages with different levels of stability. At the stage of industry maturity, firms are likely to forge fewer joint ventures encompassing higher levels of investment. Lorange and Roos (1992) argue that higher formal involvement creates higher mutual dependence and a greater requirement for trust between the partners.

- **What motivates international joint ventures?** According to Harrigan (1987) access to links in international markets are particularly important in industries where technology changes rapidly. This raises the costs of remaining innovative. Firms barely have the time to enter global markets before the technological advantage is overhauled by competitors. As an example, Harrigan uses the pharmaceutical industry in the early 1980s. Products took around eight years to develop and had an eight – ten-year patent protection before generic competitors could enter the market. To offset the costs of development, therefore, firms needed to enter new international markets rapidly before the competitive advantage expired. In this situation, joint ventures providing local market knowledge and distribution may be particularly valuable.
- **Do joint ventures set up for different purposes have different characteristics?** Research proposes that joint ventures may overcome lack of capital, lack of technological ability or lack of local knowledge. Glaister, Husan and Buckley (1998) suggest that co-operative behaviour begins early in the product development cycle. For this reason, they differentiate between the initial research, development and production phase and the second marketing phase. Partnerships in basic R&D are relatively unlikely because of the commercial sensitivity of innovations. For new applications of existing technologies and entry into new (and often international) markets joint venture agreements can provide valuable access to resources. As firms move beyond R&D and production into marketing agreements, earlier research by Buckley and Casson (1988) suggests that firms might be more likely to renege on joint venture deals. Possible reasons include the fact that difficulties become more apparent as deadlines loom and the project is tested in its final market. This finding seems to be supported by Glaister, Husan and Buckley (1998), in that more research/development and production joint ventures exist than do marketing joint ventures.
- **Multinational or global players may be at the centre of a complex web of international**

alliances. In this respect, managing these relationships may pose challenges similar to those presented in the Network sections of this book. Harrigan (1987) describes firms as being at the 'hub' or centre of a 'spider's web' of agreements. If technology lifecycles continue to shorten (as described more fully in Chapter 3) this web of less binding relationships may be a more effective means of gaining flexible access to transitory advantages.

Creating Successful Joint Ventures

The literature in this area is large and growing. A number of different approaches are proposed, but some unifying themes can be identified.

■ **Value of each partner's contribution**. The potential advantages of partnership are not always realized. One reason may be difficulties in valuing ahead of time the contribution that each partner can be expected to make. If the contribution is technology-based, start-up problems might, for example, reduce the ultimate commercial value of a technology. Thorough plans and valuation prior to partnership is advised where possible. If the anticipated benefit involves knowledge or other intangible assets, then hard and fast valuation may be complex.

■ **Partner screening**. It is easy to rush into an agreement, but not so easy to sever a relationship. For this reason, caution is advised. Joint venture relationships are often likened to marriages and the 'marry in haste, repent at leisure' axiom may prove only too true! Although potential partners might be identified from secondary sources, a process of face-to-face interviews and learning about potential partners is advised before entering any agreement. Identification of several different partners will allow firms to assess relative merits.

■ **Learning about partners**. A stepwise, or gradual, scale of involvement may allow partners to learn more about each other before entering binding agreements. This 'courtship' may make it easier for either side to draw back of the proposed benefits are not forthcoming.

Similarly, the 'upgrade' stages may allow the possibility of further negotiation on any areas of difficulty.

■ **Development of trust**. A number of measures are suggested to aid the development of trust between partners. These include open and honest discussion of goals for the co-operation and frequent re-appraisal of the progress of the venture (Lorange and Roos 1993). Harrigan (1987) also suggests that clear measures of 'success' be should identified upfront in order that the performance of the venture can be evaluated on an objective basis.

■ **Acceptance of the 'separate existence' of jointly owned ventures**. If the co-operative agreement involves the existence of a standalone unit it is important that the sponsoring organizations accept that this unit may take on a character and culture of its own. In doing so, the unit may diverge, at times, from either of its founding organizations. This may be a sign of the success, not the failure of the enterprise. It does add to the complexity, however, of managing relationships between the jointly owned venture and its parents.

THE NETWORK PERSPECTIVE

The Network as an Organizational Type

Chapter 1 introduces the fact that there are two different schools of network literature – networks as an organizational mode that is between markets and hierarchies (Thorelli 1986; Jarillo 1988) and 'markets as networks'. The majority of this book takes the latter view that networks are a fact of existence in markets. In this chapter, however, to be consistent with its focus on mode of international operation, the network is discussed as an organizational type, rather than as a world-view.

There are a range of ways in which two parties can deal with each other. These span a spectrum from trading in a 'free' market through to dealing with each other as two separate organizations. Dealing as organizations is referred to in the literature as 'hierarchy' or 'bureaucracy' (Williamson 1975; Ouchi 1980).

If two parties trade in a free market, dealings between the two may fail if the cost is higher than carrying out the same activity within an organization (see previous sections for a review of internalization and transaction costs theories). A firm might, for example, decide to purchase cake mix from a supplier rather than making it itself. If, however, quality problems with the supplier result in costly write-offs, then firm might decide to produce cake mix itself on future occasions.

Ouchi (1980) identifies two main benefits of an organization over the free market:

1. Employment of individuals means that the firm can direct their actions more than it can those of individuals outside the firm.
2. The organization creates an atmosphere of trust because employees develop shared goals and learn that good performance is rewarded.

Despite the benefits of organizations, they can also become complex, rigid and unresponsive. A set of individuals programmed to accept a certain recipe for new product development, for example, may overlook certain types of opportunities. Employees of a multinational food manufacturer said that as a result of past new product failures, the firm wished to identify new product opportunities only within existing product categories. This kind of strategic directive is common in organizations. It may, however, limit the innovation identified in Chapter 3 as key to success in international marketing.

An increasing number of authors argue that collaboration may not only reduce costs, but may also increase the flexibility of an international operation (Perlmutter and Heenan 1986; Porter and Fuller 1986; Contractor and Lorange 1988; Hamel, Prahalad and Doz 1989; Doz 1992). For a fuller discussion of the benefits and challenges of collaborative relationships, see the Relationship section of this chapter.

Some authors go beyond suggesting single collaborative relationships to stress the benefits of collaboration with a number of other parties. This type of collaboration results in loosely connected organizational forms that have been variously referred to as 'international coalitions' (Porter and Fuller 1986), 'constellations' (Lorenzoni and Ornati 1988) or 'industrial systems constellations' (Perlmutter and Heenan 1986), 'clans' (Ouchi 1980) or 'quasi-firms' (Eccles 1991). Thorelli (1986), Miles and Snow (1986) and Jarillo (1988) refer to them as 'strategic networks'.

This section uses the term 'network' to refer to this type of organization, but reviews the contributions of literature using other names for the same phenomena, too.

The strategic network is an organizational type that lies somewhere between the free market and the organization. As Thorelli (1986, p. 37) explains:

> at one end of the spectrum is what we would call the open market. At the other we find the firm which is relatively self-sufficient in terms of vertical of functional integration. In some ways these distinctions are analogous to Williamson's (1975) markets and hierarchies, although he would likely include as part of 'markets' a number of in-between forms where we would rather apply the generic term networks.

By this definition, a network is a type of organization that the firm can choose if it is appropriate. It has a number of characteristics:

■ Its boundaries are 'fuzzy' or unclear. Although definitions vary, a common definition of boundaries is that of a 'focal net' (Cunningham and Culligan 1991) containing 'relations above a certain minimum degree of closeness to a focal or "hub" firm'.
■ Within the network, flows of power, information, money and other utilities may all be exchanged between network members (Thorelli 1986). In international marketing terms, local market information, technology and social exchanges may be valuable drivers of the network's existence.
■ The network is held together by trust and mutual gain, rather than hierarchy or contract.
■ Its membership may change over time.
■ Given the loose nature of the relationships and the informal nature of the connections, networks may be more flexible than organizations while creating more trusting interactions than occur in the free market.

Miles and Snow (1986) suggest that networks offer a flexible organizational type for turbulent environments. This suggests that networks may be a suitable organizational choice for international marketers operating in turbulent conditions (see Part II on International Marketing Strategies and in particular Chapter 6 for a fuller discussion of the implications of discontinuous change).

Networks may also confer other benefits. Lorenzoni and Ornati (1988) highlight the contribution to innovation offered by constellations of small firms in the Italian textile industry. These small firms may have less rigid recipes, be closer to their customers and are more likely to be led by entrepreneurs than are larger rivals. In retailing, small retailers may combine to form buying associations to increase their power relative to large competitors.

When debating the value of carrying out international marketing activities externally, rather than within the organization, Robinson (1986, p. 2) concludes:

> it boils down to which value-added links are most likely to enjoy international economies of scale...if performed by external specialist firms, economies which may swamp the benefits derived from the internalization of the transaction.

If operation in a network is feasible, then, as an organizational choice, it offers a number of benefits that may be attractive to international marketers. Operation in strategic networks may, however, increase risk and decrease control of an individual firm. The firm does not have sole discretion over international marketing decisions. It can, however, more readily sever its connection with the network than can a firm engaging in more formal type of collaborative relationship.

CASE STUDY 7.1   BOHOMIN STEEL WORKS[1]

Until the dramatic events of November 1989, when the Czech people, led by students and dissident writers, crowded into Wenceslas Square, Prague, to protest against Soviet oppression, Czechoslovakia had been under communist rule for 41 years. The spirit of the Czech people in rallying to support the revolutionary cause drew worldwide attention.

For the Czech Republic, the years since liberalization have been no less momentous. The transition from centrally planned to free market economy brought many changes. In 1991 the newly formed Czech and Slovak Federal Republic split into separate Czech and Slovak states. In October 1993, the Czech Republic was accepted as an associate member of the EU and is now seeking full membership. Among the former COMECON countries, the Czech Republic vies with Hungary as the nation which has progressed furthest in its reforms. A key part of the reform process in the Czech Republic has been the mass privatization of the previously state-owned monopolies. This has been achieved by issue of vouchers to Czech citizens, with which they can purchase shares in their chosen company. While this has proved a rapid way of decentralizing control, it has not been without critics. In some instances, people have taken loans to purchase shares in companies which have no experience of competition, and flounder in the free market within a short period.

One firm which has successfully completed the first phase of privatization and now operates as an independent company is Bohomin, a major producer of pressed steel goods and wires. Berlin entrepreneurs A. Hahn and H. Eisner set up the Bohomin factory in 1885, to manufacture nails and screws. The location of the plant, 12 kilometres from Ostrava on the Czech–Polish border, was seen to be advantageous, both because of the local availability of raw materials and because of the excellent road and rail links with Northern, Eastern and Southern Europe.

In 1896 the firm merged with wire producer, Moravian-Silesian Co., to become a limited company. In the following years, the plant expanded to become the largest producer of wires in the country. After the Second World War, Bohomin set up plants to manufacture pressed steel castings for a variety of purposes. Currently, Bohomin has six manufacturing plants: wires, cables and ropes, radiators and generators, pressed steel goods, railway wheels and undercarriages and wire meshes. Since liberalization, Bohomin has experienced radical changes. It has lost its guaranteed Soviet markets, and now has to compete in the international market. In practice, Bohomin has much to recommend it. The low wage costs in Czech Republic allow it to price its products at below world prices, for comparable quality. Bohomin has already achieved ISO 9001 quality certification. It has a go-ahead management team, who are currently in the process of a second rights issue to raise funds to modernize the plant. Indeed, the entire management team is in the process of improving its own managerial ability by studying for an In-Company MBA through Prague International Business School.

At the same time, there are some significant issues which Bohomin will have to resolve in order to ensure its future profitability. A significant proportion of the formerly guaranteed markets in Russia and Slovakia have been lost, for which replacements must be found. Bohomin gains a significant proportion of its sales through export. The industry sectors in which Bohomin operates are characterized by high levels of competition. Within the EU, protectionist measures in the steel and predominantly state-owned railway industries limit the access which they can gain to customers. The steel cast panels which Bohomin sells to automotive manufacturers are subject to ever-increasing quality and delivery requirements. Bohomin's ability to compete on cost may be eroded as the Czech economy moves forward and wage levels become comparable with the rest of Europe. Moreover, it is heavily reliant on supplies of oil and coal, which are still bought from Russia at less than world market price.

However, as a result of the privatization process new potential markets have opened up for Bohomin within the Czech Republic and former COMECON countries. COMECON (the Commission for Mutual Economic Aid) may no longer exist, but opportunities arise from the new economic groupings of the Visegrad countries (the Czech and Slovak Republics, Hungary, Poland), the revived Hapsburg grouping (Austria, Italy, the Czech and Slovak Republics, Poland) and the EU.

Indeed, in some of their market sectors Bohomin have little choice but to compete internationally. Czech Railways is replacing less rolling stock as shifting priorities have resulted in less governmental expenditure on infrastructure. The board of directors of Bohomin considers it unlikely that the situation will change in the foreseeable future. However, possible privatization of the railway systems in a number of other countries may open up new international markets. Bohomin also make wheels and undercarriages for trams and light railways. Increasing concern about traffic density has made this a growth area in recent years.

The market for automotive panels is almost exclusively international. Even Skoda, the leading Czech car manufacturer, is now in partnership with Germany's VW. The leading firms in the automotive industry are primarily multinationals, who make tough demands on their component suppliers. Bohomin supply some international automotive firms in Russia and Italy, but they would like to expand their business in this area.

One major problem which Bohomin faces is that the majority of its plant is very old. Accordingly it is expensive in terms of maintenance and also oriented towards previous production patterns. Bohomin have a massive capacity for the production of semi-finished and finished wires. Their finished wires are made to an extremely high specification and are capable of competing internationally on quality.

As their market is changing, Bohomin will have to rethink the way in which they operate. Orders were previously organized centrally through the state-controlled system. Order quantities were large and quality relatively unimportant. Bohomin had little knowledge about their final customers. The firm deals with the EU via one distributor, but currently has no direct links with potential customers. New private distribution channels such as builders' merchants are springing up in the Czech Republic. However, meeting the requirements of these channels would require Bohomin to supply much smaller order quantities. Order lead times may have to be reduced and consistent quality standards assured. In some geographic areas,

Strengths	Weaknesses
Broad customer base	No experience of marketing
Skilled workforce	Low profitability
International quality	
Certification	Not marketing-led
Management dynamism	
Opportunities	**Threats**
Pursue differentiation on quality	World recession
Restructure to cut costs	Protectionism
Find new Western markets supplies	Disruption of raw material competition
Find new private customers (domestic)	
Form a joint venture	
Find new suppliers	

Figure 7.2   SWOT analysis: Bohomin

Bohomin would have to decide on the most appropriate mode of international operation.

As part of their MBA marketing course, the Board of Directors of Bohomin arrived at the SWOT analysis of their firm shown in Figure 7.2.

The management team recognizes that they have, as yet, little experience in analyzing their business. They have also relatively little internal data on which products have been responsible for their profitability to date.

At this stage in their development, the management team at Bohomin is anxious to make the best strategic choices. It is currently deciding on the priorities for allocating resources between the different areas of its product portfolio. This requires an analysis of the product areas with the best potential for the future. Several Czech firms have entered joint ventures with foreign partners. A number of the Board members favour this option,

as it seems to them that this will provide Western managerial skills. If an EU partner is chosen, it may also offer access to markets currently blocked by protectionist measures. However, this suggestion raises considerable concern among other Board members, who fear the loss of autonomy which may be associated with this course of action.

QUESTIONS

1. Assess the potential of Bohomin to compete internationally.
2. What would be the advantages and disadvantages of a joint venture for Bohomin?
3. What other strategic options do Bohomin have?
4. What would be your preferred internationalization strategy, and why?

SUMMARY

In Chapter 7 we have explored the different types of international operation. The advantages and disadvantages of the different modes are identified, revealing a trade-off between investment and

hence risk, flexibility and the level of control that international marketers wish to have over operation in different international markets.

NOTE

1. This case is intended as a basis for discussion rather than to illustrate effective or ineffective handling of a business situation. © Sue Bridgewater 1994.

BIBLIOGRAPHY

Anderson, E. (1990) 'Two Firms, One Frontier: On Assessing Joint Venture Performance', *Sloan Management Review*, 31, 2: 19–30.

Anderson, E. and Gatignon, H. (1986) 'Modes of Foreign Entry: A Transaction Cost Analysis and Propositions', *Journal of International Business Studies*, 12, 3: 25–34.

Buckley, P. J. and Casson, M. (1976) *The Future of the Multinational Enterprise*, Macmillan.

Buckley, P. J. and Casson, M. (1988) 'A Theory of Co-operation in International Business', in Contractor, F. J. and Lorange, P. (eds), *Co-operative Strategies in International Business*, Lexington Books: 31–53.

Caves, R. E. (1971) 'International Corporations: The Industrial Economics of Foreign Investment', *Economica*, February: 1–27.

Contractor, F. and Lorange, P. (eds) (1988) *Co-operative Strategies in International Business*, Lexington Books.

Cunningham, M. T. and Culligan, K. (1991) 'Competitiveness through Networks of Relationships in Information Technology Product Markets', in Paliwoda, S. J. (ed.), *New Perspectives in International Marketing*, Routledge.

Doz Y. (1992) 'The Role of Partnerships and Alliances in the European Industrial Restructuring', in Cool, I. C., Neven D. J. and Walter, I. (eds), *European Industrial Restructuring in the 1990s*, Macmillan.

Dunning, J. H. (1980) 'Towards an Eclectic Theory of International Production: Some Empirical Tests', *Journal of International Business Studies*, 11, 1: 9–25.

Dunning, J. H. (1988) 'The Eclectic Paradigm of International Production: A Restatement and Some Possible Extensions', *Journal of International Business Studies*, 19, 1: 1–27.

Easton, G. (1990) 'Relationships Among Competitors', in Day, G. F. and Wensley, J. R. (eds), *The Interface of Marketing and Strategy: Strategic Management, Policy and Planning*, 4, JAI Press.

Eccles, R. G. and Nohria, N. (1991) 'The Post-Structuralist Organization', *Working Paper, Harvard Business Review*.

Erramilli, M. K. (1991) 'The Experience Factor in Foreign Market Entry Behaviour of Service Firms', *Journal of International Business Studies*, 22, 3: 479–501.

Glaister, K., Husan, R. and Buckley, P. J. (1998) 'UK International Joint Ventures with the Triad: Evidence for the 1990s', *British Journal of Management*, 9: 169–80.

Hamel, G., Doz, Y. L. and Prahalad, C. K. (1989) 'Collaborate with your Competitors and Win', *Harvard Business Review*, January–February: 133–9.

Harrigan, K. (1987) 'Why Joint Ventures Fail', *Euro-Asia Business Review*, July.

Hergert, M. and Morris, D. (1988) 'Trends in International Collaborative Agreements', in Contractor, F. J. and Lorange, P. (eds), *Cooperative Strategy in International Business*, Lexington Books.

Hirsch, S. (1976) 'An International Trade and Investment Theory of the Firm', *Oxford Economic Papers*, 28: 258–70.

Hood, N. and Young, S. (1979) *The Economics of the Multinational Enterprise*, Longman.

Hymer, S. (1960) 'The International Operations of National Firms: A Study of Direct Investment', unpublished doctoral dissertation; published as *The International Operations of National Firms: A Study of Direct Investment* (1976).

Jarillo, J.-C. (1988) 'On Strategic Networks', *Strategic Management Review*, 11: 479–99.

Johanson, J. and Vahlne, J.-E. (1977) 'The Internationalisation Process of the Firm: A Model of Knowledge Development and Increasing Foreign Market Commitments', *Journal of International Business Studies*, 8, 1: 23–32.

Johanson, J. and Wiedersheim-Paul, F. (1975) 'The Internationalisation of the Firm – Four Swedish Cases', *Journal of Management Studies*, October: 305–22.

Kindelberger, C. P. (1969) *American Business Abroad: Six Lectures on Direct Invesment*, Yale University Press.

Klein, S. and Roth, V. J. (1990) 'Determinants of Export Channel Structure: The Effects of Experience and Psychic Distance Reconsidered', *International Marketing Review*, 7, 5: 27–38.

Knickerbocker, F. T. (1973) *Oligopolistic Reaction and the Multinational Enterprise*, Harvard University Press.

Lorange, P. and Roos, J. (1993) *Strategic Alliances: Formation, Implementation and Evolution*, Blackwell.

Lorenzoni, G. and Ornati, O. A. (1988) 'Constellations of Firms and New Ventures', *Journal of Business Venturing*, 4, 2: 133–47.

Mascarenhas, B. (1982) 'Coping with Uncertainty in International Business', *Journal of International Business*, Fall: 87–98.

Miller, K. D. (1992) 'A Framework for Integrated Risk Management', *Journal of International Business*, Summer: 311–31.

Miles, R. E. and Snow, C. (1986) 'Organizations. New Concepts for New Forms', *California Management Review*, 28: 62–73.

Ouchi, W. G. (1980) 'Markets, Bureaucracies and Clans', *Administrative Science Quarterly*, 25, 1: 129–42.

Perlmutter, H. V. and Heenan, D. A. (1986) 'Cooperate to Compete Globally', *Harvard Business Review*, March–April: 1.

Porter, M. E. and Fuller, M. B. (1986) 'Coalitions and Global Strategy', *Competition in Global Industries*, Harvard Business School Press: 315–44.

Robinson, R. D. (1986) 'Some Competitive Factors in International Marketing', in Cavusgil, S. T. (ed.), *Advances in International Marketing*, JAI Press: 1–20.

Shama, A. (1995) 'Entry Strategies of US Firms to the Newly Independent States, Baltic States and Eastern European Countries', *California Management Review*, 37, 3: 90–108.

Shama, A. (1996) 'Cracking the Former Soviet Bloc Markets: An Empirical Study', *International Journal of Management*, 13, 2: 184–92.

Simyar, F. and Argheyd, K. (1987) 'Export Entry and Expansion Strategies', in Rosson, P. J. and Reid, S. D. (eds), *Managing Export, Entry and Expansion*, Praeger: 228.

Thorelli, H. B. (1986) 'Networks: Between Markets and Hierarchies', *Strategic Management Review*, 7: 37–51.

Vernon, R. (1966) 'International Investment and International Trade in the Product Cycle', *Quarterly Journal of Economics*, 80: 190–207.

Williamson, O. E. (1975) *Between Markets and Hierarchies: Analysis and Antitrust Implications*, Macmillan.

Williamson, O. E. (1981) 'The Economics of Organization: The Transaction Cost Approach', *American Journal of Sociology*, 87, November: 548–77.

THE PROCESS OF INTERNATIONALIZATION

Objectives

The issues to be addressed in Chapter 8 include:

1. Internationalization as a process
2. Two models of the internationalization process – simultaneous and sequential models
3. Particular characteristics of the internationalization process in different types of firms, e.g. small and large firms, retailers and service firms
4. The portfolio of investment decisions made by international marketers
5. The network perspective on the internationalization process

After reading Chapter 8 you will be able to:

1. Understand the dynamics of increasing international operation
2. Identify the drivers of international expansion and those factors that may inhibit international marketers in this process
3. Contrast simultaneous and sequential models of internationalization
4. Distinguish between the internationalization process in different types of firms
5. Understand the alternative network perspective on internationalization

INTRODUCTION

This chapter first explains why internationalization should be viewed as a process. Secondly, it studies two models of this process. While
some firms, like AuditCo (see Box 8.2, p. 144),
expand rapidly into new international markets
and use high investment modes of operation on
entry others, such as ComputerCo (see Box 8.1,
p. 141) enter more gradually using low levels of
investment to establish the potential of the market
before expanding their operations. The arguments
underlying the former (simultaneous) and latter
(sequential) models are explored. The chapter analyzes particular characteristics of the internationalization process of different types of firms. Small
firms, service firms, large international and retail
organizations are contrasted to see which model
more accurately explains their behaviour.

From a relationship perspective, the links
between the investment decisions of a firm are
explored. The alternative network view of internationalization is also studied to see what it adds
to understanding of firms' decisions. The chapter
concludes by studying CigaretteCo's internationalization choices so that managers understand the
complex influences on the internationalization
process.

THE TRADITIONAL PERSPECTIVE

The Process of Internationalization

Viewing internationalization as a process rather
than as isolated investment decisions offers a fuller
understanding of the international expansion of
firms. A firm may make successive decisions to

enter, expand, or retract from investments in a market. Moreover, it may enter a number of international markets one after another or in parallel. Each individual decision to enter or exit a market or to change mode is an episode in an ongoing process. Case Study 8.1, on CigaretteCo (p. 154), shows a situation in which understanding previous episodes in the international expansion of a company plays an important role in understanding the whole process.

A number of models of the internationalization process have been proposed. These models can be broadly divided into *sequential* and *simultaneous* models. Sequential models of the internationalization process identify different stages of internationalization, taking a firm from its first international activity to a high degree of internationalization. A number of different sequential models have been proposed that use different criteria to identify the steps, or stages, along the way.

Sequential Models of Internationalization

Perlmutter's 'Tortuous Evolution' of the Multinational Firm

Perlmutter (1969) bases the stages on the 'cultural orientation' of the firm. Three distinct orientations are identified. In the 'ethnocentric orientation', the domestic culture dominates the firm. A polycentric orientation is achieved when the distinction between the domestic and 'foreign' culture becomes blurred. Geocentric orientation refers to the stage at which the firm operates as a multinational or global player. These stages are used to infer different choices of international marketing strategy:

- An 'early internationalist' with an ethnocentric orientation is more likely to serve its markets by export or an agent. It may wish to retain high levels of control over all international marketing activity because it perceives high levels of risk.
- A 'more experienced internationalist' with a polycentric orientation is likely to have a range of organizations across markets globally, or within a region. It may have devolved some control and make greater use of co-operative

agreements, such as licensing agreements and joint ventures. The firm generally perceives lower risk in international marketing decisions.

- A very experienced or 'global' player with a geocentric orientation is likely to have global scope and a complex matrix of international organizations. The firm may no longer be strongly associated in customers' minds with any particular country. Some authors suggest that at this stage in its development, the firm may opt to take higher control over its operations with wholly owned or majority stake investments to protect valuable assets, such as brands, service quality and proprietary technologies.

Innovation-Related Models

Andersen (1993) classifies models of the internationalization process into 'innovation-related' models and the 'Uppsala Internationalization' model. The 'innovation-related' models, exemplified by Bilkey and Tesar (1977), Cavusgil (1980) and Czinkota (1982) focus on the learning sequence involved in internationalization as an innovation for the firm. A firm may move on in the process when it has learned enough to overcome its uncertainty about doing so.

The Uppsala Model

Probably the best known model of the internationalization process is that of the Uppsala School. This is most closely associated with the Nordic studies of Johanson and Wiedersheim-Paul (1975) and Johanson and Vahlne (1977). It studies internationalization in terms of the mode of operation and the international markets served. The Uppsala model describes a sequential progression from export to sales and then manufacturing subsidiaries. Johanson and Wiedersheim-Paul (1975) also suggest that firms will invest in countries which have progressively higher psychic distance (factors which inhibit the flow of information between markets).

Although the Uppsala model was based on data from Nordic markets, it has since been validated in a number of other markets (Dichtl, Leboid, Köglmayer and Müller 1990; Sullivan and Bauerschmidt 1990; Calof and Viviers 1995).

One of the key arguments of the Uppsala model is that the uncertainty of international markets can be overcome only by experiential and market-specific knowledge (Johanson and Vahlne 1977) (see Chapter 6 for a fuller discussion of classifications of knowledge types). On this basis, Johanson and Vahlne believe that the firm cannot build on experiences it has had in other international markets. Nor can it gain market knowledge by employing key individuals who possess this knowledge. Critics have challenged this underlying assumption of the Uppsala model.

According to the Uppsala model, the firm faces high levels of uncertainty on first entering an international market. These favour entry via low 'commitment'[1] modes of operation, such as export or use of an agent, distributor or joint venture partner. As the firm increases its knowledge and understanding of the market, it may increase its commitment by establishing a sales and, ultimately, manufacturing subsidiary. The sequential process involves not only deepening commitment within each country, but also a gradual broadening of the firm's geographic focus.

The CigaretteCo Case Study (p. 154) shows a firm following this type of incremental expansion in East and Central Europe (CEE). The firm aims to move from its initial investment in a representative office in Ukraine to a manufacturing joint venture when it has gained sufficient knowledge about the market's potential.

This incremental, or sequential, process of internationalization is also typified by the example of ComputerCo's entry into East and Central Europe (Box 8.1). ComputerCo has had long-term involvement in Hungary and Poland using a distributor and export, respectively, and invested in these countries only later when market potential was improved by liberalization.

Theoretical Analysis of the Uppsala Model

The Uppsala model of internationalization proposed two dimensions, in which firms might increase their commitment to a market:

- **The establishment chain**. This refers to the sequence of international operational types used. According to the Uppsala model, this sequence involves a progression from (1) sporadic exports to (2) exports via a foreign intermediary, such as an agent or distributor, (3) exports via a wholly owned sales subsidiary, (4) a mix of exports and foreign direct investment (FDI) in the form of a subsidiary with assembly activities to (5) a wholly owned full production facility (Forsgren and Johanson 1975).
- **Geographic sequence**. Firms are assumed to move from a market with low, towards markets with higher, psychic distance. (See Chapter 2 for a fuller discussion of psychic distance.)

Box 8.1   ComputerCo

ComputerCo is a British-based multinational producer and distributor of computers with over 60 years of international experience. It has a broad portfolio of investments in East and Central Europe. These include a direct trading subsidiary in Russia and a joint venture to assemble computers. ComputerCo has had 20 years of experience in the USSR. However, it recognizes that the 'rules' of operation in the region are no longer the same: 'the rules of operation in the Soviet Union were complex [but] once you had learned them, they were easy to play. It is has become a lot more difficult since liberalization. It is hard to determine what the new rules are.'

Liberalization sparked increased investment activity by ComputerCo in Eastern Europe. Investments in Hungary, Poland, the Czech Republic, Bulgaria, Romania and Kazakhstan followed. Entry into Ukraine took place via an independent distributor in 1992.

The choice of entry using a distributor in Ukraine was motivated by the partner's local knowledge. The local partner is part of the Diaspora, Ukrainian nationals who had migrated from the area and have returned since liberalization. He combines cultural and linguistic understanding of Ukraine with Western business experience. The firm anticipates that, longer-term, it may enter a joint venture in Ukraine, as there is clear market potential.

Later work into incremental internationalization (Luostarinen 1979; Hörnell and Vahlne 1982) suggests a third dimension of progression, evolution in terms of the product offered.

- **Product offered**. The range of products offered to a new foreign market tends to begin with goods, but services, systems and know-how are gradually added until a complete problem-solving package is on offer.

Petersen and Pedersen (1997) identify three alternative explanations for why firms may show this gradual international expansion, particularly in terms of the mode of operation used:

1. **Export sales growth**. Micro-economic theory suggests that a producer will switch from using an agent or distributor to hierarchy when the scale economies from the latter exceed the costs. In other words, firms will switch when the benefits are greater than the costs. Buckley and Casson (1985) suggest that it is most cost effective to enter via a distributor and switch to a production operation later.
2. **Accumulation of financial and management resources**. Amongst a list of barriers to markets, Porter (1980) lists the large capital requirements required. Although Porter refers to entry into an industry, Petersen and Pedersen extend the concept to entry into a new international market. As initial entry costs are high, a firm may need to use a low investment mode, such as an agent or distributor, while accumulating the funds to invest. This argument is

Table 8.1 Ranking of explanations of incremental entry mode behaviour

Explanations of incremental entry mode behaviour	% of firms ranking the explanation as important
Increase of sale volume in foreign markets	53
Acquisition of knowledge about foreign markets	30
Intensification of global competition	28
Accumulation of financial resources	15

Source: Petersen and Pedersen (1997)

used particularly in explaining the expansion of small firms, which tend to be resource constrained (Buckley 1989) (see p. 148 for a fuller discussion of the internationalization process of small firms).

3. **Increased global competition**. Petersen and Pedersen (1997) suggest that global competitive activity will cause firms to adjust the way they serve foreign markets over time. As competition increases, the potential financial consequences of not protecting global technologies and brands may outweigh the costs of investment in a higher control organizational type (see the discussion of control in Chapter 7 on Mode of International Operation).

Based on findings from Danish companies, Petersen and Pedersen (1997) ranked the various explanations of incremental entry patterns (see Table 8.1).

From this it appears that basic economic drivers, followed by knowledge acquisition and global competition, are the principal causes of incremental internationalization.

Motivations for Entry

It should be noted that Petersen and Pedersen (1997) identify limitations in previous validation studies of the Uppsala model:

1. They include international operations that are not motivated by market seeking behaviour
2. Leapfrogging is too broadly defined
3. The studies do not take into account that firms can expand using the same mode over time; this might be the case, for example, in the retail sector where firms may use franchise as a mode but expand the number of individual outlets within the country.

1. **Market seeking and other motivations for entry**. Three motivations for entry into international markets are identified by Petersen and Pedersen:

   - Market seeking
   - Resource seeking
   - Technology seeking.

To these may be added motivations identified by Bridgewater, McKiernan and Wensley (1995) for multinational corporations in Ukraine:

- Client-following
- External contract seeking

Firms with different motivations may exhibit different entry behaviour.

- **Market seeking**. Concerned at available market size and macro-level stability.
- **Resource seeking**. A firm seeking resources such as oil or gas, for example, will enter markets that have these resources and use the type of operation necessary to gain access to these. Once the initial scientific and business cases for entry into the market are established, the firm may have little choice but to invest in extraction, refineries and pipelines to exploit the resource opportunities.
- **Technology seeking**. Similarly, if the firm wishes to capitalize on technological skills available in a market, a minimum requirement might, for example, be a licensing agreement with a local partner. FDI may be necessary to gain access to the technology.
- **Client-following**. Business-to-business service firms entering Ukraine had followed international customers into the market. Given that retention of global accounts was dependent on maintaining high levels of service, the business-to-business service firms felt that they had little option but to invest in a wholly owned subsidiary in the country.
- **External contract seeking**. In the same sector, entry into a number of CEE markets was dictated by the availability of contracts funded by international economic institutions and aid agencies, such as the World Bank, the IMF and the EU, to provide managerial and economic guidance to local firms and governments. The terms of these contracts often specified a minimum level of investment in the market. A local office was often necessary to guarantee the successful execution of the contract.

From discussion of the alternative motivations for entry into international markets it becomes apparent that firms will not always have discretion over which mode of operation they use or even which geographic market they enter. Including these firms whose behaviour is dictated by motives other than market penetration in studies of incremental internationalization may distort the results.

2. **Leapfrogging is too broadly defined**. In order to determine what is meant by 'leapfrogging', it is first necessary to identify the stages of the establishment chain. The original Uppsala model supposes that use of an agent or distributor precedes establishment of a sales and marketing subsidiary. Modes such as export using a home-based salesforce, is not considered as a first step. Yet Petersen and Pedersen (1997) find this to be the most widely used form of initial international operation.

   In their comprehensive review of the literature, Welch and Luostarinen (1988) argue for the existence of a wide range of potential paths. Many of these show incremental progression, although not in the exact sequence suggested by the Uppsala model. The number of firms which really leapfrog or miss stages must take into account the range of possible incremental paths.

3. **Individual entry modes may show gradual expansion**. A firm may increase its involvement within a particular type of international operation. For example, the proportion of a market targeted by a distributor or export salesforce may increase, although the mode of international operation does not. The firm may increase the level of its investment in an existing subsidiary. It might invest in a new production line or upgrade its computer systems. These increases in commitment are not apparent if only mode of operation is studied.

   Benito and Welch (1994, p. 12) argue for more detailed study of individual firms' activities to gain a full picture of international expansion:

   Understanding of the [internationalization] process probably requires a more detailed case by case analysis, and a move away from simplistic pattern measures, from which wide-ranging inferences about process are sometimes drawn.

Testing the Concept of Geographic Sequence

A number of studies have found that firms do not enter countries in order of their psychic distance. Not all of these studies, however, have differentiated between market seeking and other motivations for entry. As has been discussed above, firms entering to gain access to resources or as a reaction to the entry of an international customer may have their choice of market dictated by the availability of resources of the actions of the customer, respectively. Further questions arise over the choice of a scale of psychic distance (see Chapter 2 for the classifications, which have been proposed to measure psychic or cultural distance).

Simultaneous Models of Internationalization

Studies of the internationalization process have also suggested the existence of simultaneous models. These are based on arguments of global convergence. As can be seen in Chapter 4, global interlinkage of economies has broken down national boundaries:

> On a political map, the boundaries between countries areas clear as ever. But on a competitive map, a map showing the real flows of financial and industrial activity, those boundaries have largely disappeared. (Ohmae 1990, p. 54)

Proponents of global convergence, such as Levitt (1983), argue that increased ability to travel and communicate globally have made customers' tastes more similar wherever in the world they are. Levitt sees evidence of this in growing similarities in the fashion and music preferences of youth around the world, and to the existence of global products such as Coca Cola and Sony Walkman. Serving these global markets with standardized products or services may offer valuable economies of scale and scope. While critics believe that Levitt's views exaggerate the extent of homogenization and the savings it may offer, nonetheless a number of authors (Quelch and Hoff 1986; Douglas and Wind 1987; Ohmae 1990; Riesenbeck and Freeling 1991) suggest some degree of standardization can offer savings.

If tastes are becoming more similar, and communication and travel easier, then the uncertainty, which Johanson and Vahlne (1977) associated with entry into new international markets must have reduced. Casson (1994) suggests that this may favour simultaneous, rather than sequential models of internationalization. Riesenbeck and Freeling (1991) show that the speed of international expansion of new brands has reduced from around 20 years for the traditional, sequential or 'waterfall' process to 1–2 years for simultaneous or 'sprinkler' launches. These findings seem to support a simultaneous model of international expansion. AuditCo (Box 8.2) is an example of a

---

Box 8.2   AuditCo

AuditCo was created by the merger of two of the big eight accounting firms in 1987 and in 1995 ranked as the second largest of the 'Big Six' globally. It has been involved in international operations since the late 1940s. As it provides business-to-business services, it has links with other firms around the world. The size of such customers is such that AuditCo is very concerned to protect its business by offering consistent levels of international service: 'Business is centred mainly on international clients. AuditCo must offer world-wide service in order to develop relationships with these clients across markets.' Any reduction in customer service might result in the loss of accounts to its international rivals. When entering Ukraine, AuditCo opted to take a majority stake in a joint venture with a local partner. The local partner provided necessary knowledge of the turbulent Ukrainian market.

AuditCo set up an office in Hungary in 1987. The success of this venture, and the subsequent liberalization of the market, resulted in rapid expansion, during 1990, into the Czech and Slovak Republics, into Poland and into Moscow. As the Moscow office was established 18 months before the Ukrainian subsidiary, experienced individuals from this subsidiary identified a likely joint venture partner. The decision to enter Ukraine was prompted by the US Headquarters, which has the strongest links with the international client. Subsidiaries in Germany and Britain, which were near to the target market, were also involved in the investment decision.

firm which has internationalized rapidly within the East and Central European region.

While AuditCo has had international experience spanning a considerable time, its entry into the East and Central European region shows virtually simultaneous entry and use of high commitment modes of operation on entry.

Limitations of Simultaneous Models

Critics of the simultaneous model question the assumptions on which it is based. Both the standardization literature and simultaneous models are based on the idea that the similarity between people in different countries has increased and that uncertainty, in consequence, has decreased. However, critics suggest that while there may be some convergence in tastes, there is little evidence of homogenization (Douglas and Wind 1987). Views range from convergence allowing global success for some 'high-technology' and 'high-touch' luxury items (Ohmae 1985) to the counter arguments of Toffler (1970) that sophisticated consumers are demanding greater customization.

A common criticism is that simultaneous market entry may be possible for large firms with high levels of resources but is not feasible for smaller or less experienced firms. The question of whether small firms can internationalize as rapidly as larger firms is considered more fully on p. 148.

In summary, while both sequential and simultaneous models offer some interesting insights into the internationalization process, neither can be universally applied to all industry sectors and sizes of firms. The following section reviews some of the principal influences on manufacturing and service firms and on retailers, on large multinational and global firms and on small firms.

Manufacturing Firms

The models presented in the preceding discussion are largely based on manufacturing firms. Whether firms follow a sequential or simultaneous process of internationalization depends in part on demographic factors such as size and level of international experience. As suggested above, large, more highly internationalized firms may internationalize more rapidly and use high commitment modes on entry. However, the pattern varies between sectors. High 'commitment' foreign investment in the chemical industry requires much higher levels of capital expenditure in exploration, pipelines and refineries than high 'commitment' investment in a manufacturing plant in an industry, such as tobacco or household goods. Firms in industry sectors where FDI involves higher levels of capital outlay are more likely to use a low commitment organization before taking this step.

Some variation in the internationalization process can be seen between firms in the same sector who are broadly comparable in terms of size and international experience. These differences may relate to the nature of the firm's competitive advantage and strategy for delivering this to the market. For example, the Case Study on CigaretteCo on p. 154 shows that more risk averse firms may not enter a market initially with a manufacturing operation. A lower commitment mode of operation might be preferred on first entry into a new international market. In contrast, the family-owned US multinational, Johnson Wax (Box 9.1) takes a pioneering approach and tends to enter international markets more rapidly using higher levels of investment than do sector rivals.

Service Firms

The term 'services' is used to encompass a spectrum from highly intangible services, such as holidays, to services which have a tangible element, such as software, creating architectural plans or producing accounts. Erramilli (1990) calls the first of these 'soft' services and the latter 'hard' services. Soft services cannot be separated from the service provider, while the tangible output of hard services can be delivered across borders.

The distinction between hard and soft services provides a useful insight into the issues which service firms face in the internationalization process.

■ **Hard services** can use export, knowledge agreements or FDI. An accountant or architect can receive a commission from an international customer, work on this in their home market and later deliver the final accounts or plans to the customer. The Internet, video conferencing and other technological advances have improved the ability to provide such services across international borders. In this way, hard services can be exported,

- **Soft services** are inseparable from the service provider. Accordingly, the minimum level of international operation required is a knowledge agreement such as a franchise. Well known examples of soft services franchised internationally are McDonalds restaurants and Best Western hotels.

As described in Chapter 7, Erramilli (1991) finds a 'U-shaped' rather than linear progression for service firms as the level of international experience increases. Both firms with little and high levels of international experience opt for high commitment investment modes. Erramilli puts this down to the level of control which the firms wish to have over their international operations. Firms with little international experience may wish to retain control, while those with high levels of experience may wish to protect brands or service quality. It is noticeable that while McDonald's use franchises in most countries, they initially enter new international markets by investment in a joint venture.

Välikängas and Lehtinen (1991) suggest that firms in different types of service industry will pursue different internationalization strategies. Firms such as McDonald's, with a mass-market focus, aim for consistent service quality, which can successfully be delivered through a franchise, provided the procedures are clearly established and policed. However, specialist services require the greater levels of control provided by foreign direct investment.

Studies of the internationalization process of services show that service firms are more likely to encounter non-tariff barriers (NTBs) (Dahringer and Mühlbacher 1991). Suggestions to overcome NTBs include:

- Encapsulate the service in a product. Examples include designer clothes or software.
- Use technological advances to deliver the service remotely.
- Use customer 'pull' by creating distinctively better services or by superior management or marketing ability, which customers demand to have.

Retailers

The retail sector mirrors trends seen in other mature sectors. A recent spate of mergers and acquisitions (MrAs) has created a smaller number of more powerful global competitors (Tordjman 1995). US giant Wal Mart's acquisition of Asda in the UK is the latest in a series of strategic moves that propel retailers into the international domain overnight.

International retailers are particularly attracted by the opening up of mega-markets, such as those of China and East and Central Europe, with large populations and attractive long-term growth potential. However, these growth opportunities may be hampered by the ongoing process of political and ethnic fragmentation seen in Eastern Europe and latterly in the former Yugoslavian markets.

Retailers have tended to be viewed as reluctant internationalists who expand internationally as a reaction to triggers rather than entering into the process proactively. In the 1990s, however, studies pointed to more proactive internationalization strategies by retailers (Alexander 1990; Williams 1992). Globalization of retailers is set to create significant changes within the retail sector. A pattern of consolidation and shakeout is likely to accompany the global development of larger players. The development of two of the most global retailers – Wal Mart and Carrefour is described in Box 8.3.

Studies of the globalization phenomena are reviewed by Burt (1995), who identifies two approaches – geographic and strategic – to studying the phenomenon. The largest strand of literature is that taking a geographic approach (Kacker 1985; Hamill and Crosbie 1990; Fernie 1992; Sternquist 1997). Geographic studies tend to focus on the flows of international activity by retailers from or to a particular geographic region, or the specific challenges of retail operation within a particular region or market (Piercy and Alexander 1988; Qiang and Harris 1990; McGoldrick and Ho 1992; Clarke and Rimmer 1997; Wrigley 1997).

Within the strategic domain, the dominant focus is the motive for internationalization of retailers. In his synthesis of the literature on motivations,

Box 8.3   Global Retail: Battle of the Titans?

In their book provocatively entitled *'Store Wars'*, Corstjens and Corstjens (1995) describe the growing size and global presence of retailers as creating a battle for both mindspace and shelfspace. While for many years retailers were considered relatively unsophisticated in comparison with the manufacturers of brands, recent years have seen a radical shift in the relative importance of the retail sector.

One area of enormous change is the development of a global presence among a small number of the larger retailers. This retail revolution has seen large retailers such as Wal Mart second largest in the world with sales of $118 billion in 1999 and Carrefour at number 14 with sales of $30 billion in 1999 (*FT 500* report, January 1999) emerge on the global stage. The highly publicized acquisition of rival chains (Wal Mart of Asda in the UK and Carrefour of its French rival Promodes) have drawn attention to the aggressive ambitions of these new retail giants. This has prompted smaller and less international retailers to press for rapid international growth themselves as a mentality of 'eat or be eaten prevails.'

To date this international expansion seems to be bringing financial benefits to the bold. On 9 May 2000, Wal Mart announced record sales and income: 'Sales for Wal Mart's international division jumped from £3291 million to $7197 [for quarter 1 2000] – an increase of 118.7% on the previous year. Operating profit for the international division jumped from $62 million to $149 million for the same period last year. This represents an increase of 136%', <*www.walmartstores.com/newsstand*>.

Benefits for retailers also accrue from global sourcing initiatives that accompany their increased size and geographic coverage. The geographic scope of Wal Mart and Carrefour as of May 2000 is shown in Table 8.2.

As suggested by strategies for global sourcing, this globalization and consolidation is likely to have wide-reaching implications for retailer – supplier relationships. Pressures from Wal Mart for 'Every day low prices' will put pressure on suppliers to harmonize the prices of branded products – or else prepare arguments to defend price premiums in particular countries. Similarly, Carrefour's demands for private label products may force suppliers to reconsider branding policies. Other pressures on suppliers include the challenges of serving more sophisticated global retailers who expect co-ordinated global marketing from suppliers.

As yet, neither Wal Mart or Carrefour has entered the home market of its rival. Each firm is still heavily reliant on sales from the home market. As both players now contest key markets in Latin America and Asia-Pacific, however, the day may not be far away when the Battle of the Titans really begins. What type of fallout might face suppliers then?

Table 8.2   Wal Mart and Carrefour: geographic scope, 2000

No. of countries		Which countries
Wal Mart	9	USA, Canada, Brazil, Mexico, Puerto Rico, South Korea, China, UK, Germany
Carrefour	22	France, Spain, Greece, Portugal, Turkey, Italy, Poland, Belgium, Czech Republic. Brazil, Mexico, Colombia, Chile, South Korea, Thailand, Taiwan, China, Malaysia, Indonesia, Hong Kong, Singapore

Alexander (1995) draws a useful distinction between 'push' and 'pull' triggers of retailer internationalization and reactive and proactive strategic responses to these. Initial research into the internationalization of retailing suggested (Treadgold 1990) that retailers were more likely to be pushed into internationalization. The research of Alexander (1990) and Williams (1992) redresses the balance by highlighting the importance of pull factors, which prompt proactive internationalization strategies.

In order to reach their customers, retailers typically have a large number of stores in each country, and therefore the costs of penetrating each country are high (Williams 1992; Whiteside 1992; Dawson 1994). This has led researchers to suggest that their internationalization process should be studied separately.

Degree of Internationalization

Discussion has centred on the question of how the extent of internationalization of retailers should be measured. Treadgold (1988, 1990) uses *geographic dispersion* as a measure. This relates to the *number of countries* in which the firm operates. As sales in some countries are small, it may actually be more accurate if the percentage of the retailer's sales overseas is also taken into account. This is *export intensity* as proposed by Cavusgil (1977). For retailers, Tordjman (1995) adds the measure of single or multi-format operation within the market to assess the number of segments per market, in which the firm operates.

Some retailers, e.g. Carrefour, have more than one format such as supermarkets and hypermarkets, or serve more than one sector with different retail brands. This is the case for Kingfisher, which uses its B and Q and Castorama chains to serve the Do-It-Yourself market, Woolworth's for confectionery and Darty for electrical goods. While being multi-format may increase the complexity of international operation, it does not prevent the firm from attaining a high performance.

Given the high costs of penetrating each market, it is perhaps not surprising that retailers tend to expand within each market incrementally. This incremental internationalization does not, however, involve increasing the commitment or control of the mode, but of broadening the *geographic coverage* within the market.

International retailers do not appear to follow the progression from culturally similar to culturally dissimilar markets. Retailer Metro Makro has a greater number of stores in the transitional economy of Poland, which it entered recently, than in either Switzerland or the UK.

Multinational and Global Firms

The distinction between multinational and global firms in this chapter is that the latter are *geocentric* (Perlmutter 1969, see Chapter 15 for a fuller discussion) and may have more standardized global activities. Firms which are highly internationalized

may have made significant investments in brands, in creating technological advantages or in developing international customer relationships. For these firms, damage to brand value or the loss of a customer does not only have an impact in one market, but potentially across a large number. So great may be the potential impact of any damage to reputation that the firm is likely to opt for high commitment modes to retain control of the operation to prevent this happening. The international experience of these firms may reduce the level of uncertainty they face, as they can draw lessons from other similar markets (Forsgren 1989). Moreover such firms have sufficient resources that they may view the expenditure required for foreign direct investment as relatively low:

> When firms have large resources the consequences of commitments are small. Thus big firms or firms with surplus resources can be expected to make larger internationalisation steps. (Johanson and Vahlne 1990, p. 12)

A key feature of the internationalization behaviour of larger firms is that of 'leapfrogging', that is skipping some of the steps in the establishment chain. Evidence that this ability relates to the size of the firm is, however, contradictory. Larger firms may be more likely to leapfrog (Johanson and Vahlne 1990). In seeming contradiction, leapfrogging is not found to be significantly lower for smaller firms (Benito and Gripsrud 1992; Ali and Camp 1993). One conclusion may be that all firms may skip steps and that this is determined by other factors.

Small Firms

If external finance is not available, expansion of small firms can be financed only by profits, which may be limited. However, management constraints may be the most significant difference between small and large firms. Shortage of management time may lead to 'short cuts in decision-making and information gathering which can be disastrous' (Buckley 1989, p. 93).

In small firms, decisions are more likely to be championed by individuals and opportunities may be pursued without evaluation of alternatives, in order to minimize the costs of information gathering.

One consequence may be that small firms opt to enter first those markets where there are lower levels of uncertainty. Given these resource constraints, small firms might seem likely to follow the sequential pattern of market entry suggested by the Uppsala model (Johanson and Wiedersheim-Paul 1975; Johanson and Vahlne 1977). Petersen and Pedersen (1997, p. 120) note that:

> In accordance with Johanson and Vahlne 1990, it is assumed that the internationalisation model will apply primarily to small and medium-sized firms.

Indeed, Coviello and Munro's useful review of studies of SME internationalization (1997) identifies a number of studies which classify the process into sequential stages (Hakam, Lau and Kong 1993; Calof and Viviers 1995), although some of these omit stages or propose amendments (Chang and Grub 1992; Rao and Naidu 1992).

On the other hand, the globalization literature suggests that changes in the global business environment may have also have reduced the uncertainty of entering new international markets for small firms. The literature increasingly highlights the existence of global niches (Bonaccorsi 1992; Chang and Grub 1992). Buckley (1989) suggests that small firms may be at no disadvantage compared to larger rivals in specialized markets with few economies of scale. Given the possibilities of raising capital externally, or else co-operating with other firms to gain access to scarce resources (Bonaccorsi 1992; Hansen, Crillesple and Gencturk 1994; Kaufmann 1995), small firms may also be able to internationalize more rapidly than the

---

Box 8.4   Simultaneous or Sequential Internationalization: Small Firm Experiences

Investigation of internationalization patterns in 44 small, high-technology firms in the UK provides useful insights into both sequential and simultaneous models. Analysis of the firms on the basis of their age size and degree of internationalization revealed three distinct clusters. The three groups were:

- **Group 1**: relatively new companies with a relatively small number of employees and turnover with high export intensity.
- **Group 2**: relatively new companies also with a relatively small number of employees and turnover with a low export intensity[1].
- **Group 3**: older companies with a larger turnover and number of employees with a mid-level export intensity.

Analysis of the three groupings showed distinctively different patterns of internationalization:

- **Overall internationalization has become more rapid**. While the firms studied were not all international from inception, the younger firms began the process more rapidly than did the older ones. Group 1 firms have achieved a higher level of international success than their older group 3 equivalents.

- The ability of these 'young' firms to expand internationally may confirm the existence of **global niches** in the high-technology sectors in which they operate (Bonaccorsi 1992; Chang and Grub 1992).

- A question arises as to why group 2 firms (comparable in age and size to those in group 1) are relatively less successful both internationally and in terms of their profitability. This may be attributable to the relative haste with which they entered successive markets after a late start. Moreover these firms expanded into other regions more rapidly. One might conclude that they did so **too rapidly**. The geographic scope which they cover may be achieved at the expense of developing sales in each individual country.

Note: Export intensity is the percentage of sales which are overseas. This measure is considered to be the most robust measure of the degree of internationalization (Cavusgil 1977). See the section on retailer internationalization for a fuller discussion.

Source: Based on Stray, Bridgewater and Murray (2001).

Uppsala model suggests. Indeed, Oviatt and McDougall (1994) suggest that many new small firms are international from their inception. Such new international ventures, they argue, arise because in the current environment:

> An internationally experienced person who can attract a moderate amount of capital can conduct business anywhere in the time it takes to press the buttons of a telephone, and, when required, he or she can travel virtually anywhere on the globe in less than a day. Such facile use of low-cost communication technology and transportation means that the ability to discover and take advantage of business opportunities in multiple countries is not the preserve of large, mature corporations.

Box 8.4 looks at a sample of small, high-technology firms to see whether they follow a sequential or simultaneous process of internationalization.

THE RELATIONSHIP PERSPECTIVE

Aharoni (1966) argues that international investment decisions should not be viewed in isolation, as each decision influences later ones. If a firm enters a country using a distributor, but then disagrees over the terms of the contract, it may not to make any further investment in the country. Were this decision to be viewed in isolation, the full explanation for it might not be apparent.

Retailer–Supplier Relationships

In order to operate successfully in an increasingly global market, retailers are adapting their strategic priorities, expanding their international operations and mastering the challenges of international operation. This internationalization of retailing inevitably raises challenges for those firms who supply them. In the channels literature, the focus in the 1980s and 1990s has moved from studies of conflict the development of long-term 'win–win' relationships (Håkansson and Wootz 1979; Håkansson 1982). This shift is mirrored in the international retailing literature. In the Introduction of their special issue of the *European Jour-*

nal of Marketing on retailer internationalization, Brown and Burt (1992, p. 5) point out the implicit message of early marketing textbooks that retailer intermediaries were:

> an impediment to the free flow of merchandise and information, a necessary evil between producers and consumers, a barrier to the implementation of the marketing concept.

Yet in recent years, the role and importance of retailers in channel relationships have shifted. Together with industry concentration, retailers have advanced in terms of their marketing ability. Important understanding of consumers now resides with the retailer and retailer brands poses a significant challenge to manufacturer brands. In sum, the marketing ability of retailers is as good, if not better, than that of suppliers (Brown and Burt 1992). These changes make it imperative for suppliers to understand the implications of retailer internationalization.

Relationships Between Small and Large Firms

The small high-technology firms studied in this chapter show an increasing ability to expand internationally, and to succeed, alone. A particular type of co-operative relationship has existed between small firms like these, which have developed promising technologies, and larger partners, which have the resources and international experience to exploit these globally.

The relationship is characterized by differences in size (and power) between the partners. As the basis of small, high-technology firms' success is the technologies they have developed, they may have to defend these against their partners. The entrepreneurial character of small firms has been the subject of considerable research. More flexible, closer to the market and more likely to work cross-functionally, small firms are of increasing importance to national economies and international success (European Commission 1995; DTI 1998; Nakos, Brouthers and Brouthers 1998). Their ongoing success may be limited, however, by the availability of external funding to permit their continued growth (Buckley 1989).

THE NETWORK PERSPECTIVE

A Network View of Internationalization

Both sequential and simultaneous models of internationalization make the same assumptions about the nature of the firm. Firms exist in a 'faceless' competitive environment. Game theorists have referred to this as a 'zero-sum' game as a firm can gain (+1) only at the expense of a competitor (−1) making zero. Network theory, which has its roots in sociology rather than economics, takes a contrasting view of the firm's links with its environment (Johanson and Mattsson 1988; Axelsson and Johanson 1992; Blankenburg 1995). Network studies show firms embedded in a web of interdependent relationships with other firms and in the broader environment. This is referred to as a 'full-faced' interface with the environment. Firms operate in an environment where 'win–win' situations are possible, that is two or more firms can gain (+1) from a relationship with each other.

From a network perspective, the process of internationalization is that of *building on existing relationships* or *creating new relationships* in international markets. Definitions include:

> the way in which existing relationships in the domestic and in third markets as well as those in the entry market are utilised in the entry process. (Axelsson and Johanson 1992, p. 219)

and:

> the process whereby the strength of the relationships in different parts of the global network increases. (Johanson and Mattsson 1988)

A number of different levels of relationship play a role. The first level is that of the macro-environment. Firms embedded in a 'full-faced' environment encounter different set of challenges from those suggested for a 'faceless' environment:

> Rather than viewing the environment as a set of separate anonymous forces – political, competitive, legal, cultural, economic etc. – all the actors are considered bearers of diverse interests, power and characteristics. It is in the meetings in the international business arena that such factors impinge on the development of business. (Johanson and Mattsson 1988, p. 2)

One of the principal challenges of entering a new international market is that developing network connections may involve restructuring the firm's network:

> To become established in a new market, that is, a network which is new to the firm, it has to build relationships which are new both to itself and its counterparts. This is sometimes done by breaking old, existing relationships, and sometimes by adding a relationship to already existing ones. (Johanson and Mattsson 1988, p. 306)

From a network perspective, internationalization involves entry into markets which each have a different web of actors and relationships. Kinch (1992) highlights the difficulties of breaking into advanced economies where the actors tend to have long-established and stable relationships. A new entrant might find it difficult to form links with a distributor who is not supplying products for one of his competitors. At the opposite end of the scale, if the network of relationships in the host market is rapidly changing, as in emerging markets, there may appear to be greater opportunities, but it may be difficult to identify appropriate partners and attractive investments. TelecomCo in Box 8.5 is an example of a firm finding it difficult to understand the networks in a new market.

The second type of relationships which influence the process of internationalization are *between* organizations. A complex web of relationships may have a bearing on the decisions which a firm makes. Firms may stand in different relation to each other in different international markets:

> Competitors in one market co-operate in another and are suppliers and customers to each other in a third. (Johanson and Mattsson 1988, p. 313)

> A Swedish firm might increase its penetration in a South American market because of its relationship in Japan with an internationalising Japanese firm. Other examples of such international interdependence are 'big projects' in which design, equipment, supply, construction, ownership and operation can all be allocated to firms of different national origin. (Johanson and Mattsson 1988, p. 315)

Box 8.5 TelecomCo

TelecomCo expanded into Europe and the USA in the late 1960s. By 1991, 44 per cent of its sales were outside the UK. TelecomCo takes a risk averse approach to international expansion, but the decline of its 'cash cow' in the UK dictates rapid entry into markets which are less technologically developed. The firm has a successful joint venture in Moscow and had been studying the potential of Ukraine for two years before winning a contract to supply the Ukrainian government with equipment to modernize the telecommunications infrastructure. An export representative went out to Ukraine in 1993. Since then, he has been assessing market potential with a view to setting a joint venture.

A number of business opportunities seemed open to the representative TelecomCo. Yet he found it difficult to find out to whom he should speak or what procedure he should follow: 'There is so much political instability that you can sign an agreement with someone one week, who will not be there next week. Then they say that the previous agreement was invalid and ask for a bribe. Success is possible if you are prepared to pay the right people.'

Twice, he was asked to make payments in order to ensure the smooth running of the authorization process. On each occasion, Head Office refused to sanction any such payment as they felt it might damage their international reputation.

Finally, the local representative produced a business idea, which he believed would work in Ukraine. However, Head Office had decided that the risks for the firm were too great. In March 1994, the representative was about to leave Ukraine, en route to a new posting in Azerbaijan. TelecomCo were withdrawing in the face of worsening market conditions, but might reconsider investment at a future stage. The representative of TelecomCo felt that he had gained personal knowledge of the conditions in Ukraine, but it was difficult to convey the fact that business was possible there to Head Office. From a distance the level of uncertainty seemed unacceptable.

Finally, relationships *within* the organization may influence the process. Multinational corporations and global firms may have relatively large subsidiaries in a number of countries. Decision making in this type of organization may take place at the subsidiary level rather than always at the centre. Forsgren (1989) argues that when this happens there may be cultural distance between different parts of the firm as well as with the host market. Individuals and subsidiaries that are further away from the target investment may perceive it as higher risk than those who are closer and have better understanding.

An instance of this can be seen in the case of TelecomCo (Box 8.5). When the firm made decisions about further investment in Ukraine, the local representative considered there to be less risk than did Head Office who were further away. In Box 8.2 AuditCo's subsidiaries in Germany and the UK played a role in the entry into Eastern Europe. Once the Moscow office was established, it helped with later investments in the region.

From a network perspective, relationships at the macro-, inter-organizational and firm level all play a role in investment decisions and each decision is influenced by others, which have gone before.

THE INTERNATIONALIZATION PROCESS

A range of firm, industry and country factors influences each international investment decision. International business theory proposes sequential and simultaneous models of process of internationalization.

These take different views of the level of uncertainty involved in internationalization. Sequential models see new international markets as uncertain and suggest entry into more culturally similar markets first. Simultaneous models build on the convergence of customer tastes which they believe to reduce the uncertainty of international markets. Provided the firm has sufficient resources, the barriers to more rapid internationalization and entry via foreign direct investment are lower.

Network theory provides an alternative view of internationalization. Greater attention is paid to the web of relationships which influence investment decisions. From a network perspective, internationalization is the process of forming relationships in new international markets. This may involve building on existing relationships in the home, host or a third country.

CASE STUDY 8.1 THE INTERNATIONALIZATION PROCESS OF CIGARETTECO IN CENTRAL EUROPE

In Hungary, the three main production facilities for cigarettes were privatized in the course of 1991. By the end of 1991, two large plants, Pecs and Egri, had gone to BAT and Philip Morris, respectively, and a third, Debrecen, went to R. J. Reynolds in January 1992. The privatization of the Czech tobacco industry had been announced in September 1991. Competition was equally fierce and the process of selecting the preferred bid complex. A preliminary tender for the largest target, Tabak, the Czech manufacturing enterprise with five factories around the country, attracted bids from both Philip Morris and R. J. Reynolds (BBC Monitoring Service Eastern Europe, 16 April 1992). The Czech government then announced a public competition, in which:

> any company which submitted a proposal by 20th January 1992 could take part. Competing plans were also submitted by BAT, Rothmans, the Seita company of France and Reetsma of Germany. The conditions for bidding for A. S. Tabak included a commitment to maintain the enterprise as a single unit and a pledge not to lay off any workers of the company for the next five years. (BBC Monitoring Service Eastern Europe, 16 April 1992)

The final decision, to sell the factory to Philip Morris for $104 million plus $140 million in modernization over the next year was fiercely contested by its rivals, as it gave Philip Morris monopolistic control over the Czech market. Reetsma subsequently reached a successful agreement with Slovak International Tabak (*CTK Business News*, 21 April 1992).

The Polish market has three main producers, Cracow (33 billion cigarettes), Radom (30 billion) and Poznan (22 billion), which accounted for 90 per cent of total sales in 1992 (*Gazeta Bankowa*, 26 April 1992). Until mid-1992, four production licences had been granted by the agriculture ministry. The volume of imports was also controlled, by the Ministry of Foreign Economic Relations (*Reczpospolita*, 15 July 1992). The restricted access to this large potential market heightened Western rivalry.

As a result of the competition for investment targets in the Czech Republic, Hungary and Poland, some of the smaller players in the industry missed out. CigaretteCo was one of those who felt that it had 'lost out' compared to its larger rivals. With the breakdown of the Soviet Union in late 1991, however, it was determined to make up for its failure to invest in Central Europe. It was not alone. The *Central European* (1 August 1993) stressed that:

> the world's top cigarette companies are queuing up to acquire control of Almaty Tobacco Kombinat (ATK), the only cigarette producer in the central Asian republic of Kazhakstan, which is being sold in the country's first hard currency privatisation transaction.

CigaretteCo exported to Eastern Europe prior to liberalization, but everything was channelled centrally via Moscow. After liberalization, the firm was interested in exploring the potential of the region, which was considered to be a 'virgin' market which, together with China and Vietnam, was one of the last remaining areas for global competitors to contest. Initial interest in Eastern Europe was prompted by large, unsolicited orders from Poland. As this market was one of those which appeared important, CigaretteCo set up a local office and began studying the next tier of markets.

In both the Czech Republic and in Hungary, CigaretteCo was outbid by larger rivals. Therefore, it moved its focus of attention to the Former Soviet Union. CigaretteCo established a joint venture to set up a greenfield manufacturing site in St Petersburg. While the market was seen to be unstable, gaining even a small market share would compensate for the risks, which it knew to be high. The company's concern was more at assessing the size of the opportunity, to see if these risks were justified. The next choice of market in the Former Soviet Union (FSU) was between Ukraine, Kazhakstan and Uzbekistan. These were seen as possible first steps toward entry into the larger, but more turbulent Russian market.

Ultimately, CigaretteCo's aim was to set up a local production facility, because products were too expensive if imported. Lower commitment options, such as a representative office, were contemplated only as an interim solution, if it were felt that further market information was required before making this commitment. There was a clear *prima facie* case for entry into Ukraine. The market was large, and in 1991 was widely heralded as having better potential for reform than Russia or the Southern Republics. The company had originally served Ukraine by exporting products manufactured in the UK. However, the production costs of these were higher than the selling price of locally produced products. The decision to invest in the market was made in December 1992 and a representative office was set up. Throughout the summer of 1993, the firm gathered information on market size and possible joint venture partners. Two of the larger tobacco firms were in the process of signing manufacturing agreements but, given its smaller size, CigaretteCo did not wish to rush in. Market information from secondary sources was contradictory. The legislation surrounding investments was confusing. Moreover, market conditions in Ukraine worsened considerable during this period. A primary research survey of the market revealed that while consumers were keen to buy 'status brands', they had low levels of disposable income.

As a result they were likely to buy local products, for everyday use. In the late summer of 1993, CigaretteCo decided against setting up a manufacturing operation in Ukraine. The Southern Republics, and Russia itself, now appeared to have greater stability and potential than Ukraine.

QUESTIONS

1. To what extent do you think CigaretteCo's interest in Ukraine was influenced by its experiences in Central Europe?
2. Why did it choose to enter using a 'low commitment' entry mode?
3. What type of international operation did CigaretteCo ultimately wish to use in Ukraine and why?
4. What factors influenced the firm's decision to look at Russia and the Southern Republics in preference to Ukraine?

SUMMARY

In Chapter 8 we have examined the way in which international marketers expand operations. We have explored the forces that drive, and inhibit, this process together with the different models of this internationalization process that are proposed.

Distinctive characteristics of internationalization for different types of firms are identified. The network view of internationalization is appraised to understand the contributions that this offers international marketers.

NOTES

1. The concept of commitment is not clearly defined but seems to equate to the total investment the firm makes in the market. Total investment may involve more than only financial investment. A firm might have committed time to selection of a distributor or joint venture partner. It may have made a highly publicized market entry and stand to damage its reputation – and market value – if seen to retract from the country.

BIBLIOGRAPHY

Aharoni, Y. (1966) *The Foreign Investment Decision Process*, Harvard University Press.

Alexander, N. (1990) 'Retailers and International Markets: Motives for Expansion', *International Marketing Review*, 7, 4: 75–85.

Alexander, N. (1995) 'Internationalization: Interpreting the Motives', in McGoldrick, P. J. and Davies, G., *International Retailing: Trends and Strategies*, Pitman.

Ali, A. J. and Camp, R. C. (1993) 'The Relevance of Firm Size and International Business Experience to Market Entry Strategies', *Journal of Global Marketing*, 6, 4: 91–108.

Andersen, O. (1993) 'On the Internationalization Process of Firms: A Critical Analysis', *Journal of International Business Studies*: 209–29.

Axelsson, B. and Johanson, J. (1992) 'Foreign Market Entry – The Textbook versus the Network View', in Axelsson, B. and Easton, G. (eds), *Industrial Networks: A New View of Reality*, Routledge.

Benito, G. R. G. and Gripsrud, G. (1992) 'The Expansion of Foreign Direct Investments: Discrete Rational Choices or a Cultural Learning Process?', *Journal of International Business Studies*, 23, 3: 461–76.

Benito, G. R. G. and Welch, L. (1994) 'Foreign Market Servicing: Beyond Choice of Entry Mode', *Journal of International Marketing*, 2: 7–27.

Bilkey, W. J. and Tesar, G. (1977) 'The Export Behaviour of Smaller Sized Wisconsin Manufacturing Firms', *Journal of International Business Studies*, 3, Spring – Summer: 93–8.

Blankenburg, D. (1995) 'A Network Approach to Foreign Market Entry', in Möller, K. and Wilson, D. (eds), *Business Marketing: An Interaction and Network Perspective*, Kluwer Academic: 375–410.

Bonaccorsi, A. (1992) 'On the Relationship between Firm Size and Export Intensity', *Journal of International Business Studies*, 23, 4: 605–25.

Bridgewater, S., McKiernan, P. and Wensley, J. R. (1995) 'Strategic Investment Decisions by Western Firms in Ukraine: The Role of Relationships in Home and Host Market Networks', *Journal of East–West Business*, 1, 3: 17–35.

Brown, S. and Burt, S. (1992) 'Retail Marketing: International Perspectives – Introduction', *European Journal of Marketing*, 26, 8/9: 5–7.

Buckley, P. J. (1989) 'Foreign Direct Investment by Small and Medium-Sized Enterprises: The Theoretical Background', *Small Business Economics*, 1: 89–100.

Buckley, P. J. and Casson, M. (1985) *The Economic Theory of the Multinational Enterprise: Selected Papers*, Macmillan.

Burt, S. (1995) 'Retail Internationalisation: Evolution of Theory and Practice', in McGoldrick, P. and Davies, G. (eds), *International Retailing: Trends and Strategies*, Pitman.

Calof, J. L. and Viviers, W. (1995) 'International Note: Internationalization Behaviour of Small- and Medium-Sized South African Enterprises', *Journal of Small Business Management*, October: 71–9.

Casson, M. (1994) 'Internationalization as a Learning Process: A Model of Corporate Growth and Geographic Diversification', in Sapsford, J. and Balasubramanyam, V. N. (eds), *The Economics of International Investment*, Edward Elgar.

Cavusgil, S. T. (1977) 'A Proposed Conceptualization of International Marketing Activities and Some Observations', *Studies in Development*, 16, Summer: 28–42.

Cavusgil, S. T. (1980) 'On the Internationalization Process of Firms', *European Research*, 8, November: 273–81.

Chang, T. and Grub, P. D. (1992) 'Competitive Strategies of Taiwanese PC Firms in their Internationalization Process', *Journal of Global Marketing*, 6, 3: 5–27.

Clark, I. and Rimmer, P. (1997) 'The Anatomy of Retail Internationalisation: Daimaru's Decision to invest in Melbourne, Australia', *The Service Industries Journal*, 17, 3: 361–82.

Corstjens, J. and Corstjens, M. (1995) *Store Wars: The Battle for Mindspace and Shelfspace*, John Wiley.

Coviello, N. and Munro, H. (1997) 'Network Relationships and the Internationalization Process of Small Software Firms', *International Business Review*, 6, 4: 114–35.

Czinkota, M. R. (1982) *Export Development Strategies: US Promotion Policies*, Praeger.

Dahringer, L. and Mühlbacher, H. (1991) 'Marketing Services Internationally: Barriers and Management Strategies', *Journal of Services Marketing*, 5, 3: 5–17.

Dawson, J. A. (1994) 'Internationalisation of Retailing Operations', *Journal of Marketing Management*, 10, 3: 267–82.

Department of Trade and Industry (DTI) (1998) 'White Paper', *Our Competitive Future: Building the Knowledge Economy*.

Dichtl, L. E. M., Liebold, M., Köglmayr, H. G. and Müller, S. (1990) 'International Orientation as a Precondition for Export Success', *Journal of International Business Studies*, 1: 23–40.

Douglas, S. and Wind, Y. (1987) 'The Myth of Globalization', *Columbia Journal of World Business*, Winter: 19–29.

Erramilli, M. K. (1990) 'Entry Mode Choice in Service Industries', *International Marketing Review*, 7, 5: 50–61.

Erramilli, M. K. (1991) 'The Experience Factor in Foreign Market Entry Behaviour of Service Firms', *Journal of International Business Studies*, 22, 3: 479–501.

European Commission (1995) *Green Paper on Innovation*, Brussels.

Fernie, J. (1992) 'Distribution Strategies of European Retailers', *European Journal of Marketing*, 26, 8/9: 35–47.

Forsgren, M. (1989) *Managing the Internationalisation Process: The Swedish Case*, Routledge.

Forsgren, M. and Johanson, J. (1975) 'Internationell foretagsekonomi', Norstedts, Stockholm, cited in Petersen, B. and Pedersen, T. (1997) 'Twenty Years after – Support and Critique of the Uppsala Internationalisation Model', in Björkman, I. and Forsgren, M. (eds), *The Nature of the International Firm*, Copenhagen Business School Press.

Håkansson, H. (1982) *Industrial Marketing and Purchasing of Industrial Goods: An Interaction Approach*, Croom Helm.

Håkansson, H. and Wootz, B. (1975) 'Supplier Selection in an International Environment: An Experimental Study', *Journal of Marketing Research*, 12, 1: 46–63.

Hakam, A. N., Lau, G. T. and Kong, S. B. (1993) 'The Export Behaviour of Firms in Singapore: An Application of the Stage of Internationalization Model', *Asia-Pacific Journal of Marketing and Logistics*, 5, 1: 1–20.

Hamill, J. and Crosbie, J. (1990) 'British Retail Acquisitions in the US', *International Journal of Retail and Distribution Management*, 18, 5: 15–20.

Hansen, N., Gillespie, K. and Gencturk, E. (1994) 'SMEs and Export Involvement: Market Responsiveness, Technology and Alliances', *Journal of Global Marketing*, 7, 4: 7–27.

Hörnell, E. and Vahlne, J.-E. (1982) 'The Changing Structure of Swedish Multinational Companies', *Uppsala Working Paper*, 1982, 12, University of Uppsala.

Johanson, J. and Mattsson, L.-G. (1988) 'Internationalisation in Industrial Systems – A Network Approach', in Hood, N. and Vahlne, J.-E. (eds), *Strategies in Global Competition*, Croom Helm.

Johanson, J. and Vahlne, J.-E. (1977) 'The Internationalisation of the Firm: A Model of Knowledge Development and Increasing Foreign Market Commitments', *Journal of International Business Studies*, 8, 1: 23–32.

Johanson, J. and Vahlne, J.-E. (1990) 'The Mechanism of Internationalisation', *International Marketing Review*, 7, 4: 11–24.

Johanson, J. and Wiedersheim-Paul, F. (1975) 'The Internationalisation of the Firm – Four Swedish Cases', *Journal of Management Studies*, October: 305–22.

Kacker, M. P. (1985) *Transatlantic Trends in Retailing*, Quorum.

Kaufmann, F. (1995) 'Internationalization via Co-operation – Strategies of SME', *International Small Business Journal*, January–March: 27–32.

Kinch, N. (1992) 'Entering a Tightly Structured Network – Strategic Visions or Network Realities', in Forsgren, M. and Johanson, J. (eds), *Managing Networks in International Business*, Gordon & Breach.

Levitt, T. (1983) 'The Globalization of Markets', *Harvard Business Review*, May–June: 92–102.

Luostarinen, R. (1979) *The Internationalization of the Firm*, Acta Academic Oeconomica Helsingiensis.

McGoldrick, P. J. and Ho, S. S. L. (1992) 'International Positioning: Japanese Department Stores in Hong Kong', *European Journal of Marketing*, 26, 8/9: 61–73.

Nakos, B., Brouthers, K. D. and Brouthers, L. E. (1998) 'The Impact of Firms and Managerial Characteristics on Small and Medium-Sized Greek Firms' Export Performance', *Journal of Global Marketing*, 11, 4: 23–47.

Ohmae, K. (1985) 'Becoming a Triad Power: The New Global Corporation', *The McKinsey Quarterly*, Spring: 2–25.

Ohmae, K. (1990) 'Managing in a Borderless World', *Harvard Business Review*, May–June; reprinted in Buzzell, R. B., Quelch, J. A. and Bartlett, C. A. (eds), *Global Marketing Management: Cases and Readings*, Addison Wesley, Longman: 53–68.

Oviatt, B. M. and McDougall, P. P. (1994) 'Toward a Theory of International New Ventures', *Journal of International Business Studies*, Spring: 45–64.

Perlmutter, H. (1969) 'The Tortuous Evolution of the Multinational Corporation', *Columbia Journal of World Business*, January–February: 9–18.

Petersen, B. and Pedersen, T. (1997) 'Twenty Years After – Support and Critique of the Uppsala Internationalisation Model', in Björkman, I. and Forsgren, M. (eds), *The Nature of the International Firm*, Copenhagen Business School Press.

Piercy, N. and Alexander, N. (1988) 'The Status Quo of the Marketing Organisation in UK Retailing: A Neglected Phenomenon', *The Service Industries Journal*, 8, 2: 155–75.

Porter, M. E. (1980) *Competitive Strategy: techniques for Analyzing Industries and Competitors*, Free Press and Macmillan.

Qiang, G. and Harris, P. (1990) 'Retailing Reform and Trends in China', *International Journal of Retail and Distribution Management*, 18, 5: 31–9.

Quelch, J. A. and Hoff, E. J. (1986) 'Customizing Global Marketing', *Harvard Business Review*, May–June.

Rao, T. R. and Naidu, G. M. (1992) 'Are the Stages of Internationalisation Empirically Supportable?', *Journal of Global Marketing*, 6, 1/2: 147–70.

Riesenbeck, H. and Freeling, A. (1991) 'How Global are Global Brands?', *The McKinsey Quarterly*, 4: 3–18.

Sternquist, B. (1997) 'International Expansion of US Retailers', *International Journal of Retail and Distribution*, 25, 8: 262–68.

Stray, S., Bridgewater, S. and Murray, G. (2001) 'The Internationalisation Process of Small, Technology-based Firms: Market Selection, Mode Choice and Degree of Internationalization', *Journal of Global Marketing*, 15, 1: 7–30.

Sullivan, D. and Bauerschmidt, A. (1990) 'Incremental Internationalisation: A Test of Johanson and Vahlne's Thesis', *Management International Review*, 30, 1: 19–30.

Toffler, A. (1970) *Future Shock*, Bantam Books.

Tordjman, A. (1995) 'European Retailing: Convergences, Differences and Perspectives', in McGoldrick, P. J. and Davies, G., *International Retailing: Trends and Strategies*, Pitman.

Treadgold, A. (1988) 'Retailing without Frontiers', *Retail and Distribution Management*, 16, 6: 8–12.

Treadgold, A. (1990) 'The Developing Internationalisation of Retailing', *International Journal of Retail and Distribution Management*, 18, 2: 4–11.

Välikängas, L. and Lehtinen, U. (1991) 'Strategic Types of Services and International Marketing', *International Journal of Service Industry*, 5, 2: 72–84.

Welch, L. and Luostarinen, R. (1988) 'Internationalization: Evolution of a Concept', *Journal of General Management*, 14, 2: 34–55.

Whiteside, M. B. (1992) 'Internationalization of Retailing: Developing New Perspectives', *European Journal of Marketing*, 26, 8/9: 74–9.

Williams, D. (1992) 'Motives for Retailer Internationalization: Their Impact, Structure and Implications', *Journal of Marketing Management*, 8, 269–85.

Wrigley, N. (1997) 'British Food Retail Capital in the USA – Part 2: Giant Prospects?', *International Journal of Retail and Distribution Management*, 25, 2: 48–58.

PART IV

THE INTERNATIONAL MARKETING MIX

Having discussed the international marketing context and its implications for international marketing strategies, the book now moves on to discuss how these strategies might be implemented. A number of marketing decisions must be made to implement marketing strategies. These relate to:

- Product
- Place
- Price
- Promotion.

In international marketing terms, decisions on the standardization of brands and products and on the type of organization appropriate for different international markets raise the first two to strategic prominence. Accordingly, the challenges of brand and product decisions (Chapter 5) and place (Chapters 6–8) are covered in Part III of this book. Part IV reviews the issues relating to the remaining two marketing mix elements – price and promotion – from traditional, relationship and network perspectives.

INTERNATIONAL PRICING

Objectives

The issues to be addressed in Chapter 9 include:

1. The factors that influence international pricing strategies
2. The particular challenges arising from these factors for international marketers
3. Countertrade and other pricing issues that arise from the inter-relationships between pricing decisions made in different international markets
4. The difficulties of grey – or parallel – market activity and ways in which international marketers might respond to these.

After reading Chapter 9 you will be able to:

1. Identify the distinctive characteristics of pricing in international marketing
2. Gain an overview of international pricing strategies and the implications of differentiated pricing strategies
3. Understand relationships that are based on barter and exchanges other than money
4. Explore the issue of grey markets
5. Evaluate the options available to international marketers in dealing with grey market activity.

INTRODUCTION

In international markets, pricing strategy is complicated by differences between countries in exchange rates, inflation, international laws and cost structures. This chapter begins by using Weekly's framework (1991) to discuss the factors that influence international pricing strategies.

The impact of prices charged in one market on those in other markets is discussed from a relationship perspective. Countertrade relationships, where goods or services are traded for other goods and services rather than currency, are also explored. These are particularly prevalent in emerging or other blocked markets.

The network perspective considers the impact of the complex web of interrelationships that influence global pricing strategies. The existence of international buying groups is discussed. The effect of a pricing decision in one market on grey market activity, the legitimate transfer of goods between

markets by agents, is shown. If, for example, a firm set its prices low in one country in order to penetrate the market or match competitor prices, it may trigger grey market activity. An example of the grey market phenomenon can be seen in the automobile industry where cars are transferred from the lower priced Belgian market into the higher priced UK market. Similarly the network of actors involved in countertrade relationships are explored.

THE TRADITIONAL PERSPECTIVE

Market Oriented Pricing

Setting prices is one of the most critical decisions facing international marketers. As Cavusgil (1988) notes: 'Price is the only marketing variable that generates revenue.' All the same, it is one of the

Table 9.1   Who determines the price and
               on what basis?

	Who?	On what basis?
Cost-plus	Producer	Total cost and desired margin
Competitor parity	Competitors	Existing products or services
EVC	Customers	Value of benefits provided

Table 9.2   International pricing

- Limiting Factors
  - Price controls
  - Parallel markets
  - Exchange rates
  - Competition

Range of managerial discretion – PRICING STRATEGY

- Limiting factors
  - Competition
  - Anti-dumping laws
  - Exchange rates
  - Inflation
  - Costs of operation

Source: Weekly (1991). © 1991 with permission of
Elsevier Science

least researched issues in international marketing
(Baker and Ryans 1973; Terpstra 1983).

For domestic markets, marketing proposes three
methods of pricing. First, calculation of total operating costs and additional of a profit margin. This
is known as *cost-plus*. Secondly, setting of prices in
comparison with competitors' prices with a strategic analysis of the implications of undercutting or
charging a premium relative to these. This is
known as *competitor parity*. Finally, a calculation
of the price which the market is prepared to pay
for benefits over and above competitors' products
or services. This is known as *economic value to the
customer* (EVC).

Marketers tend to propose EVC as the ultimate
basis of pricing as it stems from the customer.
Competitor issues are seen as important considerations. However, while costs must be covered,
cost-plus is seen as inferior, given that it is producer driven and does not take into account value to
the customer (see Table 9.1).

International Pricing Strategies

Similar underlying choices underpin international
pricing. Weekly (1991) classifies the influences on
international pricing into limiters on the top and
bottom end of the possible range (see Table 9.2)

At the bottom end of the range lie the costs of
operation. These are complicated in international
marketing by issues of inflation and exchange rates.

Inflation

Price rises in line with inflation in different markets impact upon the marketer. Although inflation
causes prices to rise, the profit realized by the
producer does not. An extreme case of inflationary pressures is seen in markets characterized

by hyperinflation (more than 100 per cent per
annum). In these markets, the price to the customer may change from day to day. To retain
the same level of profit the firm may need to
change its prices on a regular (sometimes even
daily basis). The example of Johnson Wax in Box
9.1 gives an example of the challenges facing international marketers in inflationary markets.

Exchange Rates

Although a firm can decide its international pricing
strategy and method, the real value this delivers
will be affected by the rate of exchange between
its own currency and that of the host market.
Press coverage of the strengthening pound's effect
on British exporters demonstrates the challenges
which this may present (Box 9.2).

As can be seen in Box 9.2, rising exchange rates
mean that to maintain the same level of profit
prices must increase and may become prohibitively expensive compared to local market equivalents. Within limits, international marketers can
protect themselves against sudden fluctuations in
exchange rates, when buying international goods,
by *hedging* – buying currency ahead when rates
are favourable to them – rather than buying currency at spot rate – the rate, which happens to
prevail when they need to buy the currency.
Cavusgil (1988) points to the fact that exchange
rates fluctuations are cyclical, such that firms who

Box 9.1   Johnson Wax in Ukraine

Johnson Wax, Ukraine, is a subsidiary of SC Johnson and Son Ltd. It is a family owned multinational is based in Racine, Wisconsin, in the USA. It is a large player, worldwide, in the household products and cleaners market.

In the 1930s, SC Johnson was the first US chemical company to invest in South America. By the early 1980s there were only three areas in which Johnson Wax was not yet present: India, Pakistan and the USSR. The firm began to look at ways of entering the Soviet Union, one of the possible targets. When, in 1988, the majority control of foreign investments was allowed, Johnson Wax decided to enter and began the process of finding a suitable joint venture partner. At that time all negotiations were channelled via Moscow. Johnson Wax's partner, however, was in Kiev, which became part of Ukraine on the dissolution of the Soviet Union in late 1991.

Johnson Wax's strategy is simple: 'To be there before the others and develop a volume/cost competitive advantage in order to build up strong barriers to late entrants.'

A number of adjustments were needed for the firm to succeed in Ukraine. Some basic product formulations, such as liquid starch, were revived to meet market needs. Prices were set in the temporary local currency, the Karbovanet, in order that they might reach the majority of the market. Goods priced in dollars could be purchased only at special 'dollar shops' and could be afforded by only a small minority of Ukraine's 66 million population. At that time, competitors, such as Procter and Gamble were pricing in dollars. Johnson Wax achieved significant penetration of the market: 'Priced at roughly 30 per cent of their Western counterparts, [their products] were "gobbled up" by "a market screaming for new products," (*Business Central Europe*, February 1994).

Despite this promising start, however, the fortunes of Johnson Wax plummeted as the process of transition to a free market economy stalled. The Karbovanet failed to hold parity even with the rouble, with which its value was originally aligned. The financing of massive compensatory credits to striking miners fuelled inflation. In 1993, *The Economist* quoted an inflation rate of 72 per cent per month, an aggregate 5800 per cent per annum (23 October 1993).

Worse still, as state distribution channels crumbled, a type of parasitic trader developed who took commission for arranging a deal, but added no value. This additional mark-up caused prices to soar relative to local products. Legislative measures were subject to frequent change. The VAT levied upon the firm's products fluctuated from 0 per cent to 20 per cent to 28 per cent and back to zero. Taxes could be anything up to 90 per cent of revenue, not profit. All this, as Ukrainian citizens saw the value of their savings wiped out and their buying power decrease sharply. At one stage, to cope with the escalating prices, Johnson Wax were having to change the prices of their goods every few days.

---

find themselves at an advantage when their currency is undervalued will suffer when their currency is overvalued. Despite the long-term balancing out of exchange rate fluctuations, Cavusgil suggests some strategies which international firms might pursue under different exchange rate conditions (see Table 9.3).

Some of the strategies highlighted in Table 9.3 may not be feasible for the firm or may contradict the firm's international marketing strategy. For example, the firm may not be able or willing to switch its production and sourcing between markets in the short term and may have a global advertising agency or pricing policy. Nonetheless, the range of options open to international market-ers highlights both the fact that the firm can minimize the impacts of exchange rate fluctuations and that price is also interrelated with other variables such as product quality and features, promotion and speed of market penetration.

Host Country Legislation

Both at the top and bottom end of the range of possible prices, international marketers may be faced by host country legislation. At the bottom end of the range, firms may encounter anti-dumping legislation, which prevents them from selling below a certain price. This type of legislation tends to be used for certain sectors, such as transport and

---

Box 9.2   Sterling on Steroids: The Impact on UK Exporters

'A year ago, the idea that sterling might be worth more than DM3 was regarded with horror by *economists* and industrialists alike. Now this has become a reality. That raises the following questions. Is the strong pound here to stay? If it is, can the economy live with sterling at that level?' (Adams 1998a).

Since late 1996 the rise of the pound against other currencies continued virtually unabated. By late 1998, the pound stood at its highest level for 10 years, against a basket of currencies, more than 30 per cent higher than two years previously. In parallel with this rise of sterling, UK exports fell to their lowest levels for 15 years. In the face of lost orders, redundancies and factory closures the 'strong pound' was frequently blamed.

Among those attributing declining exports to exchange rates were both small and large firms. As Graham Hayward, Managing Director of Scottish, Grampian Brands knitwear company said: 'The export and tourist market for Scottish knitwear is continuing to be adversely affected by the strength of sterling' (Adams 1998b). Similarly, Rover cars blamed the loss of 1,500 jobs in UK car plants to the strength of sterling (Bolger 1998).

Commentators, however, note that, while exchange rates clearly play a role in making a country's products affordable or expensive, the impacts of exchange rate variation can be bolstered by long-term currency hedges (Simonian 1998). In some cases, declining fortunes may not only be as a result of the strong pound. They may mask other problems. Nonetheless, Adams (1998c) concludes wryly: 'Two years on from sterling's massive appreciation on the world's currency markets, experts are divided over the effect on UK trade. Some think it will be bad. The rest think it will be worse.'

Sources: Adams, R. (1998a) 'Sterling on Steriods', *Financial Times*, 1 April; Adams, R. (1998b) 'Export Order hit Fifteen-Year Low', *Financial Times*, 29 May; Bolger, A. (1998) 'Rover Blames 1,500 Job Cuts on Strong Pound', *Financial Times*, 23 July; Simonian, H. (1998) 'Rough Ride is not Due just to the Strong Pound', *Financial Times*, 24 July; Adams, R. (1998c) 'Manufacturing Exports Slowly Throttled by Sterling's Upward March', *Financial Times*, 7 August.

Table 9.3   Exporter strategies under varying currency conditions

When domestic currency is WEAK	*When domestic currency is STRONG*
Stress price benefits	Engage in non-price competition by improving quality
Expand product line and add more costly features	Improve productivity and engage in vigorous cost reduction
Shift sourcing and manufacturing to domestic market	Shift sourcing and manufacturing overseas
Exploit export opportunities in all markets	Give priority to exports to relatively strong currency countries
Conduct conventional cash-for-goods trade	Deal in countertrade with weak-currency countries
Use full-costing approach, but use marginal-cost pricing to penetrate new/competitive markets	Trim profit margins and use marginal cost pricing
Speed repatriation of foreign-earned income and collections	Keep the foreign-earned income in host country, slow collections
Minimize expenditures in local, host currency	Maximize expenditures in local, host country currency
Buy needed services (advertizing, insurance, transportation etc. in domestic market)	Buy needed services abroad and pay for them in local currencies
Minimize local borrowing	Borrow money needed for local expansion in local market
Bill foreign customers in local currency	Bill foreign customers in their own currency

Source: Cavusgil (1988)

---

utilities, and is designed to protect domestic suppliers. In contrast, firms may be prevented from charging over a certain price in some markets.

Again, this is more prevalent in certain sectors, such as food, and is intended to protect the interests of host market consumers.

Range of Managerial Discretion

When costs and other variables that may affect the level of profit are accounted for, managers are left with a 'range of managerial discretion' (Weekly 1991). This range is bounded top and bottom by consideration of the competitive impacts of pricing decisions. When it prices above or below competition, a firm signals its quality and the benefits which it believes it offers relative to its competitors. Pricing below competitors, if the firm offers superior benefits, represents excellent value for money for customers and may be a suitable strategy if a firm wishes to penetrate the market. In contrast, pricing above competitors for lesser, or comparable, levels of benefit represents poor value for money and may result in the firm at best skimming, or even failing to win, customers in a market.

In other words, the range of managerial discretion must also take into account economic value to the customer (EVC). Firms can charge at the upper end of the price range only if they offer *superior benefits for which the customer is prepared to pay*. The firm's products or services must add value to the customer.

Cavusgil suggests a range of possible pricing strategies for international markets. These include:

1. **Rigid cost-plus strategy**. Among US firms in the late 1980s, this cost-plus margin approach was still preferred by a majority of firms, presumably because of its simplicity. Cavusgil suggests that firms may be intimidated by the complexities of pricing in international markets and may wish to keep their pricing strategy simple. A major limitation of this strategy is that the final customer price may be prohibitively expensive compared to local products. When entering Ukraine, a British cigarette manufacturer suggested that they would ultimately have to manufacture in the market in order to compete. While their products were superior in quality to those produced locally, the cost price of their cigarettes was higher than the final price of locally produced brands. The difference in price using a cost-plus pricing strategy was felt to be too great to make inroads into the market.

2. **Flexible cost-plus strategy**. This variation on cost-plus allows for price variations in special circumstances. Porter (1990) points to strong domestic demand and rivalry as causes of competitive advantage in particular countries. Intense local competition can mean that sophisticated local customers expect high value and as low as possible prices from international competitors. Some international firms lower their prices in particular markets simply to compete with domestically produced products. An example of this might be for firms wishing to penetrate East Asia in microelectronics or the USA with a software product. Cavusgil argues that flexible cost-plus is useful to counter competitive pressures or exchange rate fluctuations.

3. **Dynamic incremental strategy**. This strategy argues that fixed costs are sunk costs – they have been spent and are therefore disregarded from the pricing calculation. The important issue is to set a price which the market will bear and, therefore, make back sufficient revenue to offset fixed costs and make a profit. In this case, Cavusgil suggests that only variable and international sales costs should be counted in the cost calculation. The price level should be consistently monitored and, if necessary, adjusted in line with market fluctuations.

It must be noted that these are all variations on cost-plus strategies, although some competitive forces are considered. To complete the consideration of international pricing strategies, competitor parity and economic value to the customer strategies for international markets should also be considered.

4. **Competitor parity**. The prices charged by a firm will clearly be measured in comparison with both locally produced and other international products and services. Dependent on the relative value customers will decide whether or not to buy. It should be borne in mind that exchange rate fluctuations will affect firms of different nationalities

differently. Hence, British firms complaining at the strength of the pound might be doubly concerned at the loss of value of the Euro. Competitor products priced in Euros might, for example, appear better value in East Asia without British or Euro zone firms changing their prices.

Firms may also choose to send deliberate, rather than the above accidental signals, to a target market. One multinational food firm was keen to penetrate the East and Central European (CEE) region in order to gain first mover advantages over international rivals. Accordingly, it priced its products lower than in Western Europe in order to gain maximum market share quickly. Hout, Porter and Rudden (1985) highlight the fact that global or highly internationalized firms have a greater degree of flexibility in their pricing strategies than domestically, or regionally-based competitors.

Aggressive global players might lower prices, at the extreme even to less than costs, to gain market share or force competitors out of the market. A local competitor would not be able to match these prices. Global firms might, however, offset low prices in one market with profits from markets with fewer growth prospects or less competitive market conditions. In BCG terms, profits from 'cash cow', or mature, markets might be used, in the short term, to strengthen position in rapidly growing 'problem children' markets.

5. **Economic value to customers**. In international terms, pricing at the level which individual markets will bear maximizes global profitability. On a market-by-market basis, a firm may look at its costs, its competitive position and the level and sophistication of market demand to make a judgement on appropriate price levels. The resulting prices may be significantly different. Moreover, a wide range of variables will influence the prices which can be attained (Box 9.3).

As can be seen in Box 9.3, firms operating in a range of international markets can make different choices about the extent to which they will standardize prices globally. Tailoring prices to local market conditions should, in theory, result in highest overall profit levels. A range of other factors may, however, complicate matters:

■ **Common currencies**. The introduction of the Euro as a common European currency has a number of implications for international marketers. Firms which have been pricing differentially within Europe now find that price comparisons are more complex. Of course, nothing has really changed. Intelligent Euro-consumers with calculators could always work out there the best value cars, or wine or computers could be purchased – a steady flow into the UK of cars from Belgium and wine from France testifies to that. Adoption of the Euro by the countries in the EU, and the prospect of further countries joining still makes a difference, however. The message of price differences is more likely to be realized when prices are all marked in Euros. International

---

Box 9.3   The Impact of Channels to Market for Home Fashion Products in the UK and France

In the mid-1980s, home fashion products in the UK were priced significantly lower than those in France because of different distribution systems. While many French consumers shopped for home fashion products in specialist stores, the majority of sales in the UK were through large retail multiples. Specialist stores in the UK accounted for a relatively small proportion of sales. The power of the retail chains in the UK had forced down prices. In France, on the other hand, prices were much higher to allow margins to be made by both wholesalers and specialist stores in the channel to market. As French consumers shopping in specialist stores were also less price sensitive than UK consumers shopping in large retail stores, manufacturers could also make higher profits in France than in the UK.

marketers are under pressure from both consumers and industrial customers and retailers to iron out the differences. As Leszinski (1995, p. 266) comments:

> As Europe moves forward toward a single market, lack of attention to pricing is a serious problem. The stakes are unusually high...On average, a 1 per cent price increase results in a 12 per cent improvement in a company's operating margin. This is four times as powerful as a 1 per cent increase in its volume. But the sword cuts both ways. A price decrease of 5–10 per cent will eliminate most company's profits. As the single market develops, decreases of this magnitude can easily happen: the existing price differentials across Europe for some products are in the range of 20–40 per cent.

The advent of common currencies, together with more open access to global product information via the Internet, increases the pressure for international marketers to harmonize prices. Box 9.4 gives an example of this type of pressure.

- **The Internet**. As discussed more fully in Chapter 3, the growth in Internet shopping also increases price transparency. Surfing the web globally means that consumers will increasingly be aware of price differences. Purchases may be made from the country with the lowest prices.
- **Parallel, or 'grey' markets**. The issue of parallel markets is discussed more fully in the Network section below. In essence, the prices charged in different markets cannot be viewed as a set of isolated decisions. As customers can compare between markets, so they can choose to purchase from the markets with the lowest prices.
- **International buying groups**. In some industry sectors, smaller buyers are beginning to group together in 'buying' groups. In addition to pricing differently for different markets firms are more likely to offer better prices to larger and more powerful customers. The increased bargaining power of buying groups puts pressure on suppliers to reduce, and harmonize, prices offered to firms within the group. (International buying groups are considered more fully in the Network section below.)

Box 9.4   Price Differentiation in the Automobile Industry

In 1999, European car prices, adjusted for inflation, fell between 2 and 2.5 per cent. (Miller 1999). In the past, prices in Europe had been considerably higher than those in the USA. This price differential resulted from a combination of trade barriers, high taxes and protectionist policies.

The decrease in the price of cars in Europe was partly attributed to the introduction in January 1998 of the Euro, Europe's single currency, into eleven EU countries. Customers could always have worked out price differentials by currency conversion with a calculator. Nonetheless, analysts suggest that the new price transparency within Europe has increased the likelihood that consumers would identify price differences between countries and buy cars where they were cheapest.

Another factor behind the reduction in car prices in Europe was excess capacity. The 1990s saw European car-makers, including Fiat, Ford, Peugeot, Citroen and Volkswagen reducing production sharply as the market shrank (Wagstaff 1994). New low price entrants, such as Daiwoo of Korea and Kia of China intensified competitive pressure, which squeezed prices still further. Other pressures for price harmonization within Europe included claims from consumer organizations that features of the European car market, such as the ability to designate separate dealers for each European country had led to big differences in car prices (Wolf 1992).

Echikson (1999) quoted price differences of around 30 per cent between nations for the same model. The introduction of the Euro saw the biggest differences limited to countries, such as Britain (Echikson 1999) and Denmark (Falleson 1999), who are outside the Euro zone. Although the gap between the Euro zone and America is reducing, the gap between the European countries outside the Euro zone and the rest of the world is widening. An OECD study showed Britons paying 29 per cent more for cars and motor cycles than did Americans.
Source: The Economist, 6 February 1999, p. 58.

- **Global retailers**. The 1990s saw retailers expanding their scope to become international, if not global. As retailers such as Carrefour, Ahold, Metro and Wal Mart increase the pace of international expansion, they become larger and more powerful. Moreover, they will increasingly demand one (and probably the lowest) global price.

THE RELATIONSHIP PERSPECTIVE

Countertrade

From the 1970s onwards, academics and practitioners concerned with world trade alike have recognized the increasing importance of countertrade (Veraziu 1992; Okoroafo 1993; Abdel-Latif and Nugent 1994; Kreuze 1997). International countertrade is paying, at least in part, for foreign goods or services with other goods or services (Okoroafo 1993).

In international marketing, countertrade is particularly common in relationships with developing countries (Brorson 1992; Lambroza 1993). Indeed, Hennart (1990) finds a correlation between indebted countries and the use of countertrade. Studies highlight the role that countertrade may play in helping foreign firms develop relationships with developing countries, such as those in East and Central Europe (Kindra, Stapenhurst and Strizzi 1993; Lambroza 1993; Ring 1993), Sub-Saharan Africa (Mitchell 1997) or China (Simpson 1994). Developing business relationships in such countries may be hindered by their lack of cash or a poorly convertible currency. Foreign firms, however, may be keen to enter rapidly to gain first mover advantages.

A number of explanations have been proffered for the use of countertrade in developing countries:

- Shortage of foreign currency
- Lack of convertibility of currencies
- Developing countries needing to reserve foreign currency for more pressing purposes
- Trade barriers in developed countries making it difficult for developing country producers to sell their goods for currency
- Difficulty for emerging countries to penetrate new markets.

A valuable review of countertrade issues and practice can be found in Paun (1997).

The Development of Countertrade Relationships

In relationship terms, the major difference between countertrade and other types of exchange relationships is that the seller 'provides a buyer with deliveries and contractually agrees to purchase goods from the latter to an agreed percentage of the value of his sales contract' (Brorsen 1992). In a countertrade relationship, therefore, firms are not engaged in one transaction, but in a contractual relationship, which may extend over a period of time.

The high levels of uncertainty in countertrade relationships may affect the development of trust. Negotiations may be protracted. Each firm is both a buyer and seller and, therefore, may have to play different roles. It is likely that countertrade relationships will involve a team of actors from each firm and may be of greater complexity than completing a cash deal. Firms will be engaged in buying and selling goods of which they have little experience. The final value of these goods may not be certain. Neale, Shipley and Dodds (1991, p. 20) sum up the motivation for countertrade relationships with the comment:

> Although countertrade is often costly and cumbersome, for many firms 'countertrade is better than no trade,' so long as the incremental costs are covered, or longer-term profit prospects are enhanced.

THE NETWORK PERSPECTIVE

Interrelationships and International Pricing

As, from a network perspective, firms are interrelated, the pricing decisions of one firm affect those of other firms with whom they are directly or indirectly connected. If one supplier lowers prices because of efficiency savings, or to puts pressure on competitors, pressure may be exerted upon other firms to match this price drop. Supplier *B* may find it difficult to match the price decrease because of different labour, raw material and other costs. Moreover, supplier *B* may be reluctant to do this, not only because of loss of margin with this customer, but also for fear that other customers may discover and demand the same price. Thus price changes and market conditions influencing prices charged by different nationality firms can flow through the network.

Transfer Pricing

International marketing literature often treats price as though firms begin with a blank piece of paper in deciding their pricing strategy. In reality, for many firms a number of 'rules' may exist which govern what is possible. One such set of rules existing within many multinational corporations surrounds transfer pricing:

> When a department in an MNC transfers its tangible or intangible output to another department or a subsidiary, it regards this transfer as a sale. The price that is placed on such products, services, and know-how is generally regarded as the transfer price. (Fraedrich and Bateman 1996, p. 17)

Transfer prices are those which the firm charges when *transferring goods between the subsidiaries of a multinational corporation*. Transfer prices can be set at a number of different levels:

1. Marginal cost
2. Marginal cost plus fixed margin
3. Full market rate.

The impact of each of these depends on the supply–demand dynamics of each of the markets. Tensions may also arise if the subunits are each profit centres judged on their performance by Headquarters.

If the supplier charges marginal cost when it could sell for a higher price to a customer outside the firm, then as a profit centre, the supplier loses potential profit. If the supplier charges the market rate to an internal buyer, who could buy more cheaply outside the firm, the internal customer makes less profit. The likely pressures in both of these cases are for one or the other subsidiary to sell or buy outside the firm. This is detrimental to the overall profit levels of the firm.

In consequence, many firms opt to set transfer prices at marginal price plus a fixed margin so that both supplying and buying firms can make a profit. A more responsive transfer price setting mechanism may be to look at where most value is added within the organization and allocate the percentage of profit accordingly.

Whatever mechanism is used to set transfer prices, multinational corporations must ensure that the rigidity of their rules does not result in a loss of flexibility in response to price sensitive consumers. If competitive pressures bring down market prices, the multinational corporation may need to check that its final price to market is not inflated.

Co-operative International Buying Groups

As discussed on p. 167, the creation of co-operative, international buying groups between previously competitive firms changes the dynamics of pricing within the network. Leszinski (1995) gives the example of a leading consumer goods manufacturer charging prices across Europe which differed by up to 40 per cent. The international buying group reduced this differentiated pricing to only 15 per cent. On the creation of a buying group comprising at least one major customer from each country, the distributors became aware of the range of price differences. Pressure was exerted to charge the same amount in each market. By agreeing to do this, the firm would lose revenue of SFr 100 million, which represented somewhere between SFr 10 and SFr 20 million in profits. The firm had no choice but to accept. The impact on revenues was as anticipated, although the impact on profits was reduced by rationalizing the complexity of the firm's structure for serving Europe.

A consequence of seeing firms as embedded in a network structure is the realization that firms are increasingly likely to discover and object to differential pricing. Whether prices are altered or remain at the current levels depends on the relative power of the actors concerned. Adapting Easton and Araujo's change diagram to the pressure to harmonize international prices (see Figure 9.1) shows when firms are likely to harmonize prices or retain price differentials. The impact on

| Impact on supplier | **Absorption** |
| Impact on buying group members | **Transformation** |

Figure 9.1 Pressures for price harmonization
Source: Adapted from Easton and Araujo (1992)

profit of price harmonization makes it internal to the firm's core activity. When supply exceeds demand (e.g. firms can switch to other suppliers to gain better prices), or the customer has greater power (e.g. international buying groups, international retailers) then the context is competitive. Suppliers, then, will absorb the impacts of the change (as in the case of the consumer goods firm above), while members of the buying group may find their profit potential transformed.

Pressure from larger, more international customers, retailers or coalitions, as in the above example, is likely to ripple throughout networks, dictating more frequent absorption of price changes. When firms form direct, rather than indirect, relationships by forming strategic alliances, joining professional bodies or otherwise co-operating, they are more likely to discover and object to price differentials.

Parallel Pricing or Grey Markets

Discussion of differential pricing in international markets raises one of the important implications for pricing of operation within a network. If firms price at EVC in each market, there may be significant price differences for the same product or service. If a customer can buy more cheaply in one market than in another then they, or more significantly an independent agent, may purchase large quantities of a product and transfer them across the border into a market where they are cheaper than local sold equivalents. Industry sources estimate that, in the mid-1980s, 10 per cent of IBM's PC sales and 20 per cent of Sharp Electronics' photocopier sales were through unauthorized channels (Cavusgil and Sikora 1988).

Cavusgil and Sikora (1988) calculate the cost of grey markets in lost revenue to each US firm as US$ 4 million in 1984. In some industries it was

higher. Average sales losses in the camera industry were US$7.4 million and in the watch industry US$6.5 million.

In addition to financial implications, firms may also face legal questions. If the firm sells products which conform to legal requirements in one market, but these are subsequently transferred across borders into a market where they do not, who is ultimately responsible for any legal action resulting from their sale? Examples of this issue result, for example, if an international distiller conforms to maximum or minimum alcoholic proof rates for the country, but the beverage is sold on into a market where it is illegal. The distiller may not knowingly have sold products in a market where they are not legal. The grey market distributor did, however, sell the firm's products legally in the market. Where brand reputation is at stake, it is the distiller who may ultimately be held liable.

Cavusgil and Sikora (1988) propose a number of measures open to the firm to minimize the impact of parallel markets. These include defensive measures, such as blocking routes, purchasing independent distributors engaged in grey market distribution, or identifying and refusing to service and guarantee products not bought in a particular market. As ever with static defences, the problem is that innovative competitors can breach them. Elimination of one route of grey market trading may solve the problem only briefly. If an opportunity exists, other grey market traders may take the place of the one which was prevented from selling or acquired. If sufficient obstacles are put in the way of customers, who have bought the product cheaply, but have nonetheless bought the firm's product legally, they are unlikely to make a repeat purchase. A more fruitful resolution seems, therefore, to lie in co-operation and relationship building with the final consumer. If sufficient incentive is offered to deal with the firm or its distributors in the individual market, then the customer may be prepared to pay a slight premium.

A particular impact of grey markets is the impact which they have on established relationships, such as those between manufacturer and dealer/distributor. Trust between the two may be damaged if grey market trade erodes the sales and margins which the dealer can achieve. In the case of Minolta cameras (Keegan 1998), the official German dealer found his trade affected by cameras imported into the market by the Hong Kong distributor. His complaint was that Minolta should prevent such grey market activity.

Countertrade Networks

Building on the earlier discussion, relationships involving countertrade lend themselves to further examination from a network perspective. As can be seen both from the work of Shipley and Egan (1900) and from Brorsen's consideration of countertrade relationships (1992), these relationships may involve more than just two actors. In addition to a buying and selling firm, a range of negotiating agents, resellers, government agencies and other actors may become involved. As a result, one countertrade deal may involve 'nets' of actors. In the case of counterpurchase agreements in Indonesia, Brorsen (1992) shows a complex web of actors in Indonesia, Singapore and in a range of Western countries.

Brorsen (1992) shows relationships between:

1. **Developing country trading house – Developing country trading house**. Two or more trading houses may make joint offers on countertrade deals. This may be the case when large quantities of goods are involved, or if the two have complementary capabilities necessary to fulfil the conditions of the deal.
2. **Developing country trading house – Headquarters**. Intra-firm relationships may exist between a subsidiary of a trading firm situated in the developing country and its Headquarters.
3. **Developing country trading house – Developing country producer**. The trading house will be in direct contact with the firm it represents.
4. **Developing country trading house – Developing country government**. This will occur if the countertrade agreement is with a government agency or, as in the case of Indonesia, must be conducted via a 'Countertrade' unit within the government.
5. **Developing country trading house – Other developing country government**. If the developing country operates as part of a free trade zone or other economic agreement, its government may be regulated by agreements with other governments within the economic zone.
6. **Developing country trading house – Industrialized country trading house**. The countertrade relationship is unlikely to be conducted directly with the industrialized country firm, but via its trading house. All foreign firms with trading capabilities belong in this last category (although a minority may handle countertrade within the firm if this occurs sufficiently often that a unit has been established).

The bonds which develop as a result of successful countertrade include:

- Bonds connecting **import and export activities**
- **Bonds of knowledge** – trading will involve experts in different goods and markets
- **Financial bonds** – may involve the creation of banking syndicates
- **Social bonds** – as with other types of relationships, these may be more essential to the development of trust than financial or knowledge bonds.

One criterion for selection of the successful partner would be 'the ability to negotiate and solve conflicts'.

SUMMARY

In Chapter 9 we have examined the implications of pricing in international markets. The nature of the influences on international pricing decisions have been explored. We have also presented an overview of international pricing strategy, considering the way in which decisions made in different international markets may be inter-related. Issues relating to grey market activity are explored and possible solutions suggested.

BIBLIOGRAPHY

Abdel-Latif, A. M. and Nugent, J. B. (1994) 'Counter-trade as Trade Creation and Trade Diversion', *Contemporary Economic Policy*, 12, January: 1–11.

Baker, J. C. and Ryans, J. K. Jr. (1973) 'Some Aspects of International Pricing: A Neglected Area of Management Policy', *Management Decision*, Summer: 177–82.

Brorsen, H. (1992) 'Developing Countertrade Networks', in Forsgren, M. and Johanson, J. (eds), *Managing Networks in International Business*, Gordon and Breach.

Cavusgil, S. T. (1988) 'Unraveling the Mystique of Export Pricing', *Business Horizons*, May–June; reprinted in Meloan, T. and Graham, J. (eds) (1998), *International and Global Marketing: Concepts and Cases*, 2nd edn, Irwin/McGraw-Hill.

Cavusgil, S. T. and Sikora, E. (1988) 'How Multinationals Can Counter Gray Market Imports', *Columbia Journal of World Business*, 23, 4.

Easton, G. and Araujo, L. (1992) 'Non-economic Exchange in Industrial Networks', in Easton, G. and Axelsson, B. (eds), *Industrial Networks: A New View of Reality*, Routledge.

Echikson, W. (1999) 'A Fender-Bender for the Euro', *Business Week*, 30 August 8.

Economist, The (1999) 'Britain: Expensive', *The Economist*, 6 February: 57–8.

Falleson, L. B. (1999) 'Copenhagen: Danes pay the Most for Cars', *Europe*, 385: 44–5.

Fraedrich, J. P. and Bateman, C. R. (1996) 'Transfer Pricing by Multinational Marketers: Risky Business', *Business Horizons*, January–February: 17–22.

Frank, V. H. Jr. (1984) 'Living with Price Controls Abroad', *Harvard Business Review*, March–April: 137–42.

Hennart, J.-F. (1990) 'Some Empirical Dimensions of Countertrade', *Journal of International Business Studies*, 21, 2: 41–63.

Hout, T., Porter, M. E. and Rudden, E. (1985) 'How Global Companies Win Out', *Harvard Business Review*, September–October: 98–108.

Kindra, G., Stapenhurst, S. and Strizzi, F. (1993) 'A Survey of Countertrade Practices with Eastern Europe', *International Marketing Review*, 10, 6: 61–77.

Kreuze, J. G. (1997) 'International Countertrade', *Internal Auditor*, April: 42–7.

Lambroza, S. (1993) 'Rubles and Sense', *The Journal of European Business*, 5, 2: 14–17.

Leszinski, R. (1995) 'Pricing for a Single Market', in Paliwoda, S. J. and Ryans, J. K. Jr. (eds), *International Marketing Reader*, Routledge: 266–72.

Miller, S. (1999) 'Europe's Auto Market Takes on American Look – Price Competition is Cutthroat, as GM starts to Fix Opel', *The Wall Street Journal*, 13 September, Eastern Edition, New York: A 33.

Mitchell, P. (1997) 'Alternative Financing Techniques in Trade with Sub-Saharan Africa', *Business America*, January–February, 118: 29–31.

Neale, C. W., Shipley, D. D. and Dodds, C. (1991) 'The Countertrading Experience of British and Canadian Firms', *Management International Review*, 31, 1: 19–35.

Okoroafo, S. C. (1993) 'An Integration of Countertrade Research and Practice', *Journal of Global Marketing*, 6, 4: 115–28.

Paun, D. A. (1997) 'An International Profile of Countertrading Firms', *Industrial Marketing Management*, 26, 1: 41–50.

Porter, M. E. (1990) *Competitive Advantage of Nations*, Macmillan.

Ring, M. A. (1993) 'Countertrade Business Opportunities in Russia', *Business America*, 11 January: 15–16.

Shipley, D., Egan, C. E., Neale, W., Hooley, G., and Danko, J. (1995) 'British Experience and Intentions with Joint Ventures in Hungary', *Proceedings of the Academy of International Business*, Bradford.

Simpson, J. L. (1994) 'Countertrade in a Transitional Market Economy: The Chinese Experience', *Irish Business and Administrative Research*, 18: 192–210.

Terpstra, V. (1983) 'Suggestions for Research Themes and Publications', *Journal of International Business Studies*, Spring–Summer: 9–10.

Veraziu, P. (1992) 'Trends and Developments in International Countertrade', *Business America*, 2 November: 2–5.

Wagstaff, I. (1994) 'Carmakers Shed Crocodile Tears', *Purchasing and Supply Management*, June: 28–29.

Weekly, J. (1991) 'Pricing in Foreign Markets: Pitfalls and Opportunities', *Industrial Marketing Management*, 21: 173–9.

Wolf, J. (1992) 'EC Commission Unveils Blueprint for Car Industry', *The Asian Wall Street Journal*, 30 April, 5–8.

PROMOTION

Objectives

The issues to be addressed in Chapter 10 include:

1. The challenges facing international marketers in creating effective international promotional strategies
2. The distinctive challenges of building relationships with international creative agencies
3. The integration of global promotional activity into Integrated Marketing Communications (IMC) strategies.

After reading Chapter 10 you will be able to:

1. Understand the issues facing international marketers from the 5 Ms of international promotion
2. Evaluate the distinctive challenges of creating relationships with international creative agencies
3. Understand moves to create IMC strategies.

INTRODUCTION

Developing effective international promotional strategies represents a major challenge for international marketers. Marketing communication plays a valuable role in making customers and consumers aware, interested and ultimately desirous of buying products or services. In international markets, however, cultural and other barriers may hinder communication and complicate the development of effective promotional strategies.

This chapter first reviews the issues involved in developing international promotional strategies. The challenges are classified under the headings: mix, message, miscommunication, media and money. The relationship section of this chapter discusses the distinctive challenges of building international creative agency–client relationships. In this instance longevity may be seen as stagnation, which results in less creativity.

From a network perspective, a growing body of literature looks at integration of global promo-

tional activity within the firm or between firms and a surrounding network of agencies. The contributions of the Integrated Marketing Communications (IMC) literature are reviewed. The chapter concludes with a discussion of the complex implications of global account management (GAM) initiatives between firms and their global customers.

THE TRADITIONAL PERSPECTIVE

The key to effective promotional strategies is communication. 'Noise,' anything which interferes in communication between the sender and receiver of the message, may reduce its effectiveness. Worse, it may result in miscommunication, that is customers receiving the *wrong message*. The concept of global standardization (discussed in Chapter 5) is viewed as particularly relevant to global advertisers (Buzzell 1968; Levitt 1983). The assumption that consumers are becoming globally more similar has, however, been challenged by subsequent work (Quelch and Hoff 1986; Douglas and Wind 1987). Cultural difference may have significant impact on the extent to which global promotional strategies and global marketing messages travel.

Challenges in International Promotional Strategies

In simple terms, the decision facing international marketers can be considered under five headings:

- Mix
- Message
- Miscommunication
- Media
- Money.

The following section addresses each of these areas.

Mix

There are a number of promotional tools available to any international marketer. These include personal selling, advertising, sales promotion and public relations. Depending on the nature of the industry sector and promotional objectives, these tools may be used in different combinations to create an overall promotional strategy:

- **Complex message – small number of buyers**. For complex messages and to communicate with a small number of buyers, *personal selling* may be the most effective promotional technique. This may be the case for industrial products or services, such as steel or computer solutions for businesses, which may also involve sales of large volumes to a single buyer.
- **Simple message – large number of buyers**. For simple messages targeting a large number of customers, as in consumer markets, personal selling to each potential buyer may not be feasible. In this situation, *advertising* may be the most effective promotional tool.

Sales promotion and public relations may be used in both industrial and consumer markets. Public relations may involve communication and relationship building with different actors, depending on the nature and identity of customer and stakeholders in particular markets. Sales promotion may take different forms in industrial and consumer markets. In industrial markets, this may involve demonstration of product functions at tradeshows. In consumer markets, this is more likely to include 'on pack' offers.

In international markets, the same basic influences determine the most effective promotional mix. In addition, however, others factors must be taken into account to create effective international promotional strategies.

In keeping with a multi-domestic marketing strategy, firms have traditionally tended to leave everything bar branding and packaging decisions to the discretion of local subsidiary managers. Riesenbeck and Freeling (1991), examine, however, the extent to which global standardization is possible for the *Fortune 500* firms. While standardization of strategic elements, such as branding and positioning – and, to a lesser extent, product and packaging – is possible, firms are far less standardized in the more tactical elements of the marketing mix.

Sales promotion is a tactical promotional tool. It tends to be used to achieve trial of new products or may be used to boost short-term sales, for example to balance seasonal sales variations. Sales promotion activity may be either directed at consumers or trade channels to market. There is a worldwide tendency to allocate the promotional budget away from advertising towards sales promotion. The outcome of this is reduced brand profitability as there is a dilution of attempts to build brand identity with customers. A switch to sales promotion, often in the form of price reductions, may be demanded in countries with strong channels to market.

The move towards sales promotion has a number of consequences:

- **Cost**. The cost of sales promotion has risen, often to the extent that it now exceeds advertising costs. Given that sales promotion does not build brand image, this is an increasing concern for international marketing managers.
- **Complexity**. The number of sales promotions and their complexity are increasing. For many firms co-ordination and assessment of the

effectiveness of this activity has become necessary. Local subsidiaries may have an incentive to agree to sales promotion activities to help build relationships with local retailers and build profits. Local priorities may not, in this case, align with Headquarters' promotional objectives.

- **Global branding**. As the trend towards building 'uniform' brand identities continues, consistency of the firm's communication strategy becomes an issue. Global co-ordination of promotional activity may be required to assure that brand harmony is achieved across markets. Local promotional activity may either enhance, or in some cases, detract from brand strategy. Consider the case of the ill fated 'Hoover' flight promotion (Box 10.1).

The negative publicity resulting from this type of ill-judged sales promotion may have a detrimental effect on brand image not just in one mar-

ket but across all markets who become aware of the adverse publicity. Given the financial and strategic importance of global brands to international marketers, it is perhaps unsurprising that Head Office may wish to ensure consistency and exercize some level of control.

Global or local promotional strategies?

The extent to which sales promotion activity can be controlled locally, or should be co-ordinated centrally, depends on the global or local nature of the brand. If the brand is specific to a particular market, as in the case of Nestlé's 'Crosse and Blackwell Branston Pickle' in the UK, then promotional activity can be handled locally without major risk. If, on the other hand, the brand is global in its scope, as in the case of Levi Jeans, Coca Cola or Swatch watches, then the possible consequences of inappropriate promotional activity in a particular markets are considerably higher. Kashani and Quelch (1990) refer to this as the

---

Box 10.1   Dust Up Over Hoover Promotion

It sounded too good to be true. Buy a Hoover vacuum cleaner for more than £100 and receive two free flight tickets to the USA or to a choice of six destinations in Europe!

However, the promotion did not end up as the marketing success intended by the company. In a welter of speculation as to whether the promotion had been miscalculated, consumer watchdogs became involved and bad publicity abounded (Mead and Skapinker 1992).

Some within the travel industry suggested that the promotion could not make commercial sense: 'What profit is Hoover making on that hundred pound sale? They might be making a tenner. Out of that they are paying for two tickets to America? It's bonkers' (Mead and Skapinker 1992).

So attractive was the scheme that the Hoover schemes created chaos. More than 100 000 applications were received for the European scheme alone. There was no cut off point, so even when the handling house was overwhelmed with responses, still customer requests arrived. Two other travel agents were drafted in to help with the backlog and Hoover had to mount its own 'free flight hotline' to cope with customers complaining that they had not yet received a response.

The sales uplift from the promotion was massive. Retailers suggested that this had been one of the most successful promotions ever. But what of the impact on Hoover themselves? The promotion was seemingly prompted by the need to move products. US parent, Maytag was reporting pre-tax losses of $50.2 million for the three months to the end of September 1992. The long-term commercial impacts, however, were less certain. The local papers in Scotland were apparently full of adverts for second-hand Hoovers. And consumer goodwill hit a low...Amid complaints that the conditions had altered – accommodation was tied to the free flights. This seemed to be priced higher through the promotion than when purchased directly. Furthermore, questions about flight availability were raised. A promotion designed to boost sales and create consumer goodwill seemed destined to leave a sour taste for a number of customers.

Sources: Mead, G. and Skapinker, M. (1992), 'Hoover Stirs up PR Dust Cloud over Free Flights Deal', *Financial Times*, 19 December; Mead, G. (1992) 'Consumer Body Cautions on Free Flights', *Financial Times*, 15 December.

'geographical equity' of the brand. When the geographical equity of a brand is high the need for central co-ordination of promotional activity increases.

The extent to which promotional activity should, or can, be standardized depends also on its nature. Riesenbeck and Freeling (1991) identify the fact that personal selling is the promotional tool least likely to be globally standard, as it depends on interaction between individuals. The way in which trusting, stable sales relationships are built with individuals in different markets may vary considerably with cultural differences (see Chapter 2). More strategic promotional tools, such as advertizing – or even trade promotions with the increasing globalization of retailers – are more likely to be standardized across international markets.

This type of analysis of standardization or adaptation is, however, essentially broad-brush. Within each tool, the issues at stake may be complex. Within personal selling, for example, international marketers may choose to standardize some elements, while leaving others to the discretion of the international subsidiary. Head Office is typically involved in strategic-level decisions such as the choice of sales organization. This may involve taking higher or lower levels of control over the salesforce operating in international markets (see Chapter 7 for a fuller discussion of this issue). Tactical issues, such as the setting of sales targets, recruitment of staff or training in sales techniques for a particular market, are likely to be handled locally. The following section addresses in more detail the questions in international sales strategy.

Centralized or decentralized sales strategy?

It may be beneficial to the firm if some aspects of sales strategy are centralized:

■ **Market intelligence systems**. The ability to access sales data and market research across markets provides useful background data for the individual sales manager. The latter may need to understand the strategic significance of a particular account, the sales potential (i.e. how many markets the customer operates in and what market share it might hope to achieve), together with any sales history with the firm. Increasingly, this type of market intelligence exists in in-company market intelligence systems (MIS). Central operation of MIS reduces the duplication of market research activity and avoids costly errors.

■ **Global account data**. The growing importance of global customers may make this kind of account management essential. Global customers may have their own records of dealings with a particular supplier and be less than amused if they discover that a component is being sold at different prices by different parts of the organization. While this may be justified by local market dynamics, the customer may expect the lowest price to be provided for all global transactions. In addition to ensuring consistent sales actions, central market research may also allow the sales operation in a particular country to identify products which are selling to one of their customers in another part of the world and to identify new sales opportunities (For a further discussion of global account management, see the Relationship section of this chapter.)

■ **Sales support**. Consistency in the promotional materials that support sales effort may also be beneficial. The benefits are, in part, due to cost reduction in developing creative strategies. Strategic gains may also result. If a firm decides from its segmentation analysis that customers across all or some groups seek the same benefits, then each group can be targeted with a consistent promotional campaign. Sales literature will clearly need to be translated and may have to be adapted to meet local preferences.

A number of disadvantages may also result from centralized control of the sales effort:

■ **Performance measurement?** One disadvantage of centralized control is that a local operation may not be able to maximize sales in its own market. Depending on the way the operation is assessed this may be a source of frustration for local managers. If, for example, the local office is a separate profit centre, it may not set sales targets, or may not be able to maximize sales to the accounts that are locally most attractive. Imagine a scenario where Head Office prioritizes certain global accounts. The sales that the local office gains from some of these may be small and make little profit for the local operation. Local customers, of little strategic importance to the firm, may be a more significant source of profit. These local customers may, however, not receive the sale level of sales, promotional and other support because of Head Office priorities. In this instance, centralized control may not maximize local profit.

- **Lack of flexibility**. In addition to causing resentment among sales representatives, centralized management may also result in missed opportunities if the decision making process is rigid or lengthy. If potential new business must be sanctioned by Head Office, then the time involved and limitations on prices charged by the local sales operation may result in lost chances.

Decentralizing sales may give the local sales operation sufficient autonomy to respond quickly and pragmatically to sales opportunities. It can make use of the local knowledge of its sales force to sell those products or services most likely to succeed in its own market. Hence it is more likely to reach its sales targets.

A global sales force?

Hill, Still and Boya (1991) identify five factors which influence the choice between separate and multi-market sales forces:

- Geographic and physical dimensions of individual countries
- Level of market development
- Country-level political and legal systems
- Human relations aspects of sales practices
- Local market conditions.

We shall examine each of these in some detail.

- **Geographic and physical dimensions**. Factors included under this heading include the size of the market. Hill, Still and Boya (1991) suggest that large markets warrant their own salesforce and are more likely to have a sales

organization independent of Head Office. In smaller markets it may not be economic to have specialists in different parts of the sales task. Typical consequences in small markets are that a sales representative may double as a sales engineer, or else that representatives may sell a broad range of the company's products.

- **Degree of market development**. Hill, Still and Boya (1991) suggest also that differing levels of educational, economic and social infrastructures may have implications for the recruitment and training of sales personnel. A particular problem is identified in recruiting appropriate sales staff in Less Developed Countries (LDCs). There may be strong local variation in the sources of staff. Examples cited include the use of US business school graduates in target countries by US multinationals, or reliance on military candidates in Central and Southern Africa.

- **Differing political and legal structures**. Different political and legal conditions complicate the standardization of salesforce working conditions and remuneration. For example, taxation differences may mean that multinational corporations alter the proportion of the total package which is represented by sales incentives as opposed to other benefits, such as higher levels of medical and maternity conditions.

- **Human relations aspects of personal selling and sales management**. Social and cultural differences may also determine the appropriate management of human resource issues. In Japan, length of service is the traditional determinant of the level of salary rises, rather than performance in achieving sales objectives. If commission is offered, this would also be dependent upon the combined efforts of the entire sales team rather than to the achievements of the individual.

- **Local market circumstances**. Other environmental differences may have an impact upon the features of a product or service which are likely to appeal to the market. In the home fashion industry, variation within the French market for wallpaper related to climactic differences and a propensity for customers in the warmer south to spend more on outdoor areas of the home. More expensive products and warmer colours were more attractive to the cooler northern region.

Message

As can be seen in the previous section, the basic promotional mix decisions involve discussion of the firm's broader strategic aims and their distinctive competences. In determining the level of standardization or adaptation of promotional strategy, a key consideration is whether the firm's message or messages should or can travel across markets.

Bougery and Guimares (1993) said of Levitt:

> Advertising agencies, he said, would need to align themselves globally, like their clients, to sell a 'one sight-one sound' message. After all, he said, if Marlboro and CocaCola could do it, why not every product and service? Human emotion was the same the world over, he reasoned, and could be appealed to cross-culturally in pursuit of marketing efficiency.

Criticisms of Levitt's (1983) claims for global consumer convergence are many (see Chapter 4 for a discussion of global–local strategies). Nonetheless, the standardization literature (Buzzell 1968) intially discussed the relevance of these arguments to advertizing. Do these arguments, then, hold weight in the new millennium?

The 1980s and 1990s witnessed a proliferation of global media. Satellite and digital television continue to expand in scope and channels such as CNN and MTV, among others, now have global reach. The Internet provides emerging media with global potential. Despite the availability of global media, however, the extent to which global communication is really possible depends on the extent to which the firm's promotional message has global appeal.

One method of reducing the impact of language differences between countries is the use of visual imagery. Bougery and Guimares (1993) argue that:

> Visual imagery is one of the most efficient ways of transcending all language barriers, whether these barriers lie between different languages or 'intralingually' – between different interpretations of meaning within the same language. Basing your ads on a strong visual image can also help to keep your messages consistent globally.

In the 1980s, Anheuser-Busch wanted to communicate the fact that Budweiser beer was cool and refreshing. One way in which this was achieved was by showing the beer in a frosted glass with a single drop of moisture running down the outside. The Chanel fashion house used magazine adverts showing a selection of opulent jewellery and rich fabrics to convey an image of luxury and style. To use a well-worn cliché, a picture may be worth a thousand words. The wisdom behind visual imagery is that this conveys a more powerful and precise message than does a verbal description. Research suggests that international marketers should begin thinking of their brand identity in pictures as soon as possible.

One useful framework for deciding whether or not a message can travel is that proposed by Bovee and Thill 2001. This framework suggests that different types of message may be more or less easy to transfer across markets. Ranging from the easiest to the most difficult to transfer, the authors suggest that messages can be classified as:

- Product facts and function – easiest to transfer
- Universal myths and symbols
- Basic human emotions
- Celebrities or topical news
- Humour and culturally specific – most difficult to transfer.

Huang (1998) builds on the idea that emotional appeals may travel across borders, as emotions are universal. He draws a distinction, however, between *basic* and *social* emotions. Social emotions are may be culturally specific because they are attitudes and beliefs that are learned during the socialization process. These may be specific to a particular culture. Based on a study of Benetton adverts that appeal to basic emotions (happiness, love and sadness) against those generating social emotions (humour, warmth and surprise), Huang found that the reponse was more similar for the first type of emotion.

Miscommunication

Cultural differences cause a significant proportion of the miscommunication between a firm and customers in other international markets. Dulek,

Fielden and Hill (1991) highlight some of the pitfalls for the unwary posed by cultural differences (these are discussed more fully in Chapter 2). Differences may impact on verbal and written communication. Using Hall's high and low context framework (see Chapter 2), Dulek, Fielden and Hill (1991) identify specific 'do's' and 'don't's' for international communication.

- ■ **Conversation**.
  - – Recognize that high context cultures need to know as much as possible about you and the country you represent. Conversations about yourself, your family, company, even current events may provide reassurance to customers from high context cultures who will have a greater sense of understanding of the context surrounding the interaction.
  - – Speak slowly, clearly and simply. Avoid jargon, slang and any other idiomatic phrases. These may not translate literally and may be a cause of confusion (see Chapter 2 on language).
  - – Use as many words in the local language as possible. Dulek, Fielden and Hill (1991) believe that showing willingness with a few phrases in the local language will appear as though the seller has made an effort. This may, however, be dangerous if the seller has insufficient knowledge of the language to appear polite and causes insult by using the wrong words.
  - – Body language and tone of voice are important keys. If the recipient of a message cannot understand some, or all, of the words in a message, other signals such as posture, facial expression and gestures take on a greater significance.
- ■ **Written communication**. The role played by written communication varies with the level of context of the country. When communicating in a low context country – that is one that values that what rather than the how of international marketing – written communication is proportionately more important than in a high context country. If written communication is important then, again, Dulek, Fielden and Hill (1991) identity a number of guiding rules:

- – Make the main points simply and directly.
- – Adapt to the stylistic preferences of the country. Some cultures place greater emphasis on politeness and formality than do others. Using the right level of formality may be significant not only in high context cultures, but also, for example, in the use of the polite rather than informal 'you' in the German or French languages. Use of the correct formal titles, appellation and final greeting may also alter the recipients' perception of the communication.
- – Enclose a translation, where possible, but have this back translated by a native speaker to check that the meaning has not been altered in the translation process. Even different nuances may alter the meaning of the message.

Media

The choice of media to communicate the promotional message may vary between countries. Levels of economic development may alter the percentage of households with television or radio and may invalidate these as forms of mass communication. The simplest guiding principle is to look at what exists within the market and what proportion of the target customers can be reached using this medium. After liberalization, for example, advertizing in Central Europe was achieved by posting adverts on the sides of buses and trams. Dialog, a new telephone bank in the Slovak Republic, elicited high levels of interest by using this media.

Debates over media now concern the rates of adoption of a number of new technologies. Global media such as satellite and digital television may offer effective media for communication of global messages. It might be assumed that these are most effective in reaching customers in advanced industrial economies, whose level of technological development is higher. This may not necessarily be the case. Uptake of these technologies in emerging markets is, for example, rapid. In Poland, for example, communication via e-commerce and satellite television systems has grown to significant proportions as the country has simply omitted the intermediary stages of technological development and invested in the latest technology.

The ultimate choice of media will be based not only on effective access to customers, but also on the resources of the company. In advertizing its repositioning of the Skoda brand in the UK, for example, VW decided on a total marketing budget of £5 million. With this level of budget, TV advertizing was impossible and posters on billboards were chosen as a cost-effective way of communicating with the target market.

Money

The choice of appropriate international promotion strategy depends not only on the decisions of the international marketers or the availability of effective media in different markets. Often such decisions are dictated by budgetary considerations. Firms may choose a poster campaign, rather than TV advertising, for reasons of cost efficiency – as did Skoda for the launch of the Felicia in the UK. Money, therefore, is a constraint on the choices of international marketers and cost-benefit analyses may be an inevitable part of international promotion.

THE RELATIONSHIP PERSPECTIVE

Advertising Agency–Client Relationships

As with any other type of relationship, agency–client relationships can be both long-term and trusting or else complicated by tensions and conflict. In July 1999, *Marketing* reported that 83 per cent of marketers believed that their creative agencies made a valuable contribution towards achieving marketing objectives. Figures from the Incorporated Society of British Advertisers (ISBA) (*Marketing*, 3 June 1999) placed satisfaction levels somewhat lower at 78 per cent. Around half of advertizers believe that their agency offers excellent service and slightly over half that agencies can be relied upon to keep their promises. It appears, then, that these relationships have their own particular tensions. Indeed, media coverage suggests that dissatisfaction and changes of agency are frequent.

This dissatisfaction exists on both sides of the relationship. Agencies also expressed high levels of dissatisfaction with relationships with market-ing customers: 84 per cent of agencies were frustrated at the level of client staff with whom they interacted and 90 per cent believed that problems arose from too frequent changes of opposite number within the marketing department of the partner.

Research suggests that only half of advertising agency–client relationships last longer than five years, with the average relationship length standing at between seven and eight years. The failure of these relationships is costly in financial terms and may detract from the consistency of the promotional strategy. Moreover, the breakdown of agency–client relationships tends to be public. Press coverage pores over the details of acrimonious break-ups:

> Foote Cone & Belding is trading swipes with former client Mazda Motor Corp. in yet another advertizing brawl arising from a severed relationship. The Japanese auto maker is demanding $2.5 million in damages from Foote Cone, which in turn is seeking $5 million from the client for what the agency claims are unpaid bills. The squabble is fallout from the US Federal Trade Commission's crackdown a few years ago on allegedly misleading car-lease ads. (*Asian Wall Street Journal*, 5 April 1999)

> Miller Brewing abruptly parted ways with ad agency Young and Rubicam, reassigning its Icehouse and Molson beer brands to a little-known Dallas agency called Square One. Both sides called the parting mutual. But some people familiar with the split up say that it was acrimonious. (*The Wall Street Journal*, 5 February 1999)

So the costs and adverse publicity of agency–client relationship failure suggests that long-term, stable relationships are as important here as for other types of relationship. Yet, in this area, this belief may be open to question:

- **Incompatability**. The literature has frequently asked the question why some firms remain in relationships that are not productive and fruitful:

  > Incompatibility is understandable. What's difficult to understand is why, after discovering that the relationship is not working, the parties insist on remaining involved with each other, ultimately

writing nasty memos, challenging invoices and wasting each others' time. (*Marketing News*, 6 July 1998)

This question is reminiscent of the work of Young and Denize (1994) who look at reasons for inertia in business-to-business relationships.

- **The dark side of long-term relationships?** The potential 'downside' of long-term relationships has been identified in a number of fields. In market research agency–client relationships, Moorman, Zaltman and Deshpandé (1992) find that long-term relationships may develop dynamics that hinder the development of trust, commitment and involvement. The high levels of experience which the firms gain of each other may lead both to believe that their service providers are no longer objective, or have become stale.

These findings are supported for relationships between advertising agencies and their clients (Doyle, Corstjens and Michell 1980, Michell and Sanders 1995). They may have particular relevance given that these are 'creative relationships'. If long-term relationships stagnate, does this result in unproductive creative relationships?

There are a number of reasons why advertising agency–client relationships may founder. A principal assertion for this type of relationship is that longevity may result in the agency losing its creative drive. Halinen (1997) suggests that clients perceive agents as producing 'institutionalized creativity'. While mutual adaptation and deepening links may be perceived as beneficial in some types of relationships, creative relationships may differ in this respect. Indeed, Grayson and Ambler (1999) show that this 'dark side' of long-term relationships in marketing services may reduce the influence of trust.

A second reason may be changes in the competitive context of advertizing agencies. As advertising agencies compete for contracts from a smaller number of large global players, there may be an increased tendency to accept contracts for which they are ill-suited. Similarly, the length of time involved in the review process for selecting new partners may be a disincentive to change.

Successful Creative Relationships

What constitutes a successful agency–client relationship has been defined in a number of ways. The first measure relates to creativity. Failure to achieve creativity, as seen above, is the main reason why firms wish to change agencies (Doyle, Corstjens and Michell 1980; Dowling 1994; Michell and Sanders 1995). Unilever launched a market research initiative to identify ways of raising creative standards. Procter and Gamble's 'agency renewal' process focused on improving the creative relationships themselves (*Adweek*, 17 August 1998).

An important first step in understanding how to create successful creative relationships is to understand how these differ from other types of relationships.

Where relationship development has been considered, improving creative performance to increase client satisfaction is a dominant theme (Michell 1988; Verbeke 1989). Winston Fletcher of Bozell UK Groups reflects, in considering trust in advertising agency relationships, that:

> I guess my contention that successful relationships between agencies and clients depend so completely on trust will be met with a hollow, cynical laugh . . . - the areas of trust which are unique relate – surprise, surprize – to creative work. Naturally, the client must trust the agency's creative abilities . . . Most other suppliers are required to provide unwavering consistency (even though what they produce may alter occasionally). Agencies, in contrast, are required constantly to provide new ideas even though these will normally be part of an ongoing campaign. (*Marketing*, 19 March, p. 5)

The pressure on constant creativity means that in contrast to industrial marketing relationships, successful management of advertising agency–client relationships may mean constant changes in staffing. Although it may be easy to conclude that the solution is to switch to a new partner, Michell (1988) suggests that relationships can be 'reinvigorated' by switching to a new account and creative team.

A second, and less researched, theme is that of building commitment and trust in these relationships (Halinen 1997; LaBahn and Kohli 1997; Grayson and Ambler 1999). A full discussion of trust and commitment in relationships can be found in Chapter 1. While the belief that the agency has the client's best interests at heart increases trust (Moorman, Zaltman and Deshpandé 1993) conflict, such as disputes over expenditure, deadlines or quality of creative output, reduces it. The results of conflict and lack of trust are all too apparent in the bitter splits discussed above.

The literature shows the importance of a number of issues in building trusting creative relationships:

- Trust builds over time as a result of 'productive' rather than 'negative' interactions (LaBahn and Kohli 1997).
- It may be favoured by accessibility of each partner (Wackman, Salmon and Salmon 1986) and expressing opinions (Cagley, Roberts and Richard 1984).
- Minor disagreements may be particularly beneficial in creative relationships if they improve the quality of creative output.
- Mutual adaptation may also be important. Henke (1995) suggests that agencies which cannot adapt to the needs of their clients will not succeed.
- From the client side, client firms may need to adapt the way in which they relate to their agencies. Client firms may see use of an agency as 'outsourcing' the promotional strategy rather than partnering for mutual benefit.
- If it is seen as an outsourcing agreement, a 'them and us' mentality may result. He suggests avoiding words like 'vendor' and 'supplier' which create unnecessary barriers. Similarly adversarial 'you guys' phrases and references to approaches from other agencies may create distance between the two firms.

Implementing Creative Strategies

A final aspect of agency performance involves implementing creative strategies. As with creativity, implementation is a frequent cause of dissatisfaction (LaBahn and Kohli (1997). Implementation includes the ability to operate within agreed deadlines, stay within budget limitations and operate within agreed advertising strategies.

A number of suggestions for improving creative relationships involve improvements in implementation. These may involve streamlining business processes, such as the process of approval of creative campaigns, matching the profile and seniority of individuals on each side and understanding the wide range of backgrounds of individuals involved in the relationship. Based on extensive experience on both sides of the fence, Bob Lamont comments (*Marketing News*, 22 June 1998, p. 5):

> I've learned that assignments might appear easily understood and straightforward to clients, yet the way agency practitioners deal with them is anything but. This is partly due to the unusual mix of personalities in the advertising profession. We attract all types: creatives, analyticals, introverts, extroverts, egotists, selfless servants, those who yearn to leave their mark on the world and those who'd rather not.

Defining Relationship Scope

Another challenge may be that of defining the scope of the relationship. Whether the client firm designs the promotional strategy and how this fits with the brand strategy itself, or hands this over to the agency, a major challenge is to make sure that the agency understands the basic strategic issues. The range and quality of possible solutions is likely to be significantly higher if both parties have a clear understanding of the promotional objectives. Beard (1999) finds that uncertainty about role requirements cause dissatisfaction in relationships for both the client and the agency. The existence of this kind of uncertainty for individuals who perform important 'boundary-spanning' roles may be a cause of relationship failure (see Chapter 3).

Global Creative Relationships

With the globalization of marketing strategies comes pressure for advertising agencies to be global in their scope:

> International agency networks and their relationships with global clients are driving the changes in strategy, structure and service. Clients are often the initiators of such change, as they examine their

own management set-ups around the globe and ask their agencies to do the same. (*Marketing*, 1 July 1998, p. 19).

[Boeing] The world's largest aerospace company is looking to develop an umbrella corporate imager effort, said sources. Should Boeing hold a review, it would likely invite agencies with strong international networks. (McCarthy and Kim 1998)

The pressures to be global in scope have fuelled both consolidation and mergers (Kim 1995) and less formal co-operation between agencies (Coleman 1996) in order to provide the necessary scope of service:

London-based relationship marketing company, Miller Bainbridge, has tied up with partners in three European countries to form a network of independent companies. (*Marketing*, 9 April, p. 6)

Many advertising agencies are now, themselves, global in scope. Grein and Ducoffe (1998, p. 301) conclude that:

Today many advertising agencies maintain global networks of offices that operate in countries throughout the world. The top ten agencies have control of approximately one-third of the world's advertising billings and US firms still function as the power centre of the global industry.

The stakes are high. In contemplating the threat to its global business with McDonald's, Leo Burnett faced the possibility of losing their share of McDonald's $1.8 billion advertising budget. There had been a number of unsuccessful episodes in the relationship. In January 1996, Burnett was passed over for the $75 million launch of McDonald's Arche Deluxe premium burger to rivals Fallon McElligott. In June 1996 they were responsible for an 'inexcusable' mistake resulting in McDonald's $20 million shortfall in its media plan. In June 1997 the high profile 'Campaign 55' was deemed unsuccessful (*Marketing Week*, 3 July 1997, p. 12). The knock on effect between markets places increased pressure on all subunits of an advertising agency to build successful relationships with its national counterpart:

The $35 million UK account is handled by Leo Burnett and any changes in the US are bound to have repercussions in the UK. (*Marketing Week*, 3 July 1997, p. 12)

Balanced against the needs of servicing large, global accounts are the needs of locally-based clients. Paul Wilkinson, Chairman of Rank Hovis McDougall in the UK criticized his company's advertising agency DMBandB for chasing global business at the expense of local customers who become second class citizens (*Marketing*, 1 July 1999).

Global Key Account Management

The Key Account Management concept developed from the management of national accounts. Stevenson and Page (1979) explain that national account management, adopting special marketing procedures for particular clients, has existed for decades. The basis for selecting particular customers for special attention is usually on the basis of their value of sales to the customer in volume or value terms. Other factors, such as the prestige of the account, may however also result in introduction of national account management. National account management has been associated with 'buyer concentration', that is situations where there are only a few strong customers. This may explain its prevalence for large industrial and retail customers.

As the key account management literature has developed, the emphasis has moved from selling to key accounts to managing key accounts as partners (Cahill 1998). Indeed, national account management approaches have increasingly been interchangeable with relationship marketing and management (Jackson 1985). With this changing focus, national account management has become a topic of interest to affiliates of the IMP group (Millman 1996)

Of particular interest in this book is the question of how national account management copes as important customers expand internationally. Millman (1996) defines global account management (referred to for the remainder of this section as GAM) as working with: 'multinational customers with a growing expectation of being supplied and serviced worldwide in a consistent and coordinated way.'

While Senn (1999) notes that:

> More and more customers require business solutions that can be implemented and managed consistently across their worldwide locations.

In moving from national account management to GAM, firms must move from one team with responsibility for a key account's business to spreading that responsibility across a number of different countries. Thus, GAM extends the national account management concept to more, but not necessarily to all, countries.

As Yip and Madsen describe it (1996, p. 25), GAM involves '*the most important countries for the most important customers and for the most important activities*' (emphasis online).

Making key account management global is not a simple process. Senn (1999, p. 11) reflects on the complexities of ABB's introduction of GAM:

> ABB Switzerland, for example, shortly after the merger of the Swedish Asea Group with the Swiss BBC in 1993, installed a group of Key Account Executives to co-ordinate the total business with ABB's global customers. But, taking another look at the ABB example, this was only the beginning of a long and hard trial and error process to finally achieve today's fully integrated customer planning and steering process on ABB group level through to a network of global account teams across various industries.

A key question for multinational corporations is that of why and when national account management should be turned into GAM. The first answer is that many GAM initiatives are dictated by customers and supplying firms have no choice but to engage in them.

If the firm has a choice, then a useful diagnostic is Yip and Madsen's extension (1996) of Yip's earlier (1992) globalization framework (see Figure 10.1).

Industry Globalization Drivers

Yip and Madsen identity many of the globalization drivers discussed in the macro-context (Chapters 2–4) and strategic (Chapter 5) sections of this book. The existence of global customers drives the use of GAM. When organizations are multinational and make different international marketing strategic choices in different markets they may use different suppliers and gain better or worse prices. As customers move towards global organization, they

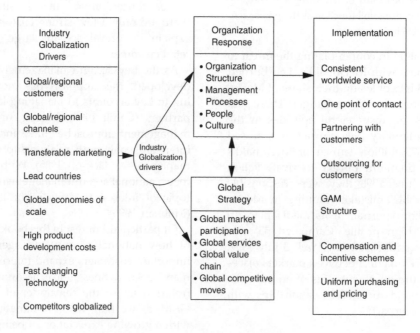

Figure 10.1   Industry globalization drivers
Source: Yip and Madsen (1996). Reprinted with permission from MCB Press

will begin to buy in a centralized, or at least a globally co-ordinated way. These global customers seek global suppliers (Ives, Jarvenpaa and Mason 1993; Yip and Madsen 1996) who can, in the words of Yip and Madsen (1996, p. 26): 'treat them as a single entity and provide consistent and seamless service across countries.'

Global customers may be final customers, or else they may be increasingly powerful global retailers (see Chapter 8 for a fuller discussion of retailer internationalization). The buying power of retailers in the channel has been demonstrated in the aftermath of US retailer Wal Mart's acquisition of Asda in the UK. Immediately prices from suppliers of Asda were forced down in line with Wal Mart's global strategy.

GAM may also be applicable to customers who are strong in a particular region, but still require consistent account handling. It should be noted that Wal Mart's acquisition of Asda marks a major step from the company's strong regional position in North America towards becoming a global player. Today's regional customers may be the global customers of tomorrow and consideration should be given to according them GAM treatment in anticipation of this.

The extent to which consistency will be an issue for global customers varies with the extent to which it has a strategy of global standardization. If the customer has developed global brands and is moving towards harmonized prices (see Chapter 9) then it may be imperative the supplier is consistent in managing the account. If the marketing strategy is one of local adaptation, then GAM may not be required.

Yip and Madsen's suggestion (1996) that GAM should be applied to 'lead countries' suggests a gradual roll-out. The supplying firm might prioritize the key markets where the customer operates an aim to provide consistent service across these as a precursor to full GAM.

Organizational Responses

The headings in Yip and Madsen's (1992) diagram can be explained as follows:

- **Organization structure** is the reporting and accountability links within an organization.

- **Management processes** are the activities, such as planning and budgeting and information systems, which make the business run
- **People** are the human resources of the global organization
- **Culture** is the set of values and rules for behaviour within the organization.

Yip and Madsen (1996) believe that changes may be required in each of these.

- **Organizational structure**. Changes to the organizational structure may include the creation of global account managers who have authority over national account managers. If, for example, an account is not very important within one country, but is globally very important, the global account manager may dictate a change of priorities to ensure that appropriate service is provided. In almost all cases, the global account manager should be located in the home country of the global customer. Exceptions would be if the account is particularly strong, or focused on entering, a particular region.
- **Management processes**. GAM is a process and it affects other processes within the business. By definition, GAM provides global co-ordination. To do this effectively, GAM may require the introduction of global information systems, global account data and global marketing strategies for these customers. The Philips Lighting IKAM (International Key Account Management) initiative made use of the company's Intranet to allow account managers in individual countries to access data on its global retail accounts. The interactive nature of the technology allows local account managers to input data on local issues that are then available both to the global account manager and to national account managers in other countries.
- **People**. As GAM is implemented by individuals within organizations, its success or failure lies largely in their hands. The importance of GAM should not be underestimated. Yip and Madsen (1996) see managers who can think globally as a potential source of competitive advantage. They argue that the GAM system can be implemented 'without adding to the headcount' as

one manager may, at first, be able to play a national and global role.

It should be noted, however, that, depending on the organization structure of the company, the global account manager should be given sufficient authority to enforce global strategies if local managers resist. Moreover, GAM, especially in the early stages of its introduction, is extremely time-consuming. This may make it difficult to succeed if global account managers have conflicting demands on their time.

- **Culture**. The composition of an organization's culture is difficult to capture. Yip and Madsen (1996) argue, however, that even when organizational structure, processes and people are in place, the GAM initiative may still founder if the culture does not support globalization. Subsidiaries used to local autonomy may openly and covertly resist moves towards standardization of their activities. To overcome these problems, top management support and more widespread communication of the reasons for GAM may be needed.

Global Strategic Response to Global Customers

GAM allows suppliers to:

- **Build global market participation**, by targeting the markets which are most important to global accounts. These may include the home markets of key accounts and their most important markets. Depending on the degree of globalization of the supplying firm this may prompt it to enter new markets or to build its position in markets, which it already serves.
- **Develop global products and services**. As the firm now has a view of global customer needs, it may be able to rationalize its product portfolio and devote a greater proportion of its research and development (R & D) and marketing budgets to developing global products and services.
- **Locate value-adding activities**. The GAM process may help to identify duplication or gaps in the way the firm adds value globally. Decisions can be made on which activities need

to be co-ordinated globally and which can be left to the discretion of local subsidiaries (see Chapter 5 for a further discussion of this issue). A supplying firm might, for example, dictate a maximum price for some key global brands, but accept that local markets price at economic value to the customer for special offerings in a particular market.

Benefits and Risks of GAM

Yip and Madsen (1996) identify a range of benefits but also a set of risks associated with implementing GAM.

Benefits include:

- **Consistency**. 'Speaking with one voice': this avoids duplication of effort and one subsidiary jeopardizing the activities of another.
- **Ability to gain revenue from customers' international expansion**. If the firm has partnering arrangements, then it will hopefully grow with its successful customers.
- **Efficiency gains and reduced costs**. These come from global economies of scale and scope.
- **Leveraging client knowledge**. If the supplier enters a market following a client it may benefit from the latter's market knowledge. This phenomenon may also work in reverse if the supplier is more international than the customer.
- **Learning from working with industry leaders**. Many global leaders are innovators in both technology and management. Partnering with this type of firm may bring a range of unanticipated benefits.
- **Raising switching costs**. Increased interdependence may build commitment and make the customer less likely to move to a supplier in whom it has less trust.

There may also be a number of *risks* involved with GAM. These include:

- **Comparison of global prices**. The global customer may have access to prices across the range of markets and demand that the lowest national price is adopted globally. One industrial producer of precision metal castings was pressurized to sell at the lowest price in the competitive South Korean market. If the customer demanded this price in all markets, different raw materials and labour cost regimes around the world would make it impossible to do this at a profit. To avoid, or at least minimize, this kind of price pressure, it is imperative that the global account manager can justify why prices may differ across markets. If this can be justified on a rational basis, such as the arguments of automotive manufacturers that developing right-hand-side drive cars for the UK is more expensive, then a premium may be accepted. As can be seen in the ruling in 1999 that cars are overpriced to the UK, manufacturers will need strong supporting evidence for any such argument.

- **Negotiating service levels**. The service level demanded in different countries may vary. Higher service levels may not be demanded in those countries where the highest price can be gained. In the case of the USA, in particular, the opposite may be true. Global contracts should be reviewed and the service card for each country should be negotiated. As described in Chapter 1, problems may be overcome if services are unbundled and firms are charged only for those service features they require.
- **Loss of autonomy of local subsidiary**. Any move towards centralized control risks a backlash from local subsidiary managers who feel that they have lost control over an activity previously carried out at subsidiary level.
- **Increased costs**. Putting the GAM system in place may have high set-up costs, both financially and in terms of time. While the long-term benefits should outweigh these, suppliers need to make resources available appropriately to ensure the success of the GAM initiative.

A common problem with global account plans is that they may be developed entirely from a *supplier perspective*. This type of plan may result in international marketers misinterpreting the strategic priorities of the customer. Senn (1997) proposes three steps to create dynamic GAM, which meet the needs of both supplier and customer:

- **Step 1**: Define goals and objectives together with global accounts. Companies decide

which customers merit this special treatment. The objectives for the account should be agreed with counterparts from the global customer team. These objectives should reflect the needs of both sides equally. This process often requires planning sessions with a GAM team from both supplier and global account employees.
- **Step 2**: Align business process towards the needs of the global accounts. Suppliers adjust their business processes to the structures of their global customers. This may involve analysis of the value added in each area of the business
- **Step 3**: Safeguard know-how and speed up learning processes

THE NETWORK PERSPECTIVE

Integrated Marketing Communications

Authors identify the study of integrated marketing communications as beginning with the seminal work of Caywood, Schultz and Wang (1991) of Northwestern University in the USA (cited in Kitchen and Schultz 1999). Integrated Marketing Communications (IMC) involves the creation of 'one sight, one sound' communication strategies (Kitchen and Schultz 1999) and can be defined as:

> a concept of marketing communications planning that recognizes the added value of a comprehensive plan that evaluates the strategic roles of a variety of communications disciplines (for example general advertizing, direct response, sales promotion and public relations)...and combines these disciplines to provide clarity, consistency, and maximum communications impact. (Schultz 1993)

Achieving this type of integration involves co-ordination of global communications strategy across countries and across the promotional mix (see the Traditional section of this chapter for a fuller discussion of promotional mix issues).

The level of integration required for IMC also varies. Some authors argue that IMC requires all aspects of promotional strategy to be handled by one firm. Kitchen and Schultz (1999) suggest that this possibility is favoured by agencies, who believe that this will reduce competition between suppliers and leave them as sole suppliers. From the client perspective, however, integration may only be closer co-operation between agencies rather than use of a sole agency.

IMC may, therefore, result in creating promotional strategies with a network of agencies and the customer. To span a sufficient geographic scope, some of the agencies may themselves have contracted alliances:

> making strategic promotional decisions through the integrated tracking, comparison and co-ordination of marketing communications across all relevant global markets, units, or offices in order to maximize both organizational learning and the efficient allocation of resources. (Gould, Lerman and Grein 1999, p. 7)

Figure 10.2 shows the type of network that might result from this approach to IMC. Some argue that advertizing agencies – as recipients of the largest proportion of the promotional budget – may play a pivotal role in IMC.

Gould, Lerman and Grein (1999) find that the choice between a single provider of all parts of the promotional mix and separate agencies may make little difference to the resulting network. Agencies providing different parts of the promotional mix often have little co-ordination between affiliate units. The network co-ordination process will be important to the success of IMC whatever organizational approach is adopted. As one advertizing agency executive concludes:

> Agencies will be expected to manage their networks as they never have before. Like an increasing number of their clients, they too will have to be transnational, collaborating and adjusting global/ local skills and resources within a responsive, interdependent network – across borders and disciplines. (Gould, Lerman and Grein 1999, p. 14)

This is the Challenge for the further development of IMC.

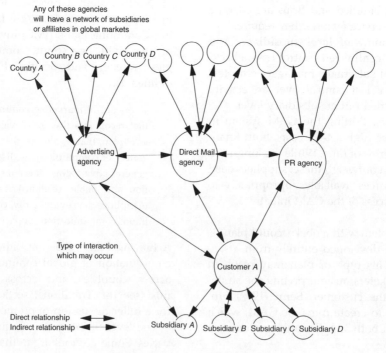

Figure 10.2   The IMC network
Source: Gould, Lerman and Grein (1999)

SUMMARY

In Chapter 10 we have examined the development of effective international promotional strategies. We have identified 5 MS mix, message, miscommunication, media and money – that are critical to international marketing success. We have identified distinctive characteristics of relationships with international creative agencies that may mean that long-term stable relationships are valued less in international promotions than in other areas of international relationships. The contributions of IMC have been examined.

BIBLIOGRAPHY

Anon. (1999) 'Miller Bainbridge Signs up for Pan-European Quartet', *Marketing*, 8 April: 6.

Beard, F. K. (1999) 'Client Role Ambiguity and Satisfaction in Client-Ad Agency Relationships', *Journal of Advertising Research*, March–April: 69–78.

Beatty, S. (1999) 'Mazda Spars with its old Ad agency – Auto Maker and Foote Cone Trade Lawsuits over Severed Relationship', *The Asian The Wall Street Journal*, 5 April: 9.

Bougery, M. and Guimares, G. (1993) 'Global Ads Say it with Pictures', *Journal of European Business*, May–June.

Buzzell, R. D. (1968) 'Can you Standardize Multinational Marketing?', *Harvard Business Review*, November–December: 102–13.

Cagley, J. W., Roberts, C. and Richard, R. C. (1984) 'Criteria for Advertising Agency Selection: An Objective Appraisal', *Journal of Advertising Research*, 24: 27–31.

Cahill, D. J. (1998) 'Using Key Accounts as Partners to Get to the Learning Organization', *International Marketing Review*, 15, 3: 205–14.

Caywood, C., Schultz, D. and Wang, P. (1991) 'Integrated Marketing Communications: A Survey of National Goods Advertisers', Medill School of Journalism, Northwestern University, unpublished report, June.

Coleman, C. Y. (1996) 'US Agencies Expand in Latin America', *Wall Street Journal*, 1 March: B5

Dignam, C. (1999a) 'A Global Outlook is Fine, But Consider the Local Business', *Marketing*, 1 July: 19.

Dignam, C. (1999b) 'Marketers Flunk the Agency Test', *Marketing*, 22 July: 22.

Douglas, S. and Wind, Y. (1987) 'The Myth of Globalization', *Columbia Journal of World Business*, Winter: 19–29.

Dowling, G. R. (1994) 'Searching for a New Advertising Agency: A Client Perspective', *International Journal of Advertising*, 13, 3: 229–42.

Doyle, P., Corstjens, M. and Michell, P. (1980) 'Signals of Vulnerability in Agency–Client Relationships', *Journal of Marketing*, 44, Fall: 18–23.

Dulek, R. E., Fielden, J. S. and Hill, J. S. (1991) 'International Communication: An Executive Primer', *Business Horizons*, January–February: 20–5.

Fletcher, W. (1998) 'A Little Trust in your Ad Agency Goes a Long Way', *Marketing*, 19 March: 5.

Gestetner, D. (1974) 'Strategy in Managing International Sales', *Harvard Business Review*, September–October: 103–8.

Gould, S. J., Lerman, D. B. and Grein, A. F. (1999) 'Agency Perceptions and Practices of Global IMC', *Journal of Advertising Research*, January–February: 7–21.

Grayson, K. and Ambler, T. (1999) 'The Dark Side of Long-Term Relationships in Marketing Services', *Journal of Marketing Research*, 36, February: 132–41.

Grein, A. and Ducoffe, R. (1998) 'Strategic Responses to Market Globalization among Advertising Agencies', *International Journal of Advertising*, 17, 3: 300–19.

Halinen, A. (1997) *Relationship Marketing in Professional Services: A Study of Agency–Client Dynamics in the Advertising Sector*, Routledge.

Henke, L. L. (1995) 'A Longitudinal Analysis of the Ad Agency–Client Relationship: Predictors of an Agency Switch', *Journal of Advertising Research*, 39, 1: 24–30.

Hill, J. S., Still, R. R. and Boya, U. O. (1991) 'Managing the Multinational Sales Force', *International Marketing Review*, 8, 1: 19–31.

Huang, M.-H. (1998) 'Exploring a New Typology of Advertising Appeals: Basic, versus Social, Emotional Advertising in a Global Setting', *International Journal of Advertising*, 17, 2: 145–68.

Ives, B., Jarvenpaa, S. L. and Mason, R. O. (1993) 'Global Business Drivers: Aligning Information Technology to Global Business Strategy', *IBM Business Systems Journal*, 32, 1: 143–61.

Jackson, B. B. (1985) *Winning and Keeping Industrial Customers*, Lexington Books.

Kashani, K. and Quelch, J. A. (1990) 'Can Sales Promotion Go Global?', *Business Horizons*, May–June: 37–43.

Kim, H. (1998) 'Unilever Polls Ad Executives', *Adweek*, 17 August: 2.

Kim, K. K. (1995) 'Spreading the Net: The Consolidation Process of Large Transnational Advertising Agencies in the 1980s and early 1990s', *International Journal of Advertising*, 14, 3:

Kitchen, P. J. and Schultz, D. E. (1999) 'A Multi-Country Comparison of the Drive for IMC', *Journal of Advertising Research*, January–February: 21–37.

LaBahn, D. W. and Kohli, C. (1997) 'Maintaining Client Commitment in Advertising Agency–Client Relationships', *Industrial Marketing Management*, 26: 497–508.

Levitt, T. (1983) 'The Globalization of Markets', *Harvard Business Review*, May–June: 92–102.

Marconi, J. (1998) 'Agency–Client Relationships Show Signs of Stress', *Marketing News*, 6 July: 14.

Marshall, S. (1997) 'Global Threat to Burnett in $600 million McDonald's Pitch', *Marketing Week*, 3 July: 12.

McCarthy, M. and Kim, K. (1998) 'Boeing Considers Global Review: Cole and Weber's $30 million account is in Jeopardy', *Adweek*, 30 November: 3.

Mead, G. (1992) 'Consumer Body Cautions on Free Flights', *Financial Times*, 15 December.

Mead, G. and Skapinker, M. (1992) 'Hoover Stirs up PR Dust Cloud over Free Flights Deal', *Financial Times*, 19 December.

Michell, P. (1988) 'The Influence of Organizational Compatibility on Account Switching', *Journal of Advertising Research*, 27, 2: 9–22.

Michell, P. and Sanders, N. H. (1995) 'Loyalty in Agency–Client Relationships: The Impact of the Organizational Context', *Journal of Advertising Research*, 35, 2: 9–22.

Millman, A. F. (1996) 'Global Key Account Management and Systems Review', *International Business Review*, 5, 6: 631–45.

Moorman, C., Zaltman, G. and Deshpandé, R. (1992) 'Relationships between Providers and Users of Market Research: The Dynamics of Trust within and between Organizations', *Journal of Marketing Research*, 29: 314–28.

Nicholas, R. (1999) 'Survey Finds Ad Agencies Still Failing Clients', *Marketing*, 3 June: 12.

Quelch, J. A. and Hoff, E. J. (1986) 'Customizing Global Marketing', *Harvard Business Review*, May–June: 59–68.

Riesenbeck, H. and Freeling, A. (1991) 'How Global are Global Brands?', *The McKinsey Quarterly*, 4: 3–18.

Schultz, D. E. (1993) 'Integrated Marketing Communications: Maybe Definition is in the Point of View', *Marketing News*, 18 January.

Senn, C. (1999) 'Implementing Global Account Management: A Process Oriented Approach', *The Journal of Selling and Major Account Management*, 1, 3: 10–15.

Stevenson, T. H. and Page, A. L. (1979) 'The Adoption of National Account Marketing by Industrial Firms', *Industrial Marketing Management*, 8: 94–100.

Thill, J. V. and Bovee, C. L. (1999) *Excellence in Marketing Communications*, (4th edn), Prentice-Hall.

Verbeke, W. (1989) 'Developing an Advertising Agency–Client Relationship in the Netherlands', *Journal of Advertising Research*, 28: 19–27.

Wackman, D. B., Salmon, C. T. and Salmon, C. C. (1986) 'Developing an Advertising Agency-Client Relationship', *Journal of Advertising Research*, 26, 6: 19–27.

Yip, G. S. (1992) *Total Global Strategy: Managing for Worldwide Competitive Advantage*, Prentice-Hall.

Yip, G. S. and Madsen, T. C. (1996) 'Global Account Management: The New Frontier in Relationship Marketing', *International Marketing Review*, 13, 3: 24–42.

Young, L. and Denize, S. (1994) 'Super-Glued Relationships: The Nature of Bonds between Professional Service Suppliers and Buyers', *Working Paper* presented at the 10th IMP Conference, Groningen, September.

PART V

REGIONAL ISSUES

This part of the book applies the issues debated in the international marketing context, strategy and mix sections to specific regions.

The part begins with a consideration of challenges of operation in the Triad. Ohmae (1990) defines the Triad as North America, Europe and Japan. Given the relationship focus of this book and the free trade links between North and Latin America, Chapter 11 begins with a consideration of international challenges in the Americas region as a whole. This is felt to be particularly relevant given proposals to create a free trade agreement spanning all of the Americas. Chapter 12 focuses on the issues in Europe, and relationships between the Single European Market (SEM) and other countries. Chapter 13 extends the third Triad member to Asia-Pacific, rather than Japan alone. The focus of this chapter is broadened for a number of reasons. First, understanding the East Asian region rather than Japan alone is relevant in appreciating the rise of the region with its 'little Dragons': Hong Kong, Korea, Singapore and Taiwan. Secondly, the East Asian Crisis showed the economic interconnections within the region. Finally, and with respect to the inclusion of Australasia, researchers from Australia and New Zealand have made a significant contribution to understanding of relationships and networks within the region as a whole. Therefore the focus of Chapter 13 is extended to Asia-Pacific.

Having addressed the issues of operation in the Triad, Chapters 14 and 15 move on to consider the international marketing challenges of emerging and Less Developed Countries (LDCs). While emerging economies are turbulent and uncertain, the size of the available markets and the potential of economic recovery makes the issues involved in realizing this potential at minimum risk of prime strategic importance. In LDCs, the distinctive nature of the markets raises a number of questions relating to appropriate levels of technology, operation in markets with lax laws and building appropriate ethical relationships with partners at different levels of economic development.

BIBLIOGRAPHY

Ohmae, K. (1990) *The Borderless World: Power and Strategy in the Interlinked Economy*, London, Collins.

THE AMERICAS

Objectives

The issues to be addressed in Chapter 11 include:

1. The application of concepts from earlier sections of the book to the Americas
2. Examination of relationships within the Americas and the dominant role of the USA in free trade agreements
3. Review studies of networks in the Americas region to identify distinctive characteristics of network structures in the region.

After reading Chapter 11 you will be able to

1. Understand the challenges facing international marketers in the Americas
2. Identify specific types of relationships that play a role in the region
3. Evaluate the contribution of network studies of the region.

INTRODUCTION

This chapter applies some of the concepts developed in the earlier sections of the book to the Americas region. The Americas encompasses both North and Latin America. Expansion of the North American Free Trade Agreement (NAFTA) to include Latin American neighbour Mexico, and further moves to create a Free Trade Area in the Americas (FTAA) by 2005 pose distinctive challenges. The expanded NAFTA agreement now spans markets with very different histories and levels of economic development.

From a relationship perspective, it is apparent that trade flows are dominated by the hub of the USA, with relatively little trade directly between Canada and Mexico. Creating a larger free trade area raises a number of issues. Deciding on membership may offer privileges to some countries at the expense of others with whom the USA has existing relationships. The Network section of this chapter discusses the interrelationships of members of potential members of the FTAA in a macro-level network. Finally, studies of networks in the Americas are reviewed to identify distinctive features of network structures in the region.

THE TRADITIONAL PERSPECTIVE

The Challenges

By most definitions, the Americas ranks amongst the most powerful regions in the world. In size, Canada (2nd), the USA (4th) and Brazil (5th) rank in the top five countries by land area and the USA (3rd) and Brazil (5th) in the top five by population size. Economically, the USA has the largest gross domestic product (GDP) in the world and Brazil (8th) and Canada (9th) also rate in the top 10. Using the United Nations 'human development index', which measures adult literacy and life expectancy to create an index of the quality of life, Canada rates highest in the world and the USA fourth highest.

Yet the Americas (Map 11.1) spans a considerable spectrum of size and economic development. While Chile (7.2 per cent), Peru (6.0 per cent), Argentina (4.9 per cent) and Colombia (4.5 per cent) ranked amongst the countries with the fastest annual growth of GDP from 1990 to 1996, Jamaica (0.8 per cent) rated amongst the slowest. While Canada (1.6 per cent), the USA (2.3 per cent), Trinidad and Tobago (3.4 per cent) and

Map 11.1   The Americas

Argentina (0.5 per cent) had among the lowest rates of annual inflation in 1996–7, Venezuela (50 per cent), Ecuador (30.6 per cent), Jamaica (26.4 per cent) and Mexico (20.6 per cent) had among the highest.

The size and economic development of the USA bring a number of challenges. It plays a dominant role in NAFTA and in efforts to integrate North American, Caribbean and Latin American countries in the FTAA by 2005. Yet it is a pluralist society with a large gap between the richest and poorest. Not everyone believes that their interests are best served by forming closer links outside North America with countries which tend to have poorer economies and cheaper labour. As G7 members, the USA and Canada also play pivotal roles in global politics.

Within NAFTA, the relative size and wealth of Canada and the USA compared with that of Mexico, poses further challenges. Canada's growth was fuelled by inflows of foreign direct investment (FDI), especially from its major trading partner the USA. Historically reliant for its economic growth on export by primary industries of agricultural produce, minerals, oil and gas and raw materials, Canada now has major secondary industries. Almost one-third of Canada's manufacturing comprises cars and related automotive products, although financial services developed strongly after 1980. Almost 80 per cent of manufacturing is based in Ontario and Quebec; East and Western Canada remain more reliant on primary sectors. Canada now has significant trade outflows, especially to the USA; such has been its growth, in international trade terms, that it now ranks as one of the top 10 manufacturing nations in the world.

Among the Latin American countries, Mexico merits separate consideration as a member of NAFTA, introduced on 1 January 1994. The door is open for the entry into NAFTA of other Latin American countries; clauses exist to allow other countries to enter at a later date and the entry of Chile was proposed as a priority. To date, however, Mexico provides the bridge between the North and Latin American regions.

The growth of the Mexican economy is of more recent date. Mexico is the third largest Latin American country, with a population of 85 million. Despite political turmoil in the early twentieth century, the post-Second World War period has seen relative political stability. Under the leadership of Carlos Salinas (1988–94), Mexico under went a transition from strict controls on foreign investment to a more favourable climate. Reforms in 1989 to encourage FDI and privatization made Mexico a major target for global industry. In particular, legislation allowing foreign firms to take equity control in 75 per cent of the economy prompted a flurry of investment activity (*The Wall Street Journal*, 14 August 1998).

Mexico has become a centre for the manufacturing operations of a number of global automotive firms, such as Volkswagen, Ford and Nissan (Hodgetts 1993). During Salinas' presidency, relations with the USA also improved. Exports from Mexico to the USA were encouraged and, in 1993, the Free Trade Agreement between the USA and Canada was extended to include Mexico. Despite their history of economic turmoil, a decade of painful market reforms may be beginning to bear fruit in the remaining Latin American countries.

The Countries of the Caribbean basin are also included in the Americas region. Since the mid-1980s, the 24 nations of the Caribbean basin (including Jamaica, Trinidad, the Dominican republic and all the Central American countries) have enjoyed strong economic and trade relations through the Caribbean Basin Initiative (CBI). Strong links have also developed between the CBI countries and the USA. US exports to the Caribbean have expanded by more than 100 per cent since the mid-1980s, while Caribbean exports to the USA increased by around 50 per cent.

Trading between the USA and the Caribbean countries was, however, adversely affected by the introduction of the NAFTA agreement. Mexican exports now enjoy more privileged access to the USA than do those from the Caribbean. Countries in the Caribbean are now forced to compete in their largest market at a significant competitive disadvantage (Bernal, *The Wall Street Journal*, 22 March 1996). The diversion of trade and investment away from the Caribbean basin has been apparent since NAFTA was introduced. Mexico has become the largest single source of US clothing exports, a sector in which other Caribbean countries were previously strong.

THE RELATIONSHIP PERSPECTIVE

Bilateral and Multilateral Free Trade Agreements

Canada–US Trading Agreements – the 'Autopact' and the Free Trade Area (FTA)

In the automotive industry, the relationship between Canada and the USA has been formalized through an 'autopact' for 30 years. By the terms of this agreement, free trade in cars assembled in Canada or the USA was permissable on condition that 50 per cent of value was added in Canada. In 1988 the extent and scope of the links between

Canada and the USA was increased by the introduction of the Canada–USA FTA.

NAFTA

The links between the Americas have been strengthened by the introduction, on 1 January 1994, of the North American Free Trade Agreement (NAFTA), which extended the FTA agreement to include Mexico. Negotiation of the NAFTA agreement began in Toronto in June 1991. This was the first time that a Less Developed Country (LDC) had entered negotiations for a FTA with two advanced economies. The ambitious agreement took the USA and Mexico from 'distant neighbours' with little contact to partners in a tripartite trading agreement with Canada.

In his account of the NAFTA negotiations, Von Bertrab (1997), in an account which pays curiously little attention to the role of Canada, nonetheless brings out the achievement in reaching this agreement given the clashes of culture, political systems and economic objectives of the partners. Agreement was reached in principle on 10 August 1992. The NAFTA agreement came into force on 1 January 1994, after its ratification by each of the member states in November 1993.

For the USA and Canada, NAFTA also represents a considerable change from the previous FTA concerning foreign investment (Rugman 1993). Three main areas of difference are:

1. Broadening the scope of the investments covered. All debt, equity and business real estate investment is covered by NAFTA.
2. The binational arbitration and dispute settlement procedures of the FTA have now been extended to cover investments. This increases their security.
3. A list of negotiated reservations to various provisions.

While NAFTA is a significant step towards trade liberalization, it does not, as yet, offer the same level of free trade as exists in the European Union (EU). Each of the partners still has its own trade laws. Moves are, however, afoot to strengthen the ties of the NAFTA agreement. Within Mexico, support has been proposed for eventual monetary union. However critics point to the 30 years which the EU spent as a Common Market before embarking on a further stage of economic integration.

While government sources deny any interest in eliminating the peso, Mexico's volatility is generally viewed as a cause for concern. A 19 per cent slide in the peso's value in 1998 took the Mexican inflation rate to 18.6 per cent, compared with a government target of 12 per cent. Analysts agree that this slide was a result of the economic crises in Brazil and Russia. Yet whether such a monetary union would resolve the problems is unclear. Argentina, whose currency is tied to the dollar through its Convertability Plan, saw interest rates rise sharply as a result of the Brazilian problems and its economy shrank commensurably. Arguments for monetary union seem more based on the fact that as Mexico has greater commercial integration with the USA than Argentina, it should also have the closest currency ties.

The Impacts of the NAFTA Agreement

The NAFTA agreements relate to particular sectors, such as clothing, textiles, automotive products and agriculture. As removal of trade barriers is being phased in, the full impacts have not yet been seen. In clothing and textiles, all tariffs will be removed over a period of 10 years. In the automotive sector, Mexico immediately reduced tariffs on cars and trucks by 50 per cent and will eliminate the remaining tariffs within 10 years. In agriculture, tariffs were removed on a range of goods when NAFTA was introduced. There is also a phased liberalization of foreign ownership. In the automotive sector, 49 per cent foreign ownership was to be allowed within three years of the agreement, 51 per cent after seven years and 100 per cent ownership after 10 years. Similar liberalization is planned for the finance and insurance sectors.

The member states of the NAFTA agreement had disparate starting points in terms of their economic wealth and growth rates. This has led theorists to propose (Rugman and Gestrin 1993) that the impacts of NAFTA on investment patterns in the USA and Canada would be neutral, whilst Mexico would draw investment away from other LDCs. These impacts are beginning to emerge.

Introduction of a new phase of legislation often creates winners and losers, but in Mexico, in particular, NAFTA has brought dramatic changes. These changes were accentuated by the peso crisis of 1994, in which reduced price Mexican firms became especially attractive to foreign investors. In 1995–6, multinational corporations invested $7 in Mexico in everything from tequila bottles to Mexico's most famous brewer, Grupo Modela, which brews Corona beer.

These changes are not restricted to Mexico. The USA has seen shifting patterns of international trade. In clothing, in the first three years of NAFTA, US imports from China, Hong Kong, Taiwan and South Korea feel from 38 to 30 per cent. In the same period, imports from Mexico more than doubled from 4.4 to 9.6 per cent (*Asian Wall Street Journal*, 16 July 1997). Indeed, analysts suggest that all of North America has benefited from the introduction of NAFTA (Weinberger 1996). Examples cited include the electronics industry, in which trade between Canada, the USA and

Mexico has risen by nearly 25 per cent since 1993.

Inter-country trade within NAFTA grew considerably in the period between 1991 and 1997, such that the USA, Canada and Mexico represent a significant proportion of each other's international trade. The bi-lateral trade between both Canada and Mexico and the USA is particularly strong: exports to the USA represent more than 85 per cent of Mexico's and over 82 per cent of Canada's total exports.

It may be noted, however, that trade between Canada and Mexico is on a far lesser scale than that of each with the USA. Canada's imports from Mexico in 1997 represented only 1.7 per cent of its total imports. This is less than their imports from either Japan (3.9 per cent) or the EU (9.0 per cent). Similarly, Mexico imported only 1.7 per event of total imports from Canada (compared with 62.5 per cent from the USA).

Despite the gains from NAFTA agreement, the rapidity of the changes has created both winners and losers (see Box 11.1).

Box 11.1 Winners and Losers After NAFTA

One example of a potential loser in the face of new NAFTA legislation lies in the booming export manufacturing or 'maquiladora' sector of the Mexican market. Under this 33-year-old programme, components were assembled duty-free for export. Around 4120 maquiladora enterprises existed in Mexico and these represented around 15 per cent of the country's GDP and employed over a million workers. Despite the recession in 1995, the gross value of production in the maquiladora sector grew by 20 per cent. Not surprisingly, Mexico was keen to protect the sector given its contribution to the national economy. On 1 January 2001, any machinery or components from sources outside the USA, Canada and Mexico lost their duty-free status. Given the growth of this sector, Mexico was keen to protect its future. As a result, the Mexican Commerce Ministry combed through lists of hundreds of components to identify the components and firms affected and determine which were deserving of exemption from the new NAFTA clause.

Foreign investors in Mexico, who bring in higher proportions of components from other regions of the world will be particularly affected by the new leg-

islation. Asian electronics producers import around a third of all components on which they will face tariffs of between 2 and 5 per cent. Around 60 components have been identified in the electronic sector which will face these new tariffs. Yet the changes in legislation on local content have also resulted in gains for Mexico. As a result of the current economic crisis in South-East Asia, many Asian firms could produce electronic equipment cheaper at home. Yet the potential changes in the legislation on local content prompts them to enter Mexico quickly. Producing in the region will be of increased importance in 2003 when NAFTA imposes tariffs on any parts which do not come from within the NAFTA region.

Manufacturing investment in Mexico rose to around $1.6 billion, of which almost 80 per cent was from Asia.

Sources: *The Wall Street Journal* (1998) 'Nafta Deadline Looms over Mexican Exporters', 11 November, Ben Fox, Eastern Edition; *The Wall Street Journal* (1998) 'Asian Firms Plunge into Mexico on Nafta's Promise – Investment Boom to Manufacturing', 14 August, Joel Millman, Eastern Edition.

Resolution of Trade Disputes

Commentators are clear that economic accord does not necessarily bring social integration between the member nations. Despite the increased opportunity for cross-border co-operation, the member states of NAFTA have struggled to retain national identity. Indeed tensions may also arise between cultural groupings within each nation. Examples include the Quebecois and other regions of Canada or the pluralist views of the different ethnic groups in the USA. Granzin *et al.* (1998) suggest that those with a greater understanding of NAFTA consider it more important. People perceiving themselves economically at risk call for job protection, and are more conservative and xenophobic in their responses to NAFTA. The gap between rich and poor in the USA is increasingly blamed on free trade, which critics blame for competition from cheap foreign labour (*The Economist*, 3 October 1998).

Not surprisingly, the potential for NAFTA to create winners and losers leads the member states to enter disputes over 'unfair' actions. The disagreements both prior to and since the introduction of the NAFTA agreement have been many and various (see Box 11.2).

This type of trade dispute has prompted discussions of what mechanisms are appropriate to resolve disputes. Since the introduction of the Canada–USA FTA in 1988, dispute resolution has taken place via the innovative Chapter 19 process. Valihora (1998) believes that this is superior to GATT's consensus-driven approach after 1947, which involves a cumbersome system of committees and rules and was prone to long delays. In contrast, Chapter 19's binational panels for the review of anti-dumping and charging extra import duties (countervailing duty) cases, such as those highlighted above, are likely to achieve speedier results. Free trade is now so widespread that the World Trade Organization (WTO) has updated the GATT mechanism, although Valihora suggests that this may still take three to four months longer than the Chapter 19 process.

Box 11.2   Chicken Arbitrage and Tomato Tariffs

Examples of trade disputes vary in scale and severity but the impacts are all too real for those who lose as a result. Mexican poultry farmers are irate at the increased smuggling of chickens from the USA into Mexico. Under the terms of NAFTA fresh and frozen chickens are subject to 240 per cent tariffs, while salted and smoked meats are subject to only 8 per cent. Mexican officials and farmers suggest that this has resulted in chickens being imported as chicken in brine intended for use in soups. Figures suggest that annual imports of this type of chicken have increased from 450 to 9000 tonnes since the introduction of the legislation in 1994 and this, claim Mexican farmers, means that imports are selling at less than local production costs. The problem, they claim, could be resolved if all chicken were subject to the same rate of tariffs.

A similar dispute has arisen over alleged 'dumping' by US exporters of beef and pork in Mexico. Beef imports from the USA have risen by 200 per cent since 1993 and pork by 40 per cent over the same period. Mexican trade officials suggest that US suppliers are selling at up to 30 per cent below cost, in defiance of the NAFTA agreement. US producers deny that any dumping is taking place, but say that this is a normal free market push by farmers who enjoy greater economies of scale and have access to cheaper feed.

Concerned about cheap Mexican imports, in 1996 the tomato growers of Florida gained the support of Mickey Kantor, America's top trade negotiator, to back their claims for safeguards. A first bill to allow this 'protection' was approved unanimously by Senate, but was later stifled by the House of Representatives. Further bills were proposed by Mr Kantor to impose extra tariffs on imports or to introduce quotas. What price free trade?

Sources: *The Wall Street Journal* (1998) 'Illegal US Chickens Flock into Mexico', Joel Millman, 24 June, New York; *The Wall Street Journal* (1998) 'Mexican Meat Producers Take on US: Dominance of Imports Prompts Cattlemen to Act', 5 November, p. A17; *The Economist* (1996) 'Rotten Tomatoes: NAFTA's Tomato Wars', 10 February.

Beyond NAFTA? Caribbean Basin Initiative (CBI) and the Caribbean Common Market (Caricom)

Since the mid-1980s, the 24 nations of the Caribbean basin (this includes Jamaica, Trinidad, the Dominican republic and all Central American countries) have enjoyed strong economic and trade relations through the Caribbean Basin Initiative (CBI). Strong links have also developed between the CBI countries and the USA. US exports to the Caribbean have expanded by more than 100 per cent since the mid-1980s, while Caribbean exports to the USA increased by around 50 per cent.

Trading between the USA and the Caribbean countries was, however, adversely affected by the introduction of the NAFTA agreement. Mexican exports now enjoy more privileged access to the USA than do those from the Caribbean. Countries in the Caribbean are now forced to compete in their largest market at a significant competitive disadvantage (Bernal, *The Wall Street Journal*, 22 March 1996).

The diversion of trade and investment away from the Caribbean basin has been apparent since NAFTA was introduced. Mexico has become the largest single source of US clothing imports, a sector in which other Caribbean countries were previously strong. As a result, trade relations between the Caribbean and the USA have begun to erode. Political discussions are under way to resolve the unintended consequences of NAFTA on the region. A period of 'NAFTA parity' lasting 10 years is proposed to allow the CBI countries to strengthen their economic position sufficiently to gain access into a hemispheric Free Trade Area of the Americas. Bernal (1996) argues that the benefits of NAFTA parity for the Caribbean and the USA are also clear. As much as 70 per cent of value added in the Caribbean clothes industry is based on US components and labour.

Any expansion of the Caribbean clothes industry has a direct impact on the USA. The introduction of a 15-country common market in the Caribbean region (Caricom) seems a good preparation for integration with the Americas, although NAFTA parity has not yet been achieved.

Latin American Co-operation

In 1995, President Clinton committed himself, at a summit in Miami, to rapid entry into NAFTA for Chile, which in turn would speed up entry for the other Latin American nations. Since then, wrangling in the White House and the US Congress preventing President Clinton from winning fast-track trade negotiating authority (*The Economist*, 11 April 1998) stalled Chile's entry. It also caused disillusionment among some in Latin America who questioned whether North America had lost interest in closer links in the Americas.

In frustration the Latin American countries began to form free trade pacts, which did not involve the USA. In addition to its participation in the NAFTA agreement, Mexico is also part of the Latin American Integration Association (LAIA) a free trade group formed in 1980 to reduce trade barriers and promote co-operation between Argentina, Bolivia, Brazil, Chile, Colombia, Ecuador, Mexico, Paraguay, Peru, Uruguay and Venezuela. LAIA's main aim is to create a Latin American common market. Given the complexity of integration between this number of countries at different stages of development, however, various subgroups have evolved.

In 1995 Mercosur, a common market agreement between the southern countries of Argentina, Brazil, Paraguay and Uruguay took steps towards eliminating most tariffs. The joint GDP of this grouping is $650 billion, 70 per cent of South America's total. In 1997, trade within Mercosur had grown by 25 per cent to $20 billion.

ANCOM (the Andean Common Market), which promotes economic integration and co-operation between Bolivia, Colombia, Ecuador, Peru and Venezuela, has seen a more than 10 per cent increase in intra-group trade, and further links are likely (*The Economist*, 11 April 1998).

The introduction of free market agreements between subsets of Latin American countries has also resulted in strong intra-regional trade and consequent growth in GDP. For example, 1998 figures show Argentina exporting 35.3 per cent of its total to other Mercosur countries (compared with only 7.8 per cent to the USA and 15.6 per cent to the EU).

It is to be noted that as a result of its NAFTA membership, Mexico has much stronger trade with North America than do the other Latin American countries. Argentina and Brazil, both members of the Mercosur Common Market Agreement have strong trade with each other and within Mercosur as a whole. The Latin American countries outside of NAFTA also have stronger trade within other groupings in the region, such as ANCOM than does Mexico.

The question of whether such regional agreements are a good thing in a globalizing economy ia a question which divides economists (*The Economist*, 22 August 1998). Critics suggest that regionalism may 'divert' trade flows and so prevent free trade. Jagdish Bhagwati from Columbia University, a prominent critic of trade blocks, describes regional trade blocs as 'stumbling blocks rather than trading blocs'. Yet the extent of diversion may be overstated. Some argue that this trade tends to be between 'natural' partners who would trade anyway. Others argue that, even allowing for trade diversion, regional trade groups make progress towards removing barriers and may merge with each other.

Free Trade Area of the Americas (FTAA)

One such potential merger between regional trading blocs forms the basis of the ambitious economic co-operation proposed by George Bush in 1990. Bush's 'Enterprise of the Americas' proposal aimed to create an all-American free trade area from Alaska to Argentina. Achieving a hemispheric agreement would remove the need for the separate Latin American and Caribbean initiatives which currently exist. Although little progress has been made in extending NAFTA, the second summit of the Americas, in Santiago in April 1998, formally opened negotiations on creating what is now referred to as a 'Free Trade Area of the Americas' (FTAA). The leaders of 34 countries met to agree an agenda of what to negotiate, and how, when and where to achieve FTAA by 2005.

Critics point to the slow progress to date suggesting, that the stumbling blocks may be too great. Some bad habits of demanding import licences and raising external tariffs have raised doubts over the commitment of Latin America to free trade, especially in the face of economic crises in South-East Asia and Brazil (*The Economist* 11 April 1998). All the same, the pace of reform among to dynamic subgroups of Latin America raises hopes that FTAA may eventually become a reality.

The 'Double Diamond' of Competitive Advantage

In the face of this integration within the Americas, research suggests that national models, such as Porter's *Competitive Advantage of Nations* model (1990) (see Chapter 4 for a fuller discussion) should be extended to acknowledge the importance of links between the countries in the region. Porter's 'diamond', for example, would link the home country 'diamond' with those of other countries within the same trading bloc.

Rugman and D'Cruz (1993) argue that, while Porter's diamond may explain the success of US, Japanese and EU multinationals, it is not applicable to small, open trading economies, which are not part of the Triad. Porter argues (1990) that sustainable competitive advantages are based upon success in the four 'determinants' of the diamond framework in the home market:

1. Factor conditions
2. Demand conditions
3. Related and supporting Industries
4. Firm strategy, structure and rivalry.

and upon the two external variables chance and the role of government.

Rugman and D'Cruz demonstrate, however, that Canada's international competitiveness cannot be explained by its home country 'diamond'. The reasons why Porter's model fails to explain key issues in Canadian international competitiveness are summarized as:

1. **Only outward FDI is seen as increasing international competitiveness**. In contrast, Canadian research shows (Rugman 1993) that 70 per cent of Canadian trade is done by

50 multinational corporations, half of whom are foreign owned. Inward foreign investment plays a significant role in Canadian international competitiveness.

2. **The role played by multinational corporations is underestimated**. If a Canadian multinational has a significant proportion of sales outside its home market then it is little affected by its home 'diamond'. On average over 70 per cent of Canadian multinational corporations' sales are in the USA.

3. **Clusters were excluded from consideration for their national importance when trade was exclusively with neighbouring nations**. On this basis the trade between Canada and the USA in car chassis manufacture is not considered, although it has had significant economic impact for both nations.

Such is the impact of the links between the USA and Canada that Rugman and D'Cruz (1993) argue for the Canadian 'diamond' to be linked with the US 'diamond' in a 'double-diamond' framework. Canada's international success lies, for example, not only in its factor advantages. It can access other factor advantages via links with the USA. Similarly, its success is built not only on the nature of related and support industries in Canada, but on the cluster of US firms with which it has links.

Considerable modifications are required to the framework to take into account the impact of free trade agreements such as Canada–USA and later NAFTA. The 'double diamond' framework argues that it would be more useful for Canadian managers to analyze a North American 'diamond' to understand the issues in Canada's international competitiveness. Free trade has brought changes which may be perceived as painful in the short-term, but the longer-term benefits in innovation and cost competitiveness are considerable.

Pressures for improved international competitiveness stemming from the North American 'diamond' include the fact that Canadian customers are learning to be as demanding as their American neighbours. This puts pressure on Canadian businesses to provide higher levels of service. Canadian subsidiaries of US multinational corporations, often built to overcome tariff barriers, find themselves in direct competition with US Headquarters and must perform well to survive. Rugman and D'Cruz see the North American 'diamond' as offering Canadian firms a step towards global competitiveness.

The limitations which Rugman and D'Cruz identify for the 'diamond' model when applied to Canada, apply equally to other small, open economies. Hodgetts (1993) applies the revised 'double diamond' framework to Mexico. The case for linking the Mexican and US 'diamonds' is comparable to that argued for Canada above. Post-NAFTA Mexico has the strongest economy in Latin America, but its economic growth is often reliant on free trade with the USA. 25 per cent of all US fruit and vegetables are imported from Mexico. The economy has been kick-started by its NAFTA links.

Hodgetts sees Mexico's international competitiveness as (1) reliant on developing innovative products and services which meet the needs not only of Mexican but also of the more demanding US customers, (2) involving learning from more advanced support industries in the USA and making full use of the physical and human resources of both countries. Again improving international competitiveness through this interlinkage of the NAFTA economies is seen as a platform for global competitiveness.

Barclay (1998) has confirmed the value of the 'double diamond' concept outside of NAFTA. This study focuses on entry into Caribbean countries by multinational corporations. The success of market entrants is not only affected by their home country 'diamond', but also by the 'diamonds' of the countries they enter. This inverted 'double diamond' shows that entrants from larger Triad countries are also affected by interlinkage of economies.

THE NETWORK PERSPECTIVE

Networks in the Americas

Macro-Level Networks – the USA as a Focal Actor

A common feature of the bilateral and multilateral relationships reviewed in the previous section is that the USA, as the largest and most powerful world player, plays a central or 'focal' role in each cluster of relationships (Figure 11.1). In this sense, it assumes the role of 'focal actor' in its network in the way described by Cunningham and Culligan (1991). This central position means that network boundaries are determined by relationships with a certain level of closeness to the focal actor.

The focal position of the USA in the NAFTA agreement is attributable to a number of historic influences. It might easily be explained by its larger population, its economic wealth and growth rate and its sophisticated customers and companies. In justifying the 'double diamond' of international competitive advantage for Canada and Mexico, respectively, Hodgetts (1993) and Rugman and D'Cruz (1993) stress the importance of the US relationship.

Through this relationship, both Canadian and Mexican firms are pressed to higher levels of performance by exposure to more demanding customers and more competitive suppliers and competitors than exist in their respective home markets. In economic terms the size of the trade flows between the USA and Canada and between Mexico and Canada is significantly larger than that between Mexico and Canada. This is denoted in Figure 11.2 by the use of thicker arrows for the larger trade flows.

The USA plays a similar focal role in the Caribbean basin (see Figure 11.2). The economic value of these relationships however, see between 1991 and 1997. Caribbean countries ascribe the reduced level of trade in sectors such as textiles to the preferential trading conditions afforded to Mexico (see p. 000). From these two examples, it is apparent that the relationships of the USA in the sepa-

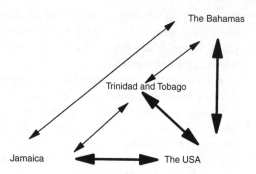

Figure 11.2   Network relationships in the Caribbean Basin

rate NAFTA and Caribbean 'nets' are interdependent. This illustrates the impact of indirect relationships on other actors within the network.

Again, the focal position of the USA is seen in terms of the economic flow (in real and percentage terms) between it and each of the other actors compared with the flow between the other actors. This phenomenon is not seen between the USA and the larger Latin American countries (with the exception of Mexico). The markedly higher economic flow between the countries who form part of the same economic groupings within the Latin American region give some indication of the level of their interdependence (see Traditional perspective for the extent of economic interdependence between NAFTA and Mercosur countries).

Network Structures in the USA

In their presentation of a network view of internationalization, Johanson and Mattsson (1988) suggest that the level of internationalization of the host country network affects market entrants. If the host market network is already highly internationalized, then firms within the market will have many relationships with actors from other countries.

The USA is an example of a host market network, which is highly internationalized. Accordingly, as suggested by Hodgetts (1993), and by Rugman and D'Cruz (1993), market entrants will face the challenges of the international competitiveness of its firms and the level of sophistication of its customers.

Figure 11.1   Network relationships in NAFTA

The particular characteristics of network structures in the USA are analyzed by both Kinch (1992) and Seyed Mohamed and Bolte (1992). Given the level of competition and the maturity of many industry sectors in the USA, the market is described as stable and 'tightly structured'. In his study of Volvo's entry into the USA, Kinch describes the characteristics of the US network. There are a small number of strong competitive actors who account for 90 per cent of the business (oligopoly). These actors follow well-established rules and the basic properties of their product offer are similar. Smaller competitors in the market tend to follow similar strategies, but suffer the cost disadvantages of smaller scale. Relationships between manufacturers, dealers, service facilities and final consumers are stable and follow established rules.

Despite the stability of the US network structures, Kinch does not, however, see this as a barrier to new entrants. In fact, conversely, tightly structured networks may be easier to enter than moderate or loose structures. This can be explained by latent discontent among the actors with the way the network operates. Given the level of similarity of strategies and structures within tightly structured networks, actors who are not favoured will lack alternatives.

A new entrant may complement the existing network by playing a different game. In the case of Volvo the vogue for imported cars had been fuelled by the entry of Volkswagen. Imported cars offered higher margins for dealers. Dealers who had a solid financial base set up new outlets to sell imported cars as well as American brands. As competition between dealers was fierce, the opportunity to distribute another high quality European brand was attractive.

In contrast, Seyed-Mohamed and Bolte (1992) suggest that it may be difficult to enter tightly structured USA networks because: 'when business interdependencies are strong the positions of the actors become closely linked by various bonds of dependencies which consequently could function as high barriers to entry to newcomers'. Long-term investments may be necessary to 'buy in' to established positions.

An important conclusion of Seyed Mohamed and Bolte's study of entry into the USA is that network structures may be 'more or less invisible' for outsiders. The unique nature of existing relationships may not be apparent to outsiders and can be understood only by operation within the network. This may have important implications for mode of entry into new international markets (see Chapter 7).

Network Structures in Canada

In her study of entry into Canada, Blankenburg (1995) outlines the interest of the Canadian authorities in introducing into Canada a national mobile phone system based on similar systems which had been successfully introduced in several areas of the USA. As it wished to favour domestic suppliers, in the early 1980s the Canadian government set down a complex set of requirements for any supplying firm. Motorola, AT&T and Nippon Electric and Swedish ERA declared themselves unable to meet the Canadian government's requirements. Only after the Cantel consortium of nine telecoms firms was formed in 1984 did entry into the Canadian market appear possible to international market entrants. The strict requirements imposed on market entrants and the high level of global competition for a route into Canada suggest that the market was 'tightly structured'. In this tightly structured market, Blankenburg's findings support Seyed Mohamed and Bolte's view. The level of competition and the relative stability of Canadian network structures make it difficult for a new market entrant to build a network position.

CASE STUDY 11.1 BANANA WARS: COMPLEX WEBS OF OLD AND NEW TRADING RELATIONSHIPS

After a generation of independence, the legacy of old colonial and the implications of new trade links with North America create complex webs to untangle for the ex-European Caribbean countries. When in February 1997 President Clinton met leaders of the Caribbean countries to sign the 'Partnership for Prosperity and Security' agreement between the USA and the Caribbean, high on the agenda was recognition of the European banana market (map 11.2).

Despite this recognition of Caribbean interests in the banana industry, links between North and Latin America brought the USA in on the side of growers of Latin American bananas. The USA threatened a trade war with the EU because it did not import enough Latin American bananas. The EU has long favoured bananas from former

European colonies in the Caribbean over those from Latin America, which are largely distributed by US companies. The dispute escalated in September 1997, the WTO upheld its findings that the EU discriminated in favour or former colonies in banana imports. By November 1998, in frustration that the EU had not acted on this ruling, the USA threatened to impose 100 per cent duties on a range of European products ranging from French cheese and wine to German coffee.

The implications of these banana wars are various. First, the WTO's dispute resolution mechanism does not seem as effective as it should be. It seems that it is possible to comply slowly, if at all. Secondly, if the large trading blocs act as if they are above the law, their arguments to other countries in favour of free trade ring hollow. Finally,

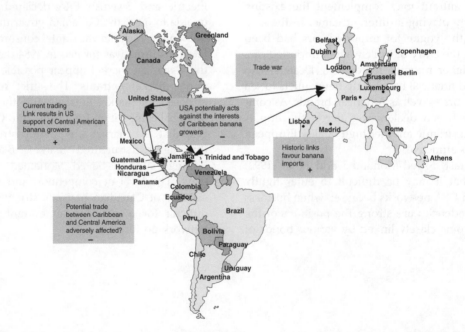

Map 11.2   Positive and negative impacts of banana wars dispute on a network of relationships

however, banana wars shows the complexities of international trade relationships. As USA has concluded bi-lateral and multilateral trading relationships with groups of countries, which have mutually exclusive interests in industries such as bananas, it is difficult to see how it can keep everyone happy.

QUESTIONS

1. What trading relationships are in the global network are revealed in the banana wars case?

2. In your estimation, which of these have been positively and which negatively affected by the banana wars dispute? Explain your reasoning.

3. What impact do you think the banana wars episode will have on the prospects of hemispheric trade in the Americas?

Source: The Economist (1997) 'Developing Fast', 13 September, *The Economist*, 'A Relic of the Empire: The Caribbean Cuts a British Link', 8 February, *The Economist*, 'Monkey Business: The Banana Trade War', 14 November.

SUMMARY

In Chapter 11 we have explored the challenges of operation in the Americas. Distinctive types of relationship in the region and their management are explored. Finally the contributions of network studies in the region are evaluated.

BIBLIOGRAPHY

Asian Wall Street Journal (1997) 'Nafta Triggers a Shift in Textile Trade – Asia's Portion of US Market Declines as Member Nations Make Gains', 16 July, E. Lachia.

Barclay, L.-A. (1998) Warwick University, unpublished PhD thesis.

Bernal, R. L. (1996) 'The Americas: A Jamaican's Case for Trade Parity with NAFTA', *The Wall Street Journal*, 22 March.

Blankenburg, D. (1995) 'A Network Approach to Foreign Market Entry', in Möller, K. and Wilson, D. T. (eds), *Business Marketing: An Interaction and Network Perspective*, Kluwer Academic.

Cunningham, M. T. and Culligan, K. (1991) 'Competitiveness through Networks of Relationships in Information Technology Product Markets', in S. J. Paliwoda (ed), *New Perspectives in International Marketing*, Routledge.

Dallmeyer, D. G. (ed.) (1997) *Joining Together, Standing Apart: National Identities after NAFTA*, Kluwer Law International.

Direction of Trade Statistics Yearbook, IMF.

Economist, The (1998a) 'Survey of World Trade: The Wages of Fear: Are Poor Countries pinching the Rich Ones' Jobs?', 3 October, P. Lane.

Economist, The (1998b) 'Finance and Economics: A Question of Preference: Do Regional Trade Agreements Encourage Free Trade?: Economic Focus: Trade Blocks', 22 August.

Economist, The (1998c) 'The Americas: The Road from Santiago: The Second 'Summit of the Americas' Opens in Chile Next Week', 11 April.

Granzin, K. L., Painter, J. J., Brazell, J. D., and Olsen, J. E. (1998) 'Public Support for Free Trade Agreements: The Influence of Economic Concerns, Group Identification and Cognitive Involvement', *Journal of Macromarketing*, 18, 1: 11–23.

Hodgetts, R. M. (1993) 'Porter's Diamond Framework in a Mexican Context', *Management International Review*, 33, 2: 41–50.

Johanson, J. and Mattsson, L.-G. (1988) 'Internationalisation in Industrial Systems – A Network Approach', in Hood, N. and Vahlne, J.-E. (eds), *Strategies in Global Competition*, Croom Helm.

Kinch, N. (1992) 'Entering a Tightly Structured Network – Strategic Visions or Network Realities', in Forsgren, M. and Johanson, J. (eds), *Managing Networks in International Business*, Gordon & Breach.

Porter, M. E. (1990) *Competitive Advantage of Nations*, Free Press.

Rugman, A. M. (1993) 'Investing in the US after NAFTA', *Ivey Business Quarterly*, 57, 4: 26–30.

Rugman, A. M. and D'Cruz, J. R. (1993) 'The "Double Diamond" Model of International Competitiveness: The Canadian Experience', *Management International Review*, 33, 2: 17–31.

Rugman, A. M. and Gestrin, M. (1993) 'The Strategic Response of Multinational Enterprises to NAFTA', *Journal of World Business*, 28, 4: 18–29.

Seyed Mohamed, N. and Bolte, M. (1992) 'Taking a Position in a Structured Business Network', in Forsgren, M. and Johanson, J. (eds), *Managing Networks in International Business*, Gordon and Breach.

Valihora, M. S. (1998) 'NAFTA Chapter 19 or the WTO's Dispute Settlement Body: A Hobson's Choice for Canada?', *Case Western Reserve Journal of International Law*, 30, 2, 3: 447–87.

Von Bertrab, H. (1997) *Negotiating NAFTA: A Mexican Envoy's Account*, Praeger.

Wall Street Journal, The (1993) 'Ford Plans Sharp Boost in Shipments between Mexico, the US and Canada', 17 December, R. L. Simison.

Wall Street Journal, The (1996a) 'The Americas: A Jamaican's Case for Trade Parity with Nafta', 22 March, L. Bernal, A13.

Wall Street Journal, The (1996b) 'Free-Trade Frustration: Latin Nations Form Pacts Leaving US on the Sidelines', *Asian Wall Street Journal*, 11 January, R. S. Greenberger and J. Friedland.

Wall Street Journal, The (1998) 'In Mexico, Support Widens in Business for Eventual Monetary Union with the US', 3 February, M. Gutschi, Eastern Edition: B7c.

EUROPE

Objectives

The issues to be addressed in Chapter 12 include:

1. The application of concepts from earlier sections of the book to Europe
2. Examination of relationships within Europe and the impact of the Single European market (SEM)
3. Review studies of networks in Europe to identify distinctive characteristics of network structures in the region.

After reading Chapter 12 you will be able to:

1. Understand the challenges facing international marketers in Europe
2. Identify specific types of relationships that play a role in the region
3. Evaluate the contribution of network studies of the region.

INTRODUCTION

In this chapter the implications of the Single European Market (SEM) are considered. The enlarged European Free Trade Area (EFTA) represents over one-third of world GDP and over 40 per cent of world trade. The region has seen considerable change in a period of increasing economic and social integration. These changes pose a number of challenges for firms within and outside of the region. Can Europe truly be considered as a single market? To what extent has convergence taken place? What are the relationship implications of the changing face of Europe?

Some of the relationship issues that emerge in the SEM are highlighted by Lessem in his Introduction to Urban and Vendemini's book on *European Strategic Alliances* (1992, p. 2):

> Competitive strategy, in effect, becomes co-operative strategy, for the company; and European bureaucracy begins to supplant national sovereignty, for the country. Realistically speaking, while Italy or Spain retains its sense of national identity, a pan-European identity emerges as a higher order phenomenon.

This chapter explores the extent to which the expected impacts of pan-European marketing have become a reality. Relationships within the SEM are studied alongside those with macro- and organisational-level actors globally.

THE TRADITIONAL PERSPECTIVE

Challenges

Defining the European Union (Map 12.1)

From initial free trade initiatives in the early 1970s, the pace of change in Europe has accelerated during the 1980s and 1990s. The new European body, the European Union (EU) came into being on 1 November 1993 after ratification of the Maastricht treaty. On this date the European Community (EC) was absorbed into the EU to form one of its three pillars: the EC, intergovernmental agreement on foreign and security matters and co-operation on immigration, asylum and law enforcement (*The Guinness European Data Book* 1994).

Map 12.1   Europe

The 15 members signing up to the EU are listed in Table 12.1.

With the EU came acceleration of free market reforms. 1 January 1999 saw 11 of the 15 EU members sinking their national currencies into a common currency. Economic progress has, however, been taking place since the introduction of the SEM in Europe in early 1993. *The Economist's*

Table 12.1   EU members, 2001

Country	Date of membership of EC
Austria	1995
Belgium	1950[a]
Denmark	1973
Finland	1993
France	1950[a]
Germany	1950[a]
Greece	1981
Ireland	1973
Italy	1950[a]
Luxembourg	1950[a]
Netherlands	1950[a]
Portugal	1986
Spain	1986
UK	1973
Sweden	1995

Note: a. Founder member
Sources: Guinness European Data Book
1994; The Economist (1999)

The World in 1999 (p. 13) commented on the introduction of the Euro, Europe's single currency, in 1998:

> Last May, when Europe's leaders picked 11 countries to join the Euro in the first wave, the mood was euphoric: economies were growing strongly, inflation had been tamed, unemployment was falling.

The Euro is predicted (*The World in 1999*, p. 41) to encourage greater convergence within Europe. Moreover, greater economic convergence should prompt calls for a common foreign and security policy.

Europe, however, has not escaped the impact of the Asian Crisis, and introduction of the single currency has involved some major changes in Europe:

> Its main impacts, which will not be fully felt until the currency itself is in circulation in 2002, will be to increase competition, to narrow prices, to save costs. Combine it with the impact of the Internet, and European business is in for a revolutionary few years. (*The World in 1999*)

The teething problems experienced en route to greater integration will have major implications for countries and companies involved in international business. Can the region really be served as one market or will separate marketing strategies still be required for each of the European countries? This question will be discussed more fully below.

Enlargement of the EU

From the late 1980s, dramatic changes unfolded on the eastern borders of the region. The liberalization of the previous Soviet satellite states of East and Central European (CEE) created a new raft of countries seeking admittance into some level of integration with the EU.

One key agenda item for the EU is its ongoing membership. Front-runners for admittance include Poland, the Czech Republic, Hungary, Slovenia and Estonia (Table 12.2). Cyprus (if the problem of division can be resolved), Malta and Latvia may soon move up the list (*The World in 1999*).

In the longer term, therefore, it appears that the EU may be much increased in size. Welford

Table 12.2   European enlargement

Potential members: the leading pack	Potential members: the second wave
Cyprus	Bulgaria
Czech Rep.	Lithuania
Estonia	Romania
Hungary	Slovak Rep.
Latvia	Turkey
Malta	
Poland	
Slovenia	

and Prescott (1994, p. 257) note that 'it is easy to envisage a Community of over 20 nations'. Advocates of this increased membership suggest that integration with Eastern European countries, in particular, may act as a defence against these countries' involvement as part of a Soviet regime. A number of obstacles have, however, also been suggested (Welford and Prescott 1994):

■ The accelerating pace of European enlargement may weaken cohesion of the Union
■ The Union may become unwieldy and cumbersome
■ Costs of integrating the CEE countries may be prohibitively expensive; the diversity of backgrounds and economic wealth may mean that such an enlarged Europe needed to change its policies on funding, or monetary union
■ The EU should deepen and consolidate its own union before admitting new members
■ Plans for the SEM did not anticipate the changes in East and Central Europe, nor closer links with the EFTA nations.

These obstacles may be sufficient to prevent further full memberships in the foreseeable future. *The Economist* notes that:

> The unpalatable truth is that, although all European governments subscribe to the strategic and moral case for admitting Poles, Czechs, Hungarians and the rest to their club, none is comfortable with the huge costs of such an expansion. And in the EU, money has always, in the end, counted for more than idealism. (*The World in 1999*, p. 14).

Given the slow progress in enlarging the EU so far, *The Economist* predicts that no further countries will become members until around 2005. Some interim agreement seems, however, likely. In 1991, Jacques Delors, then President of the European Commission, called upon the union to devise a system of *concentric rings of membership*, from full membership to looser economic and political relationships with the EU.

The Reality of Pan-European Marketing

The development of an SEM has resulted in renewed attention to the question of serving Europe as a single geographic segment (Gogel and Larreché 1989; Halliburton 1990; Halliburton and Hünerberg 1993).

Halliburton and Hünerberg (1993) suggest that pan-European segments exist for some products or services, which are 'high-tech' or 'high-touch' (luxury). Moreover, they suggest that Europe might be divided into groupings of countries, such as Anglo-Saxon North and Latin South, which are similar on the basis of macro-environmental trends.

Paitra (1991) suggests a convergence across Europe in broad social trends, such as ageing of the population, attitudes to work and increases in the number of working women and single-parent families. However, he refers to this as a 'two-level phenomenon. Significant differences exist in the level or importance of these trends between countries.

Despite this evidence of convergence, a number of studies suggest the existence of cultural differences in consumer preferences (Meffert and Bolz 1991; Diamantopoulos, Schlegelmulch and Du Preez 1995). Consequently, while there is empirical evidence to suggest that some firms have succeeded with pan-European branding and marketing strategies, there is also evidence that firms can succeed with adapted strategies (Gogel and Larreché 1989; Littler and Schlieper 1995). The example of pan-European marketing in the food industry is explored in Box 12.1.

Standardization in the Textile Industry – An Example of Pan-European Marketing?

The following section explores further the extent to which standardized marketing is possible

---

Box 12.1   The 'Euro Consumer'

At the heart of the debate over the existence of the Euro consumer lies the issue of how to segment the European market. It is generally accepted that no one type of Euro consumer exists, or will exist. Over time, however, the similarities are beginning to outnumber the differences.

1. Lifestyle. Studies have identified a number of consumer types, such as Paitra's 'traditionals', 'moderns' and 'go-betweens', which exist in different proportions in different European countries. While this approach may be useful in identifying patterns of similarities and differences, the use of such descriptive variables for segmentation runs the problem of not asking 'why' they might buy and particular product or service (see Haley 1968).

2. Segmenting the market on the basis of behavioural factors, such as usage occasion, picks up the fact that the same consumer may exhibit different behaviour on **different occasions or for different products**. A consumer might be traditional in his approach to one product but buy another internationally. A UK consumer might, for example, buy English tea, but buy wine from a number of countries within Europe.

3. Benefit segmentation. The answer to whether segments exist across European markets lies in the question of whether consumers from the different markets perceive benefits in the same product or services. As a result, demand for for some products, such as 4 × 4 cars or the Internet, may be common to a segment in each market, whereas demand for other products may be fragmented.

Sources: Based on Haley (1968); Carr and Texeraud (1993); Paitra (1993).

---

within Europe. Research findings (Bridgewater and Wu 1996) discuss the impacts on textile firms in France and the UK to see the extent to which these are similar and whether international marketing activity has changed since the introduction of the SEM.

■ **Sourcing behaviour.** The geographic source of raw materials differs between French and UK firms. While French firms source predominantly from the EU, primarily from Portugal and Greece, UK firms source more from home market suppliers and to a greater extent from South East Asia.

■ **Location of customers.** Both UK and French firms sell largely to the home market. Both do similar levels of trade within the EU. Other international activity by the French is some-what more centred on North America than that of their UK counterparts.

■ **Level of standardization.** Tables 12.3 and 12.4 show the levels of standardization of product offerings by UK and French textile firms to Europe before and after the inception of the EU. It is apparent that French firms had higher initial levels of product standardization (50 per cent compared with 40 per cent) and that, in general, firms in the clothing sectors are more standardized.

The main explanation for this initial variation is that of differences in colour and fashion preferences in member states. Successful marketing means that these customers cannot be addressed in a standardized way. Another possible explanation relates to the type of customers and customer

Table 12.3   Current level of standardization across Europe

		Standardized (%)	Mixed (%)	Adapted (%)
By nationality	UK	40.0	25.7	34.3
	France	50.0	8.3	41.7
By sector	Textile/Other	29.2	20.8	50.0
	clothing	52.8	22.2	25.0

Table 12.4   Will a greater level of standardization
be possible in future?

		Yes (%)	No (%)
By nationality	UK	67.6	32.4
	France	56.5	43.5
By sector	Textile/Other	71.2	28.8
	clothing	52.0	48.0

relationship in each sector. Firms in the textile
sector tend to supply industrial customers with
large-volume orders. Customization is common –
hence the low standardization. Firms in the clothing sector sold to end consumers primarily via
retail channels and had a higher potential to benefit from convergence in European fashion tastes.
Indeed, both sectors seem optimistic that cultural
convergence will increase within the SEM.

- **Benefits of European integration?** When
  asked their views on the benefits and disadvantages of European Integration (Tables
  12.5 and 12.6), all firms professed a belief in

greater opportunities. Both UK and French
firms agree that there has been a simplification
in buying processes. This suggests that the EU
is achieving Cecchini's goal (1988) to facilitate
more intra-European trade. In contrast, relatively little benefit was seen to accrue from
standardization either of production or of
marketing activities. Both nationalities rated
increased competition as the most negative
consequence of the SEM.

So far, French and UK firms perceive the SEM
similarly. They do, however, differ in some
respects. UK firms see increasing labour costs as
a disadvantage, while French firms are relatively
unconcerned. While enforcement of a Europe-wide
minimum wage may be in the future (Welford and
Prescott 1994) it appears that labour rates have
increased within the UK since the creation of the
Social Chapter in 1990. This may certainly have an
impact on UK firms. The extent of this may relate
to the 'positioning' of these firms in the market.
Firms with a value for money position will be more
concerned about costs.

Table 12.5   What advantages has the SEM offered your firm?

Advantages[a]	UK			France		
	Mean score	Standard deviation	Rank	Mean score	Standard deviation	Rank
Increased market opportunities	4.97	2	1	4.59	1.8	1
Simpler buying process	3.57	1.8	2	3.59	2.1	2
Standardized marketing	2.60	1.5	3	2.27	1.3	4
Lower VAT	2.57	1.7	4	2.14	1.4	5
Demand for standardized products	2.47	1.5	5	2.14	1.2	5
Reduced production costs	2.47	1.5	6	2.77	1.3	3
Savings on advertizing	1.97	1.1	7	2.00	1.3	7

Notes: UK *n* = 37 France *n* = 24
[a]Sorted by mean, where respondents rated elements on a 7-point Likert scale from 1 for unimportant to 7 for very important

Table 12.6   What disadvantages has the SEM created for your firm?

Disadvantages	UK			France		
	Mean score	Standard deviation	Rank	Mean score	Standard deviation	Rank
Increased competition	4.40	1.9	1	5.00	2.2	1
Higher labour costs	3.97	2	2	2.20	1.4	4
Higher quality products required	3.67	2.1	3	4.55	2.22	2
Lower prices obtained	3.73	2.4	4	4.40	2.0	3

Table 12.7   Has the SEM resulted in a change in your business performance?

	Performance better	Performance same	Performance worse
UK	25.0	66.7	8.3
France	20.8	70.8	8.3

Despite the perceived advantages and disadvantages of the SEM, by 1996 the majority of firms had experienced no major change in performance (see Table 12.7). Indeed, those firms whose performance had worsened tended to blame external factors, such as global recession or management mistakes. Improvements in performance, however, tended to be linked by respondents with the increase in new market opportunities identified in Table 12.5.

In summary, these data suggest that, by 1996, the SEM had either improved the performance or made no major changes for the majority of textile firms. It is not clear that a homogeneous SEM exists, especially for firms serving end consumers, although convergence might have a greater impact for these firms. Firms supplying industrial customers were, in any case, more likely to supply goods to customized orders. While standardization has not occurred to any significant extent, firms were generally optimistic that the SEM would deliver benefits.

The above example seems to be supported by other work on pan-European marketing. Some authors argue the possibility of standardizing marketing strategies for Europe (for example, Domzal and Unger 1987 argue that this may be possible for high-tech and high-touch products; Appelbaum and Halliburton 1993 argue that standardization of communications strategies may be possible). The majority, though, argue the practical difficulties of pan-European marketing concerning a distinction which, as long ago as 1962, Fournis neatly summarized as being a difference between: 'the markets of Europe or the European market?' Most commentators believe that the countries of Europe remain, and will always remain, separate markets, albeit with reduced barriers to trade.

THE RELATIONSHIP PERSPECTIVE

Europe as a Trading Bloc

The development of the SEM and its future growth prospects have prompted a body of research into the relationships between Europe and other trading blocs (Wistrich 1991; Ronkainen 1993; Egan and McKiernan 1994; Welford and Prescott 1994). Indeed the SEM has been likened, as a world force, to the USA. Wistrich (1991) contemplates the role in the world economy of a 'United States of Europe', proposing benefits for support of developing countries and stability in its relations with other advanced countries.

That the creation of trading blocs is good is not, however, universally accepted. Ronkainen (1993) suggests that trading blocs can offer benefits in creating free trade. Blocs may adopt new free trade rules faster than single countries if the free trade advocates put pressure on their trading partners. Nonetheless, trading blocs can remain a big threat to free trade.

Both Welford and Prescott (1994) and Egan and McKiernan (1994) highlight the dangers of creating a 'Fortress Europe'. Welford and Prescott (1994) draw an analogy between the creation of a few, strong global trading blocs and oligopoly (existence of a few, strong firms) in markets. In oligopolistic situations, aggressive actions by one firm may prompt aggressive responses by others. Using this analogy for competition for investment flows and economies of scale by national markets, increased integration of Europe resulted, not surprisingly, in threats of renewed protection against European imports. An example of this phenomenon is described more fully in Case Study 11.1.

A number of rules have been created to govern the interaction between the EU and its trading partners. Welford and Prescott (1994) give these as:

- **Dumping.** Some definitions of dumping include only exporting at below cost of production. Others, however, are more encompassing and include charging different prices across markets where this is not supported by variances in costs. The first of these may be construed as 'anti-competitive' although the latter is less clearly 'unfair' (Welford and Prescott 1994, p. 275). The Commission's rules on anti-dumping legislation may be construed as covering both of the above situations. If firms are wrongly penalized this may result in retaliation by foreign governments.

- **Rules of origin and content**. In global markets it can no longer be assumed that a product from a US manufacturing plant is American, or that from a European plant, European. The national origin of components, assembly and parent company may all differ. Accordingly, in 1968, the EC created guidelines to determine origin. This was defined as 'the place where the good underwent its last major transformation' (Welford and Prescott 1994, p. 276). Local content is determined from the percentage of components sourced locally. The percentage considered as 'European' ranges from 35–45 per cent for televisions through to a proposed 90 per cent for Japanese cars made in Europe.

- **Reciprocity**. Colchester and Buchan (1990) suggest that reciprocity involves open access, negotiation to ensure this access and balancing the interests of the EU and third countries. This may mean an increasing role for governments to carry out such negotiation and balance the interests of the countries concerned.

Despite these measures intended to maintain relations with other countries, some alterations in relations with other countries may be expected as a result of recent changes in Europe. Welford and Prescott (1994) differentiate between the expected impacts on different categories of countries:

- **Japan and Asia-Pacific**. Japan has seemingly been singled out by European external trade policy as a result of its growth in world markets. This growth is particularly worrying for European firms given its strength in value-added rather than commodity sectors. Japanese firms seem to have reacted positively towards the SEM with increased foreign investment flows into Europe.

- **North America**. US firms' reaction shows similar increases in investment into the region. The

reaction against the possibility of protectionism has been more vocal, most concerns seem to be based on issues of reciprosity and fears that European product standards will be decided behind closed doors to the detriment to North American firms. Canadian firms, in contrast, see the SEM as a means of decreasing reliance on the USA by boosting trade flows with Europe (Rugman and Verbeke 1991).

- **Emerging markets**. The lower competitive standards of emerging market product seem to provoke lesser concern, for example, over local content legislation than, say, for Japanese or other advanced nation products. To this extent relationships may be less affected by the advent of the SEM.

- **EFTA**. This 'second-tier' association with the EU seems to have progressively lost its privileged access. Some EFTA members, such as Austria and Finland, have become full members of the Union. Others, however, have voted against this course of action. The changing role and status of the EFTA countries may necessitate a clarification of the relationship between the EU and affiliated European trade agreements.

European Interaction Studies

One of the most valuable contributions to the understanding of firm-level relationships in Europe is that made by the Industrial Marketing and Purchasing (IMP) group. This work, from both interaction and network perspectives, provides the basis for this book. To a significant extent, therefore, contributions are reviewed under each chapter heading. The regional section of this book deals, largely, with specific relationship or network issues in application to a particular region.

A review of the IMP interaction and network studies rightly takes its place in both this Relationship and the following Network section. It should be noted that many of these works rightly form the seminal studies of interaction and networks. Accordingly this review is limited to a few indicative studies. Other seminal contributions from European authors are addressed under the relevant headings throughout the book.

The first main contribution is the Interaction model itself (see Chapter 1). This was jointly developed by pan-European researchers from a research group founded in 1976 and formed the basis of the interaction approach which was subsequently developed in a number of books (Turnbull and Cunningham 1981; Håkansson 1982; Turnbull and Valla 1986).

This approach was initially based on research into European companies. Turnbull and Valla (1986) contrast the marketing strategies for Europe used by firms in different European countries. Separate chapters identify issues in international marketing strategies and relationship development by firms from France, Germany, Sweden and Britain. The chapters have distinct characters, each determined by their analysis of the key issues in the particular country. Some important similarities are, however, identified for relationship development across Europe.

First, the nature and closeness of relationships differs with the market served. For example, relationships between British firms and French customers were seen to be of low economic importance and tended, therefore, to be shorter-lived than those in Germany and Switzerland (Cunningham 1986, p. 227). Johanson and Wootz (1986, p. 125) point to the fact that dependence of German firms is higher in relationships in France than Italy. While German firms are dominant suppliers in the Italian market, they are less so in France. Swedish firms (Håkansson 1986, p. 158) perceive German customers to be more demanding than those in Britain. Accordingly, the German market was seen as more important, although this had not altered the proportion of time and effort managers devoted to building relationships in each country. French firms differed in the relative importance attributed to each market, the perceived risks of operation in each market, assessment of each market's potential and expectations for the future (Valla 1986, p. 72).

Despite these differences, similarities are also seen in relationship-building within Europe. Hallén (1986) analyzes the empirical data across countries to provide a comparison. Relationships are compared and contrasted on the basis of their age, the dependence of the customer and the social distance between the parties:

- **Age of relationships.** One striking difference in terms of age is that British relationships with European counterparts tend to be significantly more recent than do those between firms from the other European markets studied. Hallén suggests that this may be attributable to the traditional British orientation towards building relationships in Commonwealth markets rather than Europe. This is also seen as an explanation why British research has tended to focus more on market entry than market consolidation strategies in Europe.

- **Dependence.** Strong positions in the home market change the 'power dependence relation' with the market served. In this study, 'power dependence relations' is seen to be supplying more than 50 per cent of another's customer needs. Using this measure, Swedish firms are dominant in 55 per cent of French market relationships and 56 per cent of British relationships. In contrast, German firms are stronger in Italy (63 per cent) and Britain (67 per cent), French firms in Italy (57 per cent) and British firms in France (71 per cent) and Germany (63 per cent).

- **Social and cultural distances.** The development of trust is essential to relationship development (see Chapter 1 for a fuller discussion of interaction and relationship perspectives on marketing). Social and cultural distances (chapter 2) may hinder the development of trust. Using a scale from 'close personal relations' to 'formal business relations,' IMP also assesses the extent of these distances within European relationships. Distinct differences become apparent. More than half of German firms' relationships are formal. Formal relations are, however, the exception for British firms. Differences can also be detected in how firms from the same country approach customers in different European markets. Thus, German and Swedish suppliers are more formal in relations with France than with customers from other countries.

This data from relationships with European industrial customers reinforces the importance of the national culture and characteristics of both supplier and customer. It also emphasizes the complexity and engrained nature of differences within Europe in a way that supports critics of European cultural convergence.

Strategic Alliances in Europe

In their analysis of co-operative practices in Europe, Urban and Vendemini (1992) identify three types of co-operation:

- **Adaptation co-operation**, in which the management and effectiveness of an activity are adapted. These strategies may be used to develop market share, gain access to new markets, acquire new technologies or diversify activities.
- **Functional co-operation**, which aims to rationalize the management of functions. Essentially aimed at reducing costs (increasing efficiency rather than effectiveness), this may be achieved by gaining economies of scale or by reducing costs, time or risks.
- **Co-ordination co-operation**, which harmonizes the management of a portfolio of activities to increase effectiveness. This may allow the firm to rationalize its activities, improve the profitability of new technologies or gain access to new sources of finance.

For a sample of German and Italian co-operative relationships, Urban and Vendemini find that adaptation co-operation is the most prevalent in international markets. Despite European convergence, a number of obstacles inhibit the successful operation of intra-Europe co-operative relationships. These include differences in technical standards, differences in managerial culture and linguistic difficulties. The complexity of co-operative relationships is seen to be a function of:

1. **The activity concerned in the co-operation**. The expected result, the number of functions involved, the number of products involved and the number of markets involved all increase complexity.
2. **The macro-environment in which the co-operation is conducted**. Changes in market demand, customer preferences, competitive actions,

substitutes product or service offerings and other stakeholders may increase complexity.
3. **The strengths and weaknesses** of the partners.

THE NETWORK PERSPECTIVE

As with the interaction studies reviewed above, so the 'markets as networks' literature has its roots in the work of European scholars. It should be noted that ongoing contributions in the markets as networks field have broadened in origin, with a rich vein of work emanating now from North America (Iaccobucci 1995; Wilson and Möller 1995) and Australasia (Coviello and Munro 1992; Wilkinson and Young 1999). Including markets as networks under the European section of this book is not intended to lessen the global contribution to this field. It is, however, intended as recognition of the dominant role in development of the network area played by pan-European and, particularly, Nordic network researchers.

Based on their interest in single relationships, IMP researchers began in the mid-1980s, to look at more complex patterns of interaction in networks. Early research (Johanson and Mattsson 1985; Håkansson and Johanson 1988) looks at the role of interaction in the emergence and development of industrial networks and at investment in network position. This work, among others, formed the basis of what has come to be known as the 'markets as networks' literature, which is large and growing. Many of the contributions of European markets as network scholars are presented throughout the book. This section represents a sample of recent contributions to knowledge for illustrative purposes.

Network Evolution

One of the principal characteristics of networks (identified in Chapter 1) is that they are flexible and dynamic. Stability in networks creates clear definition of network positions and long-term, trusting relationships (Mattsson 1989), frequent changes of membership are both time-consuming and costly (Hertz 1992). Nonetheless, 'structuring' in networks may make them akin to organizations, which can become rigid and unresponsive to market changes (Håkansson 1992). A key feature of the network is that new relationships can be formed and, if necessary, old relationships dissolved, so that the network can metamorphose to meet any given market situation.

This metamorphosis is seen in Håkansson and Waluszewski (1997). As demand for environmentally-friendly recycling gained pace in Sweden during the 1990s, recycled fibre was used in new, high quality applications. New actors, such as the German environmental authorities, changed the views of recycled fibre and altered the priorities for the pulp and paper industry. The new attractiveness of the recycling industry brought new players into the network. These included the acquisition by the Swedish SCA of one of the largest British collecting companies, Maybanks. A whole raft of new processors of recycled paper – de-inkers – became involved in the network. Producers of photocopiers, such as Xerox, had to adjust their copiers to cope with the dustier recycled paper. This case illustrates a number of facets of change in networks:

1. Network changes had an impact on **many different types of actors**, including recycling companies, associated technical specialists, end users and other influence groups, such as environmental lobbyists.
2. Networks are '**resource constellations**', (Håkansson and Waluszewski 1997, p. 407). No single actor controls the innovation process. The role of recycled paper is affected by perceptions of it in relation to other resources, such as new paper. Originally, recycled paper was seen as poor quality compared to new paper. When 'environmentally-friendly' became a positive label, recycled paper had advantages for some uses.
3. The changes resulted in **investments in new activities, new relationships and new resource ties**. Before the 1990s, paper collection was the primary activity. With the new popularity of recycled paper, new activities (such as de-inking), new relationships (like those with photocopier firms) and new interdependencies between the actors were created.

4. Investments created '**lock-in' effects**. Although change is ongoing, larger investments are more likely to create stability in relationships and roles in networks.
5. If a number of actors benefit from the change, **adaptation is easier and more likely to be radical**. In this case, the benefits to many existing network actors of the new popularity of recycled paper amplifies the scale of the changes. Håkansson and Waluszewski (1997, p. 408) point to the fact that: 'when a large number of actors change marginally the total effect can be multiplied.' This last finding supports Easton and Araujo's research into the role of nodes in networks (1992). If a change is central it may be absorbed and result in adaptation. If not, it may be transmitted or deflected.

The field of adaptation in networks is one of considerable interest to network scholars in the late 1990s. Research focuses increasingly on networks as dynamic structures. Håkansson (1992) identifies the need for 'heterogeneity', or the ability to find new ways of combining activities and resources. Lundgren (1992) distinguishes between 'co-ordination' or continuous change, and 'mobilization' or discontinuous change to create new resource structures and access routes. Studies of change in networks include Easton, Wilkinson and Georgieva (1997), Håkansson and Waluszewski (1997).

Network Organizations

A second dominant theme in European network studies is that of network organizational structures (Forsgren 1989; Forsgren, Holm and Thilenius 1997; Pahlberg 1997). This literature, reviewed more fully in Chapter 16, focuses on networks of relationships within the organization. Forsgren (1989) suggests that, from a network perspective, multinational corporations are not pyramid structures with a Head Office controlling subsidiaries. Rather, they are 'centre–centre' structures in which international marketing decisions may be made by established international subsidiaries. Network organizations are seen as political

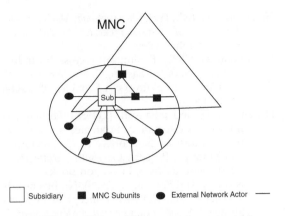

Subsidiary ■ MNC Subunits ● External Network Actor ——

Figure 12.1 The network context of a subsidiary

entities in which individuals may have different agendas, aspirations and associations with others within and outside the organization.

Research by Nordic scholars explores further the question of the interface between the network organization and its context. Forsgren, Holm and Thilenius (1997) question the extent to which the activities of a multinational corporation are linked to the local environment of its subunits (Figure 12.1).

The relationships with other subunits in the firm and external actors are shown in Figure 12.1. In the previous section, Hallén (1986) discusses the fact that different nationality subunits may have different and complex patterns of con-

tact with other firms. Each firm's network context is unique (Håkansson and Snehota 1989). From a network perspective, then, the network organization will operate in a number of different national contexts. Forsgren, Holm and Thilenius (1997, p. 480) conclude that network context is 'unique, changing and incomprehensible to outsiders'.

Recent developments in research into network organization are closer to the dynamic network studies reviewed above. The issue of 'network infusion' has been studied with respect to Swedish multinational corporations. The focus of these studies is the infusion, of product developments, technology or other changes, from subunits to other parts of the organization. In this process, changes in the network surrounding a national subunit may result in organization-wide changes.

To illustrate this phenomenon, British subsidiaries of multinational corporations in the food industry have been affected by the entry into the UK of US retailer Wal Mart. Wal Mart, in acquiring Asda, lowered its prices dramatically. This resulted in price war in the UK, with other retailers, such as Tesco, also dropping its prices. The issue of price harmonization within Europe has risen to the top of the agenda for British subsidiaries. Changes in British prices have to be agreed by Head Office as this impacts on other European markets. Hence the ripples of change have infused from British subunits back to the centre and may then result in changes in other subunits.

SUMMARY

In Chapter 12 we have explored the challenges of operation in Europe. Distinctive types of relationship in the region and their management are explored.

Finally the contributions of network studies in the region are evaluated.

BIBLIOGRAPHY

Appelbaum, U. and Halliburton, C. (1993) 'How to Develop International Advertising Campaigns That Work: The Example of the European Food and Beverage Sector', *International Journal of Advertising*, 12: 223–41.

Bridgewater, S. and Wu, J. (1996) 'Standardization and Adaption of the Marketing Strategies of UK and French Textile Firms', *Working Paper*, Warwick Business School.

Bürgenmeier, B. and Mucchielli, J. L. (eds) (1991) *Multinationals and Europe 1992: Strategies for the Future*, Routledge.

Carr, E. and Texeraud, M. (1993) 'The CIRCLE Approach Applied to Pan-European Product Strategy in the European Food Sector', in Halliburton, C. and Hünerberg, R. (1993), *European Marketing: Readings and Cases*, Addison-Wesley: 177–200.

Cecchini, P. (1988) *1992: The Benefits of the Single Market*, Wildwood House.

Colchester, N. and Buchan, D. (1990) *Europe Relaunched: Truths and Illusions on the Way to 1992*, The Economist Books, Hutchinson.

Cunningham, M. T. (1986) 'The British Approach to Europe', in Turnbull, P. W. and Valla, J.-P. (eds) (1986), *Strategies for International Industrial Marketing*, Routledge: 165–234.

Diamantopoulos, A., Schlegelmilch, B. and Du Preez, J.-P. (1995) 'Lessons for Pan-European Marketing.: The Role of Consumer Preferences in Fine-Tuning the Product-Market Fit', *International Marketing Review*, 12, 2: 38–52.

Domzal, T. and Unger, L. (1987) 'Emerging Positioning Strategies in Global Marketing', *Journal of Consumer Marketing*, 4, 4: 23–40.

Easton, G. and Araujo, L. (1992) 'Non-Economic Exchange in Industrial Networks', in G. Easton and B. Axelsson (eds), *Industrial Networks: A New View of Reality*, Routledge.

Easton, G., Wilkinson, I. and Georgieva, C. (1997) 'Towards Evolutionary Models of Industrial Networks', in Gemünden, H.-G., Ritter, T. and Walter, A. (eds), *Relationships and Networks in International Markets*, Pergamon.

Economist, The (1999) *The World in 1999*.

Egan, C. E. and McKiernan, P. (1994) *Inside Fortress Europe: Strategies for the Single Market*, Addison-Wesley.

Forsgren, M. (1989) *Managing the Internationalisation Process: The Swedish Case*, Routledge.

Forsgren, M., Holm, P. and Thilenius, P. (1997) 'Network Infusion in the Multinational Corporation', in Björkaan, I. and Forsgren, M. (eds), *The Nature of the International Firm*, Copenhagen Business School Press.

Fournis, Y. (1962) 'The Markets of Europe or the European Market?', *Business Horizons*, 5, Winter: 77–83.

Gogel, G. and Larreché, J.-C. (1989) 'The battlefield for 1992', *European Management Journal*, Spring: 132–40.

Guinness (1994) *European Data Book: Facts, Figures, Issues*, Guinness Publishing Ltd.

Håkansson, H. (1986) 'The Swedish Approach to Europe', in Turnbull, P. W. and Valla, J.-P. (eds) (1986), *Strategies for International Industrial Marketing*, Routledge: 127–64.

Håkansson, H. (ed.) (1982) *International Marketing and Purchasing of Industrial Goods: An Interaction Approach*, John Wiley.

Håkansson, H. (1992) 'Evolution Processes in Industrial Networks', in Easton, G. and Axelsson, B. (eds), *Industrial Networks: A New View of Reality*, Routledge.

Håkansson, H. and Johanson, J. (1988) 'Formal and Informal Cooperation Strategies in International Industrial Networks', in Contractor, F. and Lorange, P. (eds), *Cooperative Strategies in International Business*, Lexington Books.

Håkansson, H. and Snehota, I. (1989) 'No Business is an Island: The Network Concept of Business Strategy', *Scandinavian Journal of Management*, 5, 3: 187–200.

Håkansson, H. and Walusewski, A. (1997) 'Recycled Fibre Turning Green', in Gemünden, H.-G., Ritter, T. and Walter, A. (eds), *Relationships and Networks in International Markets*, Pergamon.

Haley, R. I. (1968) 'Benefit Segmentation: A Decision-Oriented Research Tool', *Journal of Marketing*, 32: 30–5.

Hertz, (1992) 'Towards More Integrated Industrial Systems' in Easton, G. and Axelsson, B. (eds), *Industrial Networks: A New View of Reality*, Routledge.

Hallén, L. (1986) 'A Comparison of Strategic Marketing Approaches', in Turnbull, P. W. and Valla, J.-P. (eds) (1986), *Strategies for International Industrial Marketing*, Routledge: 235–49.

Halliburton, C. (1990) 'Mega-Marketing: The European Realities', *European Management Journal*, Autumn: 365–70.

Halliburton, C. and Hünerberg, R. (1993) *European Marketing: Readings and Cases*, Addison-Wesley.

Iaccobucci, D. (ed.) (1995) *Networks in Marketing*, Sage.

Johanson, J. and Mattsson, L.-G. (1985) 'Marketing Investments and Market Investments in Industrial Networks', *International Journal of Research in Marketing*, 2:

Johanson, J. and Wootz, B. (1986) 'The German Approach to Europe', in Turnbull, P. W. and Valla, J.-P. (eds) (1986), *Strategies for International Industrial Marketing*, Routledge: 79–126.

Littler, D. and Schlieper, K. (1995) 'Development of the Eurobrand', *International Marketing Review*, 12, 2: 22–37.

Lundgren, A. (1992) 'Co-ordination and Mobilisation Processes in Industrial Networks', in Easton, G. and Axelsson, B. (eds), *Industrial Networks: A New View of Reality*, Routledge.

Mattsson, L.-G. (1989) 'Developments of Firms in Networks: Positions and Investments', in Cavusgil, S. T. (ed.), *Advances in International Marketing*, 3, JAI Press: 121–39.

Meffert, H. and Bolz, J. (1992) 'Standardisation of Marketing in Europe', in Kumar, N. and Haussman, H. (eds), *Handbuch der Internationaler Unternehmenstätigkeit*, reprinted in Halliburton, C. and Hünerberg, R. (1993) *European Marketing: Readings and Cases*, Addison-Wesley.

Möller, K. and Wilson, D. T. (1995) (eds) *Business Relationships: an interaction perspective*, Kluwer, Boston.

Ohmae, K. (1990) 'Managing in a Borderless World', *Harvard Business Review*, May–June.

Pahlberg, C. (1997) 'Cultural Differences and Problems in HQ-Subsidiary Relationships in MNCs', in Björkan, I. and Forsgren, M. (eds), *The Nature of the International Firm*, Copenhagen Business School Press.

Paitra, J. (1991) 'The Euro-Consumer: Myth or Reality?', *Futuribles*, 150: 25–35, reprinted in Halliburton, C. and Hünerberg, R. (1993) *European Marketing: Readings and Cases*, Addison-Wesley.

Ronkainen, I. (1993) 'Trading Blocs: Opportunity or Demise for Trade?', *Multinational Business Review*, 1, 1: 1–9.

Rugman, A. M. and Verbeke, A. (1991) 'Competitive Strategies for non-European Firms', in Bürgenmeier, B. and Mucchielli, J. L. (eds) (1991), *Multinationals and Europe 1992: Strategies for the Future*, Routledge: 22–35.

Turnbull, P. W. and Cunningham, M. T. (1981) *International Marketing and Purchasing*, Macmillan.

Turnbull, P. W. and Valla, J.-P. (eds) (1986), *Strategies for International Industrial Marketing*, Routledge.

Urban, S. and Vendemini, S. (1992) *European Strategic Alliances: Co-operative Corporate Strategies in the New Europe*, Blackwell Business.

Valla, J.-P. (1986) 'The French Approach to Europe', in Turnbull, P. W. and Valla, J.-P. (eds), *Strategies for International Industrial Marketing*, Routledge: 11–78.

Welford, R. and Prescott, K. (1994) *European Business: An Issue-Based Approach*, 2nd edn, Pitman.

Wistrich, E. (1991) *After 1992: The United States of Europe*, Routledge.

ASIA-PACIFIC

Objectives

The issues to be addressed in Chapter 13 include:

1. The application of concepts from earlier sections of the book to Asia-Pacific
2. Examination of relationships within Asia-Pacific and the impact of the East Asian crisis
3. Review studies of networks in Asia-Pacific to identify distinctive characteristics of network structures in the region.

After reading Chapter 13 you will be able to:

1. Understand the challenges facing international marketers in Asia-Pacific
2. Identify specific types of relationships that play a role in the region
3. Evaluate the contribution of network studies of the region.

INTRODUCTION

Through the 1990s the international community came to expect the continuation of sustained, rapid growth in the developing countries of East Asia. These expectations were shattered by the sudden emergence of financial, economic and even political disruption throughout the region in the second half of 1997. (Garnaut 1998)

T he economic success experienced by South-East Asia in the post-war period after 1945 until the mid-1990s fuelled considerable interest in the region by both marketing theorists and practitioners. A large body of research focused on the difficulties for Western firms in operating successfully in the region. This was variously attributed to high levels of competition between domestic firms in the region, to the sophisticated consumers which this had produced and to perceived tariff and non-tariff barriers (NTBs) to entry. These were a particular focus of attention in Japan.

As a result of its economic success, the 'miracle' in South Asia was much discussed as a model

for others. Since mid-1997, however, 'economic turmoil in the region has placed the achievements of decades in jeopardy' (McLeod and Garnaut 1998). This chapter looks at the literature surrounding the marketing challenges of East Asia prior to the economic crisis, at the causes underlying the crisis and at the future prospects in the region.

Defining the composition of the Asia-Pacific region (map 13.1) is complicated by the uncertain membership of economic groups such as ASEAN (the Association of South-East Asian Nations) and APEC (Asia-Pacific Economic Co-operation). Das (1997) proposes that Asia-Pacific comprises:

- **Japan** – the largest and pivotal Asia-Pacific economy
- **Australia and New Zealand**
- **South Korea, Taiwan, Hong Kong and Singapore** – the 'Little Dragons'
- **Indonesia, Malaysia, Thailand and the Philippines** – the ASEAN four
- **China** – an emerging economy that plays a role as being both large in land mass and having recorded record growth during the 1980s.

Figure 13.1 Asia-Pacific

In this book, China will be treated more fully as an emerging mega-market in Chapter 14. To the extent that it impacts on the fortunes of its neighbours and in cultural similarities in guanxi relationships it will also be discussed in this chapter.

THE TRADITIONAL PERSPECTIVE

Challenges in Asia-Pacific

The sustained and rapid economic growth of East Asia led to its being used as a model of success for other firms and economies. The period after 1945 saw a seemingly inexorable economic growth in Japan and the four 'Little Dragons' of South Korea, Taiwan, Hong Kong and Singapore. In chronicling the economic growth of Japan, Johnson (1982) notes that it:

> is the best example of a state-guided market system currently available; and Japan has itself become a model, in whole or in part, for many other developing or advanced industrial systems.

Nor was he alone in this view. Das (1997, p. 1) highlights the 'changing morphology' of the entire East Asia region with an: 'effervescent economic growth, whose rise can be traced back to the early 1960s when the Japanese economy came into its own.'

Despite the current economic crisis in East Asia, therefore, this chapter begins with a review of the lessons which management theorists proposed should be learned from the success of East Asia. Given the central importance attributed by Das and others to the rise of Japan, the discussion begins with a review of Japanese marketing.

The Japanese Miracle

Throughout the 1960s, Japan's gross domestic product (GDP) grew at more than 10 per cent per annum. Despite the influence of external events, such as the oil crisis in the 1970s, it continued to grow, largely through its export success. The four 'Little Dragons', South Korea, Taiwan, Hong Kong and Singapore grew in its shadow, eventually achieving comparable growth rates. Das (1997) pinpoints how they concentrated energies on economic growth, pragmatic macro-economic policies and rapid industrialisation as contributory factors in the region's upward spiral of success. In sum, the economic success of Japan and the 'Little Dragons' challenged the orthodoxy on economic growth and spawned a new literature on the 'Japanese miracle' (Johnson 1982; Doyle, Saunders and Wong 1992; Johansson and Nonaka 1996).

This literature identifies seven key characteristics which are associated with Japanese marketing, strategy and organizational structures:

1. **Ad hoc strategic decision-making**. While Western firms were associated with traditional, rational planning approaches (Grinyer 1971), Asian firms combined both comprehensive written plans for functional areas such as marketing, finance and operations with ad hoc strategic decision-making (Foo, Grinyer and McKiernan 1992; Foo 1997)

2. **Long-term orientation**. Doyle, Saunders and Wong (1992) contrast the Japanese style of aggressive pursuit of volume in order to build

market share and achieve economies of scale with Western short-term financial objectives.

3. **Challenging the orthodoxy**. Ambler (1995) suggests that Western firms understand some contrasts as trade-offs. For example, quality implies relatively high cost. In contrast, Japanese firms pursued a strategy of quality at low cost by building market share to drive down costs. This is attributed by Ambler to different philosophies underlying business in East and West.

4. *Keiretsu*. The term '*Keiretsu*', meaning 'line of connection' (Melville 1999) is used to describe clusters of Japanese companies around a central bank. While some have criticized these as excluding non-members, the social and business connections provided by the *Keiretsu* are also seen as contributing to the success of Japanese firms. The *Keiretsu* are discussed more fully in the Network section of this chapter.

5. **Quality of products**. Porter (1990) uses the success of Japan in microelectronics to illustrate the fact that demand from sophisticated customers used to high quality fuels ongoing innovation. Melville (1999) suggests, moreover, that the main issue in selling to Japan is raising quality to an acceptable standard. In operations, the Japanese term '*Kaizen*', or 'improvement', has become synonymous with high quality production methods. Similarly, zero-defects, Just-in-Time (JIT) and other feature of the Japanese system have been adopted globally.

6. **Marketing orientation**. Doyle, Saunders and Wong (1992) associate market orientation with the quest by Japanese firms to combine quality and value in their products and services. Japanese organizations are often held up as classic cases of marketing orientation. Johansson and Nonaka (1996) suggest that, paradoxically, this marketing orientation is achieved by being product oriented. Because Japanese firms consider marketing the business of everyone, rather than just the marketing department, engineers, designers, top managers and production employees are all involved in delivering products that customers want.

7. **Hands-on market research**. Johansson and Nonaka (1996) also identify a 'hands-on' approach to market research. They draw parallels with Hamel and Prahalad's suggestion (1994) of 'expeditionary marketing'. According to both of these concepts, customer needs can only be partially understood in the rapidly changing markets of the early twenty-first century. As a result an *iterative process of ongoing improvement* to ensure customer satisfaction is considered as contributory to success.

The East Asian Crisis

As early as 1993, clouds began to appear on the horizon for the boom economies of East Asia:

> The dragons are having to come to term with structural shifts in their economies away from traditional low-cost manufacturing. Policies to deal with higher inflation and other symptoms of overheating have also led to a cyclical slowdown, adding to the sense of despondency. (*The Economist, The World in 1993*).

In the years of sustained growth, the economies of East Asia seemed to have common features. The World Bank (1993) suggests high rates of saving and investment, a strong focus on education, sound macro-economic policy and good economic governance as features of economies as diverse as Korea, Indonesia, Singapore, Malaysia and Thailand. Yet the economic crisis in East Asia has affected some of these countries more radically than others and seems to have made clear the differences rather than the similarities between the countries of East Asia (McLeod and Garnaut 1998).

The initial shock resulted from the raised premium on investment in developing East Asia after Thailand's decoupling from the dollar 'peg'. The differences in the impact of this shock depended on the nature of the political systems, policy responses and financial institutions of the countries concerned. The 'Asian Financial Crisis' to which the world media referred was at that time a misnomer. The financial crisis was principally confined to Indonesia, Korea, Thailand and Malaysia, the countries of South Asia remained relatively unaffected. Through 1998, however, economic contraction and reduction in imports transmitted to other economies in the region.

The vulnerability of the region to widespread economic recession remained apparent:

> The past year was the most miserable that South-East Asia has suffered in a generation. 1999 could be worse; certainly it will be no better. It may be that the financial markets have seen their most panic-stricken days. The runs on regional stock-markets and currencies that began with the devaluation of the Thai baht in July 1997 have given was to what looks almost like stability. But it is like the calm of a city devastated by an air-raid. The rubble keeps piling up even as rebuilding work starts and there is still the fear of unexploded bombs. (*The Economist, The World in 1999*)

Particular fears centred on the stability of Indonesia, which is the biggest country in the region and which straddles trading routes to Japan.

'Post-bubble' East Asia

The title of this section is borrowed from Johansson and Hirano's (1996) article, referring to Japan after the East Asian crisis. While it is easy to believe McLeod and Garnaut's assertion (1998) that East Asia has gone from being a miracle to needing one, this is not universally so. Indeed, despite three to four years of negative news out of Japan, Japanese firms remain among the major global players (Johansson and Nonaka 1996). The general consensus (Johansson and Hirano 1996) seems to be that, while the bubble has burst, Japan will recover as a 'diligent and prosperous economy' (Melville 1999). Chaponnière (1995) suggests that the inaccuracy of the previous optimistic scenarios for the future of Asia preclude too much speculation about the ultimate future of the region.

THE RELATIONSHIP PERSPECTIVE

Relationships Within Asia-Pacific

At the macro-level, relationships exist between different groups of East Asian countries, between East Asia and its neighbour China, between East Asia and Australia and New Zealand and between East Asia and other countries, such as the USA and Canada through the Asia-Pacific Economic Co-operation (APEC) agreement. Some of these relationships are between countries with similar cultural roots, or shared languages. Asia-Pacific, however, is considered my many to be among the most diverse regional groupings in the world.

The rich diversity of Asia-Pacific can be illustrated using a number of indicators, including land mass, population or GDP. In terms of land mass, China alone extends over an area of 9.5 million square kilometres and has a population of over a billion people (Das 1997). Within the region there are also a number of 'micro-states', small nations in terms of land mass that may cover less than 1000 square kilometres and have populations of less than 10 million. Some countries are densely populated and others only sparsely.

Wide disparity is also found in the economic wealth of countries in the region. Japan, the region's largest economy, is an economic superpower. In 1997, Japan had a GDP *per capita* of $38 120, while small economies, such as the Philippines ($1 200 *per capita*) and Indonesia ($1 210 *per capita*) were classed as low-income economies.

The face of Asia-Pacific has changed substantially since 1945. In the early 1960s, Japan's economy was war-ravaged and China was in the middle of a revolution. Australia and New Zealand counted as prosperous, if not advanced, industrial economies. In 2001, Japan plays a dominant role in the region and, indeed, globally, while China is emerging as an economic giant. The World Bank predicts that China will in fact become the world's largest economy in the early years of the twenty-first century (Kelley and Luo 1999). In the 1990s, China became the largest exporter to the USA in 11 different product groups. Its progress is significantly linked with investments from the USA, but also from Hong Kong, Taiwan and Japan. Despite this progress, China is still viewed by some as the 'true wild card in Asia's still developing economic picture' (Henderson 1999).

This reorientation of roles in Asia-Pacific alters the political and economic landscape. At the macro-level, relationships alter. Despite predictions of a 'cautious relationship' between Australia and Asia on the election of John Howard as prime minister, Foreign Minister Alexander Downer emphasized that relations with Asia were the highest foreign policy priority. A significant proportion of relationship literature from Australia and New Zealand now focuses on building relationships with firms in East Asia (see among others Barrett and Fletcher 1999; Fu *et al.* 1999; Kriz, Purchase and Ward 1999; Purchase and Ward 1999).

Relationships in Asia-Pacific

Research tends to see relationships between Western firms and those in East Asia as problematic. Lasserre and Probert (1994) suggest that this may be a case of accepting high risks to gain high returns. Often these risks are ascribed to the significant cultural differences which may exist between partners from East and West (Tung 1991; Tse, Francis and Walls 1994; Hofstede 1997). Indeed, respect for cultural differences and knowledge of the culture and language of the partner are cited among key success criteria for negotiating success with Korean partners.

Clearly, as there are many distinctions in size and economy, so are there many cultural differences within the region. Some point to the similarities in underlying Confucian philosophy as a binding force in East Asia. Others, however, suggest that this is more prevalent in North-East than South-East Asia. Others note similarities between Sinic societies – China, Japan and Korea (Das 1997). Tung (1991), however, suggests that Korea may be culturally more different to US managers than Japan or China. The limitations of studying culture as a national phenomenon should be noted (see Chapter 2). To study relationships, cultural distance may best be studied at the personal rather than aggregate level. Managers' perceptions may vary considerably with individual experiences and education.

Nonetheless, this Relationship section begins by highlighting some of the characteristics commonly associated with East Asia. Given the importance of understanding East Asia for both Western and other Asia-Pacific countries, such as Australia and New Zealand, it is hoped that reviewing these

may offer initial insights into some of the challenges of building relationships within and with partners outside the region. Research emphasizes the relative importance of personal and corporate relationships in the Asian business environment. While Guanxi is typically identified as a Chinese phenomenon (see Ambler 1995, Chapter 3), Guanxi influences extend more broadly within the East Asian region.

A significant proportion of interaction and relationship literature is written, however, from a Western perspective. As such, it may be biased by Western assumptions. The aims of the IMP2 project (Fu *et al.* 1999) acknowledge this bias in a significant proportion of relationship literature. The IMP2 project and a growing body of work looking at Guanxi and other types of Eastern relationships attempts to redress the balance.

The role played by relationships in Asian businesses is, if anything, more significant that in Western societies. In contrast with Western businesses which tend to focus on relationships between an individual business and customer, in Asia, a more complex web of relationships may be involved. Fu *et al.* (1999) suggest that these are, perhaps, more fundamental to business development:

> in Asian cultures, relationships – and especially their social dimensions – are viewed often as a prerequisite to doing business, compared with the 'Western' model.

This view is supported by research into the business methods of different Asian societies (Redding 1990). Comparative research between firms in the East and West (Merrilees and Miller 1999) affirms the greater importance of relationships in business in the East, and Kriz, Purchase and Ward (1999) suggest that these relationships may tend to be interpersonal than between organizations.

Given the importance of relationships to doing business in Asia, this section begins with a consideration of relationship development and management in East Asia. The following section on networks builds on this to develop Kriz, Purchase and Ward's contention (1999) that networks provide a richer understanding of relationship impact on business in the region.

The Role of Relationships in Asian Societies

The central importance of relationships in Asia is related to cultural values in the region:

1. **Confucian religion**. This is often associated with a long-term orientation, patience and tolerance. Das (1997) suggests that thriftiness and personal discipline are important features of Confucianism. Ambler (1995) also suggests the idea that there is a greater tolerance of opposites (yin–yang) as being complementary (e.g. sweet and sour) rather than mutually exclusive as in Western cultures (good versus evil, black or white).

2. **Collectivism**. Hofstede (1994) differentiates between societies with *individual* and those with *collective* values. Asian countries are collective: an individual may subordinate his or her interests for the good of the group. As a result, social cohesion may be high.

3. **Ethnic and religious differences**. In contrast to the social cohesion predicted by collectivism, however, tensions may exist as a result of ethnic and religious differences within the region. While Japan, Korea and Taiwan are ethnically homogeneous, Malaysia, Indonesia, Singapore and Hong Kong are multi-racial and multi-cultural.

4. **Intense respect for bureacracy and officialdom**. Das (1997) associates this particularly with Sinic countries, Japan, Korea and China.

5. **Guanxi** (indebted personal relationships). The importance of 'kin' or other social relationships extends into business. The network section of Chapter 2 discusses Guanxi more fully. Luo (1997) offers a number of characteristics of guanxi, which are used here as a reprise of the discussion in Chapter 2. Guanxi is:

- **Transferable**. If one actor has Guanxi with another than it can introduce or recommend a friend to its partner.
- **Reciprocal**. A person who does not return a favour loses face (*mianzi*) and is thereafter seen as untrustworthy.
- **Intangible**. This is largely an unspoken commitment. The code by which actors are bound is invisible and unwritten.
- **Utilitarian** not emotional. This is an exchange of favours rather than a sentimental bond.
- **Interpersonal** rather than organizational.
- **Social**. Guanxi is based on social connections although its influence extends into the business community. To this extent, Guanxi may also govern economic and other exchanges.

Some authors argue that the values underlying Guanxi are prevalent not just in China but extend more broadly throughout East Asia. Caulkin (1996) identifies a number of characteristics of the startling growth experienced in East Asia prior to the late 1990s crisis as having their origins in China and in Chinese family businesses:

- Dynamic family-owned firms
- Driven to succeed by economic hardship
- Thrifty, self-reliant individuals
- Emigration of ethnic Chinese throughout the region
- Dense webs of relationships between families, clans or groups linked by village or language loyalties.

Guanxi values may influence the process of relationship development in East Asia. Leung, Wong and Tam (1995) apply the interaction model (see Chapter 1) of process, parties, environment and atmosphere to markets governed by Guanxi. Studying relationships between Hong Kong and China, they identify a revised framework for relationship development. Their research first identifies three factors which are important in these relationships: relationship-building, mutual expectation and information exchange.

Relationship-building, in the view of Leung, Wong and Tam, requires guanxi activities. An 'outsider', who does not have access to these connections, will find it difficult to gain access to information or otherwise build relationships. Only by becoming an 'insider' can this be gained. This can be achieved by a process, which Leung, Wong and Tam describe as:

- **Availability**. Identifying appropriate relationships.

- **Association**. Learning how to build these relationships.
- **Acceptance**. Relationship-building may result in acceptance.
- **Affordability**. This process involves time and resources. Leung, Wong and Tam (1995) suggest intermediary stages of affirmation and assurance that the relationship will succeed. These seem similar to relationship marketing's increasing relationship closeness as customers become advocates (Christopher, Payne and Ballantyne 1991).
- **Adaptation**. The final stage, as with the interaction model, is mutual commitment of the relationship partners, although this may have been achieved through a different process.

In other parts of Asia, relationship development has similar features. Purchase and Ward (1999), studying relationships between Australian and Thai partners, conclude that a firm might overcome the outsider role if they could identify an appropriate network catalyst. These catalysts might include regulatory agencies, such as the Asian Development Bank, actors in each country's government or the actions of another network member. The importance of networks of actors in this research is such that it is reviewed more fully in the Network section of this chapter.

Cross-Cultural Adjustment

An interesting topic, which perhaps arises within the East–West relationship literature from predicted cultural obstacles to relationship-building, is that of how managers of firms may adjust to different cultures (Black and Gregersen 1991). One relevant concept is that of 'anticipatory adjustment'. In this case, managers who are about to enter a new international relationship or expatriate posting may make adjustments to the new culture in anticipation.

Research proposes a set of variables that may positively influence cultural adjustment:

- **Previous international work experience**. This may help managers know what to expect.

- **Pre-departure training**. This provides information about both the assignment and the culture of the relationship partner.
- **Length of time in the host country**. There may be a brief 'honeymoon period' when the new international challenge is exciting. Once this has passed, building cultural understanding is largely a function of time and exposure.
- **Role discretion**. If the individual is allowed discretion by Head Office or other managers, then they have the flexibility to adapt then role and how it should be achieved to cultural specifics. Building successful relationships in East Asia might, for example, require building Guanxi connections which were not anticipated at the outset.

THE NETWORK PERSPECTIVE

In many of the situations discussed above, success does not mean building single, but multiple, relationships. The importance of interpersonal relationships in business in the region suggests that successful international marketing may require firms to build positions in complex webs of relationships.

Guanxi Networks

Professor Gordon Redding of Hong Kong University Business School emphasizes the fact that Guanxi is a not just a Chinese phenomenon, but extends more widely throughout the Asia-Pacific region:

> China is the classic example but the networks also cross national boundaries, providing contacts, sources of finance and influence all over Asia. (Caulkin 1996, p. 62).

Guanxi connections play a role in entering networks through East Asia. Purchase and Ward (1999) analyze the entry of Australian firms into Thai networks. Access to the network is facilitated by 'catalyst' firms. These catalyst firms might be internal to the Thai network; alternatively they might be an external firm in government or regulatory sector that already has connections in the

Thai network. In the first of these cases, access into the Thai network is facilitated by a firm which is already connected into the guanxi network. In the second, a third party at macro-level with existing network links acts as a bridge into the guanxi network.

Purchase and Ward also use the actor–activity–resource model (Håkansson and Johanson 1992; Håkansson and Snehota 1995) to analyze the way in which lasting bonds or relationships are developed in the Thai network. Bonds between actors may form as a result of links through activities or resources. The network in this case involves Australian engineering firms, and activities form the starting point for relationship development. Australian engineering firms engaged in activities that proved their technical competence before bonds were formed. It may be assumed that the important role of data collection and transfer activities in Thai networks are that these provide an opportunity for firms to engage in social exchanges and develop trust. The concept of 'network catalyst' reinforces that played by indirect relationships in networks.

An applications of Western network models to Eastern market is undertaken by the subsequent work by Kriz, Purchase and Ward (1999). The focus is broadened from networks in Thailand to networks throughout China, Hong Kong, Taiwan and other Chinese-influenced societies such as Thailand, Singapore and Malaysia. Japan and Korea are excluded on the basis that these are said more to follow Western business behaviour.

A first insight into these networks is gained from the reminder that relationships tend to be individual. These may be based on kin, friends, regions or referrals (Numazaki 1996). Björkman and Kock (1995) point to the importance of personal network connections in Chinese business. Some have argued that since the industrial revolution Western societies have moved away from interpersonal networks (Sheth and Parvatiyar 1995). Similarly, interpersonal networks have taken on a greater importance in emerging Eastern European economies where business structures are transient (Bridgewater 1999) (see Chapter 14 for a fuller discussion of networks in emerging mega-markets).

The question arises, therefore, of whether these guanxi networks will persist as firms globalize.

Kriz, Purchase and Ward (1999) suggest that relationships play a much stronger role in Asian than in Western societies. Their roots in cultural values suggest that they will do so. They may, however, evolve and metamorphose as do networks in all markets.

Keiretsu

From the early 1900s, Japan developed diversified holding companies known as *zaibatsu*. These were disdained by some, as trade was seen as lower status than military and other occupations. *Zaibatsu* tended to be based on single-family ownership (Melville 1999). As firms grew, the single-company *zaibatsu* could not provide enough finance and the structures began to break down. In the late 1940s, the *zaibatsu* were dissolved, although the tendency towards co-operative business structures remained.

Business conglomerates were formed in the 1950s and 1960s. These were now known as *Keiretsu*. These have been defined (Melville 1999, p. 11) as:

> sets of relationships between companies, loosely bound together by a continuation of both business and social obligations, as well as a desire to prosper by combining resources.

Literally, *Keiretsu* means 'line' or 'connection'. *Keiretsu* may involve supply chain links or affiliations between companies in different sectors. These are known, respectively, as *horizontal* and *vertical Keiretsu*:

■ **Horizontal** *keiretsu* are similar to diversified conglomerates although the firms are not bound together in one organization. Instead, they choose to operate as a cluster, or clan (see Chapter 7). *Keiretsu* structures involve the development of long-term co-operative relationships (Johansson and Nonaka 1996). There are many horizontal *Keiretsu*, large and small, but Melville (1999) contends that six, large bank-centred groups are the principal players. Both business and social relationships may develop. While economic transactions may happen predominantly within the *Keiretsu*, it is not exclusively so.

■ **Vertical keiretsu** are described as pyramid structures with one firm (either supplier or distributor at the top, depending on whether this is an upstream or downstream *Keiretsu*). At each level there are a greater number of smaller firms.

Keiretsu have been heralded as providing a number of benefits:

■ **Stability and structure**. *Keiretsu* relationships tend to be long-term and network composition stable.
■ **External access to resources**. Firms can overcome resource scarcity by accessing resources through *Keiretsu* partners.
■ **Flexibility**. *Keiretsu*, as is true of other network structures, may be appropriate in rapidly changing markets.
■ **Cost-benefits**. Individual organizations operating in *Keiretsu* structures may succeed with leaner structures than competitors.
■ **Resilience**. Together with flexibility and lean structures, the possibility of mobilizing pertinent ties to gain access to resources externally may give *Keiretsu* the ability to withstand difficult market conditions. Articles in the press

currently give considerable attention to the notion that the East Asian Crisis resulted in the breakdown of the *Keiretsu*. Evidence suggests that some partnerships are loosening, but others remain strong (Lincoln, Ahmadjian and Mason 1998).

Conversely, a number of criticisms have been levelled at *Keiretsu*:

■ **Opacity**. From the outside, *Keiretsu* structures may be difficult to understand.
■ **Closed markets**. A frequent criticism is that *Keiretsu* block entry into Japan by non-members (Lincoln, Ahmadijan and Mason 1998; Melville 1999).
■ **Globalization**. As firms become larger and more global, local suppliers and relationships may be required, which the *Keiretsu* do not provide.
■ **Cosy networks**. *Keiretsu* are seen by some as unable to withstand the East Asian Crisis, heightened global competition and the spiralling pace of technogical change. Whether *Keiretsu* are dissolving, trade in Japan certainly now happens outside, as well as inside *Keiretsu* (Melville 1999).

SUMMARY

In Chapter 13 we have explored the challenges of operation in Asia-Pacific. Distinctive types of relationship in the region and their management are explored. Finally the contributions of network studies in the region are evaluated.

BIBLIOGRAPHY

Ambler, T. (1995) 'Reflections on China: Re-orienting Images of Marketing', *Marketing Management*, 4, 1 23–30.

Ambler, T. and Styles, C. (1999) 'The Effect of Channel Relationships and Guanxi on the Performance of Inter-Province Export Ventures in the People's Republic of China', *International Journal of Research in Marketing*, 16, 1: 75–87.

Björkman, I. and Kock, S. (1995) 'Social Relationships and Business Networks: The Case of Western

Companies in China', *International Business Review*, 4: 519–35.

Black, J. S. and Gregersen, H. B. (1991) 'Antecedents to Cross-Cultural Adjustment for Expatriates in Pacific Rim Assignments', *Human Relations*, 44, 5: 497–515.

Bridgewater, S. (1999) 'Networks and Internationalisation: The Case of Multinational Corporations Entering Ukraine', *International Business Review*, 8: 99–118.

Caulkin, S. (1996) 'Chinese Walls', *Management Today*, September: 62–8.

Chaponnière, J. R. and Lautier, M. (1995) 'Breaking into the Korean Market: Invest or Licence?', *Long Range Planning*, 28, 1: 104–12.

Christopher, M., Payne, A. and Ballantyne, D. (1991) *Relationship Marketing*, Butterworth–Heinemann.

Das, D. K. (1997) 'The Changing Morphology of the Asia-Pacific Region', in de Bettignies, H.-C. (ed.), *The Changing Business Environment in the Asia-Pacific Region*, International Thompson Business Press.

Davies, H. J., Leung, T. K. P., Luk, S. K. and Wong, Y. (1992) 'The Benefits of Guanxi: The Value of Relationships in Developing the Chinese Market', *Industrial Marketing Management*, 24: 207–14.

Davis, H. J. and Schulte, W. D., Jr. (ed.) (1997) *National Culture and International Management in East Asia*, International Thompson Business Press.

de Bettignies, H.-C. (ed.) (1997) *The Changing Business Environment in the Asia-Pacific Region*, International Thompson Business Press.

Doyle, P., Saunders, J. and Wong, V. W. (1992) 'Competition in Global Markets: A Case Study of American and Japanese Competition in the British Market', *Journal of International Business Studies*, 23, 3: 419–43.

Economist, The (1993) The World in 1993.

Economist, The (1999) The World in 1999.

Fletcher, R. and Bohn, J. (1998) 'The Impact of Psychic Distance on the Internationalisation of the Australian Firm', *Journal of Global Marketing*, 12, 2: 47–68.

Foo, C. T. (1997) 'The Rationale for Strategic Planning in the Asia-Pacific Region: Implications for European Corporations', in de Bettignies, H.-C. (ed.), *The Changing Business Environment in the Asia-Pacific Region*, International Thompson Business Press.

Foo, C. T., Grinyer, P. H. and McKiernan, P. (1992) 'Strategic Planning in the ASEAN Region', *Long Range Planning*, 25, 5: 8–92.

Fu, H., Spencer, R., Wilkinson, I. and Young, L. (1999) 'The Recent Evolution of Business Networks in China: Two Case Studies', *EMAC Proceedings*, Berlin.

Garnaut, R. (1998) 'The East Asian Crisis', in McLeod, R. H. and Garnaut, R. (eds), *East Asia in Crisis: From Being a Miracle to Needing One?*, Routledge 3–30.

Grinyer, P. (1971) 'The Anatomy of Business Strategic Planning Reconsidered', *Journal of Management Studies*, 8, 2: 339–50.

Håkansson, H. and Johanson, J. (1992) 'A Model of Industrial Networks', in Easton, G. and Axelsson, B. (eds), *Industrial Networks: A New View of Reality*, Routledge.

Håkansson, H. and Snehota, I. (eds) (1995) *Developing Relationships in Business Networks*, Routledge.

Hamel, G. and Prahalad, C. K. (1994) *Competing for the Future*, Harvard Business School Press.

Henderson, C. (1999) *China on the Brink: The Myths and Realities of the World's Largest Market*, McGraw-Hill.

Hofstede, G. (1994) *Cultures and Organizations: Intercultural Co-operation and its Importance for Survival*, HarperCollins.

Hofstede, H. (1997) 'Foreword', in Davis, H. J. and Schulte, W. D., Jr. (ed.) (1997), *National Culture and International Management in East Asia*, International Thompson Business Press: xiv–xxiii.

Horiuchi, A. (1998) 'Japan', in McLeod, R. H. and Garnaut, R. (eds) (1998), *East Asia in Crisis: From Being a Miracle to Needing One*, Routledge.

Johansson, J. and Hirano, M. (1996) 'Japanese Marketing in the Post Bubble Era', *International Executive*, January–February: 33–51.

Johansson, J. and Nonaka, I. (1996) *Relentless: The Japanese Way of Marketing*, Butterworth–Heinemann.

Johnson, C. (1982) *MITI and the Japanese Miracle: The Growth of Industrial Policy 1925–1975*, Stanford University Press.

Jomo, K. S. (ed.) (1998) *Tigers in Trouble: Financial Governance, Liberalisation and Crises in East Asia*, Hong Kong University Press.

Kelley, L. and Luo, Y. (1999) *China 2000*, Sage International Business Series.

Kriz, A., Purchase, S. and Ward, T. (1999) 'Relationships and Networks: The Double Helix of Asian Business Practice', *Proceedings of the IMP Conference*, University College, Dublin.

Lasserre, P. and Probert, J. (1994) 'Competing on the Pacific Rim: High Risks and High Returns', *Long Range Planning*, 27, 2: 12–35.

Leung, T. K. P., Wong, Y. H. and Tam, J. M. (1995) 'Adaptation and the Relationship Building Process in the People's Republic of China', *Journal of International Consumer Marketing*, 8, 2: 7–26.

Lincoln, J. R., Ahmadjian, C. L. and Mason, E. (1998) 'Organizational Learning and Purchase-Supply Relations in Japan', *California Management Review*, 40, 3: 241–64.

Luo, Y. (1997) 'Guanxi: Principles, Philosophies and Implications', *Human Systems Management*, 16: 43–51.

McLeod, R. H. (1998) 'The East Asian Crisis', in McLeod, R. H. and Garnaut, R. (eds) (1998), *East Asia in Crisis: From Being a Miracle to Needing One*, Routledge.

McLeod, R. H. and Garnaut, R. (eds) (1998). *East Asia in Crisis: From Being a Miracle to Needing One*, Routledge.

Melville, I. (1999) *Marketing in Japan*, Butterworth–Heinemann.

Merrilees, B. and Miller, D. (1999) 'Direct Selling in the West and East: The Relative Roles of Product and Relationship (Guanxi) Drivers', *Journal of Business Research*, 45, 3: 267–73.

Numazaki, I. (1996) 'The Role of Personal Networks in the Making of Taiwan's *Guanxiqiye*', in G. G. Hamilton (ed.), *Asian Business Networks*, De Gruyter.

Porter, M. E. (1990) *Competitive Advantage of Nations*, Macmillan.

Purchase, S. and Ward, T. (1999) 'Exploratory Research into the Internationalisation Path of Technical Consultancies Embedded within an Industrial Network Approach', *EMAC Proceedings*, Berlin.

Sheth, J. N. and Parvatiyar, A. (1995) 'The Evolution of Relationship Marketing', *International Business Review*, 4, 4: 397–418.

Tse, D. K., Francis, J. and Walls, J. (1994) 'Cultural Differences in Conducting Intra- and Inter-Cultural Negotiations: A Sino-Canadian Comparison', *Journal of International Business Studies*, 25, 3: 537–55.

Tung, R. L. (1991) 'Handshakes across the Sea: Cross-Cultural Negotiating for Business Success', *Organizational Dynamics*, 19, 3: 30–40.

Whittaker, D. H. (1997) *Small Firms in the Japanese Economy*, Cambridge University Press.

World Bank (1993) *The East Asian Miracle*, Oxford, Oxford University Press.

EMERGING MEGA-MARKETS

Objectives

The issues to be addressed in Chapter 14 include:

1. The application of concepts from earlier sections of the book to Emerging Markets
2. Examination of relationships within Emerging Markets and the impact of the turbulent conditions
3. Review studies of networks in Emerging Markets to identify distinctive characteristics of network structures in the region.

After reading Chapter 14 you will be able to:

1. Understand the challenges facing international marketers in Emerging Markets
2. Identify specific types of relationships that play a role in the region
3. Evaluate the contribution of network studies of the region.

INTRODUCTION

Gaining significant market share in the growth regions of the Triad – the Americas, Europe and Asia-Pacific (discussed in Chapters 11, 12 and 13 respectively) – is complicated by intense competition in these markets between a small number of strong, global players. In the 1980s and 1990s, international marketers have become increasingly attracted to emerging markets, which have some of the fastest growing GDPs in the world. In addition, some emerging markets, such as China, India and Russia have some of the largest populations in the world. Given their strategic importance, these emerging mega-markets are attracting interest from both academics and practitioners. This interest has been fuelled by the liberalization of East and Central Europe (CEE) and by market reforms in China.

The international marketing challenges of these countries differ in a number of respects from those of mature, industrialized economies. Market potential is high, but this may be realized only in the long term. In the short term, international entrants face high levels of uncertainty and turbulent market conditions.

The Relationship section of this chapter discusses the reasons underlying the growth of joint ventures and strategic alliances as a mode of entry into the region. The Network perspective discusses the implications for entrants of loose structured, emerging market networks.

THE TRADITIONAL PERSPECTIVE

Definitions

In the late 1980s and early 1990s the phenomenon of emerging markets rose to prominence. Emerging markets, such as China, which had the fastest growing, and India, the second fastest growing, GDP in the world, represented attractive investment opportunities. These were particularly important to multinational corporations in mature industry sectors, as they represented the last markets left to contest.

During the 1980s and 1990s, interest in emerging markets was fuelled by the liberalization of East and Central Europe and by market reforms in China. The pace of transition to the market economy in these liberalized countries has varied, as has the level of success with which reform has been

Map 14.1   Emerging and mega-markets

implemented. Some critics argue that economies in transition from central planning cannot be called 'markets' and prefer to call them 'transitional economies' (TEs) or 'newly industrializing countries' (NICs) rather than emerging markets. This chapter focuses on a range of countries in the process of rapid change or 'emergence' into free markets. These include the transitional economies of East and Central Europe and the emerging 'mega markets' of Russia, China and India (Map 14.1).

Market Data

With a population of 1.2 billion people in China, just under a billion in India and around 200 million in Russia, the attraction for international marketers of these three mega-markets alone is apparent. Add to that the fact that China and India have the world's fastest GDP rates and that these markets, which as one commentator expresses it 'are short of absolutely everything', and the market opportunities in emerging markets are easy to identify.

Yet, despite this potential, the rapidity of change, the uncertainty of the transition process in previously centrally planned economies such as East and Central Europe and China poses significant risks to international marketers wishing to capitalize on these opportunities.

Opportunity and Risk in Emerging Markets

After the liberalization of East and Central Europe, the CEE economies of Hungary, the Czech and Slovak Republics and Poland moved most rapidly through the process of privatization and reform to a market economy. Not surprisingly, therefore, these were seen as offering good opportunities at moderate levels of risk. Accordingly they became the first investment targets in the region for many international marketers.

In terms of population size, however, these CEE markets are much smaller than countries further East (the Czech Republic and Hungary have population sizes of around 10 million people compared to 200 million in Russia). In some cases, they were used as a gateway to the larger, and therefore more attractive, Eastern European countries, who were less far through the process of market reform.

In press announcements of its expansion strategy for East and Central Europe, the Seagram Company Ltd (1992, 1994) described it as expansion eastwards (Box 14.1).

Together with a growth in population size towards the East of the CEE region, firms are also likely to encounter greater levels of political and economic uncertainty. The GDP *per capita*

Box 14.1   Seagram's Strategy in the CEE Countries

'This summer, after considerable ground work earlier in the year, affiliates were established in Hungary and Czechoslovakia. In population terms, these two markets are relatively small, with 10 million people each. However, both are adapting fast to western commercial business methods, with people increasingly familiar with the workings of a market economy. Seagram's strategy is to use these markets as a bridgehead into Central and Eastern Europe, as they are ideal for developing, testing and refining propositions for the total region...the next stage is to enter the Ukraine...Using the experience gained in the Ukraine market, Seagram's will then expand its operations in Russia, a market three times the size with a population of 150 million.

Source: Seagrams Press Announcement (1992).

---

figures for the countries show that, despite teething problems on the road to a market economy, the Czech, Hungarian and Polish economies have far better GDP and GDP *per capita* levels and growth than do either Ukraine or Russia. These three countries belong in the 'leading pack' (see Table 12.2) moving towards integration into the EU, while the countries less advanced in the

---

Box 14.2   Ins and Pre-Ins in Eastern Europe

A growing distinction can be seen between the 'leading pack' of five countries in the East and Central European (CEE) region – the Czech Republic, Hungary, Poland, Slovenia and Estonia – and the rest of the region. The leading five economies will eventually be accepted 'in' the EU, although agreeing the terms of entry may be a long and complex process. *The Economist* (*The World in 1999*) describes the resulting division of the region as a new curtain:

> the curtain will not be as rigid as the old one of iron. It may, howzever, seem almost as cruel. Unlike the old one, it does not run along the region's western borders, but down its middle; and it divides more by economic performance than political ideology.

Of the 'in' countries, Poland is now tipped as the 'one to watch':

> By far the biggest market for foreign investors in the region, it has also become the most dynamic. It recently overtook Hungary as the recipient of the most foreign investment in the region, and will continue to pull ahead of its neighbours as its economy motors on.

The prospects for the region's laggards, referred to by the EU as 'pre-ins' looks considerably bleaker. At one time, Ukraine was tipped as the country most likely to proceed successfully to a market economy. In December 1991, in a popular referendum, the people of Ukraine voted to become an independent state. Amid the general euphoria, the people of Ukraine looked forward to a prosperous future as a nation-state trading in the world market. Yet, despite this initial optimism, the legacy of a repressive political system and the web of infrastructural and trade links between Ukraine and the former Soviet Republics has proved difficult to disentangle. *The Economist* survey of Ukraine (May 1994) commented:

> Ukraine floated to independence on a cloud of illusions...With 52 million people, it was bigger than all the rest [of the former Soviet States] bar Russia. It had stronger hopes of quickly establishing ties with the rest of Europe than, say Kazakhstan. And it had inherited a disproportionate amount of the former Soviet Union's industry...Thus one big illusion: that Ukraine is a wealthy place. Two and a half years later, a majority of Ukrainians have still not come to terms with the fact that most of their Soviet-era dinosaurs are a liability, not a legacy.

Now Ukraine, Russia, Romania and other 'pre-ins' remain mired in the legacy of the Soviet past, while the 'ins' move forwards to a more prosperous future.

Sources: Valencia, M. (1999) 'Eastern Europe's Sad Duet', *The Economist, The World in 1999*; *The Economist*, (1994) 'Survey of Ukraine', May.

transition process still battle with the legacy of central planning (Box 14.2).

The issues faced in China and India are similarly complex, although different in nature. The 1980s and 1990s in China witnessed a series of market reforms under Deng Xiaoping. These brought market reform, although unlike East and Central Europe, these took place under the control of the Communist government. The death of Deng Xiaoping in February 1997 however, resulted in greater uncertainty about the country's political and economic prospects. President Jiang Zemin faces the twin problems of avoiding the economic crisis sweeping through South-East Asia and implementing the difficult process of sweeping lay-offs in state industry sectors (Box 14.3).

Despite shaky coalition governments in India, economic growth continues at a stable 6 per cent. There is a consensus between the parties that economic reform should continue. Given the economic problems in South-East Asia and Latin America, this suffices to make India the second fastest growing country in the world after China. It is both this growth and the population size of China and India which creates so much interest around these 'mega-markets'. With a combined population of almost 2.4 billion people, Russia, China and India are sufficiently large in population terms to be attractive to international marketers, despite the challenges which they pose. A *Financial Times* study of retailers entering Russia

states (12 October, 1992) stated that: 'The prospect of converting 400 million eager consumers into loyal shoppers is encouraging many retailers to invest in the region.'

Challenges

Few could have anticipated the speed with which the Iron Curtain would be raised in 1989, after more than 40 years of totalitarian domination of East and Central Europe. The liberalization of East and Central Europe, ongoing market reforms in the 1980s and 1990s under Deng Xiaoping in China and the emergence of a growing middle class in India presented hitherto undreamed-of opportunities for international marketers. The market potential of these 'mega-markets' in terms of population size is immense, and in the 1990s issues of entry into Russia, China and India rose to the top of the strategic agenda for both firms and academics.

As explained above, however, these markets are also very uncertain. The principal difficulty is the turbulent political and economic environment. The climate of *discontinuous change* which has characterized the international climate since the mid-1970s, is intense in all of these mega-markets as they move through the tortuous process of transition to global market economies.

Four key challenges face international marketers in mega-markets.

Box 14.3   China's Difficult Choices

The process of transition to market economy has reached a critical phase in China. China needs to stimulate its economy to provide jobs for the growing numbers of unemployed. Difficult choices lie ahead. In introducing much-needed reforms to the Chinese banking system, the government needs to call in the loans which are keeping loss-making state enterprises afloat. The 1998 economic growth rate of 8 per cent was just enough sufficient to prevent unemployment from becoming a social problem. There have been a number of isolated strikes, demonstrations and sit-ins, which may be exacerbated by planned lay-offs in a number of state

industries. In addition, the reform process in China is taking place against a backdrop of economic crisis among is neighbours. China's banks 'are as plagued with bad debt and political interference as many of their counterparts elsewhere in Asia. More than 20 per cent of loans are estimated to be unrecoverable', (*The Economist, The World in 1999*).

Any crisis in public confidence might bring a collapse of the precarious Chinese financial system.

Source: 'China's Communism, 50 years on', *The Economist, The World in 1999*.

The Legacy of Central Planning

The Communist regimes of China and the Former Soviet Union (FSU) operated centrally planned economies. From 1959 onwards in the former Soviet Union, COMECON (the Commission for Mutual Economic Aid) laid out a series of five-year plans decreeing which goods would be made, in what quantity and where in the Soviet Union. In order to achieve this, monopolistic supply and specialization of production by country and by region within the Soviet Union was encouraged. Ukraine had a significant proportion of the oil refining, chemical and nuclear power industries, while Hungary had a significant proportion of the motor industry production facilities for buses and vans, for example.

However, the centrally planned system largely failed in terms of efficiency and living standards. Even prior to the demise of the Soviet Union the socialist system within the region was foundering. This has been attributed to external factors such as the loss of trade with the liberalized Central European countries in 1989 and to industrial unrest in the region and the forced shutdown of plants for environmental reasons. Its seems likely that central planning also failed because of continued underinvestment in new technologies and because it subsidized poor quality products and inefficient plants which would not have survived in a market economy.

Privatization

A number of different models and processes of transition to a market economy can be seen. Within East and Central Europe and China the absence of a free market economy poses distinctive problems. It is not regeneration, but building of an infrastructure from grass roots level, which is required. Economic advisors fear that funding alone will not overcome the problems associated with adopting new technologies or developing an entrepreneurial spirit. Indeed, given the budget deficits which exist in many former COMECON countries, it has been argued that 'the outside world should give no financial aid, but should be generous in providing technical assistance and training' (Åslund 1991). In China, economic reform is taking place under the existing political system, whereas in East and Central Europe political changes may favour more radical economic reform.

One of the main challenges for the reform process is to create a *corporate governance structure* where none previously existed. As the government previously controlled firms, the 1990s in East and Central Europe brought a debate over appropriate management structures and models of privatization:

> The task of privatisation is to construct...a corporate governance structure and institute it in an environment in which there is a pronounced lack of available personnel and a potentially unfavourable political structure. (Frydman and Rapaczynski 1991)

The current changes to state-owned enterprises in China may well herald increased privatization.

Political Turmoil

A common feature of the emergence of all of the mega-markets is that of the political division between reformers and conservatives in government. An extreme example of the tensions which economic and political change can create, was seen in Russia in 1998. In the face of deepening financial and economic crisis, Boris Yeltsin sacked his entire cabinet, headed by young, reform-minded Sergei Kiriyenko. Kiriyenko was replaced by the re-appointment as Prime Minister of the moderate reformer Victor Chernomyrdin, who had previously been sacked and replaced for not proceeding sufficiently rapidly with market reforms (*Financial Times*, 24 August 1998). Despite the accession of Putin, the uncertain political environment in Russia continues.

In China, the death of the pro-reform Deng Xiaoping was expected by some to result in a leadership struggle. The pre-selection by Deng of his reform-minded successor Jiang Zemin seems to have allowed the process to continue and maybe even gain pace (*The Economist, The World in 1999*). In India, political divisions continue, although these do not currently seem to be impeding economic growth.

Social Unrest

The extent to which changes in political government have resulted in social unrest varies significantly, and tragically, within emerging markets. In the most extreme case, the end of communism in Central Europe resulted in the creation of new nation states. Some have divided peacefully, such as the 'Velvet Divorce' between the Czech and Slovak Republics. Others split violently, as can be seen in the continued ethnic conflicts within the former Yugoslavia. Other potential ethnic conflicts attracted attention during the political transitions of the 1990s. The possible secession of Crimea from Ukraine, the handover of Hong Kong to China and problems over nuclear testing between India, Pakistan and other world powers all created possible flashpoints.

THE RELATIONSHIP PERSPECTIVE

Since the late 1980s, determining the optimal mode of entry into Eastern and Central Europe has risen to the top of the strategic agenda for many managers. A growing body of literature analyzes and prescribes the types of operation for entry into the region (see Table 14.1). Entry mode choices are split between foreign direct investment (FDI), co-operative joint

ventures between two or more firms and use of a distributor or agent. McCarthy, Puffer and Simmonds (1993) and Shama (1995, 1996) study US firms entering the region (see Table 14.2) and show a split between these three types of entry modes. Overall a preference for entry via a joint venture with a local partner is seen, but a number of firms have also chosen to enter using low levels of investment.

Secondary data confirms that joint ventures are the predominant mode of entry into Eastern Europe. Ozawa (1994) places the number of joint ventures at 11 234 at the end of 1990. Culpan and Kumar (1994) identify 16 000 registered joint ventures on 1 January 1991. Dunning (1994) cites 25 845 in July 1991. However, it must be noted that a significant proportion of these are inactive.

Entry into Eastern and Central Europe by means of co-operative agreements can be explained in a number of ways. Johanson (1994, p. 151) suggests that:

> Given the turbulent situation in the Soviet market and the difficulties for outsiders in perceiving how the Soviet economy works, knowledge about this area is a crucial factor for the firm in entering the Soviet market.

Table 14.1 Primary research into investment in East and Central Europe

Author and date	Sample size	Nationality of home market	Nationality of target market
McCarthy, Puffer and Simmonds (1993)	42	US	FSU
Lawrence and Vlatchoukis (1993)	33	Western	Russia
Johanson (1994)	1	Swedish	USSR
Woodside and Somogyi (1994)	1	Japanese	Hungary
Benito and Welch (1994)	51	Norwegian	USSR, Central Europe, GDR
Ghauri and Henriksen (1994)	1	Norwegian	Estonia
De Wit and Monami (1994)	3	Swedish	FSU
De Mortanges and Caris (1994)	7	Dutch	Central Europe and GDR
Shama (1995)	125	Primarily US	FSU, Baltics, Central Europe
Meyer (1995a, 1995b)	268	UK and German	Central Europe
Hamill and Wersun (1996)	2	Scottish	Russia
Lehtinen (1996)	7	Swedish	Russia

Table 14.2 Entry modes used in East and Central Europe

Source	Host country	Export or distributor	Licence	Joint venture	Wholly owned subsidiary
McCarthy, Puffer and Simmonds (1993)	Russia	8	–	20	0
Shama (1995, 1996)	Russia and FSU	38	9	53	2
	Central Europe	28	11	59	2
Total		**74**	**20**	**132**	**4**

This reinforces the suggestion that Western investors perceive high levels of cultural or 'psychic' distance in entering Eastern European markets (see Chapter 2 for a definition of psychic distance and its impacts on international marketers). Moreover, justification for collaboration with a local partner seems to fit with the arguments of the strategy literature (Hamel, Doz and Prahalad 1989) that this should be the chosen type of operation where it enhances the competitive advantage of each firm (see Chapter 7 for a fuller discussion of collaborative relationships). In Eastern Europe, the benefits of local knowledge and relationships may outweigh the risk of disclosing proprietary technologies and of higher financial investment.

A dominant theme in the Eastern European literature is that of the negotiation and successful operation of these joint ventures (Lawrence and Vlatchoukis 1993; Ghauri and Henriksen 1994; Johanson 1994; Woodside and Somogyi 1994). A growing body of research also evaluates the market opportunities and obstacles identified by multinational corporations (McCarthy, Puffer and Simmonds 1993; Benito and Welch 1994; Dunning 1994; Meyer 1994, 1995a, 1995b; Shama 1995). However, this latter body of research focuses more upon what firms have decided than upon why they opted for a particular entry mode.

Among those studies explaining the choice and establishment of joint ventures in emerging markets, that of Hamill and Wersun (1996) identifies some valuable issues. Joint venture failure is particularly high in co-operation between partners from developed and developing countries (Young and Hamill 1989). The success of international joint ventures can be improved, however, by more efficient planning, negotiation and management. Areas for consideration include:

- Clear statement of **joint venture objectives and time period** for achieving these.
- **A cost/benefit analysis of the advantages and disadvantages** of the joint venture compared to alternative strategies for achieving the firm's objectives. These can be compared to the financial costs of each option.
- **Screening and evaluation of potential partners** to identify the partner that best complements the firm's objectives.

- **Achieving broad agreement on the business plan**. This should be the forum for open and frank discussions of each firm's objectives for the co-operation.
- **Negotiating the final joint venture based** on the business plan.
- Incorporating this agreement into a **formal contract**, which clearly specifies the terms of the agreement.
- **Ongoing evaluation of the performance** of the venture.

Lehtinen (1996) identifies specific issues encountered in relationship development in Russia. While there are a large number of potential customers, it is difficult to find solvent ones, and also difficult to discover who is solvent. Most Russian companies previously dealt with only one customer, the foreign trade organization. Balancing the needs of a proliferation of customers is a new issue for Russian firms. In prioritizing these customers, patterns emerge in a way similar to those observed in other markets. The most frequent repeat customers received most attention and were given some special services.

Joint Ventures and Emerging Markets

A similar tendency towards entry using international joint ventures can be seen in the Chinese market and in India. In these countries many of the reasons for entry using co-operative relationships are similar to those identified for Eastern Europe. Another factor is that joint ventures may be dictated by host market legislation, as was the case in India prior to 1985 (*Fortune*, 16 November 1992) and was also the preference of Chinese and CEE governments (Schlegelmilch *et al.* 1991; Shama 1995). Government legislation may also complicate the co-operative relationship. In India, for example, in the late 1970s, CocaCola left the market when the government tried to reduce its majority holdings in a joint venture to 40 per cent. From 1986 onwards, legislative changes which allow foreign control over investments in India have made it much more attractive as a target for international investors (*The New York Times*, 6 July 1993).

Secondly, the local partner may offer a quicker route through local bureaucracy, as in China (Johnston 1991) and in the Soviet Union (Johanson 1994, p. 151):

> Given the turbulent situation in the Soviet market and the difficulties for outsiders in perceiving how the Soviet economy works, knowledge about this area is a crucial factor for the firm in entering the Soviet market.

There is general consensus that the channel to market is the key to any company's success in China (Stern, El-Ansary and Coughlan 1996). Baldinger (1998) reports that 80 per cent of managers report distribution as one of the top three difficulties in foreign investment in China. A majority of firms (Lee, 1999, quotes 78 per cent of the US firms in China) use joint ventures as the route to market.

Lee (1999) characterizes these relationships between foreign entrants and Chinese partners as involving four key factors:

- **High uncertainty**. As a majority of joint ventures in China are of recent standing, they are still in the relationship development stage. Creation of trust in these relationships is complicated by China's transitional economy, which Nee (1992) describes as having weak capital structures, poor protection of intellectual property and an undemocratic political system. All of these contribute to a highly uncertain relationship context.
- **Low interdependence**. Lee (1999) argues that the lack of strong competitors and dominant brands in the Chinese market and the existence of many small distributors may not favour the development of interdependent relationships.
- **Transactions rather than relationships**. The combination of high uncertainty and low interdependence is equated by Frazier and Antia (1995) as resulting in one-off transactions with price the main reason for switching partners.
- **Co-operation or Conflict?** The Channels literature has seen a shift away from a focus on conflict towards an emphasis on win–win (Narus and Anderson 1989; Young and Wilkinson 1989; see Chapter 1 for a fuller discus-

sion). Research has, however, questioned whether using this type of joint venture agreement as a route to market is more likely to result in conflict or co-operation in the relationship. Use of economic sources of power, such as performance-related bonuses and rebates, tends to increase conflict. Expert and information sources exercise the greatest influence in increasing relationship satisfaction. This latter may be consistent with the extent to which Chinese partners have been cut off from the outside world, and their resultant thirst for knowledge from partners.

Use of co-operative relationships with a local partner to gain market information raises some interesting issues. In uncertain transitional and emerging economies 'knowledge' about the market may well be one type of the complementary capability for which strategists propose co-operative ventures (Hamel, Doz and Prahalad 1989). Research in Ukraine (Bridgewater 1995, 1999) suggests that the rate of change in emerging markets is such that local partners may not always have access to better market information than do foreign investors. The issue of building positions in networks in emerging markets is discussed more fully below.

THE NETWORK PERSPECTIVE

The rapid changes taking place in emerging markets also impact upon the nature of network structures. Under central planning, as commercial exchanges were controlled by the central government, the term 'network' may be inappropriate (Mattsson 1993). Relationships tended to be arm's length and indirect (see Figure 14.1). In the period of transition, the previous structures are breaking down to be replaced by new market structures and new networks of exchange relationships.

Even under central planning the notion of exchange existed. The existence of a 'grey' market suggests that transactions did occur without government intervention (Salmi 1996) and that these were nearer to free market behaviour. That these were part of ongoing exchange relationships rather than opportunistic actions seems to be sup-

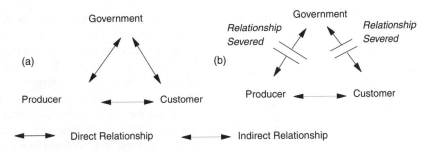

Figure 14.1 Relationships (a) under central planning, (b) in transition

ported by the importance of barter and 'fair exchange' between individual actors. Breger (1992) advises Western investors in Ukraine as follows:

> It seems impossible to carry out the most basic business functions without enlisting the help of useful Ukrainian contacts. The old system of recip-rocating favours cannot be avoided, therefore it is important to bring people on board who are bright, well-connected and resourceful. It is very difficult to go it alone.

The process of transition to a market economy has created some distinctive network issues. Boxes 14.4–14.6 illustrate these with reference to Ukraine.

Box 14.4 Network Issues in Ukraine: Dislocation

Given the size of the population, Ukraine is attractive to international firms in the mature chemical industry. Firm *A* is a French chemicals firm, which entered Ukraine with a representative office in 1991. In 1994, they were in the process of assessing whether to enter a manufacturing joint venture to make acetic acid with one of Ukraine's largest chemical firms. The potential Ukrainian partner was clearly in a survival crisis, but gave a healthy portrayal of its market and prospects to the potential Western investor as it was seeking a joint venture partner.

Under the Soviet system of production spe-cialization, the chemical industry was located in Ukraine. Ukraine has some oil and gas, mainly in Crimea, but does not have the technology to drill to the necessary depth. Its oil refining capability and the chemical industry are reliant on oil imports from Russia and Turkmenistan. All of the oil and 95 per cent of the gas necessary to run the Ukrainian acetic acid plant were previously supplied by these states at significantly less than world prices. According to the central plan, the Ukrainian firm did not know where its products were being sold. They were simply collected in the given quantity, to a given schedule. The state distribution agency or 'Glasvnab' co-ordinated and controlled the imports, exports and intermediate distribution of products, so that it, not the individual organization, had most knowledge about the Ukrainian industrial system. The information gathered by each Glasvnab was held centrally in Moscow and is therefore now lost to Ukraine. Although sales in 1992 continued vir-tually uninterrupted, in the first nine months of 1993 only 27.8 per cent of planned output was achieved because of a reduction in the volume of gas and oil supplied and a loss of former Soviet markets. The supply chain, of which this factory formed a part, was ruptured.

However, the Ukrainian firm did not know which part of its market had disappeared. Firm *A* used a student project staffed by Ukrainian nationals to fill in the gaps. Senior management disclaimed any knowledge, but other employees offered more insights. First, the financial function had some bill-ing information, which revealed the names and addresses of customers. Moreover, employees within the factory knew, from conversations with truck drivers making deliveries and collections, the approximate source of raw materials, at least in terms of country, and the location of customers. While admittedly an inexact process, a far fuller picture could be recreated from these 'pieces of the jigsaw puzzle' than had originally seemed possible.

In moving towards a market economy, former Soviet markets have had to break down the previous atrophied structures:

> Old governmental command-control structures and institutional relationships have disintegrated to a far greater degree now than they had then, creating confusion and disorder. (Manninen and Snelbecker 1993)

With the removal of government from its central controlling role, local firms are currently facing a survival crisis. They may not know the identity of their previous customers and suppliers, or where they are located. Creation of new national boundaries and the withdrawal of central planning have left actors trying to re-establish previous indirect relationships, or else with an urgent need to establish new supplier and customer relationships.

The level of uncertainty in networks in emerging markets is not only a function of high levels of macro-environmental uncertainty. The punitive totalitarian government in both China and the FSU has created an unwillingness to share information freely. Often sources are not clear and verification of facts and figures can be difficult as a result. In the above case, official data on the size of the cigarette market from two different sources varied by 29.9 billion cigarettes!

In the process of transition, a large number of new entrants into the emerging networks may be expected. Kinch (1992) describes the mature US network structures which are stable with well-established rules as 'tightly structured'. In contrast, the turbulent, opaque networks in emerging mega-markets are an extreme case of 'loose structuring'. It might initially be expected that this

---

Box 14.5   Network Issues in Ukraine: Opacity

Firm *B* is one of the smaller players in the tobacco industry. It exported to Eastern Europe, prior to liberalization, but everything was channelled centrally via Moscow. After liberalization, the firm was interested in exploring the potential of the region. Eastern Europe was seen as a 'virgin' market which, together with China and Vietnam, was one of the last remaining areas to be contested by global competitors. Initial interest in Eastern Europe was prompted by large, unsolicited orders from Poland where firm *B* eventually set up a local office. It then began looking at the next tier of countries. In both the Czech Republic and in Hungary, firm *B* was outbid by larger rivals. Therefore, it moved its focus of attention to the Former Soviet Union (FSO).

Firm *B* established a joint venture to set up a greenfield manufacturing site in St Petersburg. While the market was unstable, gaining even a small market share would compensate for the risks, which firm *B* knew to be high. It was more concerned with assessing the size of the opportunity, to see if these risks were justified. The next choice of market in the FSU was between Ukraine, Kazakhstan and Uzbekistan. Firm *B* aimed to set up a local production facility as its products were too expensive if imported. A member of staff came out from the UK to prospect the market in January 1993 and, in April, firm *B* entered the market via a representative office. This was intended only as the

first step. The subsidiary consisted of one expatriate member of staff, with a home office set up in a hotel bedroom.

Throughout the summer of 1993, firm *B* attempted to gather information on market size and possible joint venture partners. Two of the larger tobacco firms were in the process of signing manufacturing agreements. However, firm *B* felt that it should be more cautious, given its smaller size. The market information which could be gathered from secondary sources was found to be contradictory. Legislation surrounding investments was confusing. Moreover, the market conditions in Ukraine worsened considerable during this period. Primary research revealed that, while consumers were keen to buy 'status brands', they had low levels of disposable income. Therefore, they would buy only small quantities of the Western brand when a visible 'badge of capitalism' was required. They were likely to buy local products, for everyday use. The representative in Ukraine felt that conditions were alien and his principle contacts were with other expatriates and international business advisors.

In the late summer of 1993, firm *B* decided against setting up a manufacturing operation in Ukraine. The Southern Republics, and Russia itself, now appeared to have greater stability and potential than Ukraine.

Box 14.6   Network Issues in Ukraine: An Emerging Network

Firm *C* is a British-based multinational producer and distributor of computers with a broad portfolio of investment in Eastern Europe. It has 20 years of experience in the USSR, has had a distributor in Hungary since 1964 and has exported to Poland for more than 20 years. The Manager of firm C says that:

> while the rules of operation in the Soviet Union were complex, once you had learned them, they were easy to play. It is has become a lot more difficult since liberalization. It is hard to determine what the new rules are.

In Ukraine, firm *C* has chosen to form links with an independent distributor. This may eventually lead to a joint venture agreement. The local partner is an American – Ukrainian national who has the advantage of speaking the language and having a good network of contacts. He had returned to work in Ukraine with one of the international aid agencies prior to liberalization.

Largely through the efforts of the local distributor, firm *C* has developed links with local education providers in Kiev. There are high levels of information technology skills in Ukraine. Information gained through these channels is seen to be much more valuable than the secondary data which can be accessed from outside of the market. One of the difficulties for firm *C* is that it is difficult to discover how good the network relationships of the distributor are. He has some useful contacts, largely built around social relationships but it is not clear whether he is going to get firm *C* into the best positions in the emerging networks in Ukraine.

---

would provide considerable possibilities for new entrants who can find many different network positions which are available to build. On the other hand, however, the number of new entrants and the high levels of 'opacity' may make it difficult to identify which positions are attractive to build. In Box 14.6, a firm with considerable experience of the former Soviet market is still unsure whether it is building a network position which will have long-term benefits. Worse still, firm *B* is operating in Ukraine (Box 14.5), but seems unable to build relationships within the loosely structured network.

Some of the characteristics of networks in Ukraine are more broadly recognizable in former Soviet economies. In her study of Russian networks, Salmi (1996, p. 40) highlights the transformation of network structures in the process of transition:

> Before the economic reform process that started in the mid-1980s, the entire Soviet economy was controlled through a planned hierarchical arrangement...the transition to a market economy will mean the introduction of different governance structures: hierarchies, markets, networks.

The following discussion identifies some features of the traditional Soviet 'network' and the major changes which it is undergoing.

From Soviet Hierarchy to Russian Network

Under the Soviet system, Salmi (1996) describes the network as tightly structured. The roles of the main organizations under the Soviet system were clearly defined. Administrators controlled interaction between producers and distributors, production, foreign trade, etc. were handled by specialized organisations. Critics (Snehota 1995) suggest that the Soviet system was not a network structure at all, but an administered hierarchy.

In the reform process, interactions are direct, voluntary and may be with a range of new actors, such as foreign investors, joint stock companies and new local enterprises. While many of the relationships are new, Salmi (1996) like Breger (1993, p. 40) suggests that some of the new exchanges may be based on previous relationships:

> There is evidence that small enterprises are often created from earlier departments within the enterprises. These new entities characteristically combine with their earlier tasks and try to rely on their old connections.

New approaches to building positions in Russian – compared to previous Soviet networks – are required by both foreign entrants and Russian managers:

- **Context**. Russian managers are used to an inward, or production oriented, approach to business. Understanding the network context, and the need to build relationships with customers, suppliers and other actors in the new network structures, requires a different set of skills.
- **The focal net**. Salmi (1996) suggests that a first stage, for Russian managers in understanding existence in an embedded network might be to define the focal net. This would involve identifying the critical interdependencies of the firm.
- **Investing in network position**. While the concept of building relationships may be new, investment in future positions is key to future success. Salmi (1996, p. 42) suggests that some Russian firms:

> have jumped into new business possibilities, trying to proceed with numerous new firms and business ideas, while at the same time neglecting their existing business partners.

From a Western perspective:

- **Earlier investment can be inappropriate**. Investments in positions, which were right for the Soviet network may no longer be appropriate under the new system.
- **Involvement in the new networks is critical**. While it is not certain how networks will develop, information is exchanged more readily within the network than to actors who are not well connected.

- **Personal relations decrease uncertainty**. Social ties lead to the creation of trust. Although they are building new network positions, Russian and Western managers may be able to build on previous social and personal relationships to gain valuable information.

Parallels can be seen between Salmi's study of networks in Russia and the work of Törnroos (1996), which studies the development of networks in Estonia. Given the influence of the different political systems in which the Estonian and Finnish firms are embedded, the importance of political and infrastructural actors in these markets is unsurprising. As with penetration of Ukrainian networks, one route to overcoming market turbulence seems to be business and personal contacts of individual actors.

Network structures in China also retain a number of features of central planning. Fu *et al.* (1999) note a transition from the foreign trade system prior to economic reform and the current situation. Twelve Foreign Trade Corporations (FTCs) handled all exports and imports under the previous system. Specialization of the FTCs was by industry sector. In the 1980s, reform saw changes in government regulation, which allowed local firms to retain a proportion of their profits. With this change came a link between performance and rewards. FTCs benefited, but local producers became demotivated by the changes. In the 1990s, the formation of 'company groups' created vertical links with suppliers and horizontal links with other manufacturers in the same or related industries. The focus in 2000, is international rather than domestic and involves 'nets' of firms.

CASE STUDY 14.1 BUDWEISER B

Jiri Bocek took a sip of coffee and leaned back to reflect on the future of the brewery he had run for the past four years. As general director of the Budejovicky Budvar Brewery ('Budvar') in the small Southern Bohemian town of Ceske Budejovice,[1] Bocek had guided the brewery through very hectic times. Since the Velvet Revolution in November 1989 had brought democracy and a transition towards a free market for what was then Communist Czechoslovakia, events seemed to be moving at a breakneck pace for the country and for his company.

Since taking over as general director in 1991, Bocek had nearly doubled beer sales, and still demand for *Budweiser*, Budvar's beer, was greater than supply. The brewery was currently operating at maximum capacity, but still was unable to satisfy the domestic or export markets. In 1995, the company was on the verge of being privatized, after being run as a state company for almost 50 years.

The Budejovicky Budvar brewery had been established as a joint stock company in 1895 by a consortium of Czech investors. The brewery is located in the South Bohemian town of Ceske Budejovice, near the border with Austria. When Budvar was founded, Bohemia was still part of the Austro-Hungarian empire. The town's population was primarily German-speaking, so the brewery was also known by its German name, Budweiser Budvar, which means literally 'Budvar from the town Budweis'. The name 'Budvar' was created out of a contraction of the Czech '*Bud*ejovicky *Pivovar*' (or 'Budejovice Brewery').

Budvar is a small brewery by international standards, employing about 400 people, and is still State owned. The brewery produces two strengths of lager, a 12° beer (approximately 3.5–4 per cent alcohol) and a lighter 10° beer, (approximately 3–3.5 per cent alcohol). The brewery has also begun to brew an alcohol-free beer in limited quantities. Budvar's beer is known by a variety of names throughout the world, but most Westerners know the beer by the name '*Budweiser Budvar*'. In the Czech Republic it is marketed as '*Budejovicky Budvar*', although most Czechs simply refer to the beer as '*Budvar*'.

Bocek was sure that Budvar had a chance to become a strong European super premium brand, but thought this might mean partnering with a major international player. Although Budvar's management had made incredible progress, it still lacked a sophisticated marketing department and a strong international distribution network. And according to management's current plans, Budvar would still have less than 1.5 million hectolitres of production capacity by the year 2000 – nowhere near the capacity required of a major European brewery.

THE BUDEJOVICKY BUDVAR BREWERY

Budvar During the Communist Era

Budvar was nationalized in 1946, two years before the Communists took control in Czechoslovakia. The nationalization was executed by a Presidential decree of the post-war Czechoslovak government, the left-of-centre National Front. One year later, Budvar was placed under the management of a State owned brewery holding company called Ceskobudejovicky Pivovary (Ceske Budejovice Breweries). This holding company was later renamed Jihoceske Pivovary (South Bohemia Breweries). In addition to Budvar, the holding company administered a number of other breweries in South Bohemia, including the only other brewery in Ceske Budejovice, the Samson Brewery.

The Communist era was a dark period for all breweries, including Budvar. Central planners tightly controlled Budvar's production, and for two decades investment in the brewery was insufficient, which led to a degradation of the production facilities. Then, in 1967, the Communist government seemed to come to the realization that Budvar was an asset to the government in its ability to generate hard currency. The State thus embarked upon an ambitious investment programme for the brewery to modernize facilities and expand production capacity. The programme, which began in 1967, was supposed to be completed in 1982, and envisaged expanding capacity from 300 000 to 830 000 hectolitres per annum.[2]

However, soon after launching the programme to upgrade the brewery, the government realized it could not afford to fund the full investment plan. Therefore, the time frame for achieving a capacity of 830 000 hectolitres grew longer and longer. By 1982, Budvar's capacity had expanded to only 397 000 hectolitres.[3] Supply of *Budweiser* at this point was far below demand, in both the domestic and export markets. That year, in an attempt to boost hard currency earnings, the Communist government drastically cut supply of Budvar's beer on the domestic market, raising exports to over 73 per cent of production. This meant that less than 100 000 hectolitres of the Czech *Budweiser* was available in Czechoslovakia per annum.

This short supply of Budvar for the domestic market continued through the rest of the 1980s, as production capacity increased only marginally, to approximately 420 000 hectolitres per year by 1989.

Budvar After 1989

The Velvet Revolution of November 1989 marked a radical break with the past for all Czech firms, as the newly democratic government began to implement measures which were to transform Czechoslovakia from a centrally planned system to a market economy.

The period immediately after the Velvet Revolution was extremely influential for Budvar's future. The brewery's first test came when it attempted to end its long-term relationship with the foreign trade organization Koospol, which had previously handled all external trade for Budvar.

Under Communism, Czech companies were not allowed to deal directly with foreign firms, but had to employ foreign trade organizations (FTOs) to act as middle men. After 1989, many companies continued to use FTOs, which had extensive contacts and experience dealing with the West. But to Budvar, Koospol symbolized the Communist past. Moreover, Budvar felt that developing its own export department would give them more flexibility and freedom, and would be better for the long-term development of the company.

Koospol, however, was not keen to surrender its lucrative position as Budvar's exclusive exporter. After a 12-month struggle, Budvar finally ended its relationship with Koospol in January 1991. Budvar was then free to establish new distribution relationships with foreign firms.

Budvar's second and far more difficult challenge came when it sought to separate itself from the Jihoceske Pivovary. Managers at Budvar felt that bad management at Jihoceske was keeping the brewery from living up to its full potential, and thought Budvar would be better off as an independent entity. The Budvar management therefore began to lobby the government for a split from Jihoceske.

There were many opponents of the separation both at Jihoceske and within the government. Budvar was likely seen as the 'jewel' in Jihoceske's crown. Jihoceske tried to block the separation, but Budvar eventually succeeded in convincing the government that a split from the holding company was in Budvar's best interest. The existence of the trademark dispute between Anheuser-Busch (AB) and Budvar (see Case Study 5.1), and the fact that the government was unsure how and when Budvar should be privatized, probably aided Budvar's cause. The Jihoceske Pivovary was slated to be privatized in the first round of mass privatization in mid-1992, and the separation of Budvar allowed the privatization of Jihoceske to go forth as scheduled. This left the government to resolve the Budvar privatization issue separately.

After Budvar was granted independence from Jihoceske, Jiri Bocek, a Budvar manager, was appointed to run the brewery. When Bocek took over as general director, he was 35 years old. Bocek had studied brewing at the faculty of food production and chemical technology in Prague, a school that has historically trained the majority of brewmasters in the country. Bocek was not a first-generation Budvar employee. His father had once been the brewmaster there. The brewmaster is the individual responsible for controlling the composition and quality of a brewery's beer, and is a position in Bohemia which vies for importance with the local priest or doctor.

In an attempt to block Budvar's separation, Jihoceske had predicted that Budvar would not be able to succeed on its own, and would collapse in a matter of months. Instead, independence from Jihoceske Pivovary and new, young blood in top management provided Budvar with the ability to rejuvenate itself and to set in motion changes in production, sales and marketing. Bocek believes that the struggle to break away from Jihoceske brought together the management team as nothing else could have, and made them loyal and committed to the success of Budvar[4]. These qualities were often missing from the management of state-owned companies in the former Czechoslovakia.

CHALLENGES FOR BUDVAR

Expanding Domestic and Export Sales

Budvar put considerable effort into expanding sales after 1991 to better supply the domestic and export markets. Sales volumes rose from 499 000 hectolitres in 1991 to 796 000 hectolitres in 1994, a 62 per cent increase. Total 1995 sales were projected to be near 870 000 hectolitres. To achieve these sales volumes Budvar operated at or near maximum capacity almost all of the time. (Of course, these sales volumes could not have been achieved without significantly expanding capacity. The capacity expansion programme will be discussed below.)

Domestic Sales

Increasing the volume of *Budweiser* available on the Czech market was a key concern for management. As Bocek explained, 'Our objective is for the Czech people not only to read about our beer in the newspapers, but also to consume our beer.'[5] This had not been possible for the majority of Czechs, especially during the 1980s, when domestic supply had been severely cut.

Owing to the small volumes that had been sold domestically in the past, Budvar had a very weak domestic distribution network focused mainly on the local region. Management therefore had to put considerable effort into building domestic distribution for *Budweiser*. This included establishing a new distribution centre adjacent to the brewery, and purchasing additional distribution vehicles. Distribution of bottled *Budweiser* was then increased significantly to Czech supermarkets and small food shops around the country, while additional pubs were supplied with *Budweiser* on tap.

As a result of this effort, domestic sales volumes more than doubled from 1991 to 1994, rising from 160 006 hectolitres per year to 331 544 hectolitres per year. In addition, in accordance with management's objectives, domestic sales increased from 32.6 per cent of total production in 1991 to 43.9 per cent of total production in 1994.

This dramatic jump in domestic sales is all the more impressive when considering that during the early 1990s most other Czech brewers were experiencing tough competition and declining sales. Moreover, *Budweiser* was priced as a premium product, from 20 per cent to 50 per cent above most other Czech beers.

Export Sales

Export sales had always been more attractive than domestic sales for Budvar as export margins were far higher than domestic margins. But in the past export sales had been erratic, fluctuating quite significantly for each individual country in volume terms from year to year. Budvar could claim to have sales in over 80 countries around the world, but in many of these markets Budvar sold less than 500 hectolitres per annum.

Management recognized the need for a more focused approach to developing export markets.

This meant identifying Budvar's current key markets and those markets that Budvar ought to try developing in the future. Budvar then began to concentrate on building sales in these priority markets. As a result of the more focused approach to exporting, Budvar's shipments abroad rose 28 per cent between 1991 and 1994. During this period, exports actually declined as a percentage of total production from 67.4 per cent in 1991 to 56.1 per cent in 1994, as Budvar shifted a greater portion of sales to the domestic market.

While Budvar exports to over 30 countries, more than 90 per cent of export sales now come from six key markets. Germany is by far the most important export market, with 53 per cent of export volume in 1994. The UK is the second largest market for Budvar, comprising 13 per cent of sales. Budvar also exports significant volumes to Austria, the Slovak Republic, Italy and Sweden. Markets with strong future potential for Budvar include Spain and France, where Budvar had set about strengthening distribution over the past three years. Figure 14.2 shows Budvar's major export markets in 1994.

Promotion

Budvar launched its first foreign advertising campaign since the beginning of Communism in May 1995 in the UK, where sales growth was projected to be the strongest in the coming years. The campaign included print advertising and posters in bus shelters throughout the country. With the help of the campaign, Budvar expected to sell 75 000 hectolitres in 1995, a gain of 36 per cent over the previous year.

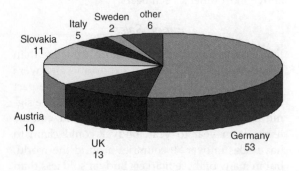

Figure 14.2   Budvar's major export markets, 1994
Source: Budvar management

Budvar's only other advertising activities are domestic. In the Czech Republic Budvar primarily advertises on billboards, on bus shelters and in 'Metro' stations, and through sponsorship of sporting events. Limited resources mean that large-scale foreign advertising is not currently possible. However, as the demand for the beer is currently greater than supply, advertising is not really necessary to sell *Budweiser*.

UPGRADING FACILITIES AND EXPANDING PRODUCTION CAPACITY

Production Capacity

Completing the modernization and expansion of production capacity which was begun in the late 1960s was the top priority of Brewmaster Josef Tolar after 1991. Tolar oversaw the expansion of Budvar's brewing capacity from 499 000 hectolitres in 1991 to 870 000 hectolitres in 1995. Figure 14.3 shows the dramatic increase in Budvar's production, after remaining relatively stable for more than a decade.

Budvar's product mix has not changed significantly since 1991. Production of Budvar's strongest beer (12° beer) declined slightly, while production of its 10° product rose. This is in response to changing consumer tastes. Also in response to emerging trends, Budvar began producing non-alcoholic beer in 1992, although production remained below 2 per cent of total beer production. The proportion of beer packaged in bottles, cans, kegs and tanks also remained virtually the same, with a slight rise in shipments of kegged beer and a slight decline in the proportion of bottled beer. This rise in kegged production reflects the shift to supplying a greater volume of beer to the domestic market, and in particular to pubs.

Management has given considerable thought to their vision for the future of the brewery. According to its plans, Budvar was to incrementally increase capacity to a level of 1 400 000 hectolitres by the year 1999. Budvar sees this as a manageable rate of growth, which will allow them to build the *Budweiser* brand both domestically and abroad. Budvar is very wary of expanding production too rapidly, having taken note of the recent blunder made by its competitor Plzenske Pivovary (Pilsen Breweries). Plzenske followed the advice of a group of Western consultants, who told the brewery that in order to become a major European player, it needed to have a 5 million hectolitre capacity. The brewery dramatically expanded capacity, but found that demand was not strong enough to keep the brewery anywhere near full capacity. Plzenske now has idle capacity and has had to cut back its ambitious expansion plans.

As a means of overcoming capacity constraints, Budvar has investigated the possibility of licensing agreements. They have negotiated arrangements with brewers in Turkey and India, but these agreements were aborted in the final stages owing to difficulties with the licensees. These licensing agreements would have offered Budvar's recipes, technical support and know-how, but would not have allowed the licensee to use the *Budweiser* name. As it stands now, *Budweiser* is registered by Budvar not only as a trademark, but also as an 'appellation of origin', i.e. a name which identifies the geographic origin of a product. The *Budweiser* name cannot legally be used by other parties (except Anheuer-Busch) unless the product is physically produced in Ceske Budejovice (Budweis).

Renovation and Expansion

Under Tolar's supervision nearly every step in the brewing process was upgraded. The capacity of the brewhouse was doubled, while exactly preserving the old brewing process. New combination fermentation and ageing tanks were added to partly replace the old 'open' fermentation process. A new filtration system from a Swiss firm was installed. A very high-tech bottling line from Italy was added, and the existing keg filling line was extended. In order to make these improvements, investment over the years 1991–94 ranged from 100 million to 200 million CZK per year (£2.5 million–£5 million). One-third of this money was spent on renovation or construction of buildings and two-thirds on equipment. A considerable amount of money was also invested in projects aimed, in Bocek's words, to restore people's pride in the brewery.[6] These projects included

construction of a modern office building which will house the sales and marketing department and top management's offices, as well as a Budvar pub, open to the public.

The Budvar brewery is now an eclectic mixture of old and new. Some of the oldest parts of the brewery are 100 years old, and make use of equipment and technology that has long since disappeared from Western breweries. However, the newer sections are now comparable in technology to the most modern breweries in the world. Certain steps in the brewing process make use of both the old and new technologies side by side. For example, fermentation of half of Budvar's total production takes place in a series of open, tiled pools which were built as part of the original brewery, while the rest of the beer is now fermented in modern stainless steel tanks which were installed over the past several years.

Not all of the old brewing equipment, however, is inferior to modern brewing technology. According to Brewmaster Tolar, Budvar conducted extensive tests before putting the new technology into use, and found that the stainless steel tanks that it planned to use for the combined fermentation and ageing of the beer were actually unsuitable for the long ageing process Budvar has historically used. Therefore Budvar will continue to use its old laggering vessels for ageing its beer.

Budvar's renovation is still incomplete, and will continue for several years. In the future, management plans to put half of total investment towards replacement of equipment and half towards expand capacity. Tolar emphasizes, however, that long-term investment plans are difficult to develop, as the brewery has yet to be privatized, and new owners may decide upon a different strategy. Budvar's investment horizon therefore currently looks only five years ahead.

FINANCIAL PERFORMANCE

While many State owned companies in the Czech Republic had never been run profitably, breweries had traditionally been cash cows. Budvar was no exception. Moreover, Budvar's exports had generated significant hard currency for the Czech government. Many breweries, however, began to

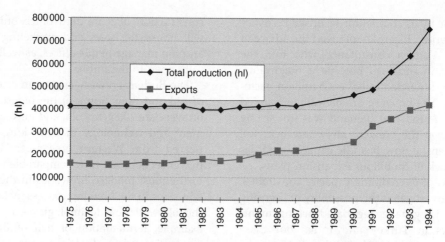

Figure 14.3   Budvar's production and exports, 1975–94
Source: Budvar management

encounter problems after 1989. In contrast, Budvar's financial picture remained encouraging. Revenue rose from 199 million CZK (£4.98 million) in 1989 to 1 100 million CZK (£27.5 million) in 1994, an increase of more than 400 per cent. Budvar's profits fluctuated over this period, but the firm's profits do not accurately reflect the performance of the company. 1992 earnings were depressed by a large one-time payment Budvar was required to make to Jihoceske Pivovar to settle up its debts with the holding company.

In addition, earnings were reduced in 1992 and 1993, owing to mandatory changes in both years in its accounting system, which brought Czech accounting practices into line with EU standards. Moreover, Budvar was investing significant amounts of funds in renovation and expansion of capacity during this period.

Budvar also experienced lower profits owing to spiralling input costs after prices were liberalized in the Czech Republic from 1 January, 1991. Rising energy costs and prices for ingredients like hops and malt cut significantly into Budvar's earnings. Despite these challenges, Budvar maintained profitability throughout the toughening economic period.

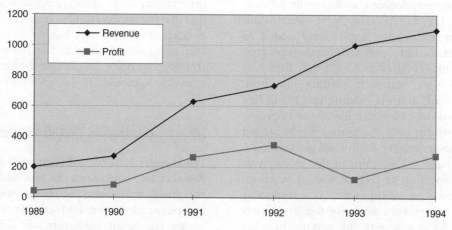

Figure 14.4   Budvar's revenues and profits, 1989–94 (million (2K))

Figure 14.4 shows Budvar's revenues and profits from 1989 to 1994.

About 70 per cent of Budvar's profits currently come from exports. However, Budvar's finance department, which consists only of the economic director, Petr Jansky, has yet to employ techniques such as hedging on currency to minimize exchange rate risk. Therefore, Budvar's financial performance is heavily dependent upon fluctuations in the international currency market.

The Czech koruna is pegged to a basket of currency made up of one-third dollars and two-thirds Deutsch Marks. Fluctuations in these two currencies cause changes in the value of the koruna *vis-à-vis* other currencies, and affect Budvar's revenues. For example, the devaluation of the Swedish krone against other major European currencies caused the value of the Czech koruna to rise against the krone. Budvar's sales dropped in Sweden as the price of Budvar rose sharply.

PRIVATIZATION

With respect to privatization, a number of large international brewers have expressed interest in a partnership with Budvar. These potential partners have pointed to the benefits that could be gained for Budvar by having access to foreign capital, and the marketing and distribution assistance of a major international brewer. But Budvar is not jumping at the possibility of a foreign partner. The prospect of unlimited access to foreign capital does excite Budvar's economic director, Petr Jansky, who says:

> If we want finance, we can go to the bank and get money anytime we want because we are a very solvent company. Domestic and foreign banks are bidding on credit to Budvar. We can choose the bank that gives us the best conditions.[7]

Director Bocek takes a more pragmatic stance:

> On the basis of our economic projections, the well being of our brewery doesn't depend on the entry of a foreign partner. However, co-operation on an international scale, which would be beneficial for both parties, is an option for us.[8]

Bocek and his management team were preparing a revised privatization plan which would be submitted to the government. They had to come to a decision as to whether they would recommend that the brewery be privatized with foreign participation, or whether a totally Czech solution was preferable. Bocek was not alone in expressing fear that selling a stake in Budvar to a foreign brewer could compromise the centuries-old traditions of the brewery and the distinctive character of the Budvar beer. He had only to look at the experience of another Czech brewery to be reminded of the potential loss of control over the brewery that could come from teaming up with a foreign partner. The English brewer, Bass plc, bought a minority stake in the Prazske Pivovary (Prague Breweries). Bocek knew that in a matter of months, Bass executives had moved into the brewery and were running the operation. People in the industry knew that it was only a matter of time before Bass acquired a controlling share in the brewery, and the Prazske Pivovary would cease to be a Czech brewery.

Although there was no guarantee that management's privatization plan would be accepted by the Czech government, Bocek knew their proposals would receive careful consideration. He also knew that the Budvar privatization would receive not only national, but international scrutiny. The privatization had to be carried out with the utmost sensitivity and fairness to the Czech people. Moreover, there was no sense in alienating any of the international players who might wish the opportunity for some form of co-operation with Budvar in the future. Ultimately, however, Bocek was most concerned with securing the best arrangement for his company.

QUESTIONS

1. Analyze the current ability of Budejovicky Budvar to compete in the European super premium beer market
2. What would be the advantages and disadvantages for Budvar of co-operation with an international partner?

SUMMARY

In Chapter 14 we have explored the challenges of operation in Emerging Markets. Distinctive types of relationship in the region and their management are explored. Finally the contributions of network studies in the region are evaluated.

NOTES

1. As the town of Ceske Budejovice was once part of the Austro-Hungarian empire, the brewery was also known by its German name, Budweiser Budvar.
2. 'Budejovicky Budvar, 100 Let' ('Budejovicky Budvar, 100 years'), company marketing materials for 100-year anniversary, 1995.
3. *Ibid.*
4. *Ibid.*
5. *Ibid.*
6. *Ibid.*
7. Masek, Ivan. 'Jiri Bocek: Anheuser-Busch je pouze jednim ze zajemcu!', *Magazin Uspech*, September 1993: 22.
8. *Ibid.*, p. 20.

BIBLIOGRAPHY

Åslund, A. (1991) 'Gorbachev, Perestroika and Economic Crisis', *Problems of Communism*, January–April.

Baldinger, P. (1998) 'Secrets of the Supply Chain', *The China Business Review*, September–October: 8–17.

Benito, G. R. and Welch, L. S. (1994) 'Norwegian Companies in Eastern Europe: Past Involvement and Reaction to Recent Changes', in Buckley, P. J. and Ghauri, P. N. (eds), *The Economics of Change in Central and Eastern Europe*, Academic Press.

Borys, B. and Jemison, D. B. (1989) 'Hybrid Arrangements as Strategic Alliances: Theoretical Issues in Organisational Combinations', *Academy of Management Review*, 14: 234–49.

Breger, B. (1992) 'Foreign Investment in Ukraine: Adventures in the New Wild West', Project for Economic Reform in Ukraine, Harvard University, August.

Brewer, T. (1993) 'Government Policies, Market Imperfections and Foreign Direct Investment', *Journal of International Business Studies*, 24, 1: 101–20.

Bridgewater, S. (1995) 'Assessing the Attractiveness of Turbulent Markets: The Case of Ukraine', *Journal of Marketing Management*, D.

Bridgewater, S. (1999) 'Networks and Internationalisation: the case of multinational corporations entering Ukraine', *International Business Review*, 8: 99–118.

Buckley, P. J. and Casson, M. (1981) 'The Optimal Timing of a Foreign Direct Investment', *The Economic Journal*, 92, 316: 75–87.

Buckley, P. J. and Ghauri, P. N. (eds) (1994) *The Economics of Change in Central and Eastern Europe*, Academic Press.

Contractor, F. and Lorange, P. (eds) (1988) *Co-operative Strategies in International Business*, Lexington Books.

Culpan, R. and Kumar, N. (1994) 'Co-operative Ventures of Western Firms in Eastern Europe: The Case of German Companies', in Buckley, P. J. and Ghauri, P. N. (eds), *The Economics of Change in Central and Eastern Europe*, Academic Press.

Daniels, J. D. (1991) 'Relevance in International Business Research: A Need for More Linkages', *Journal of International Business*, 22, 2: 177–186.

De Mortanges, C. P. and Caris, W. B. (1994) 'Investment in Eastern Europe: The Case of the Netherlands', in Buckley, P. J. and Ghauri, P. (eds), *The Economics of Change in East and Central Europe*, Harcourt Brace.

De Wit, A. and Monami, E. (1994) 'Understanding the Former Soviet Market: An Interaction Approach', in Buckley, P. J. and Ghauri, P. (eds), *The Economics of Change in East and Central Europe*, Harcourt Brace.

Doyle, P., Saunders, J. and Wong, V. (1986) 'A Comparative Investigation of Japanese Marketing Strategies', *Journal of International Business Studies*, 17, 1: 27–46.

Doz, Y. (1988) 'Value Creation Through Technology Collaboration', *Aussenwirtschaft*, 43: 175–90.

Doz, Y. (1992) 'The Role of Partnerships and Alliances in the European Industrial Restructuring', in Cool, I. C., Neven, D. J. and Walter, I. (eds), *European Industrial Restructuring in the 1990s*, Macmillan.

Dunning, J. H. (1994) 'The Prospects for Foreign Direct Investment in Central and Eastern Europe', in Buckley, P. J. and Ghauri, P. N. (eds), *The Economics of Change in Central and Eastern Europe*, Academic Press.

Economist, The (1993) 'Survey: Europe: The Implication for Western European Business', in Buckley P. J. and Ghauri P. N. (eds), *The Economics of Change in East and Central Europe*, Academic Press.

Frazier, G. L. and Antia, K. D. (1995) 'Exchange Relationships and Interfirm Power in the Channel of Distribution', *Journal of the Academy of Marketing Science*, 23, Fall: 321–6.

Frydman, R. and Rapaczynski, A. (1991) 'Privatisation and Corporate Governance in Eastern Europe: Can a Market Economy be Designed?', Project for Economic Reform in Ukraine, *Working Paper*.

Fu, H., Spencer, R., Wilkinson, I. and Young, L. (1999) 'The Recent Evolution of Business Networks in China: Two Case Studies', *EMAC Proceedings*, Berlin.

Ghauri, P. N. and Henriksen, A. G. (1994) 'Developing a Network Position in the Baltic States: The Case of Statoil in Estonia', in Buckley, P. J. and Ghauri, P. N. (eds), *The Economics of Change in Central and Eastern Europe*, Academic Press.

Hamel, G., Doz, Y. and Prahalad, C. K. (1989) 'Collaborate with Your Competitors – and Win', *Harvard Business Review*, January–February.

Hamill, J. and Wersun, A. (1996) 'Joint Ventures in Russia: The Experiences of Two Small Companies', in Nieminen, J. (ed.), *East–West Business Relationships: Establishment and Development*, International Business Press.

Healey, N. (1994) 'The Transition Economies of Central and Eastern Europe: A Political, Economic, Social and Technological Analysis', *Columbia Journal of World Business*, 29, 1: 62–70.

Jain, S. and Tucker, L. (1994) 'Market Opportunities in Eastern Europe: MNCs' Response', in Buckley, P. J. and Ghauri, P. N. (eds), *The Economics of Change in Central and Eastern Europe*, Academic Press.

Jarillo, J. C. (1988) 'On Strategic Networks', *Strategic Management Journal*, 19.

Johanson, M. (1994) 'Viking Raps – a Case Study of Joint Venture Negotiation in the Former Soviet Union', in Buckley, P. J. and Ghauri, P. (eds), *The Economics of Change in Eastern and Central Europe*, Academic Press, London.

Johansson, J. and Vahlne, J. (1977) 'The Internationalisation Process of the Firm: A Model of Knowledge Development on Increasing Foreign Commitments', *Journal of International Business Studies*, 8, Spring–Summer: 23–32.

Johansson, J. and Wiedersheim-Paul, F. (1975) 'The Internationalisation of the Firm: Four Swedish Case Studies', *Journal of Management Studies*, 12, 3: 305–22.

Johnston, W. J. (1991) 'Alternative Approach Strategies for Buyer–Seller Relations with the People's Republic of China', in S. J. Paliwoda, (ed.), *New Perspectives in International Marketing*, Routledge.

Kinch, N. (1992) 'Entering a Tightly Structured Network – Strategic Visions or Network Realities', in Forsgren, M. and Johanson, J. (eds), *Managing Networks in International Business*, Gordon and Breach.

Knickerbocker, F. T. (1973) *Oligopolistic Reaction and Multinational Enterprise*, MIT Press.

Lawrence, P. and Vlatchoukis, C. (1993) 'Joint Ventures in Russia: Put the Locals in Charge', *Harvard Business Review*, January–February: 44–54.

Lee, D. Y. (1999) 'Power Sources, Conflict and Satisfaction in a Foreign Joint-Venture Supplier and Chinese Distributor Channel', *Proceedings of the Fifteenth IMP Conference*, University College, Dublin.

Lehtinen, U. (1996) 'Relationship Marketing Approaches in Changing Russian Markets', in Nieminen, J. (ed.), *East–West Business Relationships: Establishment and Development*, International Business Press.

Manninen, K. and Snelbecker, D. (1993) 'Obstacles to Doing Business in Ukraine', *Working Paper*, Project for Economic Reform in Ukraine.

Mattsson, L.-G. (1993) 'The Role of Marketing for the Transformation of a Centrally-Planned economy to a Market Economy', *Essays in Honour of Gösta Mickwitz*, Swedish School of Economics and Business Administration, Finland.

McCarthy, D. J., Puffer, S. M. and Simmonds, P. J. (1993) 'Riding the Russian Roller-Coaster: US Firms Experience and Future Plans in the Former USSR', *California Management Review*, Fall: 99–115.

Meyer, K. E. (1994) 'Direct Foreign Investment in Central and Eastern Europe: Understanding the Statistical Evidence', *CIS–Middle European Centre Working Papers*, London Business School.

Meyer, K. E. (1995a) 'Direct Foreign Investment, Structural Change and Development: Can the East Asian Experience be Replicated?', *CIS–Middle European Centre Working Papers*, London Business School.

Meyer, K. E. (1995b) 'Business Operations of British and German Companies with the Economies in Transition: First Results of a Questionnaire Survey', *CIS–Middle European Centre Working Papers*, London Business School.

Narus, A. J. and Anderson, C. J. (1990) 'A Model of Distributor Firm and Manufacturing Firm Working Partnerships', *Journal of Marketing*, 54: 42–58.

Nee, V. (1992) 'Organizational Dynamics of Market Transition: Hybrid Firms, Property Rights and Mixed Economy in China', *Administrative Science Quarterly*, 31: 1–27.

Osawa, T. (1994) 'Japanese MNCs as Potential Partners in Eastern Europe's Economic Reconstruction', in Buckley, P. J. and Ghauri, P. (eds), *The Economics of Change in Eastern and Central Europe*, Academic Press.

Perlmutter, H. V. and Heenan, D. A. (1986) 'Cooperate to Compete Globally', *Harvard Business Review*, March–April.

Porter, M. E. (1987) 'From Competitive Advantage to Corporate Strategy', *Harvard Business Review*, May–June: 43–59.

Porter, M. E. and Fuller, M. (1986) 'Conditions and Global Strategy', in Porter, M. E. (ed), *Competition in Global Industries*, Harvard Business School Press.

Root, F. (1987) *Entry Strategies for International Markets*, Lexington Books.

Salmi, A. (1996) 'Russian Networks in Transition', *Industrial Marketing Management*, 25: 37–45.

Seagram Company Ltd. (1992) 'Central Europe: The Market of the Future', *News Release*, Corporate Communications and Public Relations Department.

Seagram Company Ltd. (1994) 'Seagrams Establishes Marketing, Sales and Distribution Operations in Ukraine and Opens Seagrams Store', *News Release*, Corporate Communications and Public Relations Department.

Schlegelmilch, B. B., Diamantopoulos, A. and Petersen, M. (1991) 'Conquering the Chinese Market: A Study of Danish Firms' Experience in the People's Republic of China', in Paliwoda, S. J. (ed.), *New Perspectives in International Marketing*, 174–201.

Shama, A. (1995) 'Entry Strategies of US Firms to the Newly Independent States, Baltic States and Eastern European Countries', *California Management Review*, 37, 3: 90–108.

Shama, A. (1996) 'Cracking the Former Soviet Bloc Markets: An Empirical Study', *International Journal of Management*, 13, 2: 184–192.

Snehota, I. (1995) Comments made on Conference Paper, 'Networks in Markets in Transition: The Case of Ukraine', presented by S. Bridgewater at the tenth IMP Conference in Groningen, Netherlands, September.

Stern, L. W., El-Ansary, A. I. and Coughlan, A. T. (1996) *Marketing Channels*, (5th edition), Prentice-Hall.

Terpstra, V. and Yu, C. M. (1988) 'Determinants of Foreign Investment of CPS Advertising Agencies', *Journal of International Business Studies*. 19, 1: 33–46.

Tesar, G. (1994) 'Assessment of Mutually Beneficial Technology: East–West Perspective', *R&D Management*, 24, 3: 199–205.

Thornhill, J. (1998) 'Yeltsin Acts to save his Presidency?', *The Financial Times*, 24 August: 1.

Törnroos, J.-A. (1996) 'New Business Development and Industrial Marketing to Estonia – A Network Approach', in Nieminen. J. (ed.), *East–West Business Relationships: Establishment and Development*, International Business Press.

Woodside, A. G. and Somogyi, P. (1994) 'Creating International Joint Ventures: Strategic Insights from Case Research on a Successful Hungarian–Japanese Enterprise', in Buckley, P. J. and Ghauri, P. N. (eds), *The Economics of Change in Central and Eastern Europe*, Academic Press.

Young, S., Hamill, J., Wheeler, C. and Davies, J. R. (1989) *International Market Entry: Strategies and Management*, Harvester-Wheatsheaf, and Prentice-Hall.

Young, L. and Wilkinson, I. F. (1989) 'The Role of Trust and Co-operation in Marketing Channels: A Preliminary Study', *European Journal of Marketing*, 23: 109–22

LESS DEVELOPED MARKETS

Objectives

The issues to be addressed in Chapter 15 include:

1. The application of concepts from earlier sections of the book to Less Developed Markets (LDCs)
2. Examination of relationships within LDCs
3. Review studies of networks in LDCs to identify distinctive characteristics of network structures in the region.

After reading Chapter 15 you will be able to:

1. Understand the challenges facing international marketers in LDCs
2. Identify specific types of relationships that play a role in the region
3. Evaluate the contribution of network studies of the region.

INTRODUCTION

Discussion of the international marketing issues encountered in the Less Developed Countries (LDCs) of Africa and parts of Asia is often neglected. Quelch and Austin (1993) suggest that this is because:

> For most Multinational Corporations (MNCs), Africa is the forgotten continent. Characterized by the media mostly in terms of political turmoil, malnutrition, and AIDS, Africa seems inconsequential as a potential market or as a low-cost manufacturing source. Yet several MNCs enjoy good, sustained profitability from their African operations.

This chapter focuses on discussion of the particular challenges of operation in Africa. Specific adaptation needs are considered, alongside the ethical issues associated with the marketing of old technologies to the region by international firms. Relationship challenges include managing relationships between partners with different levels of wealth and, in some cases, technological

development. The role of intermediary firms from emerging markets is also considered.

The Network section of this chapter considers some distinctive challenges of networks in LDCs. These include the role of intermediary partners from emerging markets, who might act as a bridge between firms from advanced and LDCs.

THE TRADITIONAL PERSPECTIVE

Defining LDCs

The most common indicator of development is that of gross domestic product (GDP) of a country (Colman and Nixson 1986). On this basis, classification of countries in terms of their development is on the basis of simple economic terms. GDP is a useful indicator. It is available for most countries and its measurement rules are clearly established. It does, however, have some limitations as a measure of development.

Map 15.1   Africa

First, GDP may be inaccurate as a measure in countries with a greater proportion of 'grey market' trade and poor statistical reporting. Moreover, international comparisons on the basis of GDP may be meaningless. Usher (1966) contends that data must take into account the dollar cost of subsistence in that country to give meaningful insights into the value of income *per capita*.

Secondly, GDP should be measured as a trend to give an indication of development. In Chapter 14, for example, the countries studied may have relatively a low GDP, but are in the process of rapid growth. On this basis they are classified as 'emerging' economies.

The most important criticism is that GDP measures only economic aspects of development. Baster (1972) points out that economic indicators place zero value on the social value of income. Particularly in poorer countries, the disparity of income distribution between urban and rural areas may be marked. GDP *per capita* shows the income split by population size, but does not reflect the range of incomes within the country. Colman and Nixson (1986, p. 10) note that it may be possible for GDP *per capita* figures for a country to improve 'apparently to signal an increase in social welfare, when in fact it has diminished'.

Although the limitations of GDP as a measure of development must be remembered, it is still the most common proxy for development and, as such, is used in this chapter. The world's LDCs in terms of GDP *per capita* in 1999 included Mozambique (GDP per capita of $84), Ethiopia ($102) and Congo ($122). As many, though not all, of the LDCs are in the African continent (Map 15.1), Africa is the focus of the discussion in this chapter.

Challenges

The Economic Constraint

Africa's poverty is one of the principal constraints on its economic attractiveness (Quelch and Austin 1993). Comparison of the growth rate of Ghana on independence in 1965 and South Korea show that the two began with a similar GDP *per capita*. In the early 1990s, however, Ghana's GDP *per capita* was less than 15 per cent of that found in South Korea. The increasing foreign debt taken on by the Sub-Saharan nations during the 1980s was a heavy drain and one of the reasons why the countries fall further and further behind. The region's share of world trade is less than half what it was in the late 1980s. This is partly because of the declining price of commodities which form the major part of exports.

In their 1984 article, Hill and Still identify a number of issues which firms must take into account when marketing to LDCs. Low levels of disposable income may have a number of ramifications. Items which are not considered luxury in wealthier countries may have to be sold in smaller pack sizes in LDCs to make them affordable. Hill and Still (1984) cite the example of cigars, which tend to be sold singly rather than in packs of six, and chewing gum, which may need to be packaged in smaller units. Most multinational corporations (MNCs) offer a selection of 'basic, versatile products' (Quelch and Austin 1993).

An ethical debate has arisen around pharmaceutical marketing in LDCs. In situations where the population cannot afford basic foodstuffs or medicines, the pricing and promotion of the products and services of international firms are subject to closer scrutiny by competitors and other stakeholders. In the controversy over the sale of infant formula in LDCs, one charge levelled at Nestlé was that mothers were persuaded to buy a product, which was unnecessary as they could breast feed free. Nestlé and other marketers of infant formula point out that mothers who themselves have dietary deficiencies might need to supplement their breast milk with another source of nutrition. Similarly, observers criticized the introduction at a premium by Ciba Geigy of an anti-malarial drug, which did not offer significant advances on other products in the market. It was felt that this might cause poor consumers to spend money unnecessarily.

Level of Technology

One of the principal challenges of less developed markets is the lack of investment in infrastructure. Transport systems, infrastructure and education may suffer from underinvestment. The level of technology which firms' design into products or services in LDCs may be different to that used in more advanced industrial economies. In some cases benefits may be offered to consumers in the country by reverting to a more basic technology. For remote rural parts of South Africa, the need for expensive batteries or mains electricity supply has been avoided by using a clockwork mechanism for radios. In Kenya, one firm prefers to use mechanical rather than electronic printers as these are simpler and therefore easier to repair.

As is noted in the discussion below of the duty of care of multinational corporations (MNCs), however, using more basic technologies where these meet the needs of the consumers delivers benefits to both seller and buyer. A subject of considerable concern in relation to LDCs is the use of obsolete or dangerous technologies, which would not be permissible in more advanced industrial economies.

One important point to note on technology is that while many LDCs lag behind more advanced nations technologically, they cannot necessarily be assumed to do so. Firms may find themselves returning to basic products and technologies in one area, but requiring leading edge technologies in others. This apparent incongruity of demand in emerging markets stems from the dispersion of income. The majority of disposable income often resides among a small minority of individuals who want advanced technology and luxury products as status symbols.

Levels of Education

The challenge of 'disparity' is particularly marked in LDCs. Distribution of wealth, living standards and other factors may differ dramatically between urban centres and more remote or rural areas. Differences in levels of education may pose a number of challenges. First, international marketers may have to take into account low literacy levels for instructions on product use and for safety instructions. One suggestion has been the use of signs and symbols rather than language. Secondly, it is suggested that hard selling and advertising may exert greater influence over less educated consumers. In part, the debate over the sale of infant formula centres on the use of promotional tools such as radio jingles. These describe infant formula as 'white man's powder that will make baby grow and glow'. Similarly, promotional use of 'milk nurses' visiting mothers in hospitals to provide samples of formula have been questioned (Murray, Gazda and Molenaar 1997).

The criticism that advertising manipulates consumers into buying things they do not need or should not have has been levelled more broadly (Schudson 1984). Research suggests that consumers in LDCs are vulnerable owing to poverty, illiteracy and lack of protection by their own governments (Gilly and Graham 1988). While host governments are often lax in their legislation to protect vulnerable consumers, a level of protection exists in some countries. Multinational corporations may need to avoid 'puffery' (inflated claims) such as 'giant', 'jumbo' and 'king' size. In India, for example, such claims have been banned to protect naive consumers (Hill and Still 1984).

■ **Appropriate for goals**. The technology should be aligned with the development goals of the host country government.
■ **Appropriateness of product/service**. The product or service should be useful, acceptable and affordable for the intended users.
■ **Appropriateness of process**. The production process should, where possible, make use of host country economic inputs. e.g. labour, raw materials.
■ **Cultural and environmental appropriateness**. All products, processes and institutional arrangements should be compatible with the host country culture and environment.

Figure 15.1   Appropriate marketing strategies
for LDCs
Source: IBRD (1976)

THE RELATIONSHIP PERSPECTIVE

In identifying relationship issues with respect to LDCs, it is important to remember that a country can be considered 'less developed' only in relation to other 'more developed' countries. Thus an important dimension of study of LDCs is that of their relationships with other more developed partners. Similarly, at the firm level, debates as to the benefits and difficulties of international trade relationships become important.

The Role of Multinational Corporations

Current debates focus on the role of multinational corporations in LDCs. A repeated demand (Terpstra 1990) is that multinationals should use 'appropriate' technology, products and marketing methods in LDCs.

The World Bank (IBRD 1976) offers a useful checklist to clarify what is meant by 'appropriate'. As there are over 100 countries which might be classified as LDCs, and each has different environmental challenges and issues, a definition of 'appropriate' is not straightforward. The World Bank identifies four dimensions (see Figure 15.1)

Multinational corporations may become involved in a number of relationships when operating in LDCs. In his study of food firms in LDCs, Berg (1972) identifies a number of reasons why multi-

nationals become involved in government nutrition programmes. These include: building relations with the host government, home government and the final consumers. This emphasis on building good relationships in LDCs is reminiscent of Kotler (1986), who proposes an additional two 'Ps' for operation in 'blocked' or hostile LDCs. These are 'Power' and 'Public relations'.

In Kotler's terms, gaining power involves winning the support of influential industry officials, legislators and government bureaucrats. These, he believes, are necessary to gain entry to and to operate in the target market. To deal with these stakeholders, the 'megamarketer' will need political skills and a political strategy. In contrast to the 'push' strategy of political negotiation, Kotler identifies the 'pull' benefits of public relations as important in LDCs. Understanding the country's cultural beliefs and values will allow the firm to 'play the good citizen' by contributing to public and worthwhile causes.

While representing pragmatic advice to multinationals wishing to enter or increase business in LDCs, the tone of Kotler's 'megamarketing' implies cynical 'role play' of concern (and behind-the-scenes political manoeuvring) as essentials of an international marketing strategy in LDCs. The issues of power and politics have grown in centrality in studies of LDCs and are, therefore, discussed more fully below.

Multinationals and Politics in LDCs

One of the more controversial aspects of international marketing in LDCs is the extent to which multinationals might be expected to compensate for, or even lobby for improvements in host government policies. Case Study 15.1 on Shell in Ogoni Land (p. 262) poses the question of the extent to which Shell should become involved in politics in Nigeria. The firm is operating within the local laws. Only by applying more stringent standards from its home, or another international, market would it intervene by appealing against the Nigerian government's actions towards the Ogoni rebels or against any other lax or controversial government policy.

Given the relative economic significance of multinationals in LDCs, however, the multinational may exert a greater level of influence than it would in a more advanced economy. Kotler (1986) advocates multinational involvement in political lobbying to advance their own and their shareholders' interests. Where, then, should the boundary fall in the areas of involvement and lobbying of a multinational in these countries? Newman (1980) gives examples of the dangers to which consumers in Malaysia were exposed in the early 1980s. In explaining the use of known carcinogens, inadequate product information and warnings and deceptive labelling respondents, foreign firms said that they were doing their best in a largely underregulated market.' In a worrying number of cases, however, they claimed 'that it was not their responsibility to act for the government' which they felt was itself exploiting its citizens.

Ethical Policy and Duty of Care

While traditional marketing suggests that firms exploit opportunities, which are presented by the legal, political and cultural features of a market, the laxness of these aspects of LDC marketing environments raises a set of moral dilemmas for international marketers. To what extent should the firm maximize its shareholders' wealth by doing business in these countries in a (legal)

way? To what extent should firms operate to the highest (or higher) standards than are required?

Amine (1998) highlights a number of scandals which have arisen from multinational corporations producing or marketing potentially harmful products in LDCs. These include the highly publicized sale of infant formula, continued sale of high tar cigarettes, pesticides and asbestos after these were legally banned in more advanced economies, and the sale of high dosage contraceptives over the counter. In pressing multinationals to become 'moral champions' in their international marketing activities, Amine says that:

> one might reasonably wonder why well-educated, professionally-trained managers, who work for companies with international reputations, might take decisions that risk provoking censure by the world's business community. Is it just the 'profit motive' run rampant? Is it merely the 'ugly face of capitalism'? Or are there other reasons that might explain the apparent willingness of Western managers to run the risk of jeopardizing the health and well-being of consumers in the developing world.

Smith and Quelch (1991) identify three levels of 'duty' to which managers of organizations should conform:

1. Avoid causing harm
2. Prevent harm
3. Do good.

They point out that the moral expectation that firms should avoid negative or harmful actions (points 1 or 2) generally meet with agreement from managers, but point 3, that firms should actively do good, is less generally accepted.

Smith (1990) identifies four 'attitudes' towards corporate social responsibility (see Figure 15.2).

The first of these attitudes equates to pursuing profit via any marketing strategy permissible by law in the target LDC. The second equates broadly to Smith and Quelch's levels 1 and 2 of duty (1991) which avoid negative actions, while the last two attitudes move into Smith and Quelch's level 3 of 'doing good'. Which attitude a firm takes seems to be a question of corporate policy. Amine argues that firms should be 'moral champions' who

1. Profit maximization and social irresponsibility

2. Profit maximization tempered by 'moral minimum stand-
    ards' which are self-regulated

3. Profit as a necessary but not sufficient goal, with positive
    action extending beyond self-regulation

4. Profit as a necessary but not sufficient goal, with positive
    action extending beyond self-regulation and champion-
    ing of political and moral causes unrelated to the cor-
    poration's activities.

Figure 15.2   Attitudes towards corporate social
responsibility
Source: Adapted from Smith (1990, pp. 56–60)

embrace a 'higher level of moral care and concern
for strangers' in LDCs (Amine 199, p. 391). It is
clear, though, that this does not mean becoming
directly involved in political or moral causes in a
foreign environment as this 'may be inappropriate
or even illegal'.

Donaldson (1996) attempts to clarify the complex
ethical issues facing multinationals, particularly in
dealing with 'vulnerable' partners as follows. he
identifies different philosophical approaches (see
Figure 15.3).

Langlois and Schlegelmilch (1998) analyze the
usage and content of the code of ethics of a sample of European and US firms to see whether
there are distinctive characteristics which seem
attributable to national differences. First, they
point to the fact that corporate ethics has attracted
far greater attention in the USA than in Europe.
This difference, they add, also extends to the content of business school curricula in the USA compared with Europe.

Earlier studies suggested that large firms were
more likely to have a code of ethics (Melrose-
Woodman and Kverndal 1976). Focusing on
these larger international firms (therefore potentially overestimating figures for the total population of firms) Langlois and Schlegelmilch found
that more (Former West) German firms (47 per
cent) than British firms (31 per cent) and French
firms (18 per cent) had a formal code of ethics.
Furthermore, the scope of the policy varied. Only
12 per cent of British firms (17 per cent of West
German and 20 per cent of French) had a written
policy on political involvement. It should be noted

1. **Cultural relativism**. No one country's ethics are better
    than another's, therefore there are no international rights
    and wrongs. Donaldson sees this 'when in Rome do as
    the Romans do' approach as tempting, especially when
    to do otherwise is to lose business.

2. **Ethical imperialism**. Do everywhere as you do at
    home. This may seem like a simple answer, but Donald-
    son highlights the possible failings of this approach
    using the example of a US manager training Saudi
    Arabian managers in handling sexual harassment
    issues in the same way that they would at home.
    Some local traditions and differences must be
    respected.

3. **Balanced approach**. Making a distinction between
    practices which are different, and those which are
    wrong. Donaldson proposes three guiding principles:

    - *Respect for core human values*. These determine
      the absolute moral threshold for all business
      activities
    - Respect for *local traditions*
    - The belief that *context matters* when deciding what
      is right and wrong.

Figure 15.3   Philosophical approaches
to international business ethics
Source: Based on Donaldson (1996)

that the percentage of US firms with a policy
towards political involvement is significantly
higher (96 per cent), perhaps suggesting differences in topical issues in the home markets of
the firms surveyed. Schlegelmilch and Robertson
(1998) substantiate the existence of differences in
the way ethical codes are adopted in different
countries and industries.

Power in Relationships Between Multinationals and LDCs

Amine (1998, p. 380) highlights the fact that relationships between international firms and their
domestic counterparts or consumers in LDCs are
often characterized by power imbalance because:

> the foreign corporation controls access to information
> about the product, its use, the likely effects of misuse,
> and the availability of safer alternatives.

This statement is written in the context of abuse of
power, and it suggests that the foreign investor
would intentionally mislead other actors with
whom it has relationships. Nonetheless, Amine's

words highlight the potential for problems arising from *power imbalance* in relationships between actors from countries at different stages of development.

Joint ventures between multinationals and local partners are the predominant type of organization used by multinationals in LDCs (Vaupel and Curham 1973, Beamish 1994). This type of joint venture has been described as a 'parent–child' relationship, where one partner dominates. The basis of the control is both financial and ownership (majority stake). The dependent partner may be governed in many aspects of operation including research and development (R&D) and marketing. Implicit in the parent–child contract is the idea that the parent might *transfer learning* to the child. In this instance, a multinational corporation forming a joint venture agreement with a local partner might not only provide capital, but also managerial and technological know-how from which its partner could improve its own skills.

Beamish (1994) identifies a set of motivations behind high and low performing international joint ventures (IJVs) between a multinational corporation and a local LDC partner. At the point of entry, many of these ventures are formed to satisfy host government requirements for local ownership. It is interesting to note that this motivation is one of the few which is common to both high and low performing IJVs. Beamish suggests that to meet this requirement almost any partner will suffice. More specific partner contributions, such as providing general and functional managers, were deemed important only in high performing IJVs. The inference from this research is that IJVs run by good local managers are more successful. One respondent explained this as being because 'a good national knows how to move around the local government bureaucracy'.

Technology Transfer in Relationships: Partners in Progress

One of the principal attractions for host country governments and joint venture partners in entering into an IJV is the possibility for transfer of knowledge. Technology is a major input requirement for economic development: over 50 per cent

of economic growth has been attributed to technological change.

Not surprisingly, therefore, since the 1960s international technology transfer has been subject to considerable enquiry by academics and practitioners. Contractor and Sagafi-Nejad (1981) highlight the fact that much technology is proprietary, i.e. owned by firms. The latest technologies, they contend, are concentrated in relatively few firms in a few industrial countries. A particular concern for LDCs is how to break their dependence on commodity, low value-added industry sectors. One answer seems to lie in acquiring technological competence in new areas. To ensure that this happens, technology transfer may be demanded by the host country government as a condition of joint venture agreements.

Yet gaining access to new technologies through technology transfer is not as simple a solution as it might initially appear. Empirical research (Lall and Streeten 1977; Contractor 1980) suggests that technology transfer may involve considerable costs for both the donor and the recipient. A number of potential problems in technology transfer to LDCs have been identified:

1. A potential **absence of suitable recipients of technology transfer**. Lack of technological knowledge or low education standards may make it difficult to identify appropriate partners.
2. Difficulties in determining an **appropriate price for the technology**. It may be difficult to value intangible assets, such as knowledge.
3. **Patents protect most vital information**, which is also concentrated within a few firms, hence the market for technology is highly imperfect.
4. The **success of the technology transfer** may be influenced by a number of factors: the type of technology, the level of dependence and the process of technology transfer.

Technology might be transferred in a number of different ways. These range from arm's length agreements to equity sharing. For the most part, US firms prefer direct investment if the technology is theirs (known as *proprietary*) rather than openly available (known as a *commodity*). Exercising direct control over foreign operations has higher costs but potentially offers higher long-term benefits (see Chapter 7 for a fuller discussion of control in international operations).

Relationships with Local Distributors

> Rarely can an African distributor supply the same service as the MNC would expect its clients to receive in the United States or Europe'. Hence, several MNCs, such as IBM and Nalco, have their own missionary salespeople and service technicians working in association with local distributors whose functions are often confined to the distribution of products. (Quelch and Austin 1993)

The relative lack of skilled labour in LDCs may represent a barrier to establishment of production facilities in the local market. The growth in free trade zones (FTZs) may improve the situation; currently, however, many multinationals import goods into the region from other proximate countries.

The use of distributors as well as joint ventures as a method of gaining access to African markets is widespread. The above quote suggests some of the issues which international marketers may face. In the era of global brands and global service guarantees, multinational firms may be concerned to protect product and service quality. Local distributors may represent an ideal method of serving the local market. To what extent, however, should multinationals impose international standards on their local partners, or accept cultural and other differences in business standards and methods?

Growing attention is paid in the literature to handling differences in *ethical standards* in multicultural relationships. One such issue surrounds the existence of illegal payments (Usunier 1993). Such payments have been given different names, 'baksheesh' in Arabic, 'dash' in Nigeria, 'chai' in East Africa. The name given to these payments offers some insights into how culturally acceptable they are. Often the term translates as 'gift' or 'consideration' rather than 'bribe'. Hence a payment which may be viewed by a partner of one nationality as illegal, or ethically unacceptable, may be part of the cultural mores in another (see Chapter 2 for fuller discussion of cultural differ-

ences and their relationship implications). 'Dash' is viewed as a fact of existence in Nigeria. Usunier contends (1993) that certain realities must be faced:

> Whether illegal payments are made and what sums are involved vary widely from one country and one industrial sector to another. They will be much more substantial, for example, in the construction industry or in Nigeria than in electronics or in Australia.

In relationship terms, problems may arise between partners when one firm takes a different view to the other. This may be exacerbated in LDCs where a distributor in Nigeria might, for example, give or accept payments, which might tarnish the multinational's international reputation. In such cases, the operating procedures of a distributor or other partner must be clearly identified. What discretion does the distributor have? What incentives or promotional tools are acceptable, and what may cause embarrassment if viewed outside the cultural context?

THE NETWORK PERSPECTIVE

To date there relatively little research has considered network structures in LDCs. Nonetheless, some studies give insights into relationship and network issues relevant to these markets.

Industry structure, competitive behaviour, technology and government policies are all heralded as causes of differences in joint ventures (Harrigan 1984). Previous research indicates a different rationale for joint venture relationships in developed and developing countries. Killing (1983) suggests that for developing countries, in order of importance, the three main reasons for creating joint ventures are:

1. Need for partner's skills
2. Need for partner's attributes or assets
3. Government persuasion or legislative requirement.

(See Chapter 7 Relationship perspective for a fuller discussion of joint venture relationships.) In less developed countries, however, Beamish (1985) identifies government legislation as the primary reason for joint ventures.

For firms from developing markets, which do not have strong competitive advantages to compensate for being 'foreign' (this view builds on the monopolistic advantage theory discussed in Chapter 7). Joint venture relationships are motivated mainly by overcoming entry barriers. Hence access to local market knowledge and business practices are the main reason for joint ventures between developing country and LDC partners.

Based on these differences in joint venture motivations and structure, it is perhaps not surprising that relationships between partners from developed countries and LDCs often founder. A number of contrasts have been drawn between these and developed country–developed country relationships:

1. **Developed–LDC relationships**. High instability rates and managerial dissatisfaction; majority control; parent–child relationship with high failure rate.

2. **Developed–developed country relationships**. More stable relationships; greater managerial satisfaction; shared control; a strong relationship between ownership and control.

3. **Developing–LDC relationships**. Minority stake by developing country partner; higher stability than experienced by developed country partners; greater understanding of context, higher likelihood of success.

In sum, predictors of success in joint venture relationships include valuing partner contributions and commitment to the relationship (Killing 1983; Beamish 1985). The size of the gap between developed and LDC partners, however, may militate against relationship development. An emerging market partner may be more realistic and knowledgeable about the challenges of operation in a LDC and, therefore, may forge more successful relationships.

Although Lee and Beamish (1995) do not posit the possibility, an inference from their findings is that network structures may develop with developing country firms as nodes between developed country and LDC partners.

CASE STUDY 15.1   SHELL IN OGONI LAND

People find it hard to feel sorry for multinational corporations. Almost by definition, they are rich, impersonal – and too free, many say, from supervision by any government. But spare a thought for he men huddling in the besieged boardroom of Royal Dutch/Shell. Just lately, the world's biggest oil company has seemed unable to do anything right. (*The Economist*, 2 December, 1995)

Shell is the largest producer of oil in Ogoni Land, Nigeria. In turn, oil produces some 80 per cent of the Nigerian government's revenues. Does this give Shell a privileged position in terms of its power in Nigeria? Some believe that Shell should have used this power to intervene in the questionable trial and hanging of nine members of the Ogoni separatist movement by the Nigerian military junta.

When, in June 1995, Shell planned to dump the Brent Spar oil platform into the sea, the public relations effects were catastrophic. Depicted as a 'despoiler of the seas' (*The Economist*, 2 December 1995), Shell realized that getting its public relations right was an important part of ongoing international success. With unfortunate timing, however, Shell hit the headlines again just six months later. Opponents suggested that the company, who had just announced a $3.6 billion natural gas project in the Niger Delta, was a supporter of the Nigerian government's decision to hang Ken Saro Wiwa and the remainder of the Ogoni Nine.

Ken Saro Wiwa, variously described as an author, environmentalist and leader of the Ogoni people, had been, in his time, a teacher, minister in a state government, grocer and property developer. He could have remained in his comfortable house in Esher, UK, but decided instead to go back to Ogoni Land. Ogoni Land is unfortunate in having much of Nigeria's oil beneath it. As a result, the farmland on which its people are dependent has been despoiled by the side effects of oil extraction. Flaring of gas, a by-product of oil extraction, has also caused damage to the surrounding land over the years. Water supplies have been subject to repeated contamination. Despite the wealth of their homeland, in terms of natural resources, the Ogoni people have remained in crippling poverty.

Most of Nigeria's rulers have either divided it religiously (into the Muslim North and Christian South) or else divided it ethnically (into the Hausa–Fulani North, Ibo East and Yoruba West.) Moreover, the Nigerian government has tried to create policies and a national identity which mask the divides. Groups such as the Ogoni, who did not fit easily into the divisions, had to 'compress their identity' into the prevailing framework. Given Nigeria's tribal past, it not surprising that the Movement for the Survival of the Ogoni People argued that Nigeria should have as many different states as it needed for political freedom of its people. Under Saro Wiwa's leadership it took on both the regime and the oil companies, demanding autonomy and compensation for the despoiling of its land. Nor is it surprising, perhaps, that the Nigerian government, fearing that Nigeria might break up, resisted these claims.

Nigeria is the largest country in West Africa. With a population of almost 100 million and rich agricultural soils, its oil reserves of around 20 billion barrels also make it potentially the richest African country. Since its independence in 1960, however, military rule has been the norm. A previous breakaway by the Eastern region resulted in the Biafran war in 1967–70, a civil war that cost a million lives and years of feud and famine.

In 1995, under General Sana Abacha's corrupt regime, repression, corruption and embezzlement were rife. Commonwealth leaders, congregated in New Zealand when Ken Saro Wiwa and his colleagues were hanged (for allegedly encouraging the murder of four moderate Chiefs in 1994), looked on aghast as a military tribunal tried and hanged the nine, their pleas for leniency going unanswered.

Unable to resolve the corruption in Nigeria, lobbyists did not, however, direct their criticism at international governments and peacekeepers, but at Shell. The size of the income which Shell's oil operations afford the Nigerian government, and its questionable history in environmental terms it makes an easy target. In Shell's defence, however, it is making considerable efforts to remedy any despoiling of the Niger delta. A $3.6 billion project for liquid natural gas is ecologically sound and stands to benefit the Nigerian people, not just its government. Shell public relations material stressed the job creation and cleaner environment which would result from the project. The revenues from the project will be long-term, and so will not immediately disappear into the pockets of the Nigerian government. Opponents of Shell argue that it may well argue that it is cleaning the environment, but it caused much of the damage in the first place. Moreover, the mere existence of the project enhances the government's position and will produce long-term revenues for it.

The crux of the debate lies in the question of whether Shell is behaving in any way which is not appropriate for a multinational corporation. It is law abiding, albeit in a corrupt regime. It didn't set, nor approve of, the Nigerian government's policies and actions. Fellow multinational corporations are rushing to enter China, with its questionable human rights, and India, which has been involved with nuclear testing. Even if Shell pulled out of Nigeria, would it not just be replaced by one of its multinational competitors?

To conclude, in *The Economist's* words (2 December 1995):

> Against such complexities, it is tempting to argue for a simple division of labour. Let governments perform the complex moral calculus; let multinationals observe international law, comply with international sanctions, observe international environmental standards, avoid outright oppression of local people – but behave otherwise as political neutrals, free to make business decisions on business criteria alone ... Shell has been accused of two kinds of sin: sins of commission and sins of omission. Their defence is stronger against the first charge, weaker on the second.

Sources: *The Economist* (1995) 'Multinationals and their Morals: It is not Only Shell's Judgement that is on Trial in Nigeria', 2 December; *The Economist* (1995) 'Saro-Wiwa's Peril/Death Sentence in Nigeria', 4 November; *The Economist* (1995) 'Nigeria Foaming', 18 November.

QUESTIONS

1. To what standards should Shell be expected to operate in Nigeria:
   (a) local laws
   (b) home market laws
   (c) the highest international standards?
2. What would be the advantages and disadvantages for Shell of adopting each of these sets of standards?
3. Should multinational corporations be expected only to avoid doing wrong, or to actively do right?
4. To what extent should Multinational Corporations engage in politics?

SUMMARY

In Chapter 14 we have explored the challenges of operation in LDCs. Distinctive types of relationship in the region and their management are explored. Finally the contributions of network studies in the region are evaluated.

BIBLIOGRAPHY

Amine (1998) 'The Need for Moral Champions in Global Marketing', in Schlegelmilch, B. (ed.), *Marketing Ethics: An international Perspective*, International Thompson Press: 380–96.

Baster, N. (ed.) (1972) *Measuring Development*, Frank Cass.

Beamish, P. W. (1985) 'The Characteristics of Joint Ventures in Developed and Developing Countries', *Journal of International Business Studies*, 23, 1: 1–27.

Beamish, P. W. (1994) 'Joint Ventures in LDCs: Partner Selection and Performance', *Management International Review*, 2: 60–74.

Berg, A. (1972) 'World Malnutrition', *Harvard Business Review*, January–February: 130–41.

Colman, D. and Nixson, F. (1986) *Economics of Change in Less Developed Countries*, 2nd. edn, Philip Allan/Barnes and Noble Books.

Contractor, F. (1980) 'The Composition of Licensing Fees and Arrangements as a Function of Economic Development of Technology Dependent Nations', *Journal of International Business Studies*, Winter: 47–62.

Contractor, F. and Sagafi-Nejad, T. (1981) 'International Technology Transfer: Major Issues and Policy Responses', *Journal of International Business Studies*, Fall: 113–35.

Donaldson, T. (1996) 'Values in Tension: Ethics away from Home' *Harvard Business Review*, September–October: 48–62.

Gilly, M. C. and Graham, J. L. (1988) 'A Macroeconomic Study of the Effects of Promotion on the Consumption of Infant Formula in Developing Countries', *Journal of Macromarketing*, 14–37.

Harrigan, K. R. (1984) *Strategies for Joint Ventures*, D. C. Heath.

Hill, J. S. and Still, R. R. (1984) 'Adapting Products to LDC Tastes', *Harvard Business Review*, March–April: 92–101.

IBRD (1976) 'Appropriate Technology in World Bank Activities', 19 July.

Killing, J. P. (1983) *Strategies for Joint Venture Success*, Praeger.

Kotler, P. (1986) 'Megamarketing', *Harvard Business Review*, March–April: 117–24.

Lall, S. and Streeten, P. (1977) *Foreign Investment, Transnationals and Developing Countries*, Macmillan.

Langlois, C. C. and Schlegelmilch, B. B. (1998) 'Do Corporate Codes of Ethics Reflect National Character? Evidence from Europe and the United States', in Schlegelmilch, B. B. (ed.) (1998), *Marketing Ethics: An International Perspective*, International Thompson Business Press: 356–79.

Lee, C. and Beamish, P. W. (1995) 'The Characteristics and Performance of Korean Joint Ventures in LDCs', *Journal of International Business Studies*, 26, 3: 637–54.

Melrose-Woodman, J. and Kverndal, I. (1976) *Towards Social Responsibility: Company Codes of Ethics and Practice*, British Institute of Management Survey Reports, 28.

Murray, J. A., Gazda, G. M. and Molenaar, M. J. (1997) 'Nestlé – The Infant Formula Incident', in Meloan, T. W. and Graham, J. L. (eds) (1997), *International and Global Marketing: Concepts and Cases*, Irwin and McGraw-Hill.

Newman, B. (1980) 'Consumer Protection is Underdeveloped in the Third World', *The Wall Street Journal*, 8 April: 23.

Quelch, J. A. and Austin, J. E. (1993) 'Opinion: Should Multinationals Invest in Africa?', *Sloan Management Review*, Spring: 107–19.

Schlegelmilch, B. B. (ed.) (1998) *Marketing Ethics: An International Perspective*, International Thompson Business Press.

Schlegelmilch, B. B. and Robertson, D. C. (1998) 'The Influence of Country and Industry on Ethical Perceptions of Senior Executives in the US and Europe', in Schlegelmilch, B. B. (ed.) (1998), *Marketing Ethics: An International Perspective*, International Thompson Business Press: 302–27.

Schudson, M. (1984) *Advertising, the Uneasy Persuasion*, Basic Books.

Smith, N. C. (1990) *Morality and the Market: Consumer Pressure for Corporate Accountability*, Routledge.

Smith, N. C. and Quelch, J. A. (1991) 'Pharmaceutical Marketing Practices in the Third World', *Journal of Business Research*, 23, 1: 113–26.

Tallman, S. B. and Shenkar, O. (1994) 'International Co-operative Venture Strategies: Outward Investment and Small Firms from NICs', *Management International Review*, 2: 75–91.

Terpstra, V. (1990) 'On Marketing Appropriate Products in Developing Countries', in McDonald, M. H. B. and Cavusgil, S. T. (eds) (1990), *The International Marketing Digest*, Butterworth-Heinemann: 177–92.

Usher, D. (1966) *Rich and Poor Countries*, Eaton Paper 9, Institute of Economic Affairs.

Usunier, J.-C. (1989) 'Interculturel: la parole et l'action', *Harvard-L'Expansion*, 52, Spring: 84–92.

Usunier, J.-C. (1993) *International Marketing: A Cultural Approach*, Prentice-Hall.

Vaupel, J. W. and Curham, J. P. (1973) *The World's Multinational Enterprises*, Harvard University Press.

PART VI

INTERNATIONAL MARKETING ORGANIZATIONS

The final part of this book looks at the implications of international marketing organization for successful international marketing strategies and actions. Studies show that market oriented organizations have a set of distinct organizational features. These include long-term orientation, measuring success in terms of market share, flat structures and cross-functional teams. Doyle (1998) argues that, while identification of market opportunities and creation of innovative innovative marketing strategies and mix are important, sustainable advantages can be created only if the organizational structure and processes favour innovation.

This book concludes, therefore, with a discussion of international marketing organization. This is reviewed from a Traditional perspective by discussion of the features of market oriented companies. From a Relationship perspective, the characteristics of organizations that build successful international relationships are reviewed, based on interaction studies (Turnbull and Valla 1986). Finally, this section explores the Network view of organizations as political entities comprised of a web of interpersonal relationships.

BIBLIOGRAPHY

Doyle, P. (1998) in Doyle, P. and Bridgewater, S. *Innovation in Marketing*, Butterworth-Heinemann.

Turnbull, P. W. and Valla, J.-P. (1986) *Strategies for International Industrial Marketing*, Routledge.

INTERNATIONAL MARKETING ORGANIZATION

Objectives

The issues to be addressed in Chapter 16 include:

1. The role of international marketing organization in the creation of international marketing strategies
2. Characteristics of market-oriented organizations
3. Characteristics of organizations that build successful international relationships
4. Organizations as webs of inter-personal relationships.

After reading Chapter 16 you will be able to:

1. Identify market-oriented organizations and understand their benefits
2. Understand the types of firms that successful in relationship development
3. Understand the implications of organizations as networks of relationships.

INTRODUCTION

Designing successful international marketing strategies for different international marketing contexts is a major challenge for the new millennium. The context and strategy sections of this book highlights the fact that sustainable advantages can be created only if firms continue to identify emerging trends and develop innovative strategies. Research suggests that in international organizations, the key to competitive advantage lies in organizational structure and processes. Work by Doyle, Saunders and Wong (1986, 1992) demonstrates the link between marketing orientation and flexible, responsive organizational structures.

The book concludes, therefore, with a review of challenges for the international marketing organization from Traditional, Relationship and Network perspectives. From a Traditional perspective, the characteristics of organizations with a market orientation are contrasted across a number of different international markets. The transition in international structures from ethnocentric to poly-, regio- and geo-centric organizational structures is also discussed.

From a Relationship perspective, the challenges are those of analyzing where the organization adds value globally. Global organizations increasingly de-couple the value chain, locating activities in different international markets. Managing internal relationships, then, may become as important to international marketing success as managing external relationships.

The Network perspective on the international marketing organization takes the Cyert and March (1963) definition of the organization as a 'political entity' comprising many individuals with different interests and agendas. Within the organization, relationships between subsidiaries and individuals within subsidiaries will play a role in the creation of international relationships (Forsgren 1989a).

Creating Marketing Oriented Organizations

Marketing orientation has been identified as a significant factor in business success (Narver and Slater 1990; Doyle, Saunders and Wong 1992). The concept of marketing orientation has been conceptualized in a number of ways. One strand of literature focuses on the ability of the firm to adapt to changing market conditions (Kohli and Jaworski 1990). According to the latter, intelligence generation, intelligence dissemination and responsiveness are the key features of marketing orientation.

Another distinct view is more action oriented (Golden *et al.* 1995). Narver and Slater (1990) propose three components of market orientation:

- Customer orientation
- Competitor orientation
- Interfunctional co-ordination.

These are predictors of two measures of success: *long-term orientation* and *profitability*.

From the above definitions it is apparent, therefore, that marketing orientation depends not only on having a marketing department, but has broader ramifications. Market orientation is a philosophy underlying business and may have implications for the way in which the firm is organized. Characteristics associated with marketing orientation include:

1. **Headquarter information systems and controls** are more likely to emphasize financial measures in product oriented companies, but market performance measures in market oriented companies.
2. **Long-term orientation**. Market oriented companies tend also to use a longer measurement period.
3. Market orientation may have **human resource implications**, as long-term success may foster confidence in employees. There is also a greater commitment to training and on-the-job development.

4. Successful companies tend to use **market focused** rather than **functional organizational structures**.
5. Market oriented companies may tailor more to **local market conditions**.

The influential series of Doyle, Saunders and Wong studies (1986, 1992) suggested that the market orientation and organizational characteristics listed above were particularly associated with Japanese firms. In a comparison of American, British and Japanese subsidiaries of multinational corporations, four out of five Japanese subsidiaries were found to have aggressive growth or market domination objectives compared to only half of the American firms and one in five of the British firms. Japanese firms tended to have aggressive volume growth targets, which they believed would enable them to be efficient in cost terms. Volume sales would create sufficient resources to sustain product development. The Western approach might produce good short-term profits. In the long term, however, firms devoting too much attention to profitability might reduce investment in innovation and brand-building (Doyle, Saunders and Wong 1992).

Successful, market oriented firms also showed real organizational differences from product oriented firms. Japanese subsidiaries showed greater local autonomy in their marketing practices. This included discretion over product range, pricing, promotion and distribution. Distinctive differences were also apparent in the attitude towards international operation. The majority of American subsidiaries showed a home country (ethnocentric) attitude. This included limited understanding of the markets to be penetrated. There was a tendency to develop products for the home market and then transfer them into international markets, despite having a poor fit with local market needs and wants.

Structurally, American companies tended to use more complex, matrix structures. National subsidiaries reported to Headquarters via divisions. Both American and British firms tended to employ functional structures where a wide range of product lines might be handled by the same business. In contrast, Japanese firms segmented organizations into smaller business units. An implication of functional structures was that managers accepted little responsibility for overall business performance. The flexibility of these structures also tended to be lower. Responsibility for overall business performance was much greater in Japanese firms. While Japanese firms used informal teamwork and empowered managers to develop marketing strategies, American organizations, in particular, tended to be hierarchical with precise job boundaries. In sum, market oriented firms showed greater clarity, commitment and shared values than did product oriented firms.

Doyle, Saunders and Wong's (1992) identification of a link between market orientation and the philosophy and organization of business has been developed by a number of subsequent studies.

More recently, organization has been shown as being equally, if not more, important in creating sustainable competitive advantages than marketing strategy (Doyle and Bridgewater 1998).

The basic challenge for marketing firms entering the new millennium is that of creating organizational structures which allow ongoing innovationand creation of sustainable advantages in rapidly changing environments (Doyle 1998).

Studies of market oriented organizations have subsequently been carried out for German firms (Doyle, Wong and Shaw 1994, Shaw 1994, 1995) and East and Central European (CEE) firms (Cox et al. 1999; Fahy et al. 1999).

In studying German firms, marketing strategies and organizational characteristics of successful firms were similar to those in the Japanese study. Successful German machine tool firms developed long-term strategies with an emphasis on market share (Shaw 1995). The success of these firms, in part, related to their ability to adapt to the changing needs of machine tool customers. When comparing the German findings with the previous American, Japanese and British results, German firms lay mid-way between the Japanese and American and British firms. German firms took a more laid back attitude to short-term profits, but were similar to other Western firms in their organization, control and reporting procedures (Doyle, Wong and Shaw 1994).

Studies of marketing orientation in CEE firms show a marked contrast with firms from free market economies. Given their roots in the central planning system, these firms have tended to be product, rather than marketing, oriented. Golden et al. (1995, p. 30) explain that state owned enterprises under central planning:

> deliver a specified level of goods and services to a state agent at a pre-determined price. As a result, customer needs are minimized and there is little need for firms to manipulate the marketing mix of their products.

Other explanations of low levels of market orientation under central planning include the lack of free competition and the fact that demand exceeds supply (Shama 1992).

In the process of transition to market economy, firms from CEE markets provide an interesting topic of study. A number of phenomena relating to the success of these firms and its determinants are found in the studies of Hooley et al. (see Hooley 1993; Shipley 1993; Cox et al. 1999; Fahy et al. 1999). Cox et al. (1999) explore the controversy over the relative impacts of macro-environment and company strategies on business performance through a study of Polish firms. Fahy et al. (1999), in a parallel study, look at the insights to be gained from resource-based views of the firm in the context of Central Europe. In the transition process, firms are moving towards market orientation. State owned enterprises remain relatively product or production oriented (Cox et al. 1999). Firms with foreign investors show the greatest long-term strategies. Privately owned firms, maybe as a result of stakeholder influences, are currently interested in short-term gains. State owned enterprises frequently face survival crises.

Studies of market orientation also help to understand the environment–strategy interface. Marketing orientation has also been proposed as a link between increasing environmental uncertainty and business performance (Conant, Mokwa and Varadarajan 1990; Manu 1993; McDaniel and Kolari 1987).

International Organization

International organizations have often been described as progressing through a series of stages. The nature and type of these stages varies.

Chapter 8 discusses the progression from exporting through to sales and manufacturing subsidiaries. Stage models have also been developed to describe the 'attitude' towards international operation and the overall structure of the firm. In their widely cited study, Stopford and Wells (1972) describe a progression from having an international division through to a global matrix using either a centralized or decentralized strategy.

In another of the better-known models, Perlmutter (1969) describes a 'tortuous evolution of the multinational corporation' through a number of stages:

1. Ethnocentric
2. Polycentric
3. Regiocentric
4. Geocentric.

We shall look at each of these in turn.

Ethnocentricity

The first stage of international development is described as *ethnocentric* (ethno- meaning 'one race', from Greek: ethnos, race). The firm's managers and attitude are largely based in the home market, and international operations tend to be closely controlled by managers in the home market. Export is the predominant mode and is most likely to be conducted using the company's own sales force.

Polycentricity

At this stage, the firm has moved beyond one market and may have managers in many (poly- meaning 'many', from Greek: polus, much).

Decisions and international marketing strategies are likely to be decided in many locations.

Regiocentricity

At this stage the organization will have such a strong presence within one region that it may no longer be strongly linked to one nationality. Decisions will be made in autonomous subsidiaries by individuals from many countries within the region.

Geocentricity

At the final stage of evolution organizations are 'geocentric' or global. In global organizations, original nationality is no longer easy to identify. In a *Harvard Business Review* article, Robert Reich (1990) argues, for example, that it is no longer easy to identify 'truly American companies'. In a follow-up article the next year (Reich 1991), the author goes on to argue that globalization of the economy is such that firms have moved beyond national allegiance to become global institutions whose success depends on developing a cadre of skilled global managers.

While stage models break down the challenges of international organization into recognizable phases, Bartlett (1986, p. 368) questions their value as they try to provide simple solutions to complex problems:

> A company cannot develop a corporation that can sense, analyze, and respond to the complexity of the international environment on the basis of a simple rule of thumb relating to product or geographic diversity.

Global Organizations: Reality or Myth?

In the same way that technological advances, increased travel and increasingly cosmopolitan tastes lend credence to arguments for global standardization (see Chapter 5, Traditional perspectives section), so the arguments of Reich (1990, 1991) have an intuitive appeal.

Perlmutter's 1969 identification of geocentric, or global, organizations, was the precursor of a number of studies of global corporations. A valuable selection of the seminal articles can be found in Porter (1986). In his Introduction to this book, Porter argues that, in the face of global competition, a firm must decide on the optimal allocation of the activities of the value chain globally. He splits these into downstream (supply and manufacturing) and upstream (distribution and sales and marketing activities). Porter argues that the latter are tied to where the customer is, while the former may, however, be decoupled and located in the most cost-efficient location. The decoupling of manufacture and sales/marketing underpins a number of definitions of global organizations.

While the arguments of Hu (1992) that multinationality is a myth are controversial and may stretch a point or two, Lorenz (1992) suggests that 'his argument may be closer to the truth than most "multinational" companies would admit'.

The main arguments of Hu's thesis are that, on a number of dimensions, the extent of globalization has been exaggerated:

■ **Geographic spread**. Definitions of multinational and global operations frequently contain a measure of geographic scope.

Hu argues that, in fact, most multinational corporations, including big names such as Du Pont and General Motors, have less than half their employees and operations outside the home market. This may be particularly the case for North American corporations, for whom the home market is sufficiently large to comprise a major share of global operations.

■ **People**. The percentage of an organization's employees from other countries represents an ever lower percentage as higher levels of the hierarchy: a 'miniscule' proportion of senior managers may be from outside the home country. A higher proportion of employees at lower levels of the organization may, however, be from local markets.

■ **Ownership and control**. Hu also argues that ownership and control remain largely national (in Perlmutter's terms 'ethnocentric' or, at most, 'polycentric'). The firm may have subsidiaries in a number of countries, but the locus of decision making may be less extensive than the spread of international operations. This may be characterized by retention of control in joint ventures. Johnson Wax were prevented, for example, from entering Ukraine (Box 9.1) while laws prevented foreign company control over international operations.

■ **Legal nationality and taxation**. In terms of legal, tax and accounting regimes, each country must be handled differently. While some similarity may, for example, exist between accounting systems based on the US, British or French codes, each country has distinctive characteristics. From this perspective, there is no such thing as a 'global' or 'multinational' corporation.

THE RELATIONSHIP PERSPECTIVE

The basis of international organization from a relationship perspective lies in Porter's distinction (1986) between the *configuration* of the organization's value chain (where in the world activities are performed) and the *co-ordination* of these activities. While configuration might be explained by economic considerations, creating effective relationships and co-ordination mechanisms within the firm is vital to organizational success.

Complex geocentric structures were identified by Perlmutter (1969) and complex, divisionalized structures were found to dominate in Western firms (Doyle, Saunders and Wong 1992). From a relationship perspective, the principal challenge is that of managing global–local tensions within the firms.

Porter (1986, p. 56) argues that technological advances will increase the ability of organizations to 'co-ordinate globally throughout the value chain'. At the same time, he suggests a tendency towards increasing global dispersion of the value chain. According to Porter, therefore, firms are moving away from ethnocentric (based on home market activities) towards geocentric organizational types, and away from multi-domestic or locally adapted strategies towards global co-ordination of value chain activities. Porter (1986, p.35) argues that:

> The essence of international strategy is not to resolve trade-offs between concentration and dispersion, but to eliminate or mitigate them. This implies concentrating and dispersing different value activities depending on industry structure, dispersing some activities to allow concentration of others, and minimizing the trade-off between concentration and dispersion by co ordinating dispersed activities.

Remembering that Doyle, Saunders and Wong (1992) identify local market responsiveness as making a positive contribution to market orientation in Japanese firms, Porter's arguments mean that global competitive advantage will increasingly depend on a firm's ability to manage *internal relationships*.

A number of different internal relationships may take on global significance for firms. Flaherty (1986) focuses on the challenges of co-ordination in international manufacturing and technology relationships. Proper co-ordination of these, she argues, has the potential to reduce costs and to enhance the effectiveness of multiple manufacturing operations. Flaherty uses the example of a US chemical manufacturer improving the operation of a US plant with knowledge gained in a European subsidiary.

Relationships might also extend downstream. Leveraging relationships between manufacturing subsidiaries might also achieve cost savings if, for example, two subsidiaries combining their purchasing activities and buy larger volumes of raw materials from the same supplier.

Chapter 5 discusses the extent to which global co-ordination is desirable and attainable in marketing. Buzzell (1968) notes a move away from multi-domestic towards global marketing strategies. Levitt (1983) argues for global standardization of marketing activities, while a number of other authors suggest that standardization of some elements of marketing strategy and mix may be desirable (Quelch and Hoff 1986; Douglas and Wind 1987; Riesenbeck and Freeling 1991). Takeuchi and Porter (1986) suggest that the key issues relate to where marketing activities are performed and how they are co-ordinated.

Co-ordination, they suggest, may take a number of forms:

- **Use of similar methods across markets**. This might involve using a global brand, positioning or service strategy across international markets.
- **Transfer of marketing know-how across countries**. Organizations might create global information systems, learn from previous market entry methods or otherwise benefit from successful, or unsuccessful, marketing activities of other subsidiaries.
- **Integration of marketing efforts across subsidiaries**. Collective marketing activities, for

example international account management activities (see Chapter 10) may involve subsidiaries working together directly. This type of activity may require organizational changes (Yip and Madsen 1996) to both structure and processes.

THE NETWORK PERSPECTIVE

From a network perspective multinational organizations may involve centre–centre relationships between subsidiaries as well as between individual actors (Forsgren 1989; Forsgren and Johanson 1992; Forsgren, Holm and Thilenius 1997; Pahlberg 1997).

Centre–centre structures may have a number of implications for international marketers:

Communication

Forsgren (1989) argues that centre–centre structures may result in psychic distance within a firm. If decisions are taken in various parts of the world, some actors will inevitably be geographically and culturally distant and less likely to understand the organization's actions:

> In a network actors have fairly clear views of their own relations with, and dependencies on, other actors and some relations of these actors to third actors although these are generally much vaguer. The views of more distant parts of the network are, however, rather unclear. Furthermore, the views of different actors may differ considerably. (Axelsson and Johanson 1992, p. 231)

Location of Research and Development Activities

The HQ–Subsidiary model of international organizations makes the implicit assumption that innovation is the responsibility of the centre. Subsidiaries are then be responsible for implementing innovations in their own country. With centre–centre structures comes a fragmentation of innovative activity.

One measure of innovation, research and development (R&D) activity, suggests that the proportion of R&D activity outside the home market has increased. Forsgren (1997) cites SKF, the Swedish ball-bearing company, which has had foreign patents for 70 per cent of its products since the early 1970s. Granstrand, Hkansson and Sjölander (1992) support this finding, suggesting that the foreign share of R&D activities stands at between 30 and 40 per cent.

The dispersion of innovative activity has both advantages and disadvantages. Advantages include the fact that the organization can capture and act upon ideas from a broad range of markets. Its ability to be close to markets increases with a centre–centre structure. Indeed, the fact that advantages accrue from operation in technologically diverse contexts is supported by a wide body of research (Nohria *et al.* 1994; Yamin 1995). Conversely, dispersion can result in duplication and inefficiency.

Control over Subsidiary Activities

A recurrent theme of international marketing literature is the need for global consistency in international marketing strategies. Yip and Madsen (1996) suggest that firms may need to adapt their international organizational structures and processes, as well as their international marketing strategies, in order to achieve this consistency. With centre–centre structures, however, comes a lowering of control over subsidiary activities (Andersson and Forsgren 1995).

SUMMARY

In this chapter we have considered the challenges for international marketers of creating market-oriented organizations capable of successfully implementing international marketing strategies. We have explore the types of organizations that are successful in relationship development and management. Finally we have studied organizations as webs of relationships and considered the implications of this view for international marketing.

BIBLIOGRAPHY

Andersson, U. and Forsgren, M. (1995) 'Using Networks to Determine Parental Control of Subsidiaries', in Paliwoda, S. and Ryans, J. K. (eds), *International Marketing Reader*, Routledge.

Axelsson, B. and Johanson, J. (1992) 'Foreign Market Entry – The Text Book vs the Network View', in Axelsson, B. and Easton, G. (eds), *Industrial Networks: A New View of Reality*, Routledge.

Bartlett, C. A. (1986) 'Building and Managing the Transnational: The New Organizational Challenge', in Porter, M. E. (1986), (ed.), *Competition in Global Industries*, Harvard Business School Press.

Buzzell, R. (1968) 'Can You Standardize Multinational Marketing?', *Harvard Business Review*, November–December: 102–13.

Conant, J. S., Mokwa, M. and Varadarajan, P. R. (1990) 'Strategic Types, Distinctive Marketing Competencies and Organizational Performance', *Strategic Management Journal*, 11, 5: 365–83.

Cox, T., Hooley, G. J., Fahy, J. and Fonfara, K. (1999) 'The Balance of Macro-Level and Company-Level Influences on Market Orientation and Company Performance in Poland', EMAC Proceedings, Berlin.

Cyert, R. M. and March, J. G. (1963) *A Behavioural Theory of the Firm*, Englewood Cliffs.

Douglas, S. and Wind, Y. (1987) 'The Myth of Globalization', *Columbia Journal of World Business*, Winter: 19–29.

Doyle, P. (1998) 'Introduction', in Doyle, P. and Bridgewater, S. (eds), *Innovation in Marketing*, Butterworth–Heinemann.

Doyle, P. and Bridgewater, S. (eds) (1998) *Innovation in Marketing*, Butterworth–Heinemann.

Doyle, P., Saunders, J. and Wong, V. (1986) 'A Comparative Analysis of Japanese Marketing

Strategies in the British market', *Journal of International Business Studies*, Spring: 27–46.

Doyle, P., Saunders, J. and Wong, V. (1992) 'Competition in Global Markets: A Case Study of American and Japanese Competition in the British Market', *Journal of International Business Studies*, 3: 419–42.

Doyle, P., Wong, V. and Shaw, V. (1994) 'Marketing Strategies of International Competitors in the UK Machine Tool Market', *Journal of Global Marketing*, 8, 2: 75–97.

Fahy, J., Hooley, G. J., Cox, T. and Beracs, J. (1999) 'Privatization and Sustainable Advantage in the Emerging Economies of Central Europe', *EMAC Proceedings*, Berlin.

Flaherty, M. T. (1986) 'Co-ordinating International Manufacturing and Technology', in Porter, M. E. (ed.) (1986), *Competition in Global Industries*, Harvard Business School Press.

Forsgren, M. (1989a) *Managing the Internationalization Process: The Swedish Case*, Routledge.

Forsgren, M. (1989b) 'Foreign Acquisition: Internalization or Network Interdependency', in Cavusgil S. T. (ed.), *Advances in International Marketing*, 3, JAI Press: 121–139.

Forsgren, M. (1997) 'The Advantage Paradox of the Multinational Corporation', in Björkman, I. and Forsgren, M. (eds), *The Nature of the Multinational Firm: Nordic Contributions to International Business Research*, Copenhagen Business School Press.

Forsgren, M. and Holm, U. (1990) 'Internationalization of Division Management in Swedish International Firms', *Uppsala Working Paper*, 1990/5.

Forsgren, M. and Johanson, J. (eds) (1992) *Managing Networks in International Business*, Gordon & Breach.

Forsgren, M., Holm, P. and Thilennius, P. (1997) 'Network Infusion in the Multinational Corporation', in Björkaan, I. and Forsgren, M. (eds), *The Nature of the International Firm*, Copenhagen Business School Press.

Golden, P. A., Doney, P. M., Johnson, D. M. and Smith, J. R. (1995) 'The Dynamics of a Marketing Orientation in Transition Economies: A Study of Russian Firms', *Journal of International Marketing*, 3, 2: 29–49.

Granstrand, O., Hkansson, L. and Sjölander, S. (1992) *Technology Management and International Business*, John Wiley.

Hedlund, G. (1986) 'The Hypermodern MNC – A Heterarchy?', *Human Resource Management*, 25, 1: 9–35.

Hooley, G. J. (1993) 'Marketing Strategy Typologies in Hungary', *European Journal of Marketing*, 27, 11/12: 80–92.

Hu, Y.-S. (1992) 'Global or Stateless Corporations Are National Firms with International Operations', *California Management Review*, Winter: 107–26.

Kohli, A. K. and Jaworski, B. (1990) 'Marketing Orientation: The Construct, Research Propositions and Managerial Implications', *Journal of Marketing*, 54, 2: 1–18.

Levitt (1983) 'The Globalization of Markets', *Harvard Business Review*, May–June: 92–102.

Lorenz, C. (1992) 'The Multinational Myth Explodes', *Financial Times*, 4 March.

Manu, F. A. (1993) 'Innovation, Marketing and Performance in European Consumer Markets', *Journal of Euromarketing*, 2, 3: 73–99.

McDaniel, S. W. and Kolari, J. W. (1987) 'Marketing Implications of the Miles and Snow Typology', *Journal of Marketing*, 51, 4: 19–30.

Narver, J. and Slater, S. (1990) 'The Effect of Marketing Orientation on Business Profitability', *Journal of Marketing*, 54: 20–35.

Nohria, N. and Ghoshal, S. (1994) 'Differentiated Fit and Shared Values: Alternatives for Managing Headquarters–Subsidiary Relationships', *Strategic Management Journal*, 15: 491–502.

Pahlberg (1997) 'Cultural Differences and Problems in HQ–Subsidiary Relationships in MNCs' in Björkmna, I. and Forsgren, M. (eds), *The Nature of the International Firm*, Copenhagen Business School.

Perlmutter, H. (1969) 'The Tortuous Evolution of the Multinational Corporation', *Columbia Journal of World Business*, January–February: 9–18.

Porter, M. E. (ed.) (1986) *Competition in Global Industries*, Harvard Business School Press.

Quelch, J. A. and Hoff, E. J. (1986) 'Customising Global Marketing', *Harvard Business Review*, May–June.

Reich, R. (1990) 'Who is Us?', *Harvard Business Review*, January–February: 53–65.

Reich, R. (1991) 'Who is Them?', *Harvard Business Review*, March–April: 77–89.

Riesenbeck, H. and Freeling, A. (1991) 'How Global are Global Brands?', *McKinsey Quarterly*, 4: 3–18.

Shama, A. (1992) 'Transforming the Consumer in Russia and Eastern Europe', *International Marketing Review*, 9, 5: 43–59.

Shaw, V. (1994) 'The Marketing Strategies of British and German Firms', *European Journal of Marketing*, 28, 7: 30–44.

Shaw, V. (1995) 'Successful Marketing Strategies: A Study of British and German Companies in the Machine Tool Industry', *Industrial Marketing Management*, 24, 4: 329–40.

Shipley, D. (1993) 'Organization for Marketing among Polish Companies', *European Journal of Marketing*, 27, 11/12: 60–80.

Stopford, J. M. and Wells, L. T. Jr. (1972) *Managing the Multinational Enterprise*, Basic Books.

Takeuchi, H. and Porter, M. E. (1986) 'Three Roles of International Marketing in a Global Strategy', in Porter, M. E. (ed.) (1986), *Competition in Global Industries*, Harvard Business School Press.

Yamin, M. (1995) 'Determinants of Reverse Transfer: The Experience of UK Multinationals', in Schiatterella, R. (ed.), *New Challenges for European and International Business*, EIBA.

Yip, G. and Madsen, T. C. (1996) 'Global Account Management', *International Marketing Review*, 13, 3.

INDEX

ABB 184
  Rihand-Delhi project 76–7
absolute advantage 58
account management, global 176, 183–7
accounting systems 271
actor-activity-resource model 227
ad hoc strategic decision-making 221
adaptation 44, 216
adaptation co-operation 215
advertising 174, 246, 255–6
advertising agency-client relationships 180–3
Africa 254
  see also less developed countries
age of relationships 214
Aharoni, Y. 114, 115, 117, 150
Ahlberg, J. 65
Alexander, N. 146–7
Ambler, T. 34–6, 181, 222, 225
American firms 268–9
  see also United States of America
Americas 193–206
  banana wars 204–5
  network perspective 201–3
  relationship perspective 195–201
  traditional perspective 193–5
Amine, L. S. 257–8, 258–9
ANCOM (Andean Common Market) 199
Andersen, O. 140
Andersen, E. 6, 127
Anderson, J. C. 7
Anheuser-Busch (AB) 96–102, 178
anticipatory adjustment 226
anti-dumping legislation 163–4
appellation of origin 97–8
Apple 43, 53
Araujo, L. 116, 118
Argentina 196
Argheyd, K. 128
Arnott, D. C. 31, 32, 41
Asda 185
Asia-Pacific 213, 220–30
  network perspective 226–8
  relationship perspective 223–6
  traditional perspective 221–3
Asia-Pacific Economic Co-operation (APEC) 223
asymmetry 44

AuditCo 144–5
Austin, J. E. 253, 260
Australia 223–4
automobile industry 167
autonomy, local subsidiary 187
autopact 195–6
Axelsson, B. 35, 151, 272–3

Baldinger, P. 238
Ballantyne, D. 8, 9
banana wars 204–5
Bångens, L. 116, 118
Barclay, L.-A. 201
barcodes 86
Barley, S. R. 67
Bartlett, C. A. 270
basic emotions 178
Bass plc 249
Bateman, C. R. 168
Beamish, P. W. 259, 260–1
Beckermann, W. 29
beef 198
behavioural segmentation 210
'Belarus' tractor 28
benefit segmentation 210
Benito, G. R. G. 143
Berg, A. 256
Berry, L. L. 7
Bhagwati, J. 200
Big Six accounting firms 12, 93
bilateral trade agreements 195–6
Blair, T. 64
Blankenburg, D. 10, 203
Bocek, J. 102, 243, 245, 249
Bofors 70, 73–8
Bohn, J. 30, 31, 32
Bohomin Steel Works 134–6
Bolte, M. 91, 203
Boston Consultancy Group (BCG) matrix 109
Bougery, M. 178
boundary spanning roles 44–5
bounded rationality 127
Bovee, C. L. 178
Boya, U. O. 177–8
Brand Asset Valuator 90
brand dispute 96–102

Brand Power Grid 90
brand valuation 89
branding 88–9
  global 100–1, 175
Brazil 193
breakpoints 43
Breger, B. 239
Bridgewater, S. 38–9, 41
British firms 268
  see also United Kingdom
Brorsen, H. 168, 171
Brown, S. 150
Buchan, D. 213
Buckley, P. J. 124, 125, 126, 127, 128–9,
    130, 148, 149
Budejovicky Budvar brewery (Budvar) 243–9
  brand dispute 96–7, 101–2
Budweiser 178, 243–9
  brand dispute 96–102
bureaucracy 131
  respect for 225
Burrows, S. J. 101
Burt, S. 150
Business Environment Risk Indicators
    (BERI) 106–8
buying groups 167, 169–70
Buzzell, R. D. 85, 86

Campaign for Real Ale (CAMRA) 101
Canada 193, 195, 195–6, 200–1, 213
  network structures 203
  see also NAFTA
Canada-USA Free Trade Area (FTA) 195–6
Cantel consortium 203
capital 58–9
Caribbean basin 195, 199, 202, 204
Caribbean Basin Initiative (CBI) 195, 199
Caribbean Common Market (Caricom) 199
Carlsberg 100
Carrefour 146, 147
Casson, M. 124, 125, 126, 127
catalysts 226–7
category management 39
Caulkin, S. 225
Cavusgil, S. T. 148, 161, 162–3, 164,
    165–6, 170
central planning 235, 238, 239
centralized sales strategy 176–7
Ceske Budejovice 96, 101
Chalasani, S. 8
chance 61
Chanel 178
channels, distribution 47, 52
ChemCo 31
chemical industry 239
Chernomyrdin, V. 235
chickens 198

China
  Asia-Pacific 220–1, 223
  emerging market 231, 232, 234, 237, 238, 242
  Guanxi networks 34–5
  scenarios for the future of 119–20
ChinaWeb 51
Christopher, M. 8, 9
Ciba Geigy 255
CigaretteCo 141, 154–5
Clark, T. 114–15
classical economic trade theories 58–9
classification of national cultures 25–7
client-following motivation 143
clustering of entry 125–6
clusters 61, 201
CocaCola 237
codified knowledge 88
co-existence 93
cohesive national culture 32–3
Colchester, N. 213
collectivism 26, 225
collusion 93
colour 25
COMECON (Commission for Mutual
    Economic Aid) 235
commitment 6, 141, 155, 181–2
common currencies 64, 166–7
  see also Euro
communication 272–3
  miscommunication 174, 178–9
company groups 242
competition 93
  global 39, 142
competitive advantage of nations 59–62, 200–1
  critique of 61–2
competitor parity (pricing) 162, 165–6
competitors 115
complexity 174–5
computer industry 241
ComputerCo 141
conflict 93
Confucian religion 225
connectivity 50
consistency 85, 186
Contractor, F. 42, 259
control 85, 127–8, 271, 273
conversation 179
co-operation 93, 115–16, 128–31
  classifying co-operative ventures 129–30
  objectives of 44
  types of 215
  see also joint ventures; strategic alliances
co-ordination 216, 271–2
co-ordination co-operation 215
corporate memory 118
corporate planning 110–13
corruption 73–4, 260
cost-plus pricing 162, 165

costs 40, 174, 187
  labour costs 211
  relationship costs 89
  savings and global standardization 85
  switching costs 186
  transaction costs 88, 127
countertrade 168
countertrade networks 171
country-of-origin effects 27, 28
Cray, D. 32
creativity 181–2
  implementing creative strategies 182
cross-border virtual relationships 49–50
cross-cultural adjustment 226
Culligan, D. 11
cultural differences 29–34, 224
  Internet and 51–2
  miscommunication 178–9
  psychic distance 28–30, 31–3
cultural distance 5, 30–1, 214
  criticisms of 32–4
cultural orientation 140
cultural stereotypes 25
culture 24–37
  cross-cultural adjustment 226
  network perspective 33–5
  organizational 185, 186
  relationship perspective 28–34
  role of relationships in Asian societies 225–6
  traditional perspective 24–8
Cunningham, M. 11
customer expectations 49, 89
customer feedback 115
customer markets 9
Czech Republic 134, 154, 232–3, 244
Czinkota, M. R. 27, 28

Das, D. K. 220, 221, 225
database marketing 8, 46–7
D'Cruz, J. R. 200–1
decentralized sales strategy 176–7
decision making 221
degree of internationalization 148
Dell computers 48–9, 50, 51
Delors, J. 209
Delphi techniques 108
demand conditions 60
Deng Xiaoping 234, 235
Denize, S. 181
dependence 35, 214
description 13
Deshpandé, R. 5, 6
development
  economic 193–4
  LDCs *see* less developed countries
Dialog 179
'diamond framework' 59–62
  'double diamond' 200–1

diaspora 31
discontinuous change 105, 216, 234
discretion, managerial 165–8
dislocation 239
distance 5
  cultural 5, 30–1, 31–3
  psychic *see* psychic distance
  social 5, 214
dispute resolution 198
distribution 245
  channels 47, 52
  local distributors 260
Dobson, I. 101–2
Dodds, C. 168
Donaldson, T. 258
Donovan, 110
Douglas, S. 87
Doyle, P. 38–9, 88–9, 222, 268–9
Doz, Y. 44, 45
Drake, K. 116
Drucker, P. 39
dualism 34–5
Ducoffe, R. 183
Dulek, R. E. 178–9
dumping 198, 212–13
  anti-dumping legislation 163–4
Dunning, J. H. 124–5
Dutta, S. 39, 50
duty of care 257–8
dyads 11
dynamic incremental strategy 165
dynamic view 12, 14

East Asian Economic Crisis 119–20, 222–3
East and Central Europe 93, 269–70
  emerging markets 231–49 *passim*
  enlargement of the EU 208–9
  process of internationalization 141, 144–5,
    154–5
Easton, G. 12, 93
eclectic paradigm 124–5
economic constraint 254–5
economic development 193–4
Economic Intelligence Unit (EIU) 106–8
economic and political context 57–79
  Bofors in India 73–8
  network perspective 67–72
  relationship perspective 63–7
  traditional perspective 58–62
economic value to the customer (EVC) 162, 166
economies of scale 87
education
  levels in LDCs 255–6
  system 26
Efficient Consumer Response (ECR) 39
EFTA 213
Elkington, J. 113
Elof Hansson India 75

emerging mega-markets   213, 231–52
   Budweiser   243–9
   network perspective   69–70, 238–42
   relationship perspective   236–8
   traditional perspective   231–6
emotions   178
employee markets   9
employees   *see* human resources
endowments   58–9
   see also factor conditions
entry   114
   clustering of   125–6
   motivations for   142–3
   timing of   49
environment   21
   cultural   24–37
   economic and political   57–79
   interface with   67–8
   technological   38–56
   uncertainties   107
environmental problems, global   67
Ericsson India   75–6
Erramilli, M. K.   145–6
establishment chain   141
Estonia   242
ethical policy   257–8
ethnicity   24–5, 225
ethnocentrism   27, 140, 270
Euro   64–5, 166–7, 208
   impacts on international marketing   65–6
Euro consumer   210
European Central Bank (ECB)   64, 65
European Union (EU)   207–19
   banana wars   204
   enlargement   208–9
   members   207–8
   network perspective   215–17
   relationship perspective   212–15
   traditional perspective   207–12
exchange   5–6, 34, 48
   types of   92
exchange rates   162–3, 164
expansion   114, 143, 246–7
expatriate managers   119
expectations
   customer   49, 89
   mutual   34
experience   226
experiential knowledge   114–15
export intensity   148, 149
export sales growth   142, 245–6
exporters   164
external advisors   113
external contract seeking motivation   143

factor conditions   59–60
familiarity   27

family   24
Federal Express   51
Fein, A. J.   111
Feng Shui   24
Fielden, J. S.   179
financial resources   142
firm-specific advantages   124
   see also internalization advantages
firm strategy, structure and rivalry   60–1, 62
firm uncertainties   107
Fishburn, D.   63
fixed currencies   64
Flaherty, M. T.   272
Fletcher, R.   30, 31, 32
Fletcher, W.   181
flexibility, lack of   177
flexible cost-plus strategy   165
floating currencies   64
focal nets   11, 201–2, 242
Foote Cone & Belding   180
Ford, D.   5
Ford Motor Co.   48
foreign direct investment (FDI)   119, 125–6
Foreign Trade Corporations (FTCs)   242
foreign trade organizations (FTOs)   244
Forsgren, M.   67, 152, 216–17, 272, 273
Fraedrich, J. P.   168
fragmentation of markets   86
France   166, 214
free trade   66–7
Free Trade Area of the Americas (FTAA)   200
Freeling, A.   84–5, 174, 176
Freeman, J.   67
friendship   24–5
Frydman, R.   235
Fu, H.   224
functional co-operation   215

game theory   13, 151
Gandhi, R.   73–4
Garemo, N.   65
Garnaut, R.   220
gatekeeper   45
Gatignon, H.   127
GE-Multifactor Screen   109
Gemünden, H.-G.   43
General Agreement on Tariffs and Trade
   (GATT)   66, 198
geocentric orientation   140, 270–1
geographic dispersion   148
geographic distance   5
geographic sequence   141, 143–4
geographical equity (brand)   175–6
German firms   214, 269
Ghemawat, P.   109
Gillette Sensor   87
Glaister, K.   128–9, 130
global account management (GAM)   176, 183–7

global branding   100–1, 175
global competition   39, 142
global creative relationships   182–3
global environmental problems   67
global interlinkage of economies   63–7, 144–5
global niche strategies   40
global organizations   148, 270–1
global promotional strategies   175–6
global retailers   168
global sales force   177–8
global scope   39, 68
global standardization   84–7, 173, 174
   arguments against   86–7
   arguments for   85–6
globalization   84–7
   industry globalization drivers   184–6
Golden, P. A.   269
Gould, S. J.   188
governments   61
   countertrade networks   171
   host governments and the Internet   51
Granstrand, O.   273
Grant, R. M.   62
Grayson, K.   181
Gregory, K.   40–1
Grein, A.   183, 188
Grey, S.   31, 32
grey markets   167, 170–1
gross domestic product (GDP)   253–4
Guanxi networks   33–5, 224, 225, 226–7
Guimares, G.   178
Guinness   100
Gummesson, E.   7, 10, 91

Hådjikhani, A.   70
Håkansson, H.   5, 12, 13, 44, 46, 53–4, 70, 95, 216
Halinen, A.   181
Hall, E. T.   23–4, 26
Hallén, L.   28–9, 214
Halliburton, C.   209
Hamel, G.   222
Hamill, J.   40–1, 237
hard services   145–6
Harrigan, K.   15, 129, 130, 131
Harrison, F. L.   110
hedging   162
Heineken   100
Henders, B.   44, 46
heterogeneity   216
Heydebreck, P.   43
hierarchy   131
high-technology firms   149, 150
Hill, J. S.   177–8, 179, 255
Hkansson, L.   273
Hodgetts, R. M.   201
Hoff, E. J.   87
Hofstede, G.   23, 26–7, 32, 33, 225

Holm, P.   217
home fashion products   166
homogenization   86
Hoover 'flight' promotion   175
horizontal *keiretsu*   227
Hörnell, E.   29
host country legislation   163–4
Hu, Y.-S.   271
Huang, M.-H.   178
human development index   193
human resources   177, 185–6, 271
Hünerberg, R.   209
Hungary   154, 232–3
Hunt, S.   6
Husan, R.   128–9, 130
Hutton, J.   24–5
Hybels, R. C.   67
Hymer, S.   124
hyperinflation   162

IBM   43, 53
ideas, exploiting   85
illegal payments   260
incompatibility   181–2
incremental model of internationalization   128
India
   Bofors   73–8
   emerging market   231, 232, 234, 235, 237
individual cultural perceptions   33
individualism-collectivism   26
Industrial Marketing and Purchasing (IMP)
   Group   3–4, 10, 213, 215
industry globalization drivers   184–6
industry leaders   186
industry lifecycle   130
industry sector   130
industry uncertainties   107
infant formula   255, 255–6
inflation   162
influencer markets   9
information exchanges   34
innovation
   challenges for marketing innovation   38–9
   location of R&D activities   273
   in networks   12
innovation-related models   140
integrated marketing communications (IMC)   187–8
interaction studies   3–7
   comparison with relationship and network
      approaches   12–14
   desirability of long-term relationships   6–7
   developing relationships   5–6
   EU   213–15
   interaction processes   5
   international marketing strategy   89–91
   types of distance between suppliers and buyers   5
   see also relationship perspective
interdependency, firm   94–5

interface with the environment   67–8
internal markets   9
internalization advantages   124, 125
international buying groups   167, 169–70
international marketing organization   94, 115,
        267–75
    network perspective   272–3
    relationship perspective   271–2
    stage model   270
    traditional perspective   268–71
international marketing strategy   66, 83–104
    Budweiser   96–102
    network perspective   91–5
    relationship perspective   87–91
    traditional perspective   84–7
international pricing strategies   162–8
international technology co-operation   46
international technology networks   54
internationalization process   139–58
    CigaretteCo   154–5
    network perspective   151–2
    relationship perspective   150
    traditional perspective   139–50
Internet   167
    network perspective   50–4
    real impact of   39–42
    scenario planning   111–12, 113
    virtual relationships   46–50
Internet start-ups   50–1
inter-organizational network relationships   92–4
intra-firm relationships   see international
        marketing organization
Italy   214

Jansky, P.   249
Japan   58, 213, 221, 223
    Japanese firms   268–9
    Japanese miracle   221–2
Jarillo, J.-C.   88, 127
Jiang Zemin   234, 235
Jihoceske Pivovary   243–4, 244–5
Johanson, J.   14, 29, 67, 68, 94, 95, 114,
        140, 141, 148, 151, 272–3
Johanson, M.   236, 238
Johansson, J. K.   27, 28, 222
Johnson, C.   221
Johnson Wax   145, 162, 163
joint ventures   14–15, 128–9
    creating successful joint ventures   131
    emerging mega-markets   236–8
    improving effectiveness   130–1
    LDCs   259, 260–1
Jolibert, A. J. P.   28
Jones, C.   8

Kami, M. J.   110
Kashani, K.   175–6
keiretsu   222, 227–8

Kern, D.   108
key account management, global   176, 183–7
Killing, J. P.   260
Kin, K.   183
Kinch, N.   69, 151, 203, 240
Kindelberger, C. P.   124
Kingfisher   148
Kiriyenko, S.   235
Kitchen, P. J.   187–8
Klein, L. R.   39, 50–1
Klein, S.   125
Knickerbocker, F. T.   125, 126
Knight, F. H.   106
knowledge   113–16
    flows   116–18
    inter-relationships   115–16
    know-how   116–17, 118
    know-what   116–17
    know-why   116–17, 117–18
    leveraging client knowledge   186
knowledge economy   116
knowledge networks   116–18
Kockums   77–8
Kogut, B.   30–1, 42
Koospol   244
Kotler, P.   70, 98, 256, 257
Kriz, A.   227

labour   58–9
labour costs   211
Lamont, B.   182
land   58–9
Langhoff, T.   33
Langlois, C. C.   258
language   24
large firms: relationships with small firms   150
    see also multinational corporations (MNCs)
Latin America   199–200, 202
Latin American Integration Association
        (LAIA)   199
leapfrogging   143, 148
learning
    and adaptation in technology relationships   44
    knowledge and   113–16
    about partners   131
Lee, C.   261
Lee, D. Y.   238
Lee, J.-W.   91
Leemhuis, J. P.   110, 111
legislation   271
    differences and sales forces   177
    host country   163–4
    restrictions and the Internet   51
Lehtinen, U.   146, 236
Leo Burnett   183
Leontief paradox   59
Leppard, J. W.   109–10
Lerman, D. B.   188

less developed countries (LDCs) 253–64
  defining 253–4
  network perspective 260–1
  relationship perspective 256–60
  Shell in Ogoni Land 257, 262–3
  traditional perspective 253–6
Leszinski, R. 167, 169
Leung, T. K. P. 34, 225–6
Levitt, T. 32, 85–6, 144, 178
lifestyle 210
Lisbon Agreement 97
'Little Dragons' 221
local content 213
local distributors 260
local market conditions 177–8
local promotional strategies 175–6
local subsidiary autonomy 187
location-specific advantages 124
lock-in effects 216
Locke, J. 48
long-term orientation (LTO) 26–7, 221–2
long-term relationships 6–7, 181
loosely structured networks 93–4
Lorange, P. 42
Lorenzoni, G. 133
loyalty 7–8
Lundgren, A. 12, 53–4, 216
Luo, Y. 225

macro-level network relationships 91–2
Madsen, T. C. 184–7, 273
mailing lists 47
Malaysia 70–1
Mallory, G. 31, 114–15
management information systems (MIS) 39
management processes 185
managerial discretion, range of 165–8
Manninen, K. 69, 114, 240
manufacturing firms 145
maquiladora sector 197
marginal cost 169
marginal cost plus fixed margin 169
market attractiveness 105–22
  network perspective 116–18
  relationship perspective 113–16
  scenarios for the future of China 119–20
  traditional perspective 105–13
market development, degree of 177
market intelligence systems 176
market oriented pricing 161–2
market research 222
market research agencies 115
market seeking motivation 142–3
marketing orientation 222, 268–70
market size 177
markets
  changing market structure 65
  local market conditions 177–8

national characteristics 86
  as networks 10
  targeting and GAM 186
  technology and changing markets 39
Marks and Spencer 45
Mascarenhas, B. 106
masculinity-femininity 26
mass customization 39
Mateus, P. 8
Mathews, R. 110, 111, 112
matrix analysis 108–10
Mattsson, L.-G. 11, 12, 14, 68, 92, 94, 151
Mazda Motor Corporation 180
McCarthy, M. 183
McDonald, M. 109–10
McDonald's 125, 183
McDougall, P. P. 47, 150
McKiernan, P. 58
meaning 33–4
media 174, 179–80
mega-market see emerging mega-markets
Melville, I. 222, 227
Menem, President 64
Mercosur 199
message 174, 178
Metro Makro 148
Mexico 195, 196, 197, 201
  see also NAFTA
Miles, R. E. 133
Miller, K. D. 106, 107
Miller Brewing 181
Millman, A. F. 183
Minolta 171
miscommunication 174, 178–9
Mitchell, A. 8
mix, promotional 174–8
mobilization 216
mode of international operation 123–38
  Bohomin Steel Works 134–6
  emerging mega-markets 236–7
  network perspective 131–3
  relationship perspective 128–31
  traditional perspective 124–8
Möller, K. 4
money 174, 180
monopolistic advantage theory 124
Montreal Protocol 67
Moorman, C. 5, 6
Morgan, R. M. 6
motivations for entry 142–3
Motorola 114
multilateral free trade agreements 195–200
multinational corporations (MNCs) 201
  and global firms 148, 270–1
  Internet users 50–1
  role in LDCs 256–60
  stage model of evolution 270
mutual expectation 34

NAFTA (North American Free Trade
    Agreement)   195, 196–8, 199, 201
  impacts   196–7
  trade dispute resolution   198
narratives   111, 112
Narus, J. A.   7
Narver, J.   268
national culture   *see* culture
national markets' characteristics   86
natural advantages   58
Nauclér, T.   65
Neale, C. W.   168
Nestlé   89, 255
network infusion   217
network organizations   216–17
network perspective   9–16
  the Americas   201–3
  Asia-Pacific   226–8
  assessing market attractiveness   116–18
  comparison with interaction and relationship
      approaches   12–14
  cultural environment   33–6
  economic and political context   67–72
  emerging mega-markets   69–70, 238–42
  EU   215–17
  international marketing   14–16
  international marketing organization   272–3
  international marketing strategy   91–5
  internationalization process   151–2
  key themes   11–12
  LDCs   260–1
  markets as networks   9–10
  mode of international operation   131–3
  pricing   168–71
  promotion   187–8
  technological context   50–4
network positions   *see* positions, network
network structures   69–70, 93–4
  in Canada   203
  dynamic   11–12
  in the USA   202–3
New Economics of Information   87–8
New Zealand   223–4
Newman, B.   257
NHPC (National Hydro Power Corporation)   77
Nigeria   257, 262–3
Nohria, N.   9, 67
Nonaka, I.   222
non-tariff barriers   146
Normann, R.   8
NTPC (National Thermal Power Corporation)   77

objectives of co-operation   44
objects   24
O'Brien, L.   8
Ogoni Land, Nigeria   257, 262–3
Ohmae, K.   63, 68, 69, 84, 144, 191
oligopolistic reaction theory   125–6

opacity   35, 240
opportunism   127
opportunity   232–4
organization
  international marketing organization   *see*
      international marketing organization
  network as an organizational type   10, 131–3
organizational structure   90–1, 185
  network organizations   216–17
origin
  appellation of   97–8
  country-of-origin effects   27, 28
  rules of   213
Ornati, O. A.   133
orthodoxy, challenging   222
Ouchi, W. G.   131
outsourcing   88
Oviatt, B. M.   47, 150
ownership   271
  advantages   124–5

Page, A. L.   183
Pahlberg, C.   35
Paitra, J.   209
Palme, O.   73
pan-European marketing   209–12
  see also European Union
paper and pulp industry   216
parallel pricing   167, 170–1
parallel penetration   68–9
parent-child joint ventures   259
partner screening   131
  see also joint ventures
'Partnership for Prosperity and Security'
    agreement   204
Paul, R. N.   110
Payne, A.   8, 9
Pedersen, T.   142, 143, 149
perception
  individual cultural perceptions   33
  psychic distance   29–30
performance improvement   40
performance measurement   176–7
Pergau Dam Incident   70–1
Perlitz, M.   109
Perlmutter, H.   140, 270
personal relations   242
personal selling   174
Petersen, B.   142, 143, 149
Peterson, R. A.   28
Pettigrew, A. M.   106
pharmaceuticals   255
Philip Morris   86, 154
Philips Lighting   85
planning
  central   235, 238, 239
  corporate   85, 110–13
Plzenske Pivovary   247

Poland 154, 232–3
political relationships 70–2
political turmoil 235
politics 27, 177
    LDCs 256, 257, 262–3
    see also economic and political context
polycentric orientation 140, 270
pork 198
Porter, M. E. 59–62, 84, 165, 200, 222, 271, 271–2
positions, network
    building 34–5, 91–5; in international
        markets 94–5; in new national nets 52
    investment in 242
power
    imbalance 6
    LDCs 256, 258–9
power distance 26
Prahalad, C. K. 222
Prazske Pivovary 249
Prescott, K. 209, 212–13
prescription 13
price differentiation 167
price harmonization 65, 167, 169–70
pricing 161–72, 186–7
    network perspective 168–71
    relationship perspective 168
    strategies 165–8
    traditional perspective 161–8
privatization 134, 235, 249
Procter and Gamble (PRG) 52
product development 130
product lifecycles 39, 126–7
production capacity 246–7
production orientation 86–7
products
    global 186
    offered 142
promotion 173–90, 246
    challenges in international promotional
        strategies 174–80
    network perspective 187–8
    relationship perspective 180–7
    traditional perspective 173–80
protectionism 71–2, 204–5, 212
psychic distance 28–30
    criticisms of 32–4
    geographic sequence 141, 143–4
    in networks 35
public relations 174, 256
Pugh, D. S. 114–15
'pull' factors 113–14
pulp and paper industry 216
Purchase, S. 226, 226–7
purchasing agent 45–6
'push' factors 113–14

quality 222
Quelch, J. A. 39, 50–1, 87, 175–6, 253, 257, 260

Ramirez, R. 8
Rank Hovis McDougall 183
Rapaczynski, A. 235
'real time' interaction 49
reciprocity 213
recycling 216
Redding, G. 226
referral markets 9
regiocentrism 270
Reich, R. 270
related and supporting industries 61, 62
relationship, types of 93
relationship-building 33–5, 91, 225–6
relationship costs 89
relationship marketing 7–9, 91
    broader application 7–9
    comparison with interaction and network
        approaches 12–14
    definitions and origins 7
relationship perspective 3–9
    the Americas 195–201
    Asia-Pacific 223–6
    assessing market attractiveness 113–16
    comparison with network approach 12–14
    cultural environment 27–33
    economic and political context 63–7
    emerging mega-markets 236–8
    EU 212–15
    interaction studies 3–7
    international marketing 14–16
    international marketing organization 271–2
    international marketing strategy 87–91
    internationalization process 150
    LDCs 256–60
    mode of international operation 128–31
    pricing 168
    promotion 180–7
    relationship marketing 7–9
    technological context 42–50
relationship promoter 46
religion 24, 225
research and development 273
resource constellations 216
resource seeking motivation 142–3
retailers 146–8
    global 168
    relationships with suppliers 150
retailing scenarios 111–12, 113
Ricardo, D. 58
Richardson, G. B. 116
Riesenbeck, H. 84–5, 174, 176
rigid cost-plus strategy 165
Rihand-Delhi project 76–7
risk 105–6
    attitude to risk-taking 27
    balancing control and 127–8
    and opportunity in emerging markets 232–4
risk assessment models 108

risk assessment techniques   106–10
risk indices   106–8
Robinson, R. D.   133
role discretion   226
Ronkainen, I. A.   27, 28, 212
Ross-Flanigan, N.   52
Roth, V. J.   125
Rothmans Cigarettes   60
Rowntree   89
Rugman, A. M.   200–1
rules of origin   213
Russia   28, 125, 155, 237, 241–2

Sagafi-Nejad, T.   259
sales force, global   177–8
sales promotion   174–5
sales support   176
salesperson   45–6
Salinas, C.   195
Salmi, A.   241, 242
Sandström, M.   27–8
Sandvik Asia   74–5
Saro Wiwa, K.   262–3
Saunders, J.   222, 268–9
SC Johnson   60
SCA recycled fibre network   12
scenario planning   110–13
   China   119–20
   effective   112–13
Schlegelmilch, B. B.   258
Schultz, D. E.   187–8
scope
   global   39, 68
   relationship   182–3
   technology co-operation   44
Seagram Company   232, 233
Seattle free trade talks   66–7
security   48
Segev, A.   39, 50
Senn, C.   184, 187
sequential models of internationalization
      140–4
service level   187
services   7
   global   186
   internationalization process   145–6
Seyed-Mohamed, N.   91, 203
Shani, D.   8
Shell   113, 257, 262–3
Shipley, D. D.   168
Sikora, E.   170
simultaneous models of internationalization   140,
      144–5
Simyar, F.   128
Singh, H.   30–1, 42
Single European Market (SEM)   see European Union
six markets model   9
Sjölander, S.   273

Slater, S.   268
small firms   133
   internationalization process   148–50
   relationships with large firms   150
small numbers bargaining   127
Smith, A.   58, 59
Smith, N. C.   257
Snehota, I.   95
Snelbecker, D.   69, 114, 240
Snow, C.   133
Social Chapter   211
social distance   5, 214
social emotions   178
social exchange   5–6, 48
social unrest   235–6
soft services   145–6
Sony   42
sourcing behaviour   88, 210
Soviet Union   235, 241
   see also Russia
space   23–4
Srinivasan, T. S.   114
St Louis Cultural Centre   101
Stahl, S.   47
stakeholders   115
standardization
   global   84–7, 173, 174
   textile industry in EU   209–12
static view   14
stereotypes, cultural   26
sterling   164
Stevenson, T. H.   183
Still, R. R.   177–8, 255
Stopford, J. M.   270
strategic alliances   115–16
   in Europe   215
strategic decision-making   221
strategic networks   131–3
strategy   see international marketing strategy
supplier markets   9
supplier-retailer relationships   150
supporting and related industries   61, 62
supranational bodies   66–7
Sweden   214
   impact of Bofors scandal on Swedish companies
      in India   73–8
switching costs   186
SWOT analysis   114, 135, 136
symbols   25
Szymanski, D.   48, 49

Tabak   154
tacit knowledge   88
Takeuchi, H.   272
Tam, J. L. M.   34, 225–6
taxation   271
Taylor, J. W.   110
technological distance   5

technology 38–56
  level in LDCs 255
  network perspective 50–4
  relationship perspective 42–50
  traditional perspective 38–42
technology industries 53–4
technology relationships 42–50
  international co-operation 46
  issues for consideration 44–6
  virtual 46–50
technology seeking motivation 142–3
technology transfer 259–60
TelecomCo 151, 152
Tetra Pak India 75
textile industry 209–12
Thilenius, P. 217
Thill, J. V. 178
Thorelli, H. B. 10, 92, 93, 94, 132
tightly structured networks 93–4, 203
time 23, 48, 226
time distance 5
timing of entry 49
tobacco industry 60, 141, 154–5, 240
Tolar, J. 246, 247
tomatoes 198
Tordjman, A. 148
Törnroos, J.-A. 242
trade
  agreements 195–200
  classical theories 58–9
  disputes 198, 204–5
  free 66–7
trademark dispute 96–102
trading blocs 196–200, 212–13
trading houses 171
traditional perspective 13, 14, 15
  the Americas 193–5
  Asia-Pacific 221–3
  assessing market attractiveness 105–13
  cultural environment 23–7
  economic and political context 58–62
  emerging mega-markets 231–6
  EU 207–12
  international marketing organization 268–71
  international marketing strategy 84–7
  internationalization process 139–50
  LDCs 253–6
  mode of international operation 124–8
  pricing 161–8
  promotion 173–80
  technological context 38–42
training 226
transaction costs 88, 127
transactional marketing 7
  see also traditional perspective
transfer pricing 169
Treadgold, A. 148
Triad 63, 68–9, 191

Trisoglio, A. 113
trust 5–6, 34, 131, 214
  building in virtual relationships 47–50
  and commitment 6
  creative relationships 181–2
Turnbull, P. W. 4, 89, 214

Ukraine 31, 58, 69, 152, 233
  Johnson Wax 163
  market attractiveness 114
  network issues 239, 240, 241
uncertainty 105–6
  classifications 107
uncertainty avoidance 26
Unilever 85
unit of analysis 13
United Kingdom (UK) 166, 214
  British firms 268
United States of America (USA) 193, 194, 201, 213
  American firms 268–9
  banana wars 204–5
  beer market 98–9
  network perspective: focal actor 201–2;
      network structures 202–3
  trading agreements with Canada 195–6
  see also NAFTA
'United States of Europe' 212
Uppsala model 140–2
  theoretical analysis 141–2
Urban, S. 215
Uri Civil AB 77
Usunier, J.-C. 260

Vahlne, J.-E. 29, 94, 95, 114, 140, 141, 148
Valihora, M. S. 198
Välikängas, L. 146
Valla, J.-P. 4, 89–91, 214
value-adding activities 186
value chain 87–8, 271–2
  decoupling 87
value constellations 87–8
Vendemini, S. 215
Vernon, R. 126–7
vertical keiretsu 227, 228
VHS 53
Vickery, G. 116
virtual relationships 46–50
visibility 40
  in networks 35, 240
visual imagery 178
Volvo 203
Von Bertrab, H. 196

Wal Mart 6, 65, 146, 147, 185, 217
Waluszewski, A. 216
Ward, T. 226, 226–7
washing machine industry 86
Weekly, J. 162

Weitz, B.   6
Welch, L.   143
Welford, R.   208–9, 212–13
Wells, L. T.   270
Wersun, A.   237
Western Electric   42
Wiedersheim-Paul, F.   29, 140
Wilkinson, P.   183
Williamson, O. E.   127
Wilson, D. T.   4
win-win situations   13, 151
Wind, Y.   87
Winzip   51
Wistrich, E.   212
Wong, V.   222, 268–9
Wong, Y. H.   34, 225–6
World Bank   66–7, 256

World Trade Organization (WTO)   66–7, 198, 204
written communication   179

X and Y grids   111–12, 113

Yadav, S.   31, 32
Yeltsin, B.   235
Yip, G.   84, 87, 184–7, 273
Young, L.   181
Young, S.   237
Young & Rubicam   181
   Brand Asset Valuator   90

zaibatsu   227
Zaltman, G.   5, 6
Zanussi   86
zero-sum game   13, 84, 151